SIXTH EDITION

Southeast Asia
in the
New International Era

ROBERT DAYLEY

The College of Idaho

CLARK D. NEHER

Northern Illinois University

WESTVIEW
PRESS

A Member of the Perseus Books Group

Westview Press was founded in 1975 in Boulder, Colorado, by notable publisher and intellectual Fred Praeger. Westview Press continues to publish scholarly titles and high-quality undergraduate- and graduate-level textbooks in core social science disciplines. With books developed, written, and edited with the needs of serious nonfiction readers, professors, and students in mind, Westview Press honors its long history of publishing books that matter.

Copyright © 2013 by Westview Press
Published by Westview Press,
A Member of the Perseus Books Group

Find us on the World Wide Web at www.westviewpress.com.
Every effort has been made to secure required permissions for all text, images, maps, and other art reprinted in this volume.

Westview Press books are available at special discounts for bulk purchases in the United States by corporations, institutions, and other organizations. For more information, please contact the Special Markets Department at the Perseus Books Group, 2300 Chestnut Street, Suite 200, Philadelphia, PA 19103, or call (800) 810-4145, ext. 5000, or e-mail special.markets@perseusbooks.com.

Designed by Linda Mark

A CIP catalog record for the print version of this book is available from the Library of Congress
PB ISBN: 978-0-8133-4754-7 (alk. paper)
EBOOK ISBN: 978-0-8133-4755-4 (ebook)

10 9 8 7 6 5 4 3 2 1

Contents

Preface and Acknowledgments

THIS BOOK RESULTS FROM INFORMATION GATHERED DURING MANY trips to Southeast Asia. I am grateful to the National Science, Ford, and Fulbright foundations, the United States Information Agency, and the United States-Indochina Reconciliation Project for their generous assistance during the lengthier stays. I am also indebted to the faculty and staff of Chulalongkorn University, Thammasat University, Prince of Songkla University at Had Yai and Pattani, Chiang Mai University, Payap University in Thailand, and the University of San Carlos in the Philippines for their intellectual and material support of my work at their campuses.

During my career as a student of Southeast Asian politics, I have learned much from colleagues who share my interest. I am especially indebted to M. Ladd Thomas, Danny Unger, and Dwight King in the Department of Political Science at Northern Illinois University. They have provided generous intellectual and collegial counsel. Similar support has come from Ronald Provencher, Judy Ledgerwood, Susan Russell, Constance Wilson, and Mai Kyi Win, all associates of NIU's Center for Southeast Asian Studies. April Davis, Karen Schweitzer, Sandi Holloway, and Nancy Schuneman contributed outstanding administrative support, and David Oldfield, Paul Chambers, Chandra Mahajakana, Bryan Hunsaker, Todd Culp, Ted Mayer, Robert Dayley, and Warner Winborne provided superb research assistance. Both undergraduate and graduate students at Northern Illinois University have contributed to this book as well through their enthusiastic interest in the Southeast Asian region. It is gratifying to have taught these students, many of whom are now among the new generation of scholars of Southeast Asia.

Although I accept responsibility for all errors and misinterpretations, many scholars of Southeast Asia will see their ideas reflected in Southeast Asia in the New International Era. Among those scholars who have helped shape my views are David Wilson, Donn Hart, Michael Aung-Thwin, Ansil

Ramsay, Prasert Bhandachart, Bidhya Bowornwathana, Kusuma Snit-wongse, Suchit Bunbongkarn, Randy Fertel, Danny Unger, Gary Suwan-narat, David Adams, Sheldon Simon, Chai-Anana Samudavanija, Tanun Anuman-Rajadhon, Sukhumbhand Paribatra, Proserpina Tapales, John McAuliff, Anek Laothamathas, Panitan Wattanayagorn, Carolina Hernan-dez, Ross Marlay, Nara Ganesan, and Narong Sinsawasdi.

Clark D. Neher

Preface and Acknowledgments to the Sixth Edition

WHEN PROFESSOR CLARK NEHER FIRST INVITED ME TO COAUTHOR *Southeast Asia in the New International Era*, I accepted without hesitation. My deep sense of gratitude to him alone would not allow me to decline. As his student and research assistant at Northern Illinois University, where I completed doctoral work in the 1990s, I was the recipient of his superior academic guidance and his fatherly interest in the well-being of my young family. Professor Neher is the consummate scholar and gentleman. For many of his former students, he is a model professor. Accepting the challenge to extend the life of this text beyond his retirement is a small token of my personal appreciation for his years of mentorship.

The final edition of *Southeast Asia in the New International Era* authored solely by Clark Neher was the fourth edition, which went to press shortly after the events of September 11, 2001. For the fifth edition, published in 2010, I revised and updated content, added maps, included a new chapter on Timor-Leste, and added new "Resource Guides" to each country chapter to help students launch more effective Internet searches. These same features continue in the sixth edition.

For the sixth edition, the introduction and country chapters are now fully revised and updated through August 2012. I also rearranged the country chapters according to standard mainland and insular divisions of Southeast Asia. The chapters can be read in any order, and their new arrangement in no way infers their relative importance or regional significance. Readers familiar with previous editions will also notice that chapter sections on "Democratization" and "The State" have been merged for analytical reasons into a single section now titled "State-Society Relations and Democracy." This new edition also includes an updated set of maps, new data tables in chapter 1, and greater coverage of the ongoing disputes over islands in the South China Sea in the chapters on Vietnam and the Philippines. With hindsight always expanding, modest revision to existing text is necessary with each new edition but core themes and essential content remain intact. Necessary length restrictions may understandably leave some area experts troubled by relevant material not included in the book. As best as possible the book's information and analysis is pitched for readers new to the region—it is most effectively used as tool for students, professors, and professionals orienting themselves to Southeast Asia. It is not intended to be comprehensive survey. In my own undergraduate classes at The College of Idaho, I supplement this text with other books and articles to ensure greater depth and breadth than a single text or perspective allows.

I wish to thank The College of Idaho, Northern Illinois University, Payap University, the National Institute of Development Administration (NIDA), the Fulbright Foundation, and ASIANetwork for supporting my research endeavors in Asia, where I have lived, taught, and researched for more than four years. Teaching opportunities at Davidson College, St. Lawrence University, Oglethorpe University, China Agricultural University, and Payap University allowed me to exchange intellectually with wonderfully curious colleagues and students. My students at the College of Idaho are a constant source of inspiration to me. The Asian Studies programs at Weber State University, the University of Oregon, and Northern Illinois University similarly deserve acknowledgment for supporting my area studies training when I was a student. A special thanks to John Brandon (Asia Foundation), Zhiqun Zhu (Bucknell University), anonymous reviewers, and to colleagues who provided useful feedback on the fifth edition and advice on the sixth edition. For the sixth edition, Lucinda Wong supplied useful clerical support and Sarah Crain helped with research. Akshata Mehta and Shaun Mandiwana assisted with indexing. Ann Delgehausen of Trio Bookworks copyedited the entire manuscript. Throughout the process of revision and production Anthony Wahl, and Carolyn Sobczak at Westview Press provided excellent support. Most importantly, I thank my wife, Carrie, and three children, Mara, Molly, and Eliot, for sharing with me a love of Southeast Asia.

Robert Dayley

Acronyms

ADB	Asian Development Bank
AEC	ASEAN Economic Community
AFP	Armed Forces of the Philippines
AFPFL	Anti-Fascist People's Freedom League (Burma/Myanmar)
AFTA	ASEAN Free Trade Area
APEC	Asia-Pacific Economic Cooperation
APU	Angkatan Perpaduan Umnah (United Movement of the Faithful, Malaysia)
ARMM	Autonomous Region in Muslim Mindano (Philippines)
ASEAN	Association of Southeast Asian Nations
BN	Barisan Nasional (National Front, Malaysia)
BSPP	Burmese Socialist Program Party
CGDK	Coalition Government of Democratic Kampuchea
CNS	Council on National Security (Thailand)
CPP	Cambodian People's Party
CPV	Communist Party of Vietnam
CRNT	National Congress for Timorese Reconstruction Party
CSO	civil society organization
DAP	Democratic Action Party (Malaysia)
DPD	Dewan Perwakilan Daerah (Regional Representative Council, Indonesia)
DPR	Dewan Perwakilan Rakyat (People's Representative Council, Indonesia)
ECCC	Extraordinary Chambers of the Courts of Cambodia

ENC	Ethnic Nationalities Council (Burma/Myanmar)
ERVI	Election Related Violent Incident
Falantil	Forces Amadas de Libertação Nacional de Timor Leste
FUNCINPEC	United National Front for an Independent, Peaceful, and Cooperative Cambodia
Fretilin	Revolutionary Front for an Independent East Timor
ICJ	International Court of Justice
ICMI	Indonesian Association of Muslim Intellectuals
ILO	International Labor Organization
INTERFET	International Force for East Timor
ISI	import-substitution industrialization
JI	Jemaah Islamiyah
JPDA	Joint Petroleum Development Area (Timor-Leste)
JSOTF-P	Joint Special Operations Task Force-Philippines
KBL	Kilusang Bagong Lipunan (Philippines)
KNP	Khmer National Party
KPNLF	Khmer People's National Liberation Front
Lao PDR	Lao People's Democratic Republic
LDC	least developed country
LFNC	Lao Front for National Construction
LPRP	Lao People's Revolutionary Party
MAI	Multilateral Aid Initiative
MCA	Malayan Chinese Association
MDG	Millennium Development Goals
MIB	Malay Islamic Beraja
MIC	Malayan Indian Congress
MILF	Moro Islamic Liberation Front (Philippines)
MMR	maternal mortality rate
MNLF	Moro National Liberation Front (Philippines)
MP	Member of Parliament
MPR	People's Consultative Assembly (Indonesia)
NDF	National Democratic Front (Burma/Myanmar)
NEP	New Economic Policy (Malaysia)

NICs	newly industrialized countries
NLD	National League for Democracy
NLF	National Liberation Front (Vietnam)
NLHS	Neo Lao Hak Sat
NMP	Nominated Member of Parliament
NPA	New People's Army (Philippines)
NPKC	National Peace Keeping Council (Thailand)
NU	Nahdlatul Ulama (Indonesia)
NUP	National Unity Party (Burma/Myanmar)
OIC	Organization of the Islamic Conference
PAD	People's Alliance for Democracy (Thailand)
PAP	People's Action Party (Singapore)
PAS	Parti Islam Se-Malaysia (Islamic Party of Malaysia)
PAVN	People's Army of Vietnam
PDI-P	Indonesian Democracy Party-Struggle
PGNU	Provisional Government of National Unity (Laos)
PKB	National Awakening Party (Indonesia)
PKI	Communist Party of Indonesia
PKS	Prosperous Justice Party (Indonesia)
PPP	People's Power Party (Thailand); also, United Development Party (Indonesia)
PR	Pakatan Rakyat (Malaysia)
PRK	People's Republic of Kampuchea
RAM	Reform the Armed Forces Movement (Philippines)
RBAF	Royal Brunei Armed Forces
RSF	Reporters sans Frontieres
SBY	Susilo Bambang Yudhoyono
SEATO	Southeast Asia Treaty Organization
SLORC	State Law and Order Restoration Council (Burma/Myanmar)
SNC	Supreme National Council (Cambodia)
SPDC	State Peace and Development Council (Burma/Myanmar)
SRP	Sam Rainsy Party (Cambodia)
TRT	Thai Rak Thai Party

UDD	United Front of Democracy against Dictatorship (Thailand)
UMNO	United Malays National Organization
UNAMET	United Nations Assistance Mission in East Timor
UNCLOS	United Nations Law of the Sea Convention
UNDP	United Nations Development Program
UNESCO	United Nations Educational, Scientific, and Cultural Organization
UNICEF	United Nations Children's Fund
UNIDO	United Nationalist Democratic Organization (Philippines)
UNLD-LA	United Nationalities League for Democracy–Liberated Areas (Burma/Myanmar)
UNMISET	United Nations Mission of Support in East Timor
UNMIT	United Nations Integrated Mission in Timor-Leste
UNOTIL	United Nations Office in East Timor
UNTAC	United Nations Transitional Authority in Cambodia
UNTAET	United Nations Transitional Administration in East Timor
USAID	United States Aid for International Development
USDA	Union Solidarity and Development Association (Burma/Myanmar)
USDP	Union Solidarity and Development Party (Burma/Myanmar)
USSFTA	United States–Singapore Free Trade Agreement
UXO	unexploded ordnance

1

INTRODUCTION

WRITING A BOOK ABOUT CONTEMPORARY SOUTHEAST ASIA IS A challenge because the region is no longer a primary focus of international attention. Weeks go by without any major news stories about countries that only decades ago dominated the discussions of government officials and ordinary citizens. Because of the end of the Cold War, as well as events put in motion on September 11, 2001, international observers now focus their attention on other parts of the world. Moreover, the lingering trauma, disillusionment, and cynicism of the Vietnam War have kept many journalists, political scientists, and policymakers from focusing on Southeast Asia.

International news coverage of Southeast Asia remains dominated by the superficial and sensational. Images of sunny beaches, soccer-playing elephants, and "exotic" cuisine are standard fare for the reporters of the globalization era. When periodic spurts of interest in serious stories do manage to enter the global news cycle, the images are typically of tragedy, violence, and exploitation—of cyclone victims, bandanna-clad kidnappers, or underage workers in sweatshops. Less frequent but more in-depth commentaries about Southeast Asia may center on the region's transformation "from a battleground to a marketplace" or on problems of environmental degradation, but for the most part Southeast Asia's story is persistently overshadowed by conflict in the Middle East, the movements of U.S. troops, and the global rise of China.[1]

Southeast Asia's recent story is obviously more complex than sensational headlines and stereotypical images suggest. In fact, as the world turns its attention elsewhere, the 600 million people who live in the region are experiencing unprecedented socioeconomic change. New forms of wealth and poverty are emerging across the region. Wrenching conflicts over rights, identity, social justice, and power have become the everyday experience of many Southeast Asians. Although it no longer draws the international attention it once did, perhaps no region in the world is more dynamic.

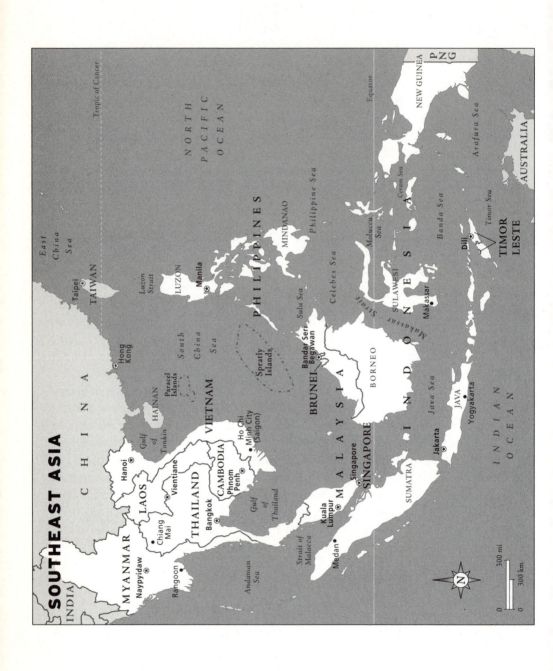

SOUTHEAST ASIA

INDIA

CHINA

MYANMAR

Naypyidaw ⊛

Rangoon •

Chiang Mai •

LAOS

Vientiane ⊛

Hanoi ⊛

Gulf of Tonkin

HAINAN

Paracel Islands

East China Sea

Taipei •

TAIWAN

Hong Kong ⊛

South China Sea

Tropic of Cancer

NORTH PACIFIC OCEAN

Luzon Strait

LUZON

Manila ⊛

PHILIPPINES

MINDANAO

Philippine Sea

Spratly Islands

VIETNAM

THAILAND

Bangkok ⊛

Gulf of Thailand

CAMBODIA

Phnom Penh ⊛

Ho Chi Minh City (Saigon) •

Sulu Sea

Celebes Sea

Bandar Seri Begawan ⊛

BRUNEI

BORNEO

MALAYSIA

Kuala Lumpur ⊛

Singapore

SINGAPORE

Strait of Malacca

Medan •

SUMATRA

Andaman Sea

Jakarta •

Java Sea

JAVA

Yogyakarta •

INDONESIA

SULAWESI

Makassar •

Makassar Strait

Molucca Sea

Ceram Sea

Banda Sea

NEW GUINEA

P N G

Arafura Sea

Timor Sea

Dili ⊛

TIMOR LESTE

AUSTRALIA

Equator

INDIAN OCEAN

N

300 mi

300 km

0

0

A new era in international relations has arisen in the past several decades with lasting repercussions for Southeast Asia. Political, economic, and social forces of unprecedented scope are currently transforming the entire region. *Southeast Asia in the New International Era* analyzes contemporary politics in the context of these new international and domestic realities from the perspectives of both the Southeast Asians and the international community. This chapter introduces the region, describes changes accompanying the new international era, and explains how standard regime labels fall short in characterizing the richness and complexity of Southeast Asian politics. Eleven country chapters follow that evaluate each country in terms of basic political history, major institutions and social groups, state-society relations and democracy, economy and development, and foreign relations. A small research guide is included at the end of each country chapter to assist readers in search of Internet-based bibliographies, socioeconomic data, research sites, and blogs on Southeast Asian countries.

INFLUENCES AND EXPERIENCES

Southeast Asia, a region of remarkable diversity, consists of eleven countries with differing histories, cultural traditions, resource bases, and political-economic systems.[2] Except for geographic proximity and a somewhat similar tropical environment and ecology, few characteristics link all these nations into a coherent whole. Nevertheless, before the international era arrived, a broad shape to a Southeast Asian political economy had developed from a few generalized influences, experiences, and social patterns described in this chapter. These influences and experiences include religious penetration by Hinduism, Buddhism, Islam, and Christianity; colonialism and introduction of political ideas from the West; the rise of nationalism associated with the struggle for independence; Japanese occupation; Cold War trauma; and regional economic transition. Shared social patterns, also outlined below, include a strong sense of the village as the primary unit of traditional identity; agricultural economies overtaken by urban-based manufacturing and service economies; and patron-client systems that influence sociopolitical interaction.

An important force shaping Southeast Asia from ancient to modern times has been the arrival and expansion of nonnative religions across the region. By supplanting local belief systems—or more often blending with them—exogenous religious influences evolved into today's seemingly endogenous value systems, which contribute to the region's diverse cultural milieu. Hinduism and Theravada Buddhism, arriving from South Asian sources, brought to the region Brahmanical notions of *deva-raja* (god-king), classical literature, such as the *Ramayana* and the *Jataka* tales, and karmic notions of rightful authority. Throughout the region, these cultural imports profoundly shaped the concept of power and the royal structures that wielded it. Mahayana Buddhism, brought from India via China, also influenced political ideals in the region, particularly in Vietnam, where social order was believed to stem from hierarchal (Confucian) relations, Buddhist cosmology, and (Taoist) naturalism. Centuries of overseas Chinese migration also spread the influence of Chinese religion and folk beliefs throughout the region, especially in urban areas where migrant communities established themselves.

Islam arrived from merchants and traders primarily from South Asia subsequent to Hinduism and Buddhism. It did not enjoy a wide presence in Southeast Asia until the fifteenth century, about the time Europeans first began to arrive with Christian traditions. Throughout insular Southeast Asia, Islam spread from island to island and from coastal ports to interior settlements. Christianity did not spread deep roots in the region, except for in the predominantly Catholic Philippines and East Timor, as well as among some enduring communities in Vietnam and Indonesia. Over the centuries of religious interaction, the eclectic, religio-royal traditions of Hinduism and Buddhism have sometimes clashed with the universalist, law-based religions of Islam and Christianity. However, tolerance and syncretism rather than conflict characterizes most of Southeast Asia's history of religious practice. Taken together, the diverse practices and beliefs of these religions, and their interaction, generate an array of cultural claims on how to organize societies politically and economically across the region.

Adding yet more complexity to this milieu of beliefs and practices was the gradual penetration of Western ideas of modernity, including "civilization," nationalism, capitalism, republicanism, democracy, and communism. Most of these foreign notions and ideologies emerged in the region during the nineteenth and early twentieth centuries, that is, during the latest phase of nearly five centuries of European influence in the region. Many of the problems of political and economic development facing Southeast Asian leaders today can be traced to colonialism.[3] The grand strategic games of imperial competition and colonial rule brought the formation of internationally recognized boundaries, which replaced the region's nonintegrated dynastic principalities that only loosely governed rural populations and upland minority groups. Foreign attempts to integrate these disparate populations often proved difficult. The imperialists eventually guaranteed new boundaries and imposed a Western sense of geographic and political order on the region.

By the late nineteenth century, national boundaries had been demarcated and the entire area of Southeast Asia, except Thailand, was in European hands. Over time, a money economy was introduced and resource extraction created large-scale industries that required skilled and unskilled laborers. Because the rural populations of Southeast Asia found industrial labor antithetical to traditional values, the colonialists imported Chinese and Indians to work in factories, tin mines, and rubber plantations. The Chinese and Indian communities were often employed as a buffer between Europeans and local populations. In many cases, laws prevented the immigrants from owning land and pushed them into the commercial sector. Urban life in colonial Southeast Asia was, in many respects, more Chinese and Indian than local or European. A discernible immigrant communalism evolved in tandem with urbanization. Hindu, Confucian, and European influences affected trade, urban architecture, art, and societal tastes and norms. From the nineteenth century forward, overseas communities (the Chinese in particular) have enjoyed economic power in Southeast Asia disproportionate to their numbers.

Among other changes, European colonists were responsible for the growth of the region's first economic infrastructure of ports, railways, and roads. Although they staffed their bureaucracies with local elites, offering education to the most gifted, the colonists failed to develop institutions of accountable governance. Serving European rather than local interests, imperial administrators exploited natural resources for export and introduced new industries and economies related to mercantilist trade in tin, rubber, tapioca, opium, spices, tea, and other valued commodities. As they extracted from mines and expanded plantations, European governors wholly neglected local socioeconomic development. Over time the cruelty, exploitation, and injustice of colonial rule bred popular resentment and put into motion a new force in the region: nationalism.

The rise of anti-imperial nationalism was the most consequential product of colonialism in Southeast Asia. Although deliberate movements against European control punctuated the entire colonial history of Southeast Asia, it was the ideological battles of the twentieth century that fed the transformative nationalism that came to define the region's future.

A traumatic experience under Japanese occupation during World War II further fueled aspirations for self-rule and independence across the region. Following Japan's surrender in 1945 to Allied forces, Europe's postwar leaders disregarded attempts by Southeast Asian leaders to declare formal independence. Eager for resources to rebuild their own war-torn economies, the colonists audaciously returned to extend control over their previously held territories: the British in Burma and Malaya; the French in Indochina (Vietnam, Cambodia, and Laos); the Dutch in Indonesia; and the Portuguese in East Timor. To legitimize their ambitions, European administrators received international recognition for their actions through postwar treaties that excluded Southeast Asians from negotiations. In 1946, the Philippines, vacated by its American occupiers of forty-seven years, joined Thailand as one of the two independent Southeast Asian countries in the early postwar period.

Resolve for independence hardened. In Burma, Indonesia, and Vietnam, nationalism became an especially potent and unifying force that led to fierce struggles for self-determination. In Malaysia and Singapore, the struggle for *merdeka* (independence) was less violent but every bit as formative in cultivating a new sense of nationalist purpose. Across the region, experiences with colonialism had differed, but the nationalist rhetoric for genuine self-governance emerged as a political lingua franca among anticolonial revolutionaries. Thailand, having escaped direct colonial rule, developed its own sense of nationhood stemming from its proud record of independence. Hoping to bind the various peoples within the borders of its constitutional monarchy, modernizing Thai elites cultivated the nationalist creed "Nation, Religion, King."

Relentless anti-imperial political activity and painfully violent episodes of engagement with colonial forces gradually produced two significant consequences for the region: the overdue withdrawal of the Europeans and the rise of a handful of charismatic, larger-than-life independence leaders, including Ho Chi Minh in Vietnam, Sukarno in Indonesia, Aung San in Burma, Tungku Abdul Rahman in Malaysia, and Prince Sihanouk in Cambodia. But even as decolonization and courageous independence leaders offered fresh hopes under sovereign statehood, a new dimension of geopolitical struggle, the Cold War, entered the scene and overwhelmed the region.

For Southeast Asians, the ironically named Cold War thoroughly destabilized the region with occupation, warfare, and even genocide. From 1945 to 1989, the effects of superpower politics led to the deaths of more than 10 million soldiers and civilians. Countless bombs and bullets from conventional warfare and unimaginable atrocities caused by zealous ideologues and murderous despots, not to mention the appalling use of chemical defoliants, produced long-term tragedy for many Southeast Asians even as their countries finally achieved true independence. The political and economic chaos of the Cold War thus not only delayed the independence of Southeast Asian states but retarded their early development by politically dividing societies, peoples, and communities.

The Cold War was fought in Southeast Asia along three interrelated dimensions: internal ideological struggle, superpower rivalry, and interstate conflict. Leftist movements embracing communist visions for state control existed in every major Southeast Asian country during this period. Competing ideological visions pitted communism against not only democratic capitalism (which scarcely existed in the region) but also right-leaning militaries, traditional monarchists, and neoimperial foreign influences. U.S.–U.S.S.R. superpower rivalry, expressed most clearly in the Vietnam War, was also affected after 1960 by the Sino-Soviet split over global communist supremacy. Ever in search of international patrons, Southeast Asian communists exploited this split to suit their largely nationalist purposes.

The meddling of three external Cold War powers in the region exacerbated existing conflicts and created new tensions. The most tragic conflict resulted in the rise of the genocidal Khmer Rouge, who, before the illegal U.S. bombing of Cambodia, had demonstrated insufficient capacity to seize Cambodian state power. China, which had supported Vietnamese revolutionaries against both the French and the Americans, turned on its former communist ally in the mid-1970s by supporting the Khmer Rouge in an attempt to outmaneuver the Soviets, who maintained support for Vietnam. China's communist leaders count among the very few diplomatic supporters of Cambodia's Pol Pot clique, which is responsible for the deaths of 1.7 million Cambodians during its three-year reign of terror.

Superpower rivalry insidiously politicized ethnic relations throughout Southeast Asia as well. During the Cold War, both communist and noncommunist governments engaged in shocking anti-Chinese violence and brutality over suspicions that ethnic Chinese harbored political loyalties to Beijing. Other ethnic minorities became the mercenaries and puppets of external powers and local opportunists, especially in the mountainous upland areas of Vietnam, Laos, and mainland Southeast Asia. In the so-called Golden Triangle—the lawless tri-border region where Burma, Thailand, and Laos meet the Mekong River and its tributaries—powerless upland minorities were recruited and coerced to do the bidding of warlords, revolutionaries, arms dealers, opium traffickers, government militaries, and CIA operatives. Forever questioned about their allegiances, and treated as pawns in the strategic calculations of more powerful actors, Southeast Asia's minorities suffered greatly during the Cold War.

The Cold War also produced new alliances and interstate conflicts between Southeast Asian states. Nonalignment, attempted by some, became an impossible position to maintain over time. Thailand and the Philippines, both noncommunist states, joined the Southeast Asian Treaty Organization (SEATO) under the tutelage of the United States. In the 1960s and '70s, both countries provided troops and territory to the United States for staging actions in Vietnam. After the Vietnam War, and the reduction of U.S. commitment to the region, noncommunist states relied more heavily on the Association of Southeast Asian Nations (ASEAN), an organization originally created in 1967 as a bulwark against growing communism in the region.

Indonesia, led initially by the charismatic Sukarno, originally claimed Cold War neutrality only to invite an internal battle between left and right forces within the country. Sukarno's failed balancing act led to the rise of the anticommunist Suharto regime, which took power after a murky 1965 coup and countercoup. Ten years later, General Suharto's Indonesian troops forcibly occupied East Timor in a bloody campaign without U.S. objections. The invasion occurred only nine days after a left-leaning organization had declared East Timor independent from Portugal. Thus, Indonesia, formerly neutral and nonaligned, turned to the U.S. as its Cold War patron and contributed to American objectives in the region.

Cambodia, which once claimed Cold War neutrality under King Sihanouk, found itself under the influence of all three major powers during the Cold War. In the wake of its secret bombing campaign, the U.S. supported Lon Nol's coup over Sihanouk in 1971 only to provoke the Chinese-backed Khmer Rouge and fuel their rise to power in 1975. Later, in January 1979, Soviet-backed Vietnam forcibly occupied Cambodia, putting it under Moscow's ultimate control. Six weeks after Vietnamese troops took control of Phnom Penh and pushed Pol Pot and his followers to jungle redoubts near the Thai border, China launched a brutal attack against Vietnam. Disastrously, both sides lost thousands of troops in the month-long conflict, in which China seized territory only to retreat after a fierce response from Vietnam's battle-tested military. China's leaders claimed victory, but Vietnamese troops stayed in Cambodia throughout the 1980s until the United Nations brokered their withdrawal.

During the 1980s, the final decade of the Cold War, the U.S. military presence in Southeast Asia included only a few bases in the Philippines. Focused on new reform efforts at home, China and the Soviet Union also began to disengage from the region. As the soldiers, operatives, and advisors of the superpowers departed, a rather unexpected but transformative force became established in the region: Japanese businessmen. Despite the fact that Japan had attacked and occupied all of Southeast Asia in World War II and that lingering resentment and fear persisted, Japan's meteoric postwar economic success brought Southeast Asia into its economic orbit. Singapore was among the first to benefit. As Japan's export-oriented economy grew, so too did its need for raw materials, petroleum, and other imports. Tiny Singapore did not produce many of these resources, but it benefited from increasing oceangoing traffic to and from Japan because of the geographical positions of its port facilities. Singapore joined South Korea, Taiwan, and Hong Kong as models of third-world economic success, known collectively as the "Asian economic dragons."[4]

In the mid-1980s, Japan's growing investments in Southeast Asia expanded rapidly as a result of the appreciating value of the Japanese yen, which made exporting from Japan expensive. Escaping the high yen, Japanese industrialists moved production to a number of Southeast Asian countries where cheap labor and favorable currency exchange rates made the region a prime export platform. All of this was timed with policy shifts in many Southeast Asian countries designed to emulate the successful export-oriented industrialization strategies of the Asian dragons and their move away from import substitution industrialization. Southeast Asian governments aggressively courted ties with Japan, causing trade volume to expand. Thailand, Malaysia, Indonesia, and to a lesser extent the Philippines each moved toward a development model of activist state guidance of private sector–driven export growth. Malaysia's prime minister appropriately dubbed the new development approach the "Look East Policy."

As economies grew and middle classes began to coalesce, new interest in democracy and political reform began to surface across the region. In 1986, Philippine president Ferdinand Marcos, a U.S. Cold War ally who had suspended democracy and manipulated law to extend his own rule, was ousted in a massive popular movement known as "People Power." Thailand also moved closer to democracy by electing its first civilian prime minister since a failed period of democracy in the mid-1970s. Even economically autarkic Burma faced new prodemocracy forces. In 1988, demonstrators forced the country's ruling military junta to schedule elections for a representative parliament. After officially changing the country's name in English to Myanmar in 1989, the elections were held in 1990 but the losing generals did not honor the results. However, with the democratic genie now out of the bottle, popular aspirations for representative government in Burma have persisted since, often provoking brutal suppression.

Elsewhere in the region, authoritarian leaders repressed growing aspirations for democracy even as the Cold War showed signs of thawing in Europe. On the communist left, Vietnamese leaders opened the economy but not its political system. On the nationalistic right, long-standing governments in Indonesia, Malaysia, and Singapore viewed greater democracy as a threat to budding economic success. Following the Cold War, public pressure for political reform would emerge as a new force that Southeast Asian governments would constantly face.

SHARED SOCIAL PATTERNS

In addition to the religious influences, colonial history, nationalist movements, and Cold War experiences that have shaped this otherwise diverse region, some observable social patterns also add definition to a Southeast Asian political economy. These generalized patterns are not universal, but they are widely shared across the region and contain elements of both "continuity and change"—a phrase commonly used among Southeast Asian specialists who are forever attempting to characterize the enduring and dynamic patterns of socioeconomic behavior in the region.

Southeast Asian nations are characterized by an agricultural base that traditionally has been the heart of everyday life. Historically, the agricultural village served as the major unit of identity for the rural population, acting as its educational, religious, cultural, political, economic, and social center. Although urban growth expanded as trade increased over time—accompanied by Indian, Chinese, Arab, and European influences on the royal and colonial centers of power—the basic economic unit for most Southeast Asians, until recent decades, has been the peasant-style family-operated farm. Generally, the family farm was part of a village economy characterized by subsistence production, with most of the farm products being consumed by the family or within the village. Experiences differed, but feudal-type arrangements across the region fed the development of landed elites, aristocrats, and royals who exploited the labor of rural populations for imperial projects—a pattern repeated later by European colonists (absent any local cultural foundations that historically ameliorated popular resentment of royal power).

Some areas of Southeast Asia today remain characterized by traditional village arrangements and subsistence agriculture, but the socioeconomic picture has grown increasingly complex. The arrival of green revolution technologies, commercial agribusiness, and rising expectations of educational opportunity and material gain defines agrarian change today. "Farmers" are replacing "peasants" in the economic sense of these terms, and life inside most villages is now fully interdependent with life outside the village due to a host of transformative factors: rural-to-urban migration, expanding nonfarm work, globalized labor markets, remittance economies, new communication technologies, and rising consumerism. Over the past fifty years, the agricultural sector's economic importance has continued to decline relative to industry and services, although employment in the sector remains considerable.

In spite of these changes, the hierarchical structure traditional to the village still finds expression in the region's political life. Southeast Asian societies, generally speaking, remain fundamentally organized into networks of superior-subordinate (patron-client) ties. These networks form the basis of political structures and affect the allocation of resources and values. In their positive expressions, these relations form "moral economies" where uneven but reciprocal relations bring mutual benefit to participants in a context of cultural appropriateness and meaning. Where there are marked inequalities in wealth, status, and control, and where resources are insufficient, those with limited access can seek alliances with individuals at a higher socioeconomic level or access to state resources. The relationship is reciprocal in the sense that the patron expects support, protection, labor, or some other service in return for dispensing benefits to the subordinate. In their pejorative interpretation, patron-client systems prop up authoritarian forms of government with vast networks designed for patrimony. The strongest networks are capable of manipulating rivals or depoliticizing opponents through co-optation and participation. Such relational asymmetry can also foster exploitation, and risks endless power struggles between elites who vie for each other's client networks.

Representative forms of democratic government in Southeast Asia thus both benefit and suffer from these patron-client systems. Such networks can link those who wield state power with ordinary citizens and, potentially, link voting constituencies with elected officials. Left unchecked, however, patron-client partiality can threaten the legitimacy of democracy through favoritism, nepotism, corruption, and abuse of official power. Throughout Southeast Asia, rising demands by individuals and groups for increased governmental accountability, transparency, and recognition of civil and political rights clash with the deep-seated impulses of power elites to defend traditional forms of patronage. Citing cultural appropriateness, Southeast Asian elites have at times fashioned regimes that are, in the name of social order, structurally designed to institutionalize state patronage.

Socioeconomically, a common pattern throughout Southeast Asia is the presence of an influential overseas Chinese business community. In most Southeast Asian urban centers, a deeply rooted overseas Chinese community discernibly, and disproportionally, influences commercial life. The experiences of such communities differ from country to country, and degrees of assimilation, hybridization, and communalization differ markedly; nevertheless, this presence influenced the course of events domestically and internationally. During the Cold War, tensions between China and Taiwan, and communists and republicans, often reproduced themselves in cities such as Jakarta, Kuala Lumpur, and Bangkok. Communist movements in the region often had a real or perceived Chinese tilt to them—a reality often proving fatal to overseas Chinese when anti-communist nationalists turned to violence, as they did in Indonesia in 1965. Having established themselves economically over time, Southeast Asia's Chinese communities were well positioned when trade and business expanded in the 1980s as a result of export-oriented policies across the region and market openness in the People's Republic of China. Around this time, overseas Chinese networks also linked Southeast Asian countries to the flourishing economies of Hong Kong and Taiwan. By the time the new international era dawned in the 1990s, many Southeast Asian Chinese were now visibly expressing their Chinese roots and identities; what was once considered a social liability emerged as a new economic asset. Moreover, powerful alliances between political leaders and wealthy overseas Chinese increasingly began to shape the political economies of the region.

The influences, experiences, and social patterns lending shape to the Southeast Asian experience described above compose only a partial set of factors able to explain the various events and trends associated with the politics of Southeast Asian countries. The country chapters that follow illustrate this fact by employing much greater sensitivity to the particular conditions, events, individuals, groups, and institutions that make up political life. Nevertheless, in addition to these shared social patterns, and the common forces of colonialism, nationalism, and the Cold War discussed above, profound changes to the international system that followed the Cold War's end now influence the political economy of the region in new and unprecedented ways.

THE NEW INTERNATIONAL ERA

An extraordinary sweep of international change occurred following the end of the Cold War in 1989. The extent of these changes, which occurred rapidly, stunned the world and irrevocably recast international relations. The major catalyst responsible for causing a break with the past was Soviet president Mikhail Gorbachev, whose policies in the 1980s put in motion the end of the bipolar conflict that had structured world relations since World War II. Gorbachev, who took the helm of the U.S.S.R. in 1985, acted on the assumption that the economically stagnant Soviet Union could flourish only if it pursued perestroika (comprehensive economic restructuring) and glasnost (opening of society). His reforms included a foreign policy of imperial disengagement, which U.S. presidents Ronald Reagan and George H. W. Bush welcomed. Populations across Western and Eastern Europe celebrated the Soviet leader's reforms. By the late 1980s, a new global optimism emanated from events being driven by the Kremlin's new agenda.

In Asia, Gorbachev's policies meant the withdrawal of Russian troops from Afghanistan, demilitarizing the Sino-Russian border, ceasing aid to Vietnam and leftist insurgencies in the region, and abandoning military bases at Cam Ranh Bay and Da Nang in Vietnam. Vietnam responded to Gorbachev's changes by seeking to restructure its own economy. Pursing a new strategy, *doi moi* (renovation), Vietnam's communist leadership began to permit free-market activity and foreign investment. These moves were in line with changes already sweeping communist China. China's leader, Deng Xiaoping, had previously broken from the failed development policies of his predecessor, Mao Zedong, and began to allow market forces to operate within communist China. During the 1980s, Deng encouraged international trade and foreign investment in China by establishing ties with Asian businesses and Western multinationals. In the new international era overseas Chinese in Southeast Asia become major conduits for business between China, Asia, and the world. The People's Republic of China, a once-feared

Cold War power in Southeast Asia, enjoyed a new economic role as a regional economic partner and a formidable export competitor.

During the new international era, the bipolar world of communists and noncommunists rapidly transformed itself into a more multipolar world where states, regions, international organizations, and nonstate actors exhibit new forms of power and influence. Although the United States stood alone as the dominant global power in the 1990s, it soon learned that relative power is far from absolute power. Asia's own rising economic influence and Europe's deepening integration with the former communist states of the old Soviet bloc created new poles of economic and political power.

The new era also became defined by increasingly assertive international bodies such as the World Trade Organization (WTO), the International Monetary Fund (IMF), and the World Bank. These organizations established and enforced the rules of globalization, often coercing struggling governments to implement their policies of market fundamentalism in the process. Nongovernmental organizations (NGOs) also proliferated across the world in the 1990s, promoting humanitarian, development, and rights-oriented causes. As for the United Nations, its increasingly visible blue-helmeted peacekeepers became symbols of a new activist (but often impotent) international community. Added to all of these new forces were powerful stateless actors tied to nefarious networks of terrorists, drug lords, and human traffickers. All of the new forces of globalization found their way into Southeast Asia during the early years of the new international era.

Although Japan had led Southeast Asia in its economic success in the closing decade of the Cold War, the East Asian economic superpower began to sink into recession, paradoxically, even as the new international era dawned. Nevertheless, ongoing Japanese investments continued to fuel a Southeast Asia boom economy that came to enjoy global renown. South Korean and Taiwanese investors, fleeing higher labor costs at home, similarly poured investments into the region. Hot money from European and American traders found its way to the region's fast and furious emerging markets.

Encouraged by Western governments, the IMF, and globalization advocates, Southeast Asian governments liberalized their financial markets, putting an end to many restrictions (and safeguards) that formerly regulated the flow of capital into and out of their countries. As a result, joint ventures and foreign-financed enterprises expanded quickly and deliberately into textiles, footwear, electronics, automobile parts, cosmetics, agribusiness, petroleum refining, and other diverse industries and manufactures. Portfolio investment poured into the region from day-traders and short-sellers in New York, London, and Tokyo. Double-digit economic growth and trade balance surpluses soon characterized the Southeast Asian "tiger economies," as they came to be known. Thailand, Malaysia, and Indonesia, and to a lesser extent the Philippines and Vietnam, all participated in the rapid economic growth unleashed by the passing of Cold War tensions and rapid liberalization of trade and financial markets.

The phenomenal economic growth rates the tigers experienced—as high as 10 percent per year during this period—fundamentally changed the Southeast Asian landscape. The most obvious change was the increase in per capita gross national product (GNP). Per capita GNP in Thailand in 1977, for example, was $300; by 1997 it had climbed to $2,970. Similar growth in per capita GNP occurred in the other countries over the same period: Malaysia, $660 to $3,531; Indonesia, $150 to $692; the Philippines, $310 to $1,049. Singapore's rose even more dramatically, from $2,120 to $24,664, hence its "dragon" status. Corresponding figures for reforming but populous Vietnam and for economically stagnant Burma, Cambodia, and Laos indicated less improvement, by contrast. By 1997, per capita GNP in these countries still averaged less than $500.

By the mid-1990s, so confident were Southeast Asians in their path to success that regional leaders began to engage the world in a debate that pitted "Asian values" against "Western values." The chief spokesmen in this debate were politicians from Singapore and Malaysia. Their contention was that because Asian culture valued social order over political freedom, it allowed economic markets to thrive even as societies remained orderly. Centuries of pent-up resentment against Western superiority unleashed itself in trans-Pacific rhetorical punches. The West's high crime rates, divorce rates, declining educational standards, and sedentary lifestyles of TV watching were cited repeatedly as evidence of American inferiority. "You Americans have this mantra about your high standard of living," argued a senior Asian diplomat, "but if standard of living means not being afraid to go outside after dark, or not worrying about what filth your children will see on all those TV channels, then our Asian societies have the higher standard."[5] The message was unambiguous: The world would be a better place if countries began to learn from Asia rather than the West. Journalists writing from New York and London countered by listing human rights injustices and corruption tied to Asian governments.

The Asian values debate symbolized the sweeping changes that had come to the region in the new international era. Political ideology, interstate war, and superpower meddling were no longer central concerns for the modern states of Southeast Asia. Instead, the key issues became economics, development, integrated markets, and stable political development. Southeast Asian societies also became more concerned with the negative effects of rapid growth, such as deforestation, pollution, traffic, corruption, and (contrary to the rhetoric of some Asian politicians) increased drug use, criminal activity, and alienation among Southeast Asian youth. Still, in the bigger picture,

Southeast Asian governments and their societies benefited by no longer building walls around their countries and isolating their economies.

The exception was Burma, which, after reneging on promised political reform and refusing to recognize the 1990 election results unfavorable to the military government, persisted in its strategy of socialist economic autarky. Burma's dreadful standard of living, however, only reinforced the dominant view in the region that interaction, not isolation, was necessary for a country to flourish. Indeed, every Southeast Asian country that tested the open-market proposition experienced unprecedented economic dynamism. The results of openness included a phenomenal rise in the people's standard of living, but success was accompanied by widening gaps between the rich and poor and unprecedented policy challenges in infrastructure, public health, and education.

The new international era also saw Southeast Asian societies transformed by new forms of communication. Television, mobile phones, Internet cafés, satellite communications, and the entire digital revolution changed the way information was spread from person to person in this new era. No longer could governments fully control information flow among the populace. In the new era, the challenge for governments became balancing the effects of technological change, foreign investment, and international trade against political demands for greater openness and governmental transparency. Another challenge that has emerged is, alas, the threat and reality of financial crisis—something that would affect all the booming countries of Southeast Asia.

A classic lesson of international political economy is that economic interdependence creates greater sensitivity and vulnerability to global markets.[6] The globalization of Southeast Asian economies had made the region's countries increasingly vulnerable to external forces and the volatility of international markets. These vulnerabilities proved to be real when the region suffered financial disaster in 1997.

In the early 1990s, China's government, already advantaged by the country's seemingly endless supply of cheap labor, devalued its currency, making its exports even more competitive than those coming from Southeast Asia. With their currencies pegged to the U.S. dollar, most Southeast Asian countries' exports consequently became more expensive than China's in international markets. China subsequently began to attract foreign investment more rapidly than Southeast Asia, and exports in the tiger economies began to level off after a decade of breakneck expansion.

By the mid-1990s, the current account surpluses enjoyed by Southeast Asian tiger economies turned into current account deficits. More foreign products and luxury goods entered local markets, causing imbalances to grow. Many remained unworried by such imbalances. The heady business environment had pundits and economists predicting further growth. But, with export opportunities slowing, Southeast Asians poured their own investment money into real estate speculation, lavish projects (such as five-star hotels and condominiums), and local stock markets. Capital inflows and easy credit also expanded, made possible by the earlier deregulation of financial and capital markets. Because local currencies were pegged to the U.S. dollar, many local borrowers denominated their loans in dollars to take advantage of lower interest rates. Over a few short years, debt obligations mounted across the Southeast Asian business community. Slowing revenues from declining exports and an oversupply of new housing and high-rise office space caused the real estate bubble to burst. Debtors began to default. Stress on financial institutions grew, and financial mismanagement of banks and investment firms began to make headlines. Corruption in both the public and private sectors drew increasing attention, and government scandals invited public criticism, especially in Thailand and the Philippines, where democratization had expanded freedom of the press since the end of the Cold War. In Indonesia, Suharto's thirty-year regime, built on performance legitimization, faced unprecedented signs of weakness.

By 1997, international investor confidence in Southeast Asia's tigers began to slip. Global currency traders, recognizing the shakiness of the region's economies, bet against the Southeast Asian currencies, undermining their worth even more. Government attempts to support the currency pegs proved futile. The result was a cascade of overnight currency devaluations from country to country, which in turn precipitated inflation, unemployment, and a massive outflow of capital from all the tiger economies. The sudden devaluation of local currencies, combined with rapid economic contraction, left local Southeast Asian investors saddled with massive loads of debt. Many investors faced the impossible task of meeting inflated repayment obligations in the face of declining revenues. Southeast Asia found itself in a full-fledged financial crisis.

Leaders in Southeast Asia responded ineffectively to the crisis, allowing the downturn to spread throughout all of Asia, eventually hurting markets across the globe. Southeast Asia's politicians seemed incapable of making the difficult decisions necessary to resolve the crisis. Instead, they hunkered down, blamed Westerners, and continued to protect cronies and undermine public-spirited technocrats. The public, more educated and savvy than ever, knew better and realized that whatever the sins of international investors, their own government and business leaders also shared the blame. The region's shell-shocked governments eventually turned to the IMF, the world's lender of last resort, to help them finance their way out of the crisis. The IMF saw itself as the economic doctor of the new international era, ready and able to administer the treatments countries needed for financial recovery. It provided multibillion-dollar loans, but only on the strict conditions that recipient governments would raise interest rates, increase tax rates, adopt strict budget austerity, and totally restructure their ailing financial sectors. It was the wrong medicine.

The IMF's ill-conceived rescue packages proved damaging to already-suffering economies. The cash liquidity the IMF provided to the stressed tiger economies largely went to pay off foreign creditors and financial institutions; it did little to spur economic growth. Government budget austerity measures exacerbated existing economic contraction, and local investment plummeted. Higher interest rates and tax burdens further inhibited local investment when it was most desperately needed. Rather than stimulate their economies with public spending, governments were bound by IMF conditionality only to starve their economies further.

Social and political disruption followed. Rampant unemployment, rapid inflation, and economic hardship turned into antigovernment protests and disorder. As a result, these once-famed emerging markets and their proud political leaders saw governments change in the wake of the crisis and IMF rescue packages. Only Singapore, with its more advanced and resilient economy, and Malaysia, whose leaders had opted to reject IMF money in favor of capital controls, survived the 1997 Asian financial crisis intact.

The 1997 Asian economic crisis shook Southeast Asia's confidence in open trade and financial globalization. Asian leaders stopped talking about Asian values. In fact, to a significant degree, the crisis set Southeast Asian countries on disparate courses that continue to the present day. Recovery patterns have differed markedly from one case to the next. Indonesia, which suffered the most severe setback, sunk into deep political crisis, ending thirty years of rule under General Suharto. The collapse of his regime led not only to greater democracy in Indonesia but also to the birth of East Timor, which had been under Indonesian occupation since 1975. Thailand, after cycling through rotations of parliamentary coalitions, eventually elected a new party (the Thais Love Thais party) whose billionaire leader turned to populist policies and ultimately ignited a political crisis that continues to this day. Philippine voters turned to an action-movie hero to manage recovery, only to throw him out of office for corruption a few years later in a reprise of People Power. Vietnam slowed its pace of reform and increased surveillance of political opponents. Then, in the wake of the Asian economic crisis and the political changes it spawned, the new international era grew even more complex as a result of terrorist attacks half a world away.

Southeast Asia's newly installed leaders faced a new, more complicated foreign policy matrix following the September 11, 2001, attacks in New York and Washington, D.C. Already worried about their sluggish economies, Southeast Asian officials now had to concern themselves with U.S.

president George W. Bush's declarations of an international "axis of evil" that tied rogue states to stateless terrorist groups. His announcement that the countries of the world were either "with us or against us" put unwanted pressure on the region's governments. Predictions by the Bush administration that Southeast Asia would become the "second front in the War on Terror" caused even wider reverberations of concern and anxiety in the region.[7]

Aside from the Philippines, which had long battled Muslim separatists in the country's south, none of the ASEAN governments enthusiastically embraced the Bush administration's view of a post–September 11 world. Thailand was a reluctant partner, and Singapore turned to the United States only pragmatically, especially after Islamist groups bombed hotels and embassies in neighboring Indonesia. Wars in Afghanistan and Iraq turned many of Southeast Asia's large Muslim populations against the United States. Over time, events (or more precisely nonevents) proved American predictions that Southeast Asia would become the second front of international terrorism erroneous. Notwithstanding the locally driven terrorist activities of long-standing irredentist Muslim organizations in southern Thailand and the southern Philippines, internationally sponsored terrorism in the region has been sporadic. Since 9/11, five dramatic bombings in Indonesia at the hands of internationally sponsored terrorists led to over two hundred deaths and hundreds of injuries. While no doubt a matter for local and international concern, the frequency and intensity of terrorism in the region is on par with that experienced by Europe. Compared to terrorist violence hotspots in the Middle East and South Asia, Southeast Asia remained relatively calm.

As government officials adjusted to a post-9/11 world and pursued policy packages with hopes of returning to the high growth rates of the previous decade, another global concern caught their attention: rising China. Southeast Asian countries continued to be outperformed economically by China throughout the first decade of the 2000s. China had become Asia's new economic power. Because of its strict currency regime and regulated foreign capital markets, China's economic competitiveness was less affected by the Asian economic crisis. With respect to its relations with Southeast Asia, China's direct and indirect influence on the region came through new free trade deals, tariff reductions, business connections, and even increased cultural influence. Almost universally, Southeast Asians were also enthralled by Beijing's impressive pageantry and execution of the 2008 Olympiad. By that same year, ASEAN's combined economies ranked as China's fourth-largest trading partner. Recent predictions forecast ASEAN to become China's top trading partner by 2015, remarkably surpassing China's trade levels with

Japan, the United States, and the European Union.[8] Adjusting to China's rise is now a top priority among all Southeast Asian governments.

Southeast Asia is now well more than a decade beyond the 1997 economic crisis. The region is showing modest levels of income recovery and general progress in overall development measures. But aggregate comparisons of basic indicators illustrate the vast economic disparities that characterize the region. In terms of economic power, performance, and poverty, Southeast Asia's economic dynamism has created a region of remarkable disparity. Tables 1.1 and 1.2 below highlight select economic and development indicators for the region.

In terms of 2011 gross domestic product (GDP) per capita, when adjusted for purchasing power parity, microstates Singapore ($59,990) and Brunei ($49,400) lead the region. Malaysia ($15,600) follows at a distant third, with Thailand ($9,700) further behind. Indonesia ($4,700) and the Philippines ($4,100) continue to rank in the middle of the pack. The remaining countries comprise the lowest tier in terms of per capita production: Vietnam ($3,300),

TABLE 1.1 Country Comparisons: Select Economic Figures

	Total Population (millions) 2011	Total GDP (nominal) $US bil. 2011 (est.)	GNI per capita (Atlas method) $US 2011	GDP per capita (PPP) $US 2011	Total Exports $US bil. 2011(est.)	Poverty rate: % below nat. pov. line 2010	GINI (higher values = higher income inequality) 2009 (est.)
Brunei	0.4	$15.6	$31,800	$49,400	$10.67	...	n.a.
Cambodia	14.3	$13.2	$830	$2,300	$5.35	31%	44.4
Indonesia	242.3	$834.3	$2,940	$4,700	$208.90	13%	36.8
Laos	6.2	$7.9	$1,130	$2,700	$1.84	27%	36.7
Malaysia	28.8	$247.6	$8,420	$15,600	$212.70	4%	46.2
Myanmar	48.3	$50.2	<$1,005	$1,300	$9.54	33%	n.a.
Philippines	94.8	$216.1	$2,210	$4,100	$54.17	33%	45.8
Singapore	5.2	$266.5	$42,930	$59,900	$409.20	...	47.3
Thailand	69.5	$345.6	$4,420	$9,700	$244.40	8%	53.6
Timor-Leste	1.2	$0.7	$2,730	$3,100	$0.18	41%	31.9
Vietnam	87.4	$123.6	$1,260	$3,300	$96.30	15%	37.6

Sources: World Bank, UNDP, ADB, CIA World Factbook

Timor-Leste ($3,100), Cambodia ($2,300), Laos ($2,700), and Myanmar ($1,300). Even with the most optimistic forecasts, it will take many decades for Southeast Asia's poorest to reach the average living standards that the region's richest countries enjoy today.

By combining 2011 World Bank income classifications with broader development indicators that consider poverty rates, education, health, access to water, and levels of corruption, the countries of Southeast Asia can be divided into four general groups:

High income/high development	Brunei and Singapore
Upper-middle income/medium-high development	Malaysia and Thailand
Low-middle income/medium development	Indonesia, Philippines, and Vietnam
Low income/low development	Cambodia, Laos, Myanmar, and Timor-Leste

TABLE 1.2 Country Comparisons: Select Development Figures

	Percentage of rural population 1975 → 2010	Human Dev. Index (HDI) value: 0.0-1.0 2011	Human Dev. Index (HDI) ranking (of 179 countries) 2011	Births attended by a skilled professional 2005 ~ 2010 (avg.)	Percentage of rural population with access to improved water 2011	Corruption ranking (of 183 countries: #1 = least corrupt) 2011	Freedom Rating (political and civil liberties) 2012
Brunei	38 → 24	0.838	#33	99%	...	#49	not free
Cambodia	90 → 77	0.523	#139	44%	58%	#164	not free
Indonesia	81 → 46	0.617	#124	73%	74%	#100	free
Lao PDR	89 → 67	0.524	#138	20%	62%	#154	not free
Malaysia	62 → 28	0.761	#61	100%	99%	#60	partly free
Myanmar	76 → 66	0.483	#149	37%	78%	#180	not free
Philippines	64 → 34	0.644	#112	62%	92%	#129	partly free
Singapore	0 → 0	0.866	#26	100%	...	#5	partly free
Thailand	76 → 66	0.682	#103	99%	95%	#80	partly free
Timor-Leste	85 → 72	0.495	#147	30%	60%	#143	partly free
Vietnam	81 → 71	0.593	#128	88%	93%	#112	not free

Sources: UNDP, World Bank, WHO, Transparency International, Freedom House

In total, the dynamic forces of the new international era have bolstered and expanded the economic power of Southeast Asia and its tremendous economic diversity. ASEAN's combined GDP of $2.3 trillion is already larger than India's and is predicted to overtake Japan's by 2028.[9] Yet, generalizing the whole region's progress in economic production and human development is increasingly challenging (and increasingly meaningless). In spite of the integration of the region's disparate economies through initiatives such as the ASEAN Free Trade Area and the Greater Mekong Subregion, the development trajectories of Southeast Asian countries seem to grow more disparate with each passing year. A similar trend of divergent paths characterizes the political regimes of the region.

COMPARING POLITICAL REGIMES

Because of the great diversity among Southeast Asian states, as well as the many influences and changes they experience over time, categorizing Southeast Asian political regimes is difficult and must be complemented by analyzing the unique attributes of each country's experience. Why this is the case is demonstrated below, and in the following chapters.

If one is primarily interested in identifying the regime types of Southeast Asia's countries, a standard approach would be to use accepted regime classifications and to analyze which countries fit those definitions. By employing Larry Diamond's sixfold typology and the widely used Freedom House ratings (*free, partly free,* and *not free*), such an analysis is possible and fairly straightforward.[10] Diamond's typology distinguishes two types of democratic regimes (*liberal* and *electoral*); three types of authoritarian regimes (*competitive, hegemonic electoral,* and *politically closed*); and *ambiguous regimes,* a residual category for systems too difficult to classify due to changing conditions or ongoing instability.

With respect to countries that label their own systems "democratic," Diamond encourages making a distinction between regimes in transition that aspire to liberal democracy from those that are *pseudodemocracies,* that is, systems where elections exist but institutional arrangements are deliberately designed to inhibit party competition, pluralism, or civil liberties.

From the perspective of Diamond's typology, Thailand, the Philippines, and Indonesia all fall within the general category of democracy. Each of these systems, however, is an *electoral democracy* and falls short of meeting the criteria to be identified as an established *liberal democracy* (where political and civil liberties exist and endure, and where changing sets of elected leaders are chosen by and accountable to an electorate through fair elections that are repeatedly held).[11]

Indonesia, one of the *electoral democracies,* is the only Southeast Asian country rated *"free"* by Freedom House in 2012. However, it is still a young and fairly untested democracy. Indonesia's political system remains deficient in some aspects of electoral fairness and durability, but, having ended Suharto's long, hegemonic rule, the country appears to be on track to becoming a *liberal democracy*, more so perhaps than either Thailand or the Philippines as of 2012.

Only a few years ago, Thailand had a pluralistic system that was approaching the definition of *liberal democracy*. In fact, Thailand was classified by Freedom House as *"free"* for seven consecutive years (1998–2005). Once a democratic beacon in the region, Thailand has since suffered from multiple electoral-driven political crises, a coup d'état, constitutional legitimacy challenges, politicized judicial interventions, and episodic clashes between civilian demonstrators and government security forces. In flux from one year to the next, Thailand saw its freedom rating swing from *"free"* to *"partly free"* to *"not free,"* and back to *"partly free"* from 2005 to 2008. Ongoing political crisis has kept its "partly free" designation in place and pushed the country into the netherworld of regime classification. Thailand, which saw its first democratic constitution appear in 1932, currently lies somewhere between an *electoral democracy* and an *ambiguous regime.*

The Philippines—not in political crisis but accurately classified as *"partly free"* by Freedom House in 2012—is also closer to an *electoral democracy* than a *liberal democracy*. This fact is discouraging given the citizens' aspirations for liberal democratic rule and the country's long experience under democratic constitutions, which dates to the 1940s. Democratic institutions in the Philippines are semidysfunctional in that they often serve as a veneer for oligarchic rule. Corruption, lawlessness, intimidation, and violence permeate politics and competitive elections for public office. The Philippines' *electoral democracy* serves elite interests over those of the broader public.

Under Diamond's typology, Malaysia is best classified as a *competitive authoritarian regime*, where a significant parliamentary opposition exists but a dominant party coalition is able to retain governmental power for decades at a time. The country is often cited as an example of an illiberal democracy. Recent developments indicate that the authoritarian features of the country's system are weakening and party dominance is under stress. The Malaysian political regime—under the weight of more intense parliamentary contestation and changing public attitudes favorable to liberal democracy—may eventually improve its current regime label.

In contrast is Singapore, where the ruling People's Action Party has perpetually inhibited the development of a significant parliamentary opposition by restricting oppositional speech, harassing government opponents, and manipulating a politicized judiciary. Singapore is a *pseudodemocracy* or, more precisely, a *hegemonic electoral authoritarian regime.* Somewhat similarly, the Cambodian People's Party, under the tight grip of strongman Hun Sen, has used extra-electoral mechanisms to intimidate opposition parties, politicians, and activists to ensure ongoing rule. Cambodia is also classified as a *hegemonic electoral authoritarian regime* within Diamond's typology.

Due to the lack of competitive elections and serious restrictions of political and civil liberties, Vietnam and Laos share classification as *politically closed authoritarian regimes*. Myanmar, which released opposition figure Aung San Suu Kyi from house arrest and allowed her and other opposition candidates to run in competitive elections, remains politically closed within the Diamond system, although it is no longer static. As in Vietnam and Laos, political pluralism does not genuinely exist in Myanmar, and new constitutional arrangements retain the military's role as the dominant political actor. Tiny Brunei, an absolute monarchy, also meets the definition of a *politically closed authoritarian regime*.

Timor-Leste, an infant state still dependent on international support and succor, is best classified as an *ambiguous regime*. Although the practice of parliamentary politics evolves and it may aspire to liberal democracy, the country's most pressing problems are political disorder and weak state capacity. Democracy enjoys general legitimacy among Timorese but electoral instability, political violence, and growing regionalism on the island undermine state development and the rule of law. With more time and experience, Timor-Leste is likely to see its regime classification change to electoral democracy.

Regime classification is useful for general comparisons, but it does not adequately portray Southeast Asian nations over time. Without supplementary analysis, regime labels are simply insensitive to the particular political structures, events, and behaviors that animate the political life of particular countries. The characteristics of political repression in Burma, Vietnam, Laos, and Brunei, for example, are different in each country, yet all are classified as *politically closed authoritarian regimes*. Similarly, the historical political experiences and trajectories of Singapore and Cambodia could not be farther from each other in almost every way, yet both share typological classification as *hegemonic electoral authoritarian regimes*. Indeed, the difference in experiences among countries that share a regime label can be greater than countries with different regime labels.

The difficulties and limitations of categorizing the Southeast Asian political systems emphasize the importance of viewing them as highly diverse and worthy of analysis from the vantage point of their unique attributes. Only more specific examination and comparative analysis can get observers beyond stereotypical images, highly generalized economic development classifications, or regime labels that obfuscate more than clarify. Building an appreciation for the political-economic realities that characterize the experiences of Southeast Asian countries requires case-by-case examination. The country chapters of this book are designed with this objective in mind and thus offer a first step toward such an exploration.

The chapters begin with Thailand, Myanmar (Burma), Vietnam, Cambodia, and Laos—the countries of *Peninsular Southeast Asia* (sometimes referred to as "Mainland Southeast Asia").[12] The book then completes the regional survey with chapters on the Philippines, Indonesia, Timor-Leste, Malaysia, Singapore, and Brunei—the countries of *Insular Southeast Asia* (sometimes referred to as "Maritime Southeast Asia").[13]

NOTES

1. The phrase to describe Southeast Asia's transformation "from a battlefield to a marketplace" was famously coined by Thai prime minister Chatichai Choonhavan at a speech to the National Press Club in Washington, D.C., June 16, 1990.

2. The conventional forms of country names are generally used throughout this book. On June 18, 1989, Burma's military rulers announced that the country's official name would (in English) henceforth be Myanmar. From 1989 until recently this name change was not recognized by those who rejected the legitimacy of Burma's military rulers. The name Myanmar was officially used in the United Nations and some official international circles but was significantly rejected by opposition politician and longtime political prisoner Aung San Suu Kyi. Previous editions of this book used Burma exclusively. In 2010, Aung San Suu Kyi was released by a new set of leaders and subsequently ran for parliament in 2011 and won a seat. Following her current practice of using both Myanmar and Burma interchangeably, the current edition of this book uses both names. At the time of writing, many governments are reevaluating relations with the country as well as diplomatic practice with respect to country name usage. This book also uses East Timor and Timor-Leste interchangeably.

3. Because this book focuses on contemporary politics it devotes little attention, unfortunately, to precolonial and colonial history. Readers will need to search elsewhere for a better understanding of historical trends and cultural foundations of the region and particular countries. A common place to begin such a study is with the classic text edited by David Joel Steinberg, *In Search of Southeast Asia* (Honolulu: University of Hawaii Press, 1987), D. R. Sardesai's *Southeast Asia: Past and Present* (Boulder: Westview Press, 2009), and *The Emergence of Modern Southeast Asia: A New History* (Honolulu: University of Hawaii Press, 2005), edited by Norman G. Owen.

4. Also called "Asian economic tigers."

5. Quoted by Kishore Mahbubani, a Singaporean scholar and diplomat, from T. R. Reid, *Confucius Lives Next Door: What Living in the East Teaches Us about Living in the West* (New York: Random House, 1999), 62.

6. See Robert O. Keohane and Joseph S. Nye, *Power and Interdependence*, 4th ed. (Boston: Longman, 2012).

7. George W. Bush, "Address Before a Joint Session of Congress on the State of the Union Address," January 29, 2002; John Gershman, "Is Southeast Asia the Second Front?" *Foreign Affairs* 81, no. 4 (July/August 2002): 60–74.

8. "ASEAN, China to Become Top Trade Partners," *China Daily*, April 20, 2012, http://www.chinadaily.com.cn/cndy/2012-04/20/content_15094898.htm.

9. This prediction was made by the reputable economic forecasting firm HIS Global Insight in 2012. See Michael Richardson, "Region Could Drive Global Economic Revival," *Japan Times Online*, August 22, 2012, http://www.japantimes.co.jp/text/eo20120822mr.html.

10. Larry Diamond is the founder and editor of the *Journal of Democracy* and is a noted regime classification expert. The typology here is taken from his article "Thinking about Hybrid Regimes," *Journal of Democracy* 13, no. 2 (2002): 21–35. Freedom House bases its ratings on a system that assigns values to indicators of "political freedoms" and "civil liberties." Visit www.freedomhouse.org.

11. Fair elections are defined as being administered in a transparent manner by neutral authorities and characterized by ballot secrecy, the impartial treatment of candidates and parties, impartial procedures for resolving complaints and disputes, and minimal political violence.

12. Thailand is the principal country of study of both authors and is treated in the book first. The order of the remaining chapters follows a rough logic that reflects the geographical, historical, and cultural ties and experiences.

13. Although part of Malaysia is located on the Thai-Malay peninsula and is geographically connected to mainland Southeast Asia, the Federation of Malaysia (which includes both peninsular and insular territories) is conventionally grouped with the countries of Insular Southeast Asia. Historically, the peoples of the southern areas of the Malay peninsula have been oriented culturally, linguistically, and economically toward island Southeast Asia more so than the mainland.

2

THAILAND

THAILAND HAS BECOME AN EXEMPLARY CASE STUDY OF HOW
third-world countries can advance economically while attempting politically to achieve stable democracy. The consequences of episodic political
instability in Thailand have not undermined the capacity of its 69.5 million
people to generate improvements in quality of life and maintain relatively
peaceful conditions. Compared with their regional neighbors, the Thais have
escaped brutal occupation, destructive revolutions, tyrannical dictatorship,
and the setbacks of protracted war. Since 1932, when they first adopted constitutional monarchy, the principal project of the Thai people has been to develop a modern economy in tandem with a workable democracy.

Today, Thailand ranks among Southeast Asia's "tiger economies" and is
considered an economic success story with wide global recognition. This
success stems from a history of astute adaptation of those aspects of modern-
ization and development that were appropriate to traditional Thai ways, especially adaptations that ensured the maintenance of two key cultural
institutions: Buddhism and monarchism. Throughout their history, as citizens of the only Southeast Asian nation never to have been colonized, the
Thais never had a foreign culture forcibly thrust upon them. Instead, they
have searched, adapted, and struggled to create their own path to economic
and political development amidst the dynamic influences of a global society.

Thailand's progress toward political liberalization and democracy is all
the more striking given that for centuries the government was autocratic in
form and spirit. Power was the privilege of a small elite as well as of absolute
monarchs who were not accountable to the people and whose authority was
enhanced by an aura of divinity attached to the highest levels of office.
Those who ruled were believed to possess superior ability and moral excel-
lence. Common citizens exhibited little interest in affairs beyond their own
villages. Vestiges of elite rule remain embedded in Thai political culture, but
rising expectations and new norms of democratic practice reflect a deepening

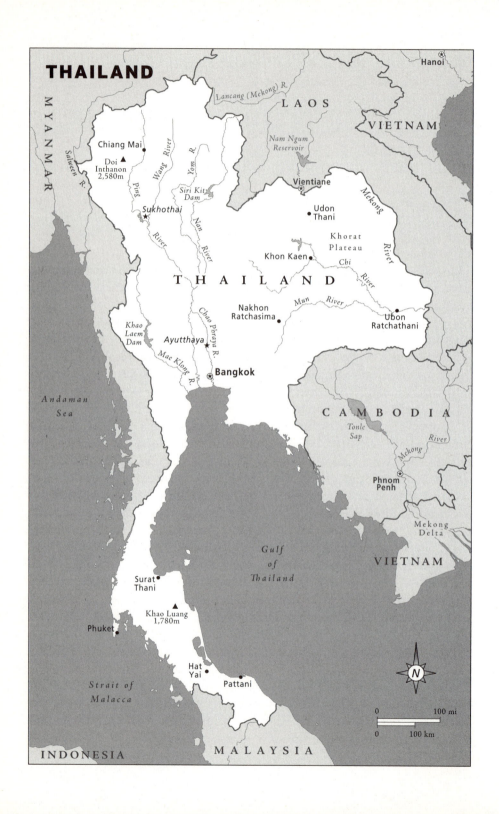

preference for political participation, accountable government, and recognition of human rights.

The Sukhothai Kingdom (c. 1238–1350) was the first Thai-controlled kingdom in history. In this formerly Khmer-ruled area, the Thais absorbed the cultures of the Khmers, Mons, Hindus, and Chinese and began the assimilation process that is important even today for understanding modern Thai society. Buddhism and Brahmanism flourished among the Thais during the Sukhothai era. Characterized in Thai textbooks as an idyllic golden age, its nurturing kings boasted "fish in the water; rice in the fields," built exquisite temples to support thousands of monks, and maintained a sizeable elephantry to protect the kingdom.[1] The Sukhothai Kingdom expanded and retracted, depending on the fortunes of military campaigns, until the long Ayutthaya period (1350–1767) began.

The Thais adapted much from the Hindu-influenced Khmers, who dominated the region from the ninth through the fourteenth century. In particular, Thai kings were transformed from paternalistic guardians into autocratic god-kings with the attributes of a Brahmanic deity. The perception of the kings as *deva-raja* (god-kings), remains even today as an important element of the veneration shown the king by his subjects. Notwithstanding this aura of godliness, Thai kings did not enjoy absolute power but were limited by court factionalism, competition for power, and an assumption of kingly virtue.

During the Ayutthaya period, important institutions were established that still influence Thai society. A feudal-like *sakdina* (field power) system was introduced that provided structure and hierarchy to the social and political relationships of the Thais. As dictated by officials in its walled capital city along the Chaophraya River, virtually all persons in the Ayutthaya kingdom were given *sakdina* rankings according to the amount of land (or number of people) they controlled. The ranking determined the salary of officials, the deference due them, and their labor obligations to the state. Although the quantifiable character of the *sakdina* system had ended by 1932, the informal hierarchical nature of the system has endured as an element of Thai society.

The destruction of Ayutthaya's capital by invading Burmese in 1767 was a traumatic event in Thai history. The political-social system was torn asunder. Despite the near-total destruction of the kingdom, the Thais displayed remarkable recuperative powers and in a short time resumed life under a new centralized government in Bangkok led by the Chakri Dynasty. Some of the Chakri kings were reform oriented—systematizing administrative structures, freeing slaves, bringing in highly educated technocrats, and ensuring the continued independence of the nation from Western colonialists. From 1851 through 1910, two legendary Chakri monarchs, King Mongkut and his son King Chulalongkorn, advanced significant reforms to modernize Siam—as it was then known to the world.[2] The present king, Bhumibol Adulyadej, is the ninth of this dynasty.

Even after the 1932 revolt, which overthrew the absolute monarchy and established a constitutional monarchy, politics remained in the hands of a small elite group, now mostly civilian bureaucrats and military generals with little competition or balance from forces outside the bureaucratic arena. The military, which emerged as the country's dominant institution, has controlled political power in Thailand for about fifty of the past seventy-five years. From 1932 to 1973, Thailand's political system was a classic bureaucratic polity. The basis of political power was highly personalized and subject to informal political manipulations and loyalties. It was also very unstable. A cycle of military control followed by weak parliamentary government, constitutional crisis, and coup d'état emerged and began to characterize Thai politics over time.[3]

Thailand entered the modern period at the end of World War II in considerably better shape than most of its Southeast Asian neighbors. Having acquiesced to Japanese occupation (and thereby having suffered little war damage) and not having fought a debilitating struggle for independence, Thailand was relatively secure and stable. Initially after the war, Thailand seemed headed toward a constitutional system of parliamentary democracy, but the army soon took power.

The most influential of the early postwar leaders was Marshal Sarit Thanarat, the army commander in chief who became prime minister in 1957, declared martial law, and ruled dictatorially for six years. He was the first prime minister to make economic development the cornerstone of his rule. His successor, Marshal Thanom Kittikachorn, followed in Sarit's footsteps by keeping the military in firm control of every aspect of government and by pursuing economic development. During both administrations, the legislature was impotent, political parties were for the most part forbidden to form, and corruption was rampant. These leaders also cooperated with the United States during the Vietnam War, providing logistical support, Thai troops, naval bases, and airfields that were used throughout the Cold War campaign against communists in the region.

In response to the low level of political accountability and the high level of corruption, the "Great Tragedy" of October 14, 1973, occurred when the citizenry rose against Thanom and his government. Upon his orders, the military massacred hundreds of unarmed protesters at Democracy Monument in Bangkok, a bloody event that resonates in Thai society to this day. Thanom and his ruling partners were subsequently forced into exile at the behest of King Bhumibol. The king then followed their expulsion by appointing the first civilian government since the immediate postwar period. Thailand's next experience with democracy thus began as a result of courageous student protests with the king's support.

The 1973 revolt raised the expectations of many Thais that fundamental economic reforms would be carried out. The succeeding three-year period, however, coincided with a worldwide recession and with inflation that temporarily ended the country's improving economic growth. Hence, the hopes of many Thais that democracy would improve their lives were dashed by an economic situation over which the new government had little control. Aside from establishing a minimum wage and some new funds for rural development, little was accomplished during this period.

The civilian government was also faced with an international and regional situation over which it had little control. The change to communist governments in Vietnam, Laos, and Cambodia in 1975 and the rise of insurgency throughout the Thai countryside shocked many Thais, who felt that only an authoritarian, military-dominated government could deal effectively with these threats. Because Thailand's traditional security ally, the United States, was withdrawing from Southeast Asia, the civilian government renewed ties with China in hopes of counterbalancing a rising Soviet-backed Vietnam. This destabilizing state of flux added to the uncertainty many Thais felt. Thai society was polarized between left and right, driven by the effects of Cold War politics in the region.

Democratic civilian rule lasted only until October 1976, when the military again overthrew the government, proclaimed martial law, and abrogated the constitution. Sparking the takeover was another massacre of students, at Thammasat University in Bangkok, in which scores of unarmed students were brutally executed in a crackdown jointly conducted by military and right-wing paramilitary forces. Predictably, the new military leaders adopted a strong anticommunist agenda. Many of their targets were leftist students and the civilian politicians of the previous government. Fearful of the military, thousands fled into the countryside, joining peasant insurgents. The leftist coalition of intellectual urbanites and rural revolutionaries, however, never materialized into a massive insurgency capable of usurping state power, as similar coalitions had in neighboring countries. The ongoing presence of the covert Communist Party of Thailand and its associated insurgency, however, allowed for successive Thai governments, generals, and bureaucrats to justify strict national security policies and harass opponents in the name of anticommunism—a practice that continued until the end of the Cold War and beyond.

The military remained the dominant government institution until 1988. Under General Prem Tinsulanond's prime ministership, the country began to liberalize politically into a type of semidemocracy. Prem included civilian technocrats in his cabinet and relied on the freely elected legislature for support of his programs. Despite two coup attempts against him, he remained in power from 1980 until 1988, when he voluntarily stepped down.

Chatichai Choonhavan was the first elected member of Parliament (MP) to become prime minister since the 1973–1976 period. Chatichai assumed his new position following the 1988 elections, when his political party, Chart Thai (Thai Nation), received the largest plurality of votes and Prem refused to accept another term as prime minister. The smooth transition from Prem to Chatichai reflected new optimism about Thailand's evolution toward democracy.

Chatichai had served as minister under previous administrations and held a reputation as a big-business playboy. However, as executive, he initiated a number of highly popular policies, such as raising the salaries of government officials as well as the minimum wage for laborers, banning the indiscriminate cutting of trees, and standing up to the United States on trade and other economic issues.

Chatichai's idea to transform Southeast Asia from a "battleground into a marketplace" was especially popular with the business community, which sought to open economic ties with Vietnam, Cambodia, and Laos. His policies were supported by his coalition majority as well as by military leaders, at least initially. Nevertheless, the problems of patron-clientism and corruption continued to be important parts of the political process. The phenomenal economic growth of the late 1980s, fueled by East Asian investors, had brought large amounts of capital into the Thai economy. These new resources became the targets of public officials who sought them for private gain.

Thai citizens became increasingly skeptical about Chatichai's professed concern for the majority, which had not gained from the economy's high growth rates. Many Thais viewed his cabinet as primarily concerned with big-business interests. On February 23, 1991, hopes that Thailand was beginning to institutionalize democratic-civilian processes were dashed when a military coup d'état ousted Chatichai's government and restored military power.

The military claimed that its primary motivation for the coup was the pervasive corruption of the sitting politicians. Thai newspapers, unencumbered by censorship, had been reporting for months on the rampant corruption among top-level cabinet members. Huge telecommunications projects, massive road and elevated commuter railway ventures, cable television contracts, and new oil refineries became well-known examples of multibillion-dollar deals arranged and managed (or mismanaged) by Chatichai government ministers whose primary aim was to perpetuate their own power base and personal wealth. Coup leaders announced these politicians had become "unusually wealthy." Coup leaders also cited the rise of a "parliamentary dictatorship" as another reason for the takeover, complaining in particular about rampant vote buying. A more direct cause for the coup, however, was a pattern of slights carried out by Chatichai and perceived by military leaders as threats to their traditional prerogatives.

Immediately after seizing power, military leaders abrogated the constitution, dismissed the elected government, and set up the temporary National Peace Keeping Council (NPKC). The NPKC, led by Army Commander in Chief Suchinda Kraprayoon, gave itself the powers of martial law and became the arbiter of public policy.

Initially, the people greeted the 1991 coup with acquiescence, though not enthusiasm, and there were no public protests or demonstrations. The NPKC moved quickly to establish an interim constitution and to name Anand Panyarachun, a distinguished civilian, as prime minister. His appointment was a sign that the military believed the populace would not tolerate direct military rule for long. Anand's appointment was universally praised, reflecting his impeccable status and reputation as a diplomat, administrator, and businessman. Coup leaders emphasized their commitment to policy continuity in economic matters. Political parties were retained, and a national legislative assembly was established to approve a new constitution and arrange for an election. For the overwhelming majority of Thais, the coup changed nothing except the names of the kingdom's top government leaders.

New parliamentary elections were scheduled for March 22, 1992. During the interim, the junta gave Anand wide leeway in running the government but also asserted its views forcefully regarding the promulgation of the new constitution. The final document returned Thailand's legislative body to its former system, in which the appointed upper house of Parliament was given equal power with the elected lower house in matters of policymaking. Anand's administration also set forth policy measures supporting privatization, trade liberalization, deregulation of the economy, a value-added tax, infrastructure projects, and constraints on labor unions.

For the March 1992 polls, military-backed parties, which were close to General Suchinda, formed a joint campaign scheme to minimize competition and elect promilitary candidates. On the other side were parties opposed to continued military dominance in Thai politics. If elected, they pledged to amend the constitution so it reduced the role of the military and bureaucracy. A chief leader of this latter group of parties was Bangkok governor Chamlong Srimuang, who had given up his gubernatorial position to lead a new party, Palang Dharma (Moral Force). Chamlong, a former military officer, enjoyed an reputation for being incorruptible, which was unique in the Thai political establishment. He campaigned wearing an indigo farmer's shirt and cultivated an austere image as a faithful member of Santi Asoke, a new Buddhist sect that rejected superstitious practices and demanded a strict lifestyle of celibacy, vegetarianism, and material sacrifice.

The campaigns reflected many of the problems that have surrounded Thai elections to the present day: party jumping, vote buying, and ineffective monitoring of candidate behavior. The run-up to the election included poll-watch volunteers who attempted to monitor individual candidates' campaign expenses, which were limited to $40,000. Radio, television, newspapers, and banners featured slogans designed to discourage people from vote buying and "selling their freedom." Although vote buying occurred throughout the kingdom, poll watchers reported only a few cases of outright fraud, such as ballot-box stuffing.

The March 1992 elections resulted in a narrow victory for parties aligned with the NPKC. Ironically, the coalition government the election produced included many "unusually wealthy" politicians of the ousted Chatichai government. Embarrassingly, the first nominee for prime minister this coalition proposed had his name withdrawn after the U.S. State Department confirmed it had denied him a visa because of alleged drug trafficking in the politician's business base in northern Thailand, in the vicinity of the infamous Golden Triangle. The promilitary parties then nominated coup leader General Suchinda, who had previously promised that he would never seek the prime ministership. In what many Thais referred to as "the second coup," General Suchinda accepted the nomination and, in the process, reversed the steps Thailand had taken toward democracy. To express dismay, some 50,000 protesters demonstrated against the new government following the announcement of Suchinda's appointment.

The anti-Suchinda demonstrations grew larger in the days that followed, bringing well over 100,000 Thais onto Bangkok streets in May 1992. Led by Chamlong and opposition leaders, mobile-phone-carrying urbanites, members of the middle class, and white-collar professionals demanded that Suchinda step down. Many began a hunger strike around Democracy Monument, site of the 1973 mass demonstrations. Although the Cold War in Southeast Asia had ended years before, Suchinda anachronistically claimed that the demonstrators were pawns of "communist elements" that sought to end Thailand's constitutional monarchy. Tension built, and the size and intensity of the protests grew.

In an episode eerily reminiscent of 1973 and 1976, Thai soldiers filed into Bangkok upon Suchinda's orders and began indiscriminately shooting into the defenseless crowds. Suchinda's troops also took control of the country's media and communications networks, but demonstrators with cameras and handheld video equipment recorded the violence and broadcast the images outside of Bangkok via fax machines and videotape. The unprecedented and effective method of spreading uncensored information undermined the military's standard practice of propagandizing coup events to manipulate Thai and global opinion. Although the full count is not known, hundreds of people died from soldier-fired weapons in the crackdown of "Black May 1992," a tragic product of Suchinda's hubris and miscalculations.

The public's reaction to the massacre was one of overwhelming sadness and anger. Suchinda had not recognized that public expectations of civilian rule and participatory democracy had become the new norm. Many Thais were profoundly embarrassed by the violent turn of events. In the new international era, when many countries were moving inexorably toward more open and liberal regimes, Suchinda had taken Thailand in the other direction by precipitating another military coup, manipulating postcoup elections to stay in power, and authorizing a Tiananmen-style crackdown on prodemocracy protesters.

After the violence, Prime Minister Suchinda was subsequently driven from office, his legacy a disastrous forty-eight-day reign. His welcome removal came after a globally televised rebuke by King Bhumibol, who made both Suchinda and Chamlong kneel before him as he sat regally on his throne. Suchinda was reprimanded for bringing death and shame to the country. Chamlong was scolded for forcing headstrong protests that put civilians at risk. The king succeeded in ending the crisis by dismissing Suchinda, agreeing to amnesty for all persons involved in the demonstrations, and supporting constitutional amendments designed to reduce the military's dominance in politics. As in 1973, the king's intervention during a political crisis was praised by an adoring public as timely, consequential, and historic.

In a second extraordinary royal intervention related to the May 1992 crisis, the king approved the return of Anand Panyarachun as prime minister. The king's decision occurred just before the Parliament overwhelmingly passed constitutional amendments requiring prime ministers to be elected members of Parliament and reducing the role of the military-dominated Senate. Anand's appointment was met enthusiastically by most Thais, who recalled the international praise he earned for running an honest and efficient government during the previous interim period.

Anand once again acted with admirable decisiveness as an interim leader. With the king's appointment legitimizing his authority, he demoted top military leaders responsible for the violence, removed important state enterprises from military control, and scheduled a new round of parliamentary elections, announcing he would remain in office for only four months, a promise he kept.

The September 1992 elections featured 2,417 contenders from sixteen parties contesting 360 parliamentary seats. Few of the candidates were newcomers, although many jumped parties. Some parties changed their names and distanced themselves from the tainted "devil" parties affiliated with the military. The prodemocracy "angel" parties won the poll and formed a government under the leadership of a civilian politician as leader of the country. Chuan Leekpai, the soft-spoken, moderate leader of the Democrat Party from

Trang Province in the south, assumed the position of prime minister. From his offices in Government House, the country's executive center, he led a 207-seat coalition in the 360-member House of Representatives.

Chuan's immediate challenge was to find a balance between democratic rule and sensitivity to the traditional prerogatives of the military. He also faced the challenge of keeping together his fragile administration, which included leaders of the coalition parties who themselves coveted the prime ministership. Opposition leaders pointed to Chuan's lack of charisma and leadership and his lack of policy initiatives and new programs to address the growing list of problems facing the country: traffic congestion, pollution, environmental degradation, child labor, HIV/AIDS, centralized decisionmaking, water shortages, and ubiquitous corruption. In May 1995, his parliamentary coalition fell apart due to a land reform scandal in the south (a Democrat stronghold) and because of conflicting demands among the ruling coalition of political parties. New elections were called.

In the July 1995 election, about 40 million people voted. Predictably, campaign issues were vague because political parties in Thailand at the time did not articulate clear platforms or represent particular ideologies. Party hopping ensued, with competitive candidates being offered up to 5 million baht ($200,000 in 1995) to switch parties. Voters were offered 100 to 300 baht ($4 to $12) if they promised to vote for a particular candidate.

The major personality in the campaign was Banharn Silpa-archa, leader of the Chart Thai party. Party members noted Banharn's vast experience: He was a billionaire business executive with six terms in Parliament and a former minister of agriculture, industry, interior, finance, and transportation. Because he represented a rural constituency, he was viewed as someone who understood the average Thai. Banharn's campaign opponents charged that he was thoroughly corrupt, citing his nickname, "Khun Ae-Thi-Am" (Mr. ATM), given for his impressive reputation for managing huge networks of patronage. Banharn's cabinet was highly factionalized and his party coalition was unstable. He was scorned by Bangkok voters and intellectual elites who viewed him as a country bumpkin.

Banharn's administration turned out to be a disaster characterized by corruption, a lack of direction, personal dishonesty (Banharn was discovered to have plagiarized his law thesis), and economic malaise. Though he was forced to call new elections in November 1996, little changed as a result. Retired general Chavalit Yongchaiyudh, leader of the New Aspiration Party, won control, after benefiting from many members of Parliament who had defected from Chart Thai's waning star. Like Banharn, Chavalit was unpopular among Bangkok's elites and the leading newspapers, although he had achieved popularity in rural areas for his support of developmental projects in the country's northeast provinces, or Isan region. Even so, his tenure was also short-lived.

As prime minister, Chavalit faced two tremendous challenges: the passage of a new constitution, from a process that began prior to his tenure, and the 1997 Asian economic crisis, which began in Thailand during his watch. A major political crisis was averted when the Parliament overwhelmingly passed a new constitution on September 27, 1997. This approval represented the culmination of a long but inclusive process that had brought many segments of Thai society into drafting the constitution. Many observers considered it to be the most democratic constitution in Thai history, the "People's Constitution." Chavalit's support for its passage added legitimacy to his leadership and bought him some time amidst crisis conditions owing to the collapse of the Thai baht in June 1997. As a result of the crisis, rising unemployment, inflation, IMF conditionality, and a failed financial sector, Chavalit's status became increasingly tenuous. Large demonstrations opposing his leadership began.

The protests centered on Chavalit's inability to resolve the economic crisis. Under his watch, the baht had lost half its value against the dollar, the stock market had fallen precipitously, and the IMF was asked to bail out the country with a loan of some $17 billion. Most Thais blamed the political system for the economic crisis, believing that politicians were more concerned about perpetuating their own power and profiting business associates than the public good. It was thus no surprise when the embattled Chavalit announced his resignation as prime minister, an office he had held for just eleven months. The mass protest that forced his resignation was indicative of the extraparliamentary change agents of Thai politics: antigovernment demonstrations, coup d'état, royal intervention, judicial rulings, or some combination of these methods.

Chuan Leekpai, of the opposition Democrat Party, managed to forge a coalition majority and was appointed interim prime minister until new elections could be held in 1998 under new constitutional provisions. Chuan instituted reform measures to rescue the economy and mandated transparency and accountability, but the crisis continued to hurt the bulk of the population financially. IMF guidance and austerity demands proved unable to resuscitate the economy.

A new election in 2001 led to the rise of Dr. Thaksin Shinawatra, a telecommunications mogul and founder of the Thai Rak Thai (Thais Love Thais) political party. A former minister and estranged ally of Chamlong Srimuang, Thaksin was among Thailand's richest businessmen, having made his fortune selling computers to Thai government agencies and creating extensive holdings in the communications sector with mobile phones, pagers, broadcast television, and satellite communications. In a few short years, Thaksin's business empire spanned most of Southeast Asia's rapidly growing markets and his name appeared on *Fortune*'s list of the world's richest people. However, Thaksin was not a member of the traditional Bangkok bureaucratic or intellectual elite. His early career was in criminal justice, a field that had brought him to the United States for master's and doctoral degrees and then back to Thailand, where he worked in the Metropolitan Police Department. Of Sino-Thai origin and a proud son of silk traders in provincial Chiang Mai, Thaksin was ranked among the country's unrefined nouveaux riche in the eyes of Bangkok's urbane aristocrats.

Thaksin's business savvy and meteoric success, combined with his former political associations with Chamlong's Moral Force Party, seemed to combine the two qualities many common Thai voters believed were needed in an emancipator able to free them from the economic crisis and dreaded IMF loan conditions: competence and trust. What voters did not fully appreciate at the time was Thaksin's unmatchable political acumen and limitless political ambition. Indeed, his political genius enabled him to methodically create an unprecedented party machine with die-hard loyalists: the Thai Rak Thai Party (TRT). This powerful party proved so volatile that it ultimately led to another military coup, Thaksin's forced exile, and an intractable political crisis setting in motion the volatile Red Shirt–Yellow Shirt divide that continues to the present day.

Thaksin's TRT election victory in 2001 came principally from public dissatisfaction with the slow pace and uneven distribution of Thailand's economic recovery. Chuan Leekpai's Democrats had held power for much of the 1990s, and Thais criticized their recovery policies for catering to international investors first. Many Thais believed it was time for a change. Thaksin, adopting a populist platform, promised to solve the economic problems, provide funds to villages, and grant debt relief to farmers. Critical of the Democrats' embrace of IMF austerity programs and the market fundamentalism of the Washington Consensus, Thaksin offered a more Keynesian approach, where the government would stimulate the economy with its own spending programs.

Where most new Thai parties eschewed specific policy platforms, centering instead on individual politicians or single-issue concerns such as clean government or national security, Thaksin embraced a multi-issue party platform. TRT seemed to offer something for everybody. Although still orbiting around its leader as do all Thai parties built around patronage, TRT brought into politics new faces from the ranks of the nouveaux riche and academia. Because the new constitution mandated that some seats in the Parliament be filled through a party list ballot, TRT was able to pull in many new loyalists. The TRT party aggressively wooed established party bosses, provincial politicians, and members of erstwhile party factions who, after the failures of Banharn and Chavalit, sought to attach themselves to Thailand's newest rising star. Even many in the ever-expanding NGO community caught Thaksin's attention. He promised to support rural development and pledged to maintain a ban on the commercial use of genetically modified agricultural products.

TRT thus built itself as a broad coalition tied to a broad array of promises. It projected an image of self-confidence, deliberateness, and dynamism—a party suited to lead a "new Thailand" in the emerging international era of economic dangers. At its ideological core, however, Thaksin's TRT was a walking paradox: It was fiercely nationalist, but not isolationist; it was populist but also favored the business elite; it was hedged with military allies, but it was not promilitary. TRT was a classic patronage-based party network, but it offered a fresh message unwedded to staid notions of bureaucratism, moderation, or nostalgic "Thai-ness."

Thaksin almost lost his seat shortly after taking it. In April 2001, a constitutional court opened a corruption case against him because the constitutionally mandated National Counter Corruption Commission alleged that he had hidden assets while serving as a cabinet member in 1997. He was accused of transferring shares worth billions of baht to his family, servants, and close friends. Thaksin claimed he had no knowledge of the transfer of assets. If the court had found him guilty, he would have been barred from holding office for five years and required to step down as prime minister. In its ruling, Thailand's highest court acquitted Thaksin on an 8-to-7 vote. Public opinion had favored his remaining as prime minister, so the decision was popular with the general public. This incident would not be the last time Thaksin and TRT leaders would force high drama involving the Thai judicial system.

Thaksin went on to become the longest-serving civilian prime minister in Thai parliamentary history. Playing in his favor was the reformed 1997 constitution, which was purposefully designed to inhibit party jumping, foster more stable party competition, and strengthen prime ministerial authority— all in the hopes of ending the revolving doors of leadership that plagued the Parliament and Government House in the 1990s.

As prime minister, Thaksin won unprecedented support from upcountry provinces with his policies. His popular programs provided inexpensive medical care, gave loans and grants to villages, canceled and postponed debts owed by farmers, and established an asset management agency to reduce corporate debt. He also developed programs to support small and medium enterprises and he encouraged every district in the country to develop at least one exportable product or handicraft. In the world of agriculture, he championed a policy to turn Thailand into "the kitchen of the world" by funding research and development in agricultural biotechnology, and started flirting with lifting the ban on genetically engineered crops.

Using weekly radio addresses and ensuring favorable media coverage, Thaksin worked relentlessly to propagandize TRT's efforts to the public. By the end of his four-year term, Thaksin could boast of having engineered Thailand's economic recovery, reviving exports, and completing loan payments to the IMF ahead of schedule. Nevertheless, TRT's massive government spending drove concerns about the sustainability of so-called Thaksinomics. Many feared Thaksin's spending strategy was hollow and lacked investment potential, portending a false recovery. Public cynicism grew, especially in Bangkok.

Observers also took note that Thaksin's business networks were benefiting from the village loans and redistributionist schemes in rural areas. Unprecedented sales of pickup trucks, motorcycles, and mobile phones were accompanied by allegations of ties to TRT corruption and local-level scheming. Programs such as the "million cows project," designed to give "one farmer, one cow," were disparaged by opposition politicians as mere vote-buying schemes veiled as antipoverty programs. Heavy criticism also came from human rights groups and the international community for Thaksin's brutal 2003 antidrug war, which included over 2,000 extrajudicial killings. From the military's perspective, Thaksin also proved unable to keep his promise to end the ongoing separatist insurgency in Thailand's Muslim south, bordering Malaysia.

Having been sidelined by TRT's dominance, middle-class urbanites, Bangkok's elites, human rights groups, academics, Santi Asoke Buddhists, and bureaucrats formed a voracious oppositional bloc and began to demand Thaksin's removal. Thaksin responded to criticism by trying to muzzle the free media, further angering his accusers, who then charged him with dismantling democracy. In fact, some of Thaksin's most vocal critics were disillusioned TRT supporters who had turned on the party and its populist direction. Thaksin had become Thailand's most polarizing figure in decades.

In spite of mounting pressures, Thaksin Shinawatra was able to stay in power until his government's four-year term expired. With the economy back on track and rural constituents satisfied, TRT found itself in solid command for the scheduled 2005 general election. The small chance that opposition Democrats had to unseat TRT and the Chart Thai Party became even smaller after the 2004 Indian Ocean tsunami hit southern Thailand—a Democrat stronghold—weeks before the election. Thaksin's actions during the disaster won him praise from both Thais and members of the international community. Even Democrat leaders conceded that Thailand's victims could thank Thaksin for his deft handling of the crisis.

In the February 2005 general election, TRT won big—bigger than any party in the history of Thai democracy, securing 375 of 500 seats. The opposition Democrats won only 96 of the 125 remaining seats, Chart Thai won just 27, and 2 went to a minor party. TRT thus secured an unprecedented majority in the Parliament. Standard allegations of vote buying were drowned out by the obvious support rural voters expressed for TRT policies. Thaksin's party support and political machine appeared invincible. Bangkok's city voters could not foresee an election scenario in which Thaksin and TRT would lose power.

Anti-Thaksin demonstrations began in Bangkok streets in late 2005, centering on allegations of official corruption. A few months later, in a gift to Thaksin's critics, a major scandal broke, with Thaksin unambiguously caught in the middle. Having used laws crafted by his own government, Thaksin benefited from a transaction where his family sold its $1.9 billion communications empire, to a Singaporean entity, tax-free. The news was more than his critics could bear. Street demonstrations mounted, with slogans that Thaksin had not only benefited from the sale, but that his family had put the nation at risk with foreign control of Thailand's vast communications network. Thaksin, facing serious pressure, dissolved Parliament and called a snap election in an attempt to reestablish his legitimacy. Knowing that without upcountry support they would lose the election, Democrats and other opposition parties boycotted the election, publicly citing TRT vote-buying strategies and alleging that Thaksin held dictatorial ambitions.

Predictably, TRT won the April 2006 polls but was unable to establish a functioning Parliament due to the boycott and cries of illegitimate results. A deadlock ensued. With demonstrations for his ouster expanding, and a court ruling annulling election results, Thaksin was forced to take audience with King Bhumibol. Visibly shaken from the event, Thaksin agreed to step down. He arranged, however, to continue on as a caretaker prime minister, at least until new polls could be held. To his critics it was a false resignation; to his supporters it was a shrewd political victory.

His dissenters, organized under the People's Alliance for Democracy, or PAD, became enraged when they realized Thaksin would still run the country as a caretaker prime minister. Earlier contempt for Thaksin transformed into sheer hatred. Standing at the head of the anti-Thaksin movement were PAD leaders Sondhi Limthongkul, a media mogul himself, and Chamlong Srimuang, the resurrected leader of the "angel" forces of Black May 1992, Santi Asoke adherent, and founder of the defunct Palang Dharma Party, of which Thaksin was once a part. To distinguish their movement, they co-opted the royally significant color yellow and identified themselves with yellow protest signs, hats, bandannas, and T-shirts.

Added to the growing list of Thaksin's alleged sins was the most serious accusation of them all—that Thaksin sought to eclipse the *baramee* (cultural charisma) of the king himself and even coveted republicanism. For evidence, the PAD pointed to Thaksin's increasing ceremonial activities that depicted him as a head of state rather than head of government. Rumors of the royal family's disdain for the prime minister circulated. The color yellow regularly donned by the PAD faithful took on heightened symbolism; no longer did wearing yellow simply celebrate monarchy, as it had previously, it now implied support for its protection from Thaksin.

Thaksin had tried earlier during his tenure to form alliances within the royal camp, but his meddling was viewed as calculating and disingenuous. King Bhumibol's most trusted adviser, Privy Councilor Prem Tinsulanond, emanated contempt for Thaksin.[4] The charge of republican ambition was political dynamite, upping the stakes of politics to a new level. Chatichai's "unusually rich" cabinet, Banharn's faked law degree, and Chuan's land reform fiasco appeared as minor scandals in comparison.

Thaksin's greatest ally amidst the rising controversy was the democratic principle of majority rule. In 2001 and 2005, Thai voters had overwhelmingly supported him, a point he cited often. Indeed, TRT enjoyed undying support in upcountry voting districts. The decision of opposition parties to boycott the April 2006 snap election was proof that Thaksin's opponents also recognized this fact. They knew that for all their charges in labeling rural voters as uneducated, stupid, and foolish, little could be done to change electoral realities. They calculated that Thaksin's grip on power would hold as long as majoritarian elections were in the picture.

The military denied coup rumors, but with another election pending in late 2006, and yet another TRT victory virtually assured, military coup d'état did indeed return to Thailand in the early morning hours of September 19, 2006. The event was quick, bloodless, and thoroughly welcomed by members of the anti-Thaksin minority in the country who had given up on constitutional means to remove the popular leader. King Bhumibol offered no disapproval of the junta leaders' actions. While seizing power, the military muzzled the media and streamed images of the monarch on television throughout the day of the takeover. Thaksin, in New York to deliver a speech at the United Nations, never returned to Thailand. TRT ministers inside the country were ordered to report to the Sonthi Booyaratklin and other coup leaders for temporary detainment.

The country was put under martial law for months. No groups of more than five people, including political parties, were allowed to gather and discuss politics. Media restrictions were put in place. Armed troops were sent to Thaksin's home province of Chiang Mai as well as others, inhibiting any opportunity for backlash by pro-Thaksin forces. The reasons cited for the coup included corruption, the need to restore political order, and Thaksin's failed security policies over the country's restive south. The coup group announced itself as the Council for Democratic Reform under the Constitutional Monarchy, shortened later to the Council on National Security, or CNS.

Though it was never revealed officially, Thailand's public and its outside observers knew that the hands of Prem Tinsulanond had engineered the coup. As a longtime privy councilor, he emanated royal authority more than any other figure. The coup leaders garnered legitimacy shortly after its execution in personal visits to Prem's Bangkok home. Broadcasted images of top brass shaking hands with the smiling Prem on his home driveway delivered the desired message: The events had full royal sanction.

An appointed government was soon authorized. Its legitimacy rested on royal approval, Prem's backing, and support from the country's Bangkok-based, anti-Thaksin political minority. The majority voters who backed Thaksin privately expressed anger and disillusionment with Thai politics. Martial law prevented organized dissent. Political scientists inside and outside the country shook their heads in dismay: "What had seemed like a firm march toward democratic consolidation from May 1992 onward had suddenly fizzled and relapsed into military-authoritarian rule."[5]

In the fifteen months of military rule between September 2006 and December 2007, new initiatives enacted by coup leaders attempted to roll back Thaksinomics and set Thailand on a course of political reform. Nevertheless, the CNS (paradoxically) combined new fiscal austerity policies with its own quasipopulist policies in an attempt to win affection from provincial Thais and even outdo Thaksin himself. It announced totally free health care and offered extended village loan schemes. Then, in a move alarming to international investors, the CNS announced that all government decisions, including those from economic ministries, would be based on the principles of Sufficiency Economy, the royal-inspired economic theory advocating Buddhist moderation, reduced consumption, and small-scale family farming. It was a clear signal away from Thaksin's progrowth policies.

In its most substantial act, the junta abrogated the 1997 People's Constitution, viewed as culpable in fostering Thaksin's rise. A new one was hastily drafted later by a select group of appointees and put up for approval by national referendum in 2007. The junta-crafted constitution barely passed, with a weak 58 percent of the national vote; a majority of voters in the pro-Thaksin Isan region voted against it.

Ironically, new elections in December 2007 proved that the coup had resolved nothing from the perspective of anti-Thaksin forces. Thaksin may have been in exile, but his party lived on, and so did its majority support from Thai voters. Even a ruling by a constitutional court that forcibly dissolved Thai Rak Thai for past election violations could not prevent it from forming under a different name: the People's Power Party (PPP).

The PPP won the December 2007 general election and, in coalition with like-minded parties, formed a new government under Samak Sundaravej. Samak, seventy-two years old and flirting with political retirement, was a surprising choice. He was a veteran politician with an independent, *nakleng* (tough-guy) image that was long tainted by allegations of involvement in the 1976 Thammasat University massacre. During the Thaksin years, Thais viewed him as a loudmouthed TV gadfly, known for hosting a popular cooking show called *Chim Pai, Bon Pai* (*Tasting and Complaining*). With his appointment, however, the independent Samak appeared to have sold out to serve as Thaksin's puppet. After the coup, Thaksin took up residence in the United Kingdom and purchased the Manchester City Premier League football team.

By May 2008, Sondhi's and Chamlong's PAD forces were back on the streets demanding Samak's resignation and the dissolution of Parliament. Numbers of yellow-clad protesters grew by the thousands when Samak sought to undo provisions coup leaders had put into the 2007 constitution. The PAD then introduced its proposal for "New Politics," which called for reform of the country's Parliament to become 70 percent appointed and only 30 percent elected. The proposal also encouraged the full embrace of Sufficiency Economy and New Theory Agriculture—the royally conceived antipoverty strategy that recommended self-sustaining family farming and the avoidance of all debt, including investment debt for cropping. The New Politics proposal, which sought nothing less than the overthrow of majoritarian democracy, was considered a slap in the face to upcountry voters who would find themselves disenfranchised under the plan.

By August, PAD protesters audaciously seized Government House, forcing the prime minister to govern from a military base for a time. Demonstrations continued for weeks on end. The People's Alliance for Democracy disrupted parliamentary business, clogged Bangkok streets, and created a tense atmosphere in the city. Samak refused to resign but chose not to remove the protesters by force, claiming prudence and restraint. A state of emergency was nevertheless declared after bloody clashes between anti-PAD groups and PAD protestors left scores wounded and one dead. Coup rumors swirled. Just as events began to crescendo, a court ruling forced Samak to step down from his post. The charge: paid appearances on a TV cooking show while serving as prime minister.

Samak's departure resolved little. To the astonishment of the anti-Thaksin movement, the PPP rallied around a new choice for prime minister: Somchai Wongsawat, Thaksin's brother-in-law. The audacious move by the PPP infuriated PAD supporters. It also proved to be a miscalculation on the part of the PPP. Somchai was unskilled and weak as PPP's leader. Among other failures, he bungled a tense standoff with Cambodia over a long-disputed Angkor-era temple near the Thai-Cambodian border. Politicizing the dispute as if Thailand's deepest national interests were at stake, Somchai's government, as well as the PAD, used the affair to attempt to make political hay when a victory regarding the matter was implausible.

The PAD, relentless in its efforts to force TRT remnants out of power, then occupied Parliament itself, trapping elected officials inside. Prime Minister Somchai was forced to jump over the back fence of the assembly compound to escape the siege. The PAD's risky actions pushed Somchai to the edge. He dispatched police, who then engaged protesters in a serious clash that led to the death of one female protester. Sensitive to crackdowns since those in 1973, 1976, and 1992, the Thai public, nervous about government-ordered bloodshed, viewed Somchai's use of force unfavorably. Queen Sirikit attended the protester's funeral, an act that emboldened the PAD faithful.

By late 2008, the PAD announced its "final battle" to remove the pro-Thaksin PPP government from power. By the thousands, "Yellow Army" protesters moved first to occupy a government-run television station and then both of Bangkok's airports, including Thailand's new Suvarnabhumi International Airport, a Thaksin project showcase. The PAD's foolhardy seizure became front-page news in Asia, Europe, and North America. Thailand's main artery of transportation with the world was shut off. Thousands of business travelers, tourists, Haj pilgrims, and others found themselves unable to get into or out of Bangkok because of the seizures. Airport authorities scrambled to accommodate the trapped travelers, sending some to a military transport center on the eastern seaboard. Days passed without any serious attempt to remove the protesters. Surreal images were broadcast globally of color-clad PAD protesters setting up food stalls, playing badminton, and waving plastic-hand clappers at speech rallies inside Suvarnabhumi's space-age stainless steel terminal.

Prime Minister Somchai, forced to govern from Chiang Mai, refused to step down and issued calls for the PAD to withdraw before force would be employed. Subsequent orders for the police and military to remove the protesters were largely ignored. Thailand's crisis reached an impasse. Pro-Thaksin "Red Shirt" supporters of the sitting government, organized as the United Front of Democracy against Dictatorship (UDD), began to stage counterrallies around the city. Fears of confrontation grew. Expectations of a military coup to end the standoff rose with each passing day.

The siege finally ended in its eighth day, just prior to annual birthday celebrations for the monarch. As with Samak's expulsion, it was the courts that proved consequential. In an expedited case, a constitutional court ruled that the People's Power Party had violated election law during the 2007 elections, and the party was ordered dissolved. Dissolution meant Somchai was disqualified for office and had to begin a five-year ban from politics. The remaining PPP members reorganized themselves into a third incarnation of Thaksin's TRT, the Puea Thai Party, but it was unable to form a coalition government.

After the "final battle" of airport seizures, Sondhi and Chamlong declared victory and PAD protesters returned home. It was the end of what was essentially a three-year protest, begun by an unsuccessful effort to force Thaksin's resignation in September 2005. Since that time and in the name of "democracy," the anti-Thaksin movement (ignominiously) encouraged the boycott of a democratic election; a military coup d'état; the sacking of the 1997 People's Constitution; a proposal to disenfranchise the majority of the electorate; the unlawful seizure of Government House, Parliament, and the country's airports; and the politicization of Thai courts to force dissolution of the country's largest political party (twice), and the removal of three prime ministers who enjoyed the confidence of elected parliamentary majorities.

The intensity of the events left many members of Parliament weary. Party defections began spurring talks of a new government coalition led by Democrat leader Abhisit Vejjajiva, an Oxford-educated, forty-four-year-old protégé of Democrat veteran Chuan Leekpai. On December 15, 2008, Abhisit won enough votes in Parliament to become Thailand's new prime minister. Ironically, the possibility of a Democrat-led coalition surfaced only when a large faction of MPs (under the leadership of the wily Newin Chitchob) opted to switch sides, denying the opportunity for the newly formed Puea Thai Party to form a successor government. Some called the Democrats' capture of power a "silent coup." The pro-Thaksin UDD began to organize with the goal to remove Abhisit's government from office.

Red-shirted UDD demonstrators from upcountry provinces and Bangkok's urban poor launched protests in the capital that lasted over three months, largely at Thaksin's urging from abroad. His visa revoked by the United Kingdom months earlier, Thaksin now operated from countries that lacked extradition treaties with Thailand. In a series of dramatic events, the UDD protesters successfully disrupted the 2009 ASEAN summit hosted by the Thai government in the resort town of Pattaya. The UDD's actions forced Prime Minister Abhisit to the embarrassing request that his fellow Asian leaders return home. Crestfallen, Abhisit then declared a state of emergency and ordered the military to disperse the protesters, who had grown in number to over 100,000. After a handful of deaths on both sides, the UDD's leaders called off the protests but pledged to continue their fight to restore Thaksin to power. Months later, both sides actively called for new demonstrations against each other. More fractured than at any time since the polarized 1973–1976 period, Thai society teetered on the brink of major civil conflict.

Throughout 2009, Red Shirt protesters relentlessly challenged the "silent coup" and the legitimacy of Abhisit's Democrat-led coalition. In April, during the festive week of Thai New Year and the Songkran Water Festival, the

UDD staged massive rallies, and tensions raised to a fever pitch. At a bridge in Bangkok's historic government district over 120,000 Red Shirt protesters gathered, camped, and harassed the Democrat-controlled Parliament until security forces broke up the demonstrations in an event recalling the crackdowns of 1976 and 1992. More than 800 were wounded and over 25 were killed in the stand-off.

Undeterred, the Red Shirts fearlessly reorganized a year later at Ratchaprasong intersection, square in the center of Bangkok's commercial district. Encamped for weeks on end—complete with loudspeaker systems, platform stages, and even live feeds of Thaksin speaking from abroad—UDD protesters disrupted downtown traffic, business, and tourism for leverage in negotiations with the Abhisit government. The 2010 Red Shirt occupation of Ratchaprasong mirrored the PAD's "final battle" and impudent occupation of Suvarnabhumi International Airport in 2008.

The UDD's primary demand was for the dissolution of Parliament within thirty days and for new general elections to be called. The situation grew volatile. Red Shirt demonstrators erected barriers to demarcate a protest zone and, for a six-week period, engaged in skirmishes with progovernment demonstrators and police. Infighting among UDD-Red Shirt leaders left the movement with a poorly organized negotiating strategy. It was unclear the extent to which Thaksin (from abroad) was in full control or not. On May 13, a favorite leader of the more hard-line camp of Red Shirts, a rogue Thai army general, was fatally shot in the head by a gunman on a motorbike while giving a sidewalk interview to a *New York Times* reporter. That evening, after top UDD leaders first agreed to, and then rejected, Abhisit's offer to call elections in six months, the Prime Minister issued an ultimatum: leave the protest site or face security forces. Although some evacuated, many stayed. Authorities cut off all water and electricity to the area in an attempt to force the protesters out. A radical group of Black Shirts pledged to stay indefinitely and wage "civil war" if needed, though their arsenal included little more than rocks, slingshots, pipe bombs, and a small collection of assault rifles.

For the next few days, the protests transformed into a fervent but feeble armed rebellion. Pockets of young men wearing red and black hunkered down behind makeshift barricades and daringly faced off against well-armed Thai troops and riot police. Sporadic clashes erupted throughout the commercial district and other parts of the city. Graphic videos of some of the violence went worldwide, much of it posted on YouTube. Government officials claimed the armed soldiers were merely firing rounds into the air, but eyewitness reports, video footage, and forensic evidence indisputably proved otherwise. Subsequent investigations confirmed that many government soldiers exceeded rules of engagement and "frequently fired into crowds of unarmed protesters" and that snipers shot demonstrators "who were unarmed or posed no imminent threat of death or serious injury to the soldiers or others."[6]

With Bangkok's glitzy shopping malls and hotels in the backdrop, disturbing images of intense street battles, soldier-on-civilian violence, and bloodied protesters gripped the global news cycle. U.N. secretary-general Ban Ki Moon and other world leaders urged a peaceful resolution to no avail. Violence also spread to Chiang Mai and other cities where Red Shirt supporters erupted in anger by rioting and setting fire to government buildings. Over one-third of Thailand's seventy-seven provinces fell under emergency decrees. Talk of civil war mushroomed, but realistic assessments predicted a quick end to the conflict, given the overwhelming mismatch in force capability.

The end arrived on May 19 after a final push by Thai army forces into the heart of the protest site. Red Shirt leaders surrendered and were brought under immediate arrest. Defeated, angered, and hopeless, a number of cowardly Red Shirt arsonists set fire to nearby shopping malls, government buildings, and the Thai stock exchange, causing billions of dollars in damage. When it was over, central Bangkok looked like war zone and the country's collective soul was shattered, shell-shocked, and traumatized.

Ultimately, 91 people died and more than 1,800 were injured in the confrontation. Both sides share blame, and both can be criticized for employing illegal, imprudent, and immoral methods that resulted in needless injuries and tragic deaths. Arguably, the violence and chaos could have been avoided had Abhisit and UDD leaders not given up on negotiations. Before the bulk of the violence occurred, a deal to dissolve Parliament and hold new elections in November had been struck. Had UDD leaders stuck with that date, or had Abhisit been willing to move it up even after the Red Shirts balked, it is conceivable that most of the violence, destruction, and death associated with the country's worst political turmoil in decades could have been avoided. As is often the case in Thai politics, neither side could tolerate the appearance of defeat; hubris clouded judgment.

Less than a year later, on May 6, 2011, following months of recriminations, investigations, and further political difficulties—including PAD leaders turning against the Democrat-led government—embattled prime minister Abhisit Vejjajiva dissolved Parliament and called for new elections six months ahead of schedule. Thus, only eleven months after the army had been ordered to forcibly disperse protesters, the key demand of the Red Shirts for new elections was effectively realized. The 2011 general elections would be the country's ninth in nineteen years. In Thailand, where general elections are even more frequent than military coups, the impatience of the body politic to demand that events, rather than constitutional rules, dictate political change once again proved extremely costly.

The new election date, June 3, 2011, opened the door for the Red Shirt camp to enlist its most powerful weapon: the ballot box. Thaksin's family, having been stripped of half its wealth by Thai courts in 2010, proved more than capable of remaining key players in the Thai political game. Yingluck Shinawatra, the younger sister of the exiled Thaksin, was selected by Puea Thai to be its candidate for prime minister. With a background in business, and with a young, fashionable image, the forty-four-year-old Yingluck took the Red Shirt electorate by storm. As with the four previous elections following its creation, Thaksin's party machine won another resounding victory. With a 75 percent national turnout, Yingluck became Thailand's first Thai female prime minister and Puea Thai secured 253 of 500 seats and control over 53 percent of the lower house. Abhisit's Democrats came in a distant second, winning 159 seats, just less than one-third of the Parliament.

A political novice, Yingluck struggled after her election, but the strength of Puea Thai and its five coalition partners (which effectively reduced the opposition by 29 seats) gave her adequate political space. Only months into her tenure, Thailand experienced its worst spate of flooding in fifty years. Ravaging 80 percent of Thailand's provincial districts and engulfing Bangkok's suburban outskirts and industrial parks for weeks, the floods caused over 700 deaths; many other areas remained under water for weeks on end. Most estimates put the damage near $45 billion. Thailand's growth rate for 2011 dropped to 0.1 percent.

For sitting governments, the difficulties involved in managing large-scale natural disasters typically produce corresponding political damage. Despite some serious missteps by the new government, however, economic recovery marked the beginning of 2012; by mid-year the hard-hit industrial sector had recovered from the floods more quickly than expected. Pointing to ineffective policies in the restive south and Yingluck's populist (and fiscally dubious) rice-purchasing scheme, the Democrat-led opposition predictably pushed for a vote of no confidence in late 2012 in spite of her high approval ratings among Thais. These parliamentary maneuvers were followed by the formation of a new anti-Yingluck group, Pitak Siam (Protecting Siam), led by a retired general who publicly announced his desire for another coup.

In the aftermath of 2010 political violence, Yingluck pursued national reconciliation with difficulty but resisted any temptation to unilaterally arrange for her brother's return from exile—a move that would enrage the royalist Yellow Shirt coalition. Her government's strict enforcement of lèse-majesté laws drew ongoing criticism from international human rights groups but appeased the traditional elites who distrusted her as a mere puppet of Thaksin (now living in Dubai).

Perhaps most consequentially, during her first year Yingluck governed within the rule of law and, unlike her brother, never exceeded the constitutional powers granted to her. Any such misstep or abuse of power, especially related to the sensitive issue of constitutional reform, would have rapidly reignited political turmoil. Notwithstanding the inherent risks of Puea Thai's populist policies, Thailand's deep-seated political cleavages, at least through 2012, were once again being channeled through the country's historically beleaguered institutions of parliamentary democracy.

INSTITUTIONS AND SOCIAL GROUPS

Monarchy

Theoretically and legally above politics, the Thai monarch is the national symbol, the supreme patron who reigns over all, and the leader of the Buddhist religion. The monarchy's prestige and veneration have grown since the coronation of King Bhumibol Adulyadej, who is the kingdom's longest-reigning monarch and the world's longest-reigning contemporary monarch. In 2006, the Thai people celebrated King Bhumibol's sixtieth year on the throne. A year later they celebrated his eightieth birthday.

During the early decades of his reign, the king cultivated a role as a patron of rural development. He intervened publicly in politics on rare occasions, including in 1973. In the 1980s, he supported the government of Prime Minister Prem Tinsulanond during two military attempts to overthrow Prem's administration. The king's strong resistance to these coups added to his public prestige and influence. He chose not to intervene in 1991 when a coup to oust Chatichai was successfully executed.

One of the king's most important interventions occurred during the May 1992 crisis when prodemocracy demonstrators called on General Suchinda to step down as prime minister and he responded with a violent crackdown. King Bhumibol admonished the nation's leaders to settle the conflict peacefully, and he demanded the resignation of Suchinda and approved the return of Anand Panyarachun to be interim leader until elections could take place. In 2006 the king intervened again, this time admonishing Thaksin Shinawatra to step down as premier. Thaksin formally resigned but retained powers as a caretaker prime minister. Six months later, Thaksin was left in foreign exile as a result of the September 19, 2006, coup. The coup was viewed with approval by the king's most trusted privy councilor, Prem Tinsulanond.

Long-standing lèse-majesté laws shield the king and royal family from public criticism. On occasion Thai intellectuals (and foreigners) writing critically about the king or royal family members have faced charges and detention for offending the dignity of the monarch; London-style royal paparazzi do not exist in Thailand. Discretion, self-censorship, and self-imposed exile made lèse-majesté court cases fairly rare until recently. Only one case of lèse-majesté went to prosecution in 2000. In 2006, thirty charges were filed. During 2010, 478 charges were filed (some cases carry multiple charges).[7] Today, many common citizens and political figures find themselves in trouble with the law, which is prone to abuse as a political tool. In 2011, the government announced campaign rules that forbade any mentioning of the monarchy during elections. That same year it also issued a warning that anyone who "likes" or "shares" a Facebook comment insulting the Thai monarchy could face prosecution—foreigners are not except from the law and may face prosecution if they go to Thailand. The announcement governing social media came just days after a sixty-one-year-old former truck driver from Bangkok was convicted of insulting the queen via text message.[8] He died of cancer a year later while still in prison.

Squaring the practice of lèse-majesté with liberal notions of free speech remains a sensitive subject in Thailand. Many Thais see no contradiction; others favor the stability it generates over democratic values. International human rights groups have universally condemned Thailand's lèse-majesté laws as draconian and incompatible with democracy. Some argue that Thailand's "defamation regime" is a potent form of discursive power used by the state to shape how Thai society understands "Thainess."[9]

The Thais' veneration of their monarch has raised concerns about a potential succession crisis. The king elevated his daughter, Princess Sirindhorn, to the rank of *maha chakri* (crown princess), thereby placing her in the line of succession along with her brother, Crown Prince Vachiralongkorn. The crown prince has often been criticized in Thailand's rumor mill for his lack of commitment and discipline, whereas the princess has been universally admired for her dedication. However, the crown prince has become more involved in ceremonial duties and is being trained to succeed his father. Because the king is such a crucial cultural symbol, a contentious succession could undo the monarchy's stability by unleashing forces now held in check by the king's presence.

Constitutions

Thailand suffers from endless constitutional change and claims of constitutional illegitimacy. Nothing at the present time indicates that its troubled history with constitutional change will be resolved soon. Almost all of the major incidents in modern Thai political history (i.e., political crises, coups, mass protests) have included some dimension of constitutional crisis. While there is a value placed on the rule of law concept, enduring agreement on basic law has yet to be realized. Moreover, the impulse to resort to extraconstitutional means to resolve political crises (namely, military coup and royal intervention) undermines the consolidation of democratic constitutionalism and the rule of law in Thailand.

The Thai propensity for changing constitutions has been referred to as "faction constitutionalism," whereby each successive draft reflects, legitimates, and strengthens major shifts in factional dominance. Most Thai constitutions have not been considered the fundamental laws of the land; rather, they have functioned to facilitate the rule of the regime in power. Since 1932 Thailand has been governed under seventeen constitutions, of which less than half were democratic and based on the parliamentary model with the executive accountable to a national assembly. Other constitutions did not require the prime minister to be selected from members of Parliament or did not have any elected Parliament or allowance for political parties.

Led by twice–interim prime minister Anand Panyarachun in 1996–1997, a "People's Committee" that included experts, academics, and members of civil society drafted the 1997 constitution, which was perceived to be the most legitimate, inclusive, and potentially sustainable democratic constitution ever promulgated in Thailand's long constitutional history. The drafting process was transparent and included input from the public. It was designed to reduce corruption, enhance human rights, decentralize the political system, make the Senate accountable (through direct elections), separate the executive from the legislative branch (by requiring ministers to resign from the Parliament), provide the judiciary with more authority, and strengthen larger political parties and discourage weaker ones. Under its provisions, one hundred members of the five-hundred-seat Parliament were elected by a national vote from a list of party-nominated candidates, whereas the other four hundred members were elected by single-member constituencies.

Thaksin's TRT benefited from the 1997 People's Constitution, which favored larger parties and stronger central authority. As one of its first acts, the 2006 coup group abrogated the constitution after stripping Thaksin of power. The 2007 constitution later drafted by the CNS returned Thailand to a half-appointed Senate, strengthened bureaucratic commissions, and empowered the judiciary over elected officials. When the constitution was subjected to a national referendum, less than 60 percent voted in favor of it. Prime Minister Samak's attempt in 2008 to reverse some of its provisions, sparking protests, was a predictable event; as was the attempt by Prime Minister Yingluck to amend the constitution in 2012. In this most recent attempt, a court showdown over charter reform nearly toppled the Pheu Thai government. Crisis was avoided when it was ruled that Yingluck's attempts to amend the constitution did not seek to undermine the Thai monarchy but could only be pursued piecemeal.

Future political crises in Thailand will likely include elements of constitutional disagreement; claims of illegitimate provisions, promulgation, or abrogation; and the fundamental inability of enduring basic law to institutionalize. Resorting to extraconstitutional measures to resolve constitutionally driven political crises is likely to continue in the foreseeable future.

Military

Since the overthrow of the absolute monarchy, the Thai military has played the dominant role in Thai politics. Of the fifty-plus cabinets organized since 1932, more than half can be classified as military or military-dominated governments. The civilian governments, which have been the most unstable, are often replaced by military regimes following army coups.

The reasons for military dominance include the weakness of civilian governments and the fact that the military is the most highly organized institution in the kingdom. Because of perceived external and internal threats to Thai security, the military has proclaimed itself the only institution capable of protecting Thai sovereignty. Moreover, the hierarchical nature of the military is congruent with the tendencies of Thai political culture. Because Bangkok, as Thailand's primary city, dominates every aspect of the country's political and economic life, the military has needed to control only this one city in order to control the entire kingdom.

Civilian governments, especially those coalesced around provincial parties, face considerable difficulties maintaining good relations with top generals. Because the military is factionalized itself, forging alliances with one set of generals can pose trouble later. Due to their own previous military experiences, Chatichai, Chavalit, Chamlong, and Thaksin all bore ties with particular military factions that proved consequential later, altering the course of events during the political crises they each faced. Standing above all the military, of course, is the venerable privy councilor Prem Tinsulanond, the retired general with unparalleled approbation from the crown and singular influence over the direction of Thai political development.

The threat of military intervention during political crisis has remained constant in the Thai system, as indicated by events in 1991, 1992, 2006, 2008, and 2010. After Black May 1992 it appeared for a time that the Thai public had lost all tolerance for military intervention. However, the 2006 coup d'état restored the military's domestic political power. To many Thais, the coup was viewed as a desirable event. PAD leaders even went abroad to explain why coups are needed in Thailand to "restore democracy."[10] Similarly, the PAD's later attempts to spark a coup as a means to overthrow the remnants of Thaksin's political machine indicated how a certain segment of Thais remain more than ready to rely on the military as a political catalyst.

The de facto insubordination that army generals showed in 2008 to Prime Minister Somchai—ignoring his orders to clear Yellow Shirt protesters from unlawful seizures of government buildings and Bangkok's airports —illustrates the enduring independent status of the military as a political actor. Only two years later, the military willingly accepted orders from Prime Minister Abhisit to crackdown on Red Shirt protests in the violent clashes of 2010. Eight decades after it toppled the country's absolute monarchy, Thailand's military remains the country's most formidable and secure state institution. Highly politicized and forever royalist, its influence casts a long shadow on the country's political future.

Bureaucracy

For most of the contemporary era, Thailand has been a bureaucratic polity with the arena of politics within the bureaucracy itself. The bureaucracy has been the bedrock of stability in a political system where top leadership positions have changed unpredictably. Although coups may bring new factions into power, the bureaucracy continues its conservative policy role with little change in direction.

The bureaucracy's formerly exclusive role has been widened in recent years by the new role of technocrats, who have attained important positions and brought a more rational mode to policymaking. These highly trained and educated officials are more inclined to public-regarding values over traditional values of hierarchy, personalism, and security. The technocrats lost some of their luster in 1997 when the Thai economy collapsed, at least partly because they did not adequately interpret the warning signs of the coming disaster. Higher salaries in Thailand's growing private sector have increasingly depleted the talent pool in the bureaucracy that formerly boasted Thailand's best and brightest.

Over the past two decades, bureaucratic actors have lost policymaking power to extrabureaucratic groups such as Parliament, political parties, business groups, and even international financial institutions. Nevertheless, even if their past dominance of the system is gone, Thai bureaucrats remain major actors in the country's political life, as demonstrated by their sizable support for the anti-Thaksin movement and because of the stability they provide to a system with frequent changes of leadership at the top.

Parliament and Political Parties

At one time, elections in Thailand were held only when the ruling group became convinced it could control the process so that elections would merely enhance its power. Today, elections provide more meaningful choices among candidates who represent alternative ideas. Thailand's bicameral Parliament is not a rubber-stamp body for a ruling party or strongman. It became less peripheral to governmental decisionmaking thanks to a greater role granted it by Prime Minister Prem, under whose leadership the Parliament began to act independently, particularly on economic matters. Although characterized by frequent changes in its structure and membership, Thailand's national assembly is more active in engaging in public debate about important issues than other legislatures in the region.

One of the reasons Thai political life is so lively and contentious is that parliamentary power matters. Establishing a parliamentary majority, and the corresponding right of that majority to choose a prime minister and cabinet, rank among the high-stake events in the Thai political system. Because governments change so frequently, coalition forming can be more politically significant than actual lawmaking functions, which, though salient, are not prone to wide shifts in ideology following elections or change in configuration of coalition parties. Access to government coffers is crucial. Crafty veteran politician Banharn Silpa-archa once let slip that "For a politician, being in the opposition is like starving yourself to death."[11]

Though the Parliament was formerly dominated by bureaucrats, military figures, and local elites, in recent decades its membership has diversified with greater representation from the business community, provincial political families, women, and (owing to party-list ballots) technocrats, academics, and other public figures. As parties are not mass based and do not offer much by way of local-level politics, and because parties tend to center on powerful individuals with regional or national prominence, the activities of political parties generally go hand-in-hand with parliamentary activity.

It is not particularly useful to visualize Thai political parties as falling along a neat left–right political spectrum because many parties fall into the moderate or nonideological middle. Ideological platforms have not been paramount in Thai campaigns because voters tend to favor candidates who served their district or regional interests first. Thai Rak Thai differed in this respect in that its populist message appealed across districts and regions. It conceived its patronage system as national rather than local or regional. To some degree, Thaksin wanted to do for all of provincial Thailand what master politician Banharn Silpa-archa of the Chart Thai Party had done for his home province of Suphan Buri (winning for it development project after development project, year after year, and making it among the most livable rural provinces in Thailand). A key distinguishing feature of TRT was not ideology but its desire to expand patronage in wider dimensions than previous successful parties had. Another key distinction of TRT was its new "professional party" approach to electoral politics; that is, it prioritized savvy marketing of the party as a media product over rigid commitments to ideals, platforms, or maintaining cumbersome membership rolls.[12]

The Democrat Party is the longest-surviving party in Thailand, with over sixty years behind it. Its base was and remains in urban Bangkok and the country's southern provinces. Having institutionalized as a party, it weathers changes in leadership and can withstand long periods in the opposition. It tends to be a party that is either leading the government or leading the opposition. When it does lead the government, its policies tend to satisfy bureaucrats, the military, traditional elites, and international investors. The party enjoys strong relations with royal institutions, and its members often boast degrees from top institutions at home and abroad. Although it is the most institutionalized party in Thailand, the Democrats have never enjoyed a parliamentary majority. In fact, their last plurality victory occurred over twenty years ago, in 1992.

In longevity and institutionalization, the closest party to the Democrats has been the Chart Thai (Thai Nation) Party. Today, however, it is a shell of its former self. Founded in the 1970s, it drew support from military-business elites and from the central provinces of the Chao Phraya River Basin. Two of its leaders, Chatichai Choonhavan and Banharn Silpa-archa, rose to serve as the country's prime minister. It survived coups, periods when parties were banned, and numerous factional divisions and defections. What Chart Thai could not survive was the 2008 political crisis and a subsequent court ruling that dissolved the party on grounds of electoral fraud. Some of its members joined other parties; a few hung on to form the Chathaipattana Party, which today holds a mere fifteen seats in Parliament.

The July 2011 general elections not only reflected the increasing polarization of Thai politics but affirmed that the weak party coalitions that shaped Thai politics in the 1980s and 1990s were truly a feature of the past. Of the available 500 seats in the national assembly 424 (85 percent) went to only two parties: Puea Thai (265 seats) and the Democrat Party (159 seats). The remaining seats went to nine other parties, seven of which combined to occupy a meager 23 seats. A system dominated by two parties has emerged for the foreseeable future.

Thaksin's party machine, now known as Puea Thai, has won more seats than any party in five straight elections (2001, 2005, 2006, 2007, and 2011). In spite of attempts by opponents to reverse its electoral victories via military coup, constitution revision, judicial activism, PAD plots and protests, and the intimidation of its supporters by armed forces—not to mention legitimate party competition—election victories for Thaksin's camp continue with no end in sight. With virtually all other means exhausted, perhaps the most plausible scenario in which the opposition can see this party dislodged from electoral power is through Puea Thai's own failure and loss of Red Shirt support. If the past holds as any guide, then factionalism, corruption, fiscal collapse, economic decline, or constitutional crisis would be plausible factors that might someday push its supporters away. For now, however, Thaksin's political edifice shows little sign of collapse.

Party Jumping and Vote Buying

In Thai electoral politics, party jumping is virtually institutionalized into the system, as are the endless allegations of rural vote buying that accompany every election. Many Thai elites and others maintain that these practices are at the root of Thailand's political problems. The 2007 People's Constitution was designed to inhibit both practices.

Party jumping occurs due to political expediency and opportunity. Political parties wooing candidates often distribute money to attract MPs who are most electable. The practice of party jumping by candidates often falls on factional lines, where a veteran politician brings a network of client MPs to the new party with him. Party jumping and party factionalism are closely intertwined in Thailand's party system.

There is conflicting evidence as to whether vote buying is an effective means to garner votes. Losers in elections always believe it matters, but skeptical researchers maintain that no hard evidence exists to demonstrate that vote buying changes election outcomes.[13] What is generally agreed upon, however, is that the practice has been used extensively in Thai elections. To deter vote buying, the Election Commission of Thailand, a constitutionally mandated body that oversees elections, is empowered to issue referee-like "yellow cards," and "red cards" to candidates suspected of violating election rules. A yellow card allows candidates to gain office through a subsequent by-election, whereas a red card bans the candidate from holding office for five years.

Vote buying entails the following tactics: giving cash to voters in return for promises of support, serving free food and drinks at village festivals, or even promising cash to voters if the candidate they were told to vote for wins. Vote-buying networks are run by *hua khanaen* (candidate canvassers) who have close ties with village leaders, teachers, and respected elders. Voters tend to vote for those candidates close to village or town leaders who have helped out the voters in the past. If these leaders have funds from candidates to divvy up, villagers are all the more likely to support the leaders' choice. A more audacious manipulation of the electorate is the creation of illegal election lotteries and inviting voters to bet on who will win in the election. Lottery agents working for candidates then rig the odds so that voting against the candidate is virtually the same as voting to lose one's own bet.[14]

STATE-SOCIETY RELATIONS AND DEMOCRACY

Until the 1980s, scholars referred to Thai politics as a "bureaucratic polity," in which politics took place within the bureaucracy and extrabureaucratic institutions were negligible. External institutions, such as the Parliament and political parties, were deemed to have little influence over the state's policy decisions. The bureaucratic polity included the military, as many of the generals held important government posts (including the position of prime minister). The state, then, was considered strong and autonomous, independent of such societal organizations as political parties, business associations,

farmers' groups, and labor unions. The enduring pillars of the Thai state—
"nation, region, and king"—provided the ideological troika upon which state
supremacy was based. When extrabureaucratic groups began to emerge,
they were initially co-opted, manipulated, or oppressed by the bureaucracy,
which used the military as its controlling force. By integrating the military
into the political process, the government established a broad-based regime.
Utilizing both collaborative and coercive forces, the state increased its stability and capacity.

Since the student-led revolt against the military in 1973, however, Thai
political institutions have increased in number and have broadened their
bases considerably, strengthening the roles of the legislature, political parties,
and business associations while reducing direct military domination. As societal groups have come to play a more important role in Thai politics, the
state has lost some of its autonomy and consequently become weaker.

The expectation many Thai elites have for state autonomy stems at least
partially from the past success of Thai authorities in preserving the state's independence and sovereignty; that having averted colonial rule, establishing a
generally peaceful country, and meeting the basic needs of the majority of
the citizenry, the Thai state had proven its effectiveness. Nevertheless, if autonomy is a key variable for assessing strength, the Thai state is weak in the
sense that officials who make authoritative decisions are not insulated from
the state-based patronage networks upon which they depend. Thailand's
state officials are integrated into some of the country's most established networks of patron-client exchange. These relationships act as links between
bureaucrats and traditional networks in old business, agriculture, labor, the
aristocracy, and the intelligentsia. Quasi-state enterprises, including public
utilities and their organized employees, are also tied into long-standing networks of patronage that emanate from the state. The loss of these networks
threatens the erosion of associated state institutions and, thus, state strength.

Thai authorities thus expect autonomy from societal actors, especially rural citizens who have been historically more politically passive than radical.
Because rural citizens constitute about 65 percent of the population and
have made relatively few demands on the central authorities, this notion of
passivity has been central to the argument that the Thai state can (and
should) act autonomously. Many state elites began to hold the rural electorate in contempt for increasing assertiveness in the political system in the
1990s, particularly through their participation in party politics, vote buying,
and organized protests against state projects, such as rural dams. Among
traditional elites, the development of a Thai version of the agrarian myth
creates a static view of rural Thailand—a view that *chao naa* (farmer peasants), *baan* (village community), *phophiang* (sufficiency), and historically
based rural contentedness are (and always will be) the essence of "Thai-

ness." This view contrasts with Thaksin's populist assumptions that rural producers desire a modern lifestyle commensurate with that experienced by urbanites, not a return to some bucolic past measured simply by a sufficient supply of "fish in the water, and rice in the fields."[15]

Thaksin Shinawatra's TRT network of patronage worked to displace and erode many of the traditional channels of bureaucratic and state patronage. Much of the resentment state elites held toward Thaksin was due to his disruption of the business-as-usual operations of a state-society patronage apparatus that had weathered so many changes in political leadership before. Thaksin's efforts to reprioritize state goals and create new state agencies caused antipathy and confusion among traditional bureaucrats. His bold attempts provoked a forceful response. As predicted by one Thai scholar well before Thaksin's rise, the conservative alliance of the military, technocrats, and old-style business elites, when threatened, may turn to "General Prem's influence to put pressure on any government which they deemed unpopular or unresponsive to their demands."[16] Thaksin, the most skilled and powerful political figure to challenge this conservative alliance, now lives in exile, a fugitive from the Thai justice system.

A state's legitimacy is a potent factor accounting for the strength of the state. Through socialization and the deliberate exploitation of the king's popularity by whichever regime is in power, the Thai state has become identified with the king and Buddhism, resulting in an extraordinarily high level of acceptance.[17] Questions about the strength of the monarchy (as an institution) in contrast to the strength of King Bhumibol (as an individual figure) will face Thai society in the future. Absent the aura of the king to bask in, state authorities could find challenges from elected governments far more difficult to repel in the future.

Constitutionalism is a possible alternative anchor of state strength in the absence or loss of royal aura due to succession. However, until common agreement on actual constitutional arrangements is achieved, implemented, and endures political crises, much of the strength of the Thai state will depend on the monarchy and on the royal approbation of state institutions and practices.

With respect to democracy, Thailand's traditional culture, with its emphasis on deference to authority and hierarchical social relations, has not proven conducive to stable democratic rule. A considerable degree of skepticism exists among state elites about the "cultural appropriateness" of majoritarian democracy. In the past, the Thais' democratic orientations have been formalistic in the sense that they have had little depth. Other values—such as security, development, deference, personalism, and economic stability—have often taken precedence over values more directly related to citizen participation in governmental affairs.

Even as traditional notions of deference and hierarchy have given way to modern notions of political equality, the outcome in Thailand has been less a Western-style "civic culture" centered on rights and laws than a "political society" where special interests and voting blocs seek to control of the state's resources. In such a state-society arrangement, "benefits flow primarily from connections, manipulation, calculation, and expediency" rather than from "civic virtue" or claim to "universal rights."[18] Thus, conditioned by the influence of Thai political culture, attempts to democratize Thailand have produced, at best, a competitive-oriented, patronage-driven electocracy; at worst, it has created a bifurcated polity with ever-hardening cleavages between traditional elites who are accustomed to state power and populist newcomers desperate to access and allocate the state's resources so long denied to them.

The most pronounced cleavage emphasized in the study of Thai politics is between the conservative state, military, and technocratic elites (who defend bureaucratic autonomy from societal forces) and the rising rural electorate, provincial forces, and extrabureaucratic business interests (who champion power for the Parliament, political parties, and electoral majorities). It is a mistake to translate this cleavage as one between preferences for authoritarianism versus democracy. The PAD's proposal for New Politics notwithstanding, the goal to develop Thailand into a democracy has not escaped the political discourse that emanates from all corners of state and society. A discourse of democracy in Thailand has evolved from political rhetoric into societal norms since 1973 and has been further fueled by events in Thailand since the end of the Cold War.

The presence of repeated coups is not evidence that Thais, on average, do not desire democracy. Results from opinion polls taken in 2002 and 2006 (four months before the coup) revealed that eight in ten Thais were generally satisfied with democracy and believed it was "suitable" for Thailand.[19] It is meaningful that Thais often justify the country's frequent military coups to foreign audiences as necessary to "save democracy"; that mass protests are viewed as rightful democratic expressions to advance "democratic political reform"; and that constitutions are tinkered with to "enhance democracy" or to "make democracy more stable."

Thus, expectations for democracy have not only grown in Thailand, they have become the norm. To the vast majority of Thais (and even many state elites), Thai regimes lacking representative government, civil liberties, or electoral accountability are at best accepted only as temporary—as legitimate only when believed necessary to resolve political crisis.

If the issue of Thai acceptance of democratic values is not the source of Thailand's inability to consolidate democracy, other sources must exist. One source fueling Thailand's democratic instability may be the unrealistic expectations Thai society places on democratic governance. As successful democracies have learned, the utility in democracy is its ability to manage conflict, to demand government accountability, and to peacefully transfer power from one set of rulers to another. Democratic practice outside of Thailand has not escaped the hazards of abuse of power, corruption, and official mismanagement, nor does it necessarily produce democratic outcomes of equitable resource allocation. The difference between Thailand and established democracies is that the latter tend to resolve political crises without turning to extraconstitutional methods. Unrealistic expectations that democracy should be orderly, produce completely fair outcomes, and be devoid of political crisis produce disappointment and lead to justification of extraconstitutional means to solve political gridlock.

Another possible source influencing Thailand's democratic instability may be too little respect for the principle of the rule of law. Evidence for this source comes from the verbal justifications used to dismiss existing law by those who find its presence an obstacle to political goals (e.g., Thaksin's extrajudicial killings during his 2003 drug war, or elite support of military or royal intervention to resolve political crises). Such justifications can stem from a cultural milieu where power often justifies itself (through karmic beliefs of rebirth and fate) producing, in turn, a societal tolerance for rule by law, rather than the unyielding defense of the rule of law.

A final source of democratic instability may come from endless debate over constitutional arrangements. All sides in these debates tend to interpret their preferred arrangement as democratic. What the protagonists fight over are the precise institutional arrangements believed necessary to produce some magical, durable democratic order. The false assumption underneath this volatile debate is that institutional arrangements matter more than realistic expectations of democracy. It is possible that an enduring democratic order will escape Thailand as long as societal norms respecting the limits of democracy are overridden by unrealistic expectations that some perfect institutional formula for constitutional democracy actually exists. An enduring democratic order will exist in Thailand only when political losers transcend their impulse to turn to extraconstitutional military intervention, royal trump cards, or politicization of the judiciary *and* when political winners transcend the impulse to abrogate or reengineer democratic constitutions or disregard constitutional limits on executive power.

ECONOMY AND DEVELOPMENT

In the postwar period, Thailand's economic performance was unimpressive until a 1957 military coup ushered in a new set of economic policies under the authoritarian leadership of General Sarit Thanarat. During much of the

Cold War, Thailand's neighbors were embroiled in conflict and suffering economically. In this context, it can be said that Thailand "won" the Vietnam War. Where the war left Vietnam, Cambodia, and Laos economically devastated, and left the United States a weaker global power, Thailand emerged with improved economic infrastructure, roads, and airports, and also with transferred technology—a result of over a decade of U.S. military aid, development projects, and circulated cash.

During the 1970s and 1980s Thailand sustained a 7 percent rate of annual economic growth, a pace equaled by only a few other developing nations. More remarkably, the kingdom's economic growth between 1987 and 1996 averaged close to 10 percent, higher than in any other country during that period. During these boom years, inflation also stayed under 5 percent. The 1997 Asian economic crisis, which began in Thailand, brought this rapid growth to a halt. Recovery under Thaksin returned Thailand to a pattern of growth, but a sluggish economy has been the consequence of political instability since the 2006 military coup.

Coincident with these high growth rates in the boom years was an increase in the export sector, which in the late 1980s grew by almost 25 percent each year. Foreign investment also grew rapidly, with Japan, Taiwan, the United States, Hong Kong, and South Korea the leading investors. Manufacturing also replaced agriculture during this period in terms of share of the country's GDP.

Although 65 percent of the Thai people are involved in the agricultural sphere of the economy, the number of those in rice farming is decreasing. Thai farmers have diversified into crops such as vegetables, fruits, maize, tapioca, coffee, flowers, sugar, and rubber, as well as livestock. The rise of agribusiness processing and related industry has also pulled ruralites out of the fields. Although farming areas have not developed as rapidly as urban areas, the standard of living in the countryside has improved noticeably since the 1970s. Nevertheless, the urban bias of Thai economic development is clear from both the emphasis on manufacturing and the higher percentage of budget allocations centered on Bangkok.

The factors responsible for the kingdom's economic successes have included a commitment to market-oriented, export-driven policies carried out by highly trained and generally conservative technocrats, and general policy continuity. For the most part, these officials were not as steeped in personalistic, clientelist politics as were their peers in neighboring countries. Where corruption did exist, officials and politicians earning kickbacks or skimming from contracts generally plowed their ill-gained wealth back into the booming Thai economy. Moreover, although coups have been a standard mechanism for changing governments, they have rarely undermined the continuity of macroeconomic policy controlled by senior technocrats.

The vital involvement of Thailand's Chinese minority cannot be overstated as a factor explaining the vibrancy of the economy. This dynamic minority has provided leadership in banking, export-import manufacturing, industrialization, monetary policy, foreign investment, and diversification. The autonomy granted the Chinese has resulted in an entrepreneurial minority's reinvesting its profits into the kingdom, with comparatively little capital leaving the country. As investments in Asia have grown, the Chinese have used filial and cultural ties to China to expand Thai investments abroad. For much of the 1990s, the single largest foreign investor in China was a Thai agribusiness company, Charoen Pokphand, founded by overseas Chinese in Bangkok.

Population control is another factor influencing economic success. In just one generation, Thailand managed to lower its population growth rate from 3.0 percent to 0.5 percent. The decrease resulted from a massive government-sponsored education program that has changed attitudes about the optimum family size and made birth control products available throughout the kingdom. The lack of population pressure has resulted in a higher standard of living for families, higher educational attainment and literacy, and lower poverty rates. According to the United Nations Development Program, the percentage of Thai people living in poverty between 1990 and 2004 was 14 percent, compared to 27 percent in Indonesia, 29 percent in Vietnam, and 43 percent in the Philippines over the same period. In 2010, Thailand's poverty rate fell to 8 percent.[20]

During the economic boom, rules favoring the expansion of foreign investment made possible a capital influx from industrial nations. Thailand became further integrated into the world capitalist system and gained access to foreign credit and technical assistance in addition to enjoying flourishing trade relations throughout the world. Thailand has been a favorite site for production plants owned by Japanese, South Korean, and Taiwanese firms. Under pressure from foreign governments and international financial institutions, Thailand liberalized its capital markets too far, however, sowing the seeds of loose credit, bad loans, and shaky investments that contributed to the 1997 economic crisis.

The nearly three decades of sustained economic development came to an abrupt halt in mid-1997 after the Chavalit administration stopped propping up the Thai baht. Having futilely spent billions of baht from foreign reserves on a lost cause, on July 2, 1997, the government unpegged the baht from the U.S. dollar and allowed it to float. Within weeks, the currency had lost 40 percent of its value. Simultaneously, the stock market suffered a precipitous decline, losing 70 percent of its value. To strengthen the economy, the Thai government accepted a $17 billion bailout from the IMF along with strict conditionality to adhere to market fundamentalism.

Many reasons for the debacle were debated in government, business, and academic circles. The long list of culprits included poor political leadership, the refusal of recent governments to make hard decisions about fiscal responsibility, pervasive corruption that blocked important infrastructure projects and educational reform, and the undisciplined opening of the economy to foreign capital. During the boom, offshore debt had also grown steadily as Thais borrowed dollars at cheaper rates than they could borrow baht. Borrowed money was often spent on real estate and a wide range of investments that offered meager returns, such as convention centers, hotels, condominiums, and private hospitals. Bad loans flourished at the end of the boom. The baht became overvalued when the dollar gained value against the yen, making Thai labor and exports more expensive and therefore less competitive. Currency speculators then bet on the devaluation of the baht, borrowing baht at one price and selling the currency back at a devalued rate, thereby making tremendous profits.

The Thai government's hope was that the devaluation would boost exports, curb imports, and cut the current account deficit. To keep the budget balanced, the Chavalit government raised the value-added tax from 7 percent to 10 percent. Interest rates were also raised to guard against a surge in inflation. These policies were in keeping with conditionality the IMF set. Recovery did not return. Chavalit was ousted and Democrats, led by Chuan, were given the opportunity to steady Thailand's sinking economic ship. Democrat leaders also followed the general IMF prescriptions of implementing budget austerity and restoring inflows of foreign capital. It was not until the election of Thaksin Shinawatra in 2001 that the Thai government noticeably changed its response to the economic crisis.

Once elected, Thaksin moved to set up a national asset management company to buy most of the financial system's remaining nonperforming debt, estimated to be about $30 billion. He moved to restructure the agricultural sector by providing debt relief for farmers and to provide funds to villages to promote income-producing activities. The debt restructuring featured a three-year suspension on debts owed by poor farmers to the state-owned Bank for Agriculture. Grants to villages were to be about 1 million baht ($23,000) to each of the nation's 70,000 villages. The Keyesian stimulus policies worked. Inflation was generally kept in check, exports expanded, and the rural economy experienced an unprecedented flow of government money.

Following the 2006 coup, the rate of the Thai economy's recovery slowed into the 4 percent range in 2007 and 2008. Concerns over the coup group's aggressive promotion of Sufficiency Economy waned, however, as the policies associated with its promotion proved to be vague goals rather than concrete measures. The global financial crisis caused Thailand's economy to contract over 2 percent in 2009. The economy recovered in 2010 with 7.8 percent growth only to be stalled again by the massive floods of 2011. Through it all, Thailand's poverty rate has declined, but overall economic inequality remains higher than any country in Asia. In fact, in 2009 Thailand's Gini coefficient (53.6) ranked twelfth worst in the world, higher than any country with a GDP its size.[21]

The seemingly endless cycle of protests by pro- and anti-Thaksin groups since 2005 have proved harmful to Thailand's economic prospects and overall image. The recognized ability of demonstrators to disrupt government operations and paralyze Bangkok's economic infrastructure, and the repeated willingness of security forces to employ violent tactics to break up civilian protests, foster Thailand's image as a dysfunctional polity. Government instability, constitutional crisis, coup d'état, corruption, politicized courts, passionate demonstrations, and the persistent threat of political violence have altered risk assessments made by investors and tourists. More so than before, many outsiders question the fundamental commitment to the rule of law in Thailand.

Observers also worry that Thailand may be destined for a "middle-income trap." All recent governments in Thailand—Thaksin-linked governments, Sonthi's postcoup cabinet, and even Abhisit's Democrat-led coalition—have shown a commitment to populist policies. Allowing Thailand's have-nots greater access to state benefits is a logical short-term political strategy, but neglecting long-overdue public investments in education and worker productivity, failing to reform the country's regressive tax system, and doing little about endemic corruption is a formula for economic stagnation in the long run.[22]

FOREIGN RELATIONS

Thailand's current foreign relations must be seen in the context of the new international era brought on by the end of the Cold War. The most obvious manifestations of this new era include the perception that there are no regional or great-power threats to Thai security and that the U.S. security role in Southeast Asia has declined. Thailand's sustained economic development and the rise of nonbureaucratic interests in the political sphere have unambiguously pushed foreign policy into the economic realm. This development has caused the military to reduce its role in foreign policy in favor of the Ministry of Foreign Affairs, cabinet ministers, and political party leaders. The increased profile of some of Thailand's top economic diplomats has also brought the country international esteem in recent years. As global economic integration replaced the Cold War, Thailand found itself in free trade agreement negotiations with the United States, the European Union, China, and Japan. Thailand's ASEAN partners are often partners at the trade negotiation table as well.

Thailand increasingly relates to the United States as an equal rather than as a client. As the Cold War ended, Thai foreign policy lessened security dependence on the United States, asserted equidistance in its relations with allies and adversaries, and launched a dramatically new Indochina policy without seeking U.S. support. In economic relations with the United States, Thailand became more assertive in bilateral negotiations over trade, intellectual property rights enforcement, and general economic policy independence (the exception being the IMF rescue package for Thailand during the 1997 economic crisis, which U.S. officials strongly encouraged).

Major aspects of Thai-U.S. relations also include joint military exercises; cooperation on suppressing narcotics trafficking, international crime, and terrorism; coordination on refugee matters involving Burmese activists and Hmong groups fleeing Laos; and ongoing support for educational exchange and the Peace Corps. Thailand provided some logistical support to the United States' war on terror but it never became a major military partner. Cooperation in tracking suspected terrorists proved worthwhile, however, when Hambali, a top al-Qaeda–linked bomb plotter, was discovered hiding in Ayutthaya and arrested in 2003.

The single most important issue in recent Thai-U.S. relations, however, has been negotiations over a United States–Thailand free trade agreement. Initiated by Thaksin and George W. Bush at an Asia-Pacific Economic Cooperation (APEC) meeting in 2003, the agreement showed some early progress. Business communities on both sides actively promoted it, countered by an equally active resistance from Thai and international NGOs. Political instability since 2006, nevertheless, stalled progress on the agreement. Discussions for the proposed Thai-EU free trade agreement, on the other hand, have picked up under Prime Minister Yingluck.

The 2006 military coup removing Thaksin put the U.S. diplomats in an awkward position. They denounced the coup as undemocratic and harmful, yet at the same time tread carefully so as not to become the defenders, patrons, or saviors of the embattled exiled ex–prime minister. Thaksin's murky status that tied him to corruption, undemocratic practices, and alienation by Thailand's power elite weighed heavily on the U.S. position regarding the coup. The common refrain from Washington and the U.S. embassy in Bangkok was a call for the coup leaders to "return the country to democracy as soon as possible." Even with the return of elected governments, Thailand's ongoing political crisis has put Thai relations with Washington in stasis. Snubbing Thailand in favor of a visit to democratic Indonesia, Secretary of State Hillary Clinton's first diplomatic trip to Southeast Asia left Thailand—and Abhisit Vejjajiva's fledging government—off the itinerary. Barack Obama later visited Indonesia as part of the 2011 East Asian Summit in Bali, where he met with Yingluck. Months later the United States granted Thaksin a visa, prompting an online firestorm by Yellow Shirt supporters in Thailand.

Since the passing of the Cold War, abrupt changes have come to Thailand's relations with its mainland Southeast Asian neighbors as well. Chatichai's initial efforts toward normalizing relations with Vietnam, Laos, and Cambodia were followed by support for the three countries' membership in ASEAN—a feat accomplished before the 1990s concluded. Lingering border disputes with Laos were also resolved as Cold War tensions dissipated. A symbol of improving relations between the two countries was the completion of an Australian-funded bridge across the Mekong River, which forms much of the border between the two countries. It was the first of three such bridges, all of far greater economic significance to landlocked Laos than to Thailand.

Thailand's relations with Cambodia also deepened in the 1990s. Foreign investment from Thailand brought Cambodia needed foreign exchange. Thai-driven investment in textiles, mobile phones, satellite communications, and other industries contributed to Cambodia's gradual economic recovery. Other industries driven by Thai investment—border casinos, brothels, and logging operations—proved less encouraging. The degree of rising Thai foreign investment in Cambodia was demonstrated in 2003 when a popular Thai actress claimed that Cambodia's famed Angkor Wat temple complex actually belonged to Thailand. The comment sparked unruly anti-Thai riots in Phnom Penh. Images of Cambodian youths vandalizing Thai-owned businesses and interests spread anger across Thailand.

Mutual anger also erupted in 2008–2011 over Preah Vihear, an Angkor-era temple set on a cliff near the Cambodian-Thai border. Troops on both sides mobilized after Thailand objected to Phnom Penh's application to designate the temple a World Heritage Site by the United Nations Educational, Scientific, and Cultural Organization (UNESCO). Multiple skirmishes over a three-year period resulted in nationalist rhetoric, firefights, and multiple deaths on both sides. The legality of ownership of Preah Vihear had long been settled in Cambodia's favor in the 1960s by the International Court of Justice (ICJ). Much of the dispute related to conflicting claims over border demarcations in the temple area. Phnom Penh's application was approved by UNESCO in 2011 and the ICJ once again intervened by ordering each side to remove troops beyond a newly designated demilitarized zone. Tensions over the issue have since subsided.

In the new international era, Thailand also supported Burma's application to ASEAN as part of its "constructive engagement" strategy with the Burmese regime. The purpose of this approach, which countered the policies of most of the world's nations, was to reduce tensions between the two countries and to gain access to Burmese resources. The latter objective transcended any particular government that has controlled Thailand. Thaksin enjoyed strong relations with Burma's ruling junta, and Burma was the first country the 2006 coup leaders visited following Thaksin's ouster. After political reforms began in 2010 in Myanmar, the released and newly elected parliamentarian Aung San Suu Kyi traveled to Thailand in an event that irritated Myanmar's top brass. After meeting with Prime Minister Yingluck, the Nobel laureate visited cheering Burmese refugees stuck in camps near the Thai-Burma border. Even so, Thai relations with Myanmar remain driven by mutual economic interests.

Thai civilian leaders have not ignored threats to their territory. With some 3,000 miles of borders with Burma, Laos, Cambodia, and Malaysia, there are constant (but generally small) border disputes and skirmishes. The situation is complicated by smuggling, weaponry, drugs, prostitution, and refugees—especially persons fleeing from oppression in Burma. In early 2000, for example, God's Army, a ragtag group of Karen minority insurgents led by twin twelve-year-old boys, attacked a hospital in the Thai city of Ratchaburi. The Thais responded by killing the insurgents because they viewed the assault as a threat against Thai sovereignty and territory.

In regional affairs, Thailand strongly supported the post–Cold War initiative to create the ASEAN Free Trade Area (AFTA). A response to the European Union and the creation of the North American Free Trade Agreement (NAFTA), AFTA was viewed as a move to reduce economic dependence on Japan and East Asia. With a market of 320 million people in a rapidly growing region, AFTA sought to expand trade by lowering trade tariffs. AFTA's economic significance to individual countries, however, remained minimal because the partners shared similar economic and export profiles and the volume of bilateral trade each enjoyed with Japan, the United States, the European Union, and China far exceeded levels of intra-AFTA trade.

Of all the changes in the new era, China's rise as a power is arguably the most consequential international development for Thailand. Concerns about the Asian giant, however, are almost exclusively in the realm of trade competitiveness and economic relations, not direct security interests. Thailand's relationship with China improved markedly after the Vietnam War but even more so following the Cold War. In particular, the new environment expanded people-to-people contacts between Sino-Thais and Chinese business interests. Once a liability in Thai cultural circles, the Chinese heritage of prominent business families in Bangkok became a cause for celebration and resulted in visits to ancestral villages in China's coastal provinces. Cultural goodwill translated into good business.

As part of the ASEAN Plus Three process and China's initiative that launched the ASEAN–China Free Trade Agreement (ACFTA), Thailand enjoyed "early harvest" provisions of free trade with China in agriculture and other sectors by 2003, seven years before the agreement went into effect.[23] As a consequence, an increased flow of fruits and vegetables is transforming Thailand's agriculture markets, as well as stressing its environment. In northern Thailand, for example, small-scale tangerine producers have been pushed out by large, plantation-size tangerine exporters who employ low-paid Burmese migrants. Cheap produce from China also affects Thai producers.

Internationally, recognition for Thailand's economic success came symbolically in the new international era with the 2002 appointment of one of the country's top technocrats, Supachai Panitchpakdhi, as director of the WTO. The new international era has also witnessed Thai troops participate as UN peacekeeping forces in East Timor. Thailand also won praise from the United Nations for efficient handling of the 2004 Indian Ocean tsunami. Following the disaster, Thaksin Shinawatra led the international push to create an Indian Ocean tsunami warning system. In 2008, when Burma's military rulers initially refused foreign aid following Cyclone Nargis, Thailand convinced the regime to allow it to act as an intermediary to funnel aid to the country. Thai relations with Muslim states, on the other hand, are often strained due to perceptions of harsh, ineffective, and unfair policies toward Thailand's Muslim population in the deep south.

Following the 2006–2010 political turmoil—after years of general foreign policy neglect and declining status in ASEAN—Prime Minister Yingluck Shinawatra pursued an aggressive strategy of regional diplomacy. She visited every ASEAN member state except Vietnam during her first year and extended her support for the creation of an ASEAN economic community. It remains to be seen, however, if Thailand will restore its former leadership role in ASEAN, especially given the rise of a more democratic and prosperous Indonesia, the only G-20 member in ASEAN.

CONCLUSION

Thailand today is fundamentally different from what it was decades ago, when a military-dominated bureaucracy fully controlled society. Economic development, evolving expectations for democracy, and extended periods of parliamentary governance have brought new groups into the political system to challenge the traditional power elites. Conservative state elites still wield sufficient power to alter events, but unless societal norms for representative government, accountable leadership, and civil liberties disappear, Thailand's bureaucrats, generals, and royals will find constant frustration in trying to undermine societal attempts to establish democratic institutions.

At best, Thailand's political future will likely see society muddle through more weak parliamentary governments, corruption scandals, demands from traditional state elites, and threats of military coup d'état. The struggle for democratic stability would continue under this scenario even as economic growth marches forward and lifts the country's standard of living. At worst, political turmoil will return, economic inequality will continue to worsen, and the deep south will more fully erupt. Most ominously, the ailing health of King Bhumibol, and the uncertain events his passing will put into motion, could lead to an unprecedented degree of unpredictability and instability.

Thailand's future is nothing if not daunting. Reveals one Thai political scientist in the *Journal of Democracy*: "All Thais fear but do not dare say in public, that Thailand's future is up for grabs. What happens after the current king leaves the scene could be the most wrenching crisis yet."[24] Another confirms that "the monarchy's future looks precarious indeed," and that reforms will be necessary after the current king's passing—a scenario likely to produce political crisis.[25] Over their modern history, the Thais have escaped occupation, revolution, tyranny, and interstate war. What they cannot escape is cyclical political crisis, perpetual constitutional change, and the uncomfortable sense that 1932's promise of democracy seems as distant as ever.

NOTES

1. The phrase "fish in the water; rice in the fields" is known by virtually all Thais. It is taken from Stone Inscription no. 1, an archeological artifact claimed to be discovered by kings of the current Chakri dynasty.

2. These reforms later became the backdrop of the popular twentieth-century stage musical *The King and I*, based on the apocryphal tales of English tutor Anna Leonowens. All print, stage, and film versions of her stories are officially banned in Thailand for offending the dignity of the Thai monarchy.

3. Thai political scientist Chai-Anan Sumudavanija is famously credited with first describing this pattern, or Thailand's vicious cycle of coup d'état.

4. Paul Handley, *The King Never Smiles: A Biography of Thailand's King Bhumibol Adulyadej* (New Haven, CT: Yale University Press, 2006), 425–426.

5. Thitinan Pongsudhirak, "Thailand Since the Coup," *Journal of Democracy* 19, no. 4 (October 2008), 143.

6. Human Rights Watch, *Descent into Chaos: Thailand's 2010 Red Shirt Protests and Government Crackdown* (New York: Human Rights Watch, 2011), 82–83, http://www .hrw.org/sites/default/files/reports/thailand0511webwcover_0.pdf. Many details in this section are drawn from this documented report.

7. Tania Branigan, "Thailand Cracks Down on 'Insults' to Royal Family," *The Guardian*, August 29, 2011, http://www.guardian.co.uk/world/2011/aug/29/thailand-crackdown-in- sults-royal-family.

8. "Thai Facebook Users Warned Not to 'Like' Anti-Monarchy Groups," *The Guardian*, November 25, 2011, http://www.guardian.co.uk/world/2011/nov/25/thai-facebookers -warned-like-button.

9. David Streckfuss, *Truth on Trial in Thailand: Defamation, Treason, and Lèse-Majesté* (New York: Routledge, 2011).

10. James Ockey, "Thailand in 2006: Retreat to Military Rule," *Asian Survey* 47, no. 1 (January/February 2007): 139.

11. Quoted in Kevin Hewison, "Political Change in Thailand: Democracy and Participation" (London: Routledge, 1997), 31.

12. Duncan McCargo and Ukrist Pathmanand, *The Thaksinization of Thailand* (Copenhagen: NAIS Press, 2005), 77–79.

13. Robert B. Albritton and Thawilwadee Bureekul, "The State of Democracy in Thailand," paper presented at the Conference on the Asian Barometer, Taipei, Taiwan, July 2008, p. 1.

14. Pasuk Phongphaichit and Chris Baker, *Thailand's Boom and Bust* (Chiang Mai: Silkworm Books, 1998), 250–251.

15. Robert Dayley, "Thailand's Agrarian Myth and Its Proponents," *Journal of Asian and African Studies* 46, no. 4 (August 2011): 342–360.

16. Chai-Anan Samudavanija, "Old Soldiers Never Die, They Are Just Bypassed: The Military, Bureaucracy, and Globalisation," in *Political Change in Thailand: Democracy and Participation*, ed. Kevin Hewison (London: Routledge, 1997), 56.

17. Joel S. Migdal, *Strong Societies and Weak States: State-Society Relations and State Capabilities in the Third World* (Princeton, NJ: Princeton University Press, 1988).

18. Andrew Walker, *Thailand's Political Peasants: Power in the Modern Rural Economy* (Madison: University of Wisconsin Press, 2012), 22–23.

19. Albritton and Bureekul, "The State of Democracy in Thailand," 4–5.

20. See Table 1.1 in chapter 1.

21. "Country Comparison: Distribution of Family Income—GINI Index," CIA World Factbook, https://www.cia.gov/library/publications/the-world-factbook/rankorder /2172rank.html.

22. Peter War, "A Nation Caught in the Middle-Income Trap," *East Asia Forum Quarterly* 3, no. 4 (October/December 2011): 4–6.

23. Robert G. Sutter, *Chinese Foreign Relations: Power and Policy since the Cold War* (Lanham, MD: Rowman & Littlefield, 2008), 269.

24. Thitinan, "Thailand Since the Coup," 149.

25. Patrick Jory, "The Crisis of Thai Monarchy," *East Asia Forum Quarterly* 3, no. 4 (October/December 2011): 13–14.

RESOURCE GUIDE

Two useful tools for bibliographic and other information on Thailand are available from the University of Leeds at www.polis.leeds.ac.uk/thaipol/resources/bibliography, and Australia National University's WWW Virtual Library: www.gksoft.com/govt/en/th.html. The University of California–Berkeley maintains a useful portal for digital and print resources on Thailand: www.lib.berkeley.edu/SSEAL/SoutheastAsia/seaelec.html. Northern

Illinois University's Southeast Asia Digital Library includes a range of useful links that cover government, academic, and research institutions specific to Thailand: http:// sea.lib.niu.edu. The University of Wisconsin–Madison Libraries similarly maintains a list of digital and print resources on Thailand: www.library.wisc.edu/guides/SEAsia /collections/UW.html.

The Royal Thai Government's official English language Web site is www thaigov.go.th/en/index.php. An excellent source for economic and public policy information and statistics is the Thailand Research and Development Institute, at www .tdri.or.th. For articulation and assessment of Sufficiency Economy, see the Thailand Human Development Report 2007 at www.undp.or.th/download/NHDR2007bookENG .pdf. For information on environmental, agricultural, and international trade issues from a civil society perspective, visit the BioThai Foundation at www.biothai.net. A useful and well-documented account of the 2010 Red Shirt Protests is available from Human Rights Watch at www.hrw.org/sites/default/files/reports/thailand0511webwcover_0.pdf.

Daily online news sources in English include the *Bangkok Post* at www.bangkokpost .com and the *Nation* at www.nationmultimedia.com. Both of these sites have useful searchable archives of back issues. Useful blogs on Thai politics include http:// bangkokpundit.blogspot.com and the *New Mandala*, an active blog on Thai and Southeast Asian politics maintained by researchers from Australian National University, at http://asiapacific.anu.edu.au/newmandala. Links to Thai television, including some broadcast news in English, are available at www.siamtv.info.

3

MYANMAR (BURMA)

ON JUNE 18, 1989, THE MARTIAL LAW GOVERNMENT OF BURMA declared that the country's official name (in English) would henceforth be Myanmar. Officially, the move attempted to separate the country from its colonial past and to internationalize a locally used name ostensibly more inclusive of the country's non-Burmese minorities. Critics viewed the name change as little more than a ploy by the military junta to legitimize its repressive rule. Respecting the wishes of persecuted opposition groups within the country, many foreign governments, news organizations, and scholars rejected the name change and continued to refer to the country as Burma. Most international organizations and non-Western governments adopted the country's new name, but usage of either name elsewhere inherently carried with it political overtones.[1]

Around 2010, Burma's ruling generals surprisingly began reforming the state's governing institutions and opened political space for opposition parties to legitimately participate in the country's politics. The Republic of the Union of Myanmar, as it is now formally called, remains far from pluralist, but the increasing acceptance of its new name parallels the military's deliberate (and welcome) steps toward political reform. A commensurate relaxation of long-standing economic sanctions by Western governments has also accompanied the country's post-2010 tilt toward democracy. Burma's two names—and all that they imply domestically and internationally—symbolize the country's challenge of ethnic diversity as well as Burma's story of promise, disappointment, tragedy, and potential.

Burma, like other Southeast Asian countries, is diverse, but uniquely so. About a dozen major ethnic groups and scores of smaller minorities make up more than one-third of the total population of 48 million. For the Chin, Kachin, Shan, Karen, Wa, Rakhine and other minority groups, there has long been ethnic sensitivity to the dominant position of Burmans, or Bamah, the country's largest ethnic group. Geographically, most ethnic minority

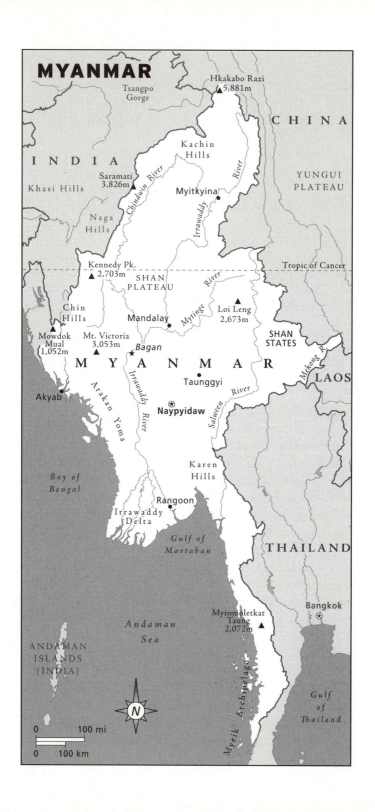

groups live in the frontier terrains along the country's mountainous perimeter, and most Bamah populate the country's grain-producing center, which is fed by the massive Irrawaddy River. More than any other feature, Burma's geodemography—its large core majority group surrounded by a mosaic of divergent minority groups—influences and shapes the country's politics.

In the international era, most Southeast Asian countries embraced the opportunity for economic development and political liberalization following the collapse of Cold War tensions. Burma has been the clear exception. Characterized by ethnic conflict, economic stagnation, and political oppression, Burma has yet to achieve *pyidawtha*—the ideal peaceful, pleasant, and prosperous society. Failure to reach this goal has been all the more tragic because the nation is rich in natural and human resources and because the Burmese came close to securing their political rights in 1988 when they revolted against their military leaders in a short "Rangoon Spring" only to see the uprising brutally quelled by armed government troops.

The 1988 revolt was not the first time the Burmese had struggled for their rights. In January 1948, the Burmese won their independence after several years of demonstrations and often-violent opposition to over sixty years of British rule. The independence struggle was led by the Thakin movement, a group of anti-British nationalists headed by Aung San, the father of modern Burma and a fiery nationalist who received his training in Japan during World War II after the Japanese had occupied Burma. Subsequently, the movement turned against the Japanese as their occupation became increasingly repressive. Aung San, who was expected to be Burma's first head of state, was assassinated in 1947 and thus became the nation's martyred hero.

The Thakin movement became the core of the Anti-Fascist People's Freedom League (AFPFL), a united front group opposed to the Japanese. AFPFL forces cooperated with the British to oust the Japanese and then turned against the British in the struggle for independence. The AFPFL negotiated independence and formed the country's first parliamentary government in 1948 under the leadership of forty-one-year-old U Nu.

The period from 1948 to 1958 was known as the "Time of Troubles." The well-organized minority ethnic groups opposed the government's move toward a national state and instead supported establishing autonomous states for each group. The Shans, Karens, and other groups rose against the central authorities, precipitating a struggle that began an ongoing civil war. Ethnicity-based antigovernment sentiment and conflict thus troubled the country in its early years of independence and remains a central element of Burma's military-dominated politics.

The second major postindependence problem concerned the poorly trained civil service, which was not able to carry out government programs effectively. U Nu's government had proclaimed a socialist policy that required a high degree of centralized administration, but the Burmese bureaucracy floundered, causing severe political and economic disturbances. U Thant, one of U Nu's closest advisors, was unavailable to fully assist in postindependence rebuilding, being tied up in New York as the third UN secretary-general. Absent independence martyr Aung San and the pragmatic U Thant, the charismatic U Nu struggled to guide Burma's Parliament and bureaucracy. Poor governance added fuel to ethnic resentments and a rising communist movement.

By 1958, Burma's political condition was so chaotic that U Nu turned the functioning of the government over to the Tatmadaw (the military), led by General Ne Win, who was also a leader of the Thakin independence movement and a compatriot of Aung San. Following this "constitutional coup," a caretaker administration stabilized the cost of living and controlled the black market. Exports were increased and corruption was temporarily halted. Ne Win's government reorganized the bureaucracy to make it more efficient and restored a semblance of law and order. Corruption within the bureaucracy was uncovered, and violent crime and gangsterism were rooted out in the countryside. The caretaker military government also stepped up its campaign against ethnic rebels and a growing threat from communists. Throughout all of this activity, the press and courts remained free and independent.

Despite the success of the Tatmadaw's caretaker government in a number of areas, in 1960 the electorate chose to return to U Nu for leadership. Again, however, he was not able to control the economy. U Nu's leadership was based on his charismatic religious qualities and reputation for impeccable honesty, but he was a poor day-to-day administrator. The nation was reeling from multiple rebellions among minority groups, and therefore a large share of the central budget was allocated to internal security, but U Nu concentrated on establishing Buddhism as the state religion.[2] U Nu believed Buddhism was the best defense against rising sympathy for communism within Burma. His efforts to conceptualize an idealistic vision of a Burmese welfare state based on Buddha's teachings were not matched by a parallel plan for implementation and administration.

The military, which perceived that the civilian government was weak and dependent upon Western-style political institutions that were incompatible with Burmese culture, carried out a coup on March 2, 1962, led by Ne Win. This seizure of power, which was rapid, nonviolent, and without major challenge, began an era of military rule that has continued for over four decades. Ne Win disbanded the Western-style Parliament, banned political parties, and restricted civil liberties. Hundreds of thousands of ethnic Indians living in Burma, a legacy of British rule, were forced back to India and East Pakistan. He then devised a program of radical economic and political policies called the "Burmese Way to Socialism," which included nationalizing major industries, schools, rice mills, small and large businesses, and financial institutions. His program to install a centralized state monopoly of the means of production was designed to ensure control of a united Burma.

To mobilize support for the socialist program, Ne Win established the Burmese Socialist Program Party (BSPP), organized to reach down to the village level along hierarchical lines but with all power remaining firmly at the party's military-dominated top echelon. The party's main function was to legitimize army rule. To keep Western "bourgeois decadent" ideas from infiltrating Burma, Ne Win arrested those who opposed his policies, restricted travel to Burma by foreigners, and ended academic freedom at the universities. His move toward a neutralist foreign policy took the form of isolationism.

In January 1974, Burma became the Socialist Republic of the Union of Burma after the electorate had passed the new socialist constitution. Although Ne Win discarded his military uniform in 1971 and became the "civilian" president of the new government, the military continued to be the dominant political force. Ne Win nominally stepped down as president in 1981 but retained his more powerful position as head of the BSPP. In that position, he was able to continue his dominance over political and economic policymaking. Influencing Ne Win's decisions were his beliefs in astrology and numerology. The policies emanating from the military junta became increasingly erratic.

In the summer of 1988, hundreds of thousands of farmers, urban workers, students, monks, and civil servants took to the streets of Burma's major cities to demonstrate against their government leaders. This revolt was the culmination of years of frustration and disgust at the failures of the military government to bring development to Burma. Although rich in natural resources, Burma had been humiliated by the UN decision in 1987 to declare it one of the world's least-developed nations. The revolt was also a response to the pervasive suppression of the people's political rights since 1962, when the military had assumed all political power.

A more immediate cause of the revolt was the 1987 decision of Ne Win's administration to declare valueless some 80 percent of the Burmese money in circulation. Any kyat note over $1.60 in value became instantly worthless. As part of the policy, the junta unexpectedly ordered that old notes be replaced by new ones divisible by nine, Ne Win's lucky number. Kyat notes denominated in nine, forty-five, and ninety appeared in circulation. Sudden demonetization, justified as a measure to undermine black-marketeers and control inflation, adversely affected the entire population, rich and poor. The bulk of the working economy was sustained by the black market (the government's socialistic economy having collapsed), so the demise of this unofficial market was seen as a catastrophe. Moreover, no recompense was given to holders of kyat notes above the maximum allowed; in effect, then, the savings of the entire population were wiped out. The price of food skyrocketed, and even government supporters began to grow uncomfortable with the country's direction.

The incident that sparked the 1988 revolt occurred in a tea shop when students and other patrons squabbled over the choice of music tapes being played. When the police arrived, a student was killed. Thousands of his schoolmates later returned to avenge their colleague's death, but they were met by weapons and security police. In a particularly dreadful incident, forty-one students were herded into a police van, where they suffocated in the intense heat. More demonstrations and security clashes occurred during the ensuing weeks. Unofficial estimates of student deaths from beatings, bayonet stabbings, and suffocation were in the hundreds, but the government blandly announced a total of only two student deaths.[3]

In the midst of the unrest, General Ne Win gathered with leaders in a special session of the BSPP Central Committee. In an alarming speech, he took responsibility for the student deaths and resigned his post as party chairman in favor of General Sein Lwin. Most astonishingly, Ne Win called for a popular referendum on a return to multiparty democracy. He also warned, ominously, that future mob disturbances would invite the use of military force. The party rejected the idea of the referendum but agreed to accept his resignation and the appointment of Sein Lwin, known as the "the Butcher" for his 1974 decision to violently quell demonstrations by grief-stricken students honoring U Thant's death.

Ne Win's moves sparked more demonstrations and more killings by security police. Students, distrustful that Sein Lwin could ever lead reform, began to mobilize, joined by dockworkers, laborers, and members of the general population. Sporadic protests erupted in Rangoon and other major cities. Then, on August 8, 1988 (i.e., 8/8/88), the army followed through on Ne Win's warning. Sein Lwin ordered the use of lethal force against the demonstrators. Dozens were killed on the initial night of the crackdown, but the violence hardened the protesters' resolve. Mass demonstrations continued for five consecutive days, as did the lethal violence. In yet another shameful incident, government soldiers shot and killed a group of exhausted doctors and nurses in front of Rangoon General Hospital.[4]

International outcry followed the junta's crackdown on the "8888 Uprising," as it became known. The U.S. government was one of the first to issue a protest and became a visible symbol of democratic government; thus, the grounds of the U.S. embassy in Rangoon became an important site for antigovernment demonstrations. Other governments condemned the crackdown as well. Demonstrations in Rangoon and in Mandalay grew to more than a million people.

Facing mounting protests, Sein Lwin abruptly resigned, and the army began to withdraw from Rangoon five days after its slaughter had begun. Maung Maung, a civilian academic and Ne Win's personal biographer, was appointed president. For a brief time, a sense of victory swept the population and suggested that regime change was possible. Opposition politicians emerged after years of suppression and began to discuss plans for action. Aung Sun's daughter, Aung San Suu Kyi, visiting Burma from her home in London, began to offer public speeches encouraging reform. Top diplomats signed an open letter calling for an end to Burma's isolationism.

Then, just as systemic change seemed within reach, a series of cascading events redirected Burma's historical course. The civil administration collapsed, and the police went on strike. Prisoners were released, and a sense of insecurity developed among the public. Revolutionary-style protests grew in size and audacity, and a number of government offices were stormed by unruly crowds. An attitude of recrimination surfaced. In a few cases, "suspected government agents were gruesomely beheaded or hacked to death in front of cheering crowds."[5] Burma faced the prospect of a bloody social revolution.

With the knowledge that the military's dominance was in jeopardy, army commander in chief General Saw Maung, ostensibly on orders from Ne Win, crushed the revolt and restored the military to power on September 18, 1988. The military's coup was not against an opposition government, as none existed, but was against the civilian facade government under Maung Maung that the army itself created. The violent coup was followed by the arrest of demonstrators, the censorship of all forms of communication, and the flight of tens of thousands of students to the nation's borders to escape the military and organize for a future rebellion. Altogether, some 3,000 Burmese lost their lives in their attempt to end military rule.

Saw Maung, taking his orders from Ne Win, established the State Law and Order Restoration Council (SLORC) to endure "until anarchy and demonstrations could be brought under control." SLORC, consisting of generals who were loyal to Ne Win, was given responsibility for administering the state. Ruling by martial law, SLORC brutally suppressed regime opponents even as it announced plans for a new election to be held in May 1990. SLORC argued that its harsh policies were necessary because of an alleged collusion between the Burmese Communist Party and the U.S. Central Intelligence Agency, which was the cause of demonstrations and antigovernment dissidence. Aung San Suu Kyi, who formed the National League for Democracy (NLD) in the days following the uprising, was placed under house arrest for having been "manipulated" by communists and foreign intelligence agencies. SLORC also argued that a highly centralized, military-oriented administration was necessary to ensure the country's continued unity in the face of potential rebellion by minority ethnic groups. None of these explanations were accepted by the vast majority of Burmese, who were extremely angry that their people's revolt had been crushed. The Tatmadaw, once a symbol of stability in Burma, became a hated organization.

Reports from Burma were few during 1989 and 1990 because SLORC did not allow foreign journalists or scholars into the country. However, sketchy reports suggested that SLORC was violating the Burmese people's human rights by silencing writers, banning assemblies, and forcefully moving some half a million people from their homes with the aim of breaking up prodemocracy neighborhoods and areas favorable to opposition leader Aung San Suu Kyi. The relocation of urban residents in late 1989 from cities to satellite towns was particularly egregious; it was justified by SLORC as a "beautification measure."

Despite these human rights violations, SLORC organized the May 27, 1990, election to choose legislators in the Pyithu Hluttaw (People's Assembly), the sole organ of legislative authority. Under the election law, each constituency was to elect one representative. Some 492 constituencies, determined by population size, were to choose representatives; seven constituencies of ethnic minorities, however, were not allowed to vote because of "security" threats in their regions. SLORC believed the election could be controlled to ensure that progovernment forces would prevail. In fact, the government was given the power to censor the speeches and publications of parties and candidates. Television time was limited to one ten-minute period per party during the entire campaign, and statements had to be submitted for approval seven days in advance. Candidates who gave speeches that had not been scrutinized and approved by the authorities were imprisoned.

Popular opposition leaders were harassed and kept from participating in the election. Aung San Suu Kyi, for example, was disqualified, as were former prime minister U Nu and another prominent opposition leader, former general Tin Oo. All of these leaders were placed under house arrest. Progovernment candidates who joined the successor party of the BSPP, the National Unity Party (NUP), received government funds for campaigning, but funds were not available to opposition leaders. The authorities banned outdoor assemblies and relocated citizens from their voting constituencies to ensure a progovernment vote.

Despite these measures, and in an extraordinary display of independence, the oppositionist National League for Democracy (NLD) won more than 80 percent of the seats (396 of 485) in the Pyithu Hluttaw. The NUP won only 10 seats, losing even in areas dominated by the army. Such a sharp rebuke of the martial law government was unexpected by junta leaders. Even months after the election, the military still refused to turn the government over to the newly elected legislators, even though the latter were ready to install a new constitution based largely on the country's last democratic constitution of 1947. Although the Burmese had expressed their anger toward the military government and their support for democratic rule through their vote, the regime in power was unwilling to act in compliance with the people's will.

Although world reaction to SLORC's oppression was strongly critical, the military continued to jail opposition leaders, dominate every facet of society, and isolate the regime from global currents. When in December 1991 Aung San Suu Kyi received, in absentia, the Nobel Peace Prize for standing up to the military junta, many believed that SLORC could not withstand the negative worldwide publicity. However, despite global condemnation and economic sanctions, SLORC dug in even deeper, claiming that freeing the Nobel laureate would threaten the nation's peace and tranquility.

In 1992, General Saw Maung stepped down as chairman of SLORC and was replaced by General Than Shwe, who was the nation's military commander and minister of defense. The new leader released some five hundred political prisoners, although the principal oppositionists were not freed. Colleges and universities were reopened, and a constitutional convention was called. The latter was viewed as a sham by both the Burmese people and foreign observers, who pointed out that the convention was dominated by the military and that the leading opposition leaders were still in jail. The convention met in January 1993 but did nothing to undermine military rule. Indeed, the conference specifically approved a leading political role for the army in the country's future governance.

During the postelection period, SLORC persisted in denying elected parliamentarians their rightful seats. In response, 250 would-be delegates formed a "parallel government" outside of the country in December 1990: the National Coalition Government of the Union of Burma. It called for the release of Aung San Suu Kyi and all other political prisoners, the transfer of power to those properly elected, and a halt to the civil war. But the military rulers ignored their requests.

Sometime in 1994 the generals realized that SLORC's policy of isolation had brought devastation to Burma. They allowed small openings in the economy, but the lack of capital, the poor infrastructure, and the disdain for the regime by much of the world made change difficult. Nevertheless, in the mid-1990s Burma's economic growth rate improved, ending the total stagnation of previous decades. Foreign entrepreneurs, mainly Asian, began setting up investments, and a "Visit Myanmar Year" promotional campaign was launched. New hotel projects changed the face of Rangoon. The opening did almost nothing to improve the standard of living of the people, among the world's poorest, most of whom led subsistence lives. Corruption, an inflated bureaucracy, political mismanagement, and the continued imprisonment of the democracy leaders were all reasons for the ongoing economic problems.

In July 1995, Aung San Suu Kyi was "released" from house arrest. In reality, she was guarded closely to ensure that she and her followers would not jeopardize SLORC's control over the nation. The government felt compelled to release her because of foreign pressures stemming from her extraordinary international reputation as a democrat. She was also released as an inducement to convince foreign nations to invest in Burma, and because the generals had decimated her National League for Democracy. Although thousands of Burmese citizens came to hear her speak, Aung San Suu Kyi was effectively silenced. Her talks were not allowed to be broadcasted or printed in the government-controlled press. Indeed, the press attacked Aung San Suu Kyi daily. In 1997, when her British husband, Michael Aris, was near death from prostate cancer in Great Britain, Burma analysts believed the junta would show compassion by allowing him to spend his last days with his wife. However, he was denied a visa, and she was reluctant to leave Burma, fearing she would not be allowed to return. Aris died in Britain in 1999 while Aung San Suu Kyi remained under house arrest.

Throughout the 1990s, SLORC allowed no discussion of the key issue: Which was the more legitimate institution, SLORC or the NLD? The election results remained ignored by the government, which continued to rule in a despotic manner. Political opponents were jailed or executed. Military officers replaced civilians at all levels of the bureaucracy. Most political parties remained banned. E-mail and Internet communication were permitted in the country but only under tight control by censors. The military junta was able to sign cease-fire agreements with a number long-standing ethnic rebel groups, but for those still engaged in civil war, such as the Karens, the military stepped up its suppression, forcing hundreds of thousands to flee to Thailand, where they languished as refugees in terrible living conditions.

In an attempt to improve its international image, SLORC officials renamed the ruling council in 1997 the "State Peace and Development Council" (SPDC). SPDC policies remained virtually the same as those of SLORC. Although the SPDC partially liberalized trade and investment, most new foreign investment permitted into Burma explicitly benefited state officials who doubled as businessmen.

In 2000, a special UN envoy attempted to bring about talks between the government and the democracy leader Aung San Suu Kyi, who was under house arrest for the second time. Speculation emerged that a new breakthrough and compromise could lead to an opening of the nation. By mid-2001, however, talks broke down. Months later, Aung San Suu Kyi was released from house arrest and allowed to travel within Burma. In 2003, while she was touring Depayin, a provincial town in upper Burma, a violent clash erupted between NLD sympathizers and the government. Opposition leaders claimed the confrontation led to seventy deaths, whereas the government reported only four. Prodemocracy groups accused the government of orchestrating the Depayin massacre. Soon afterward, NLD leaders were arrested and Aung San Suu Kyi's third detention began.[6]

Intrigue within the military has also punctuated Burmese politics. Following an alleged coup attempt by Ne Win's son-in-law in March 2002, Ne Win was placed under house arrest by Than Shwe. Months later, at age ninety-one, Ne Win died at his home on Inya Lake. The military junta refused to recognize Ne Win's passing with a state funeral or official salute of honor. In Myanmar's Tatmadaw, intergenerational despotism had fully arrived. Burma's prospects for political change appeared bleak.

In August 2003, only months after the Depayin massacre, newly appointed prime minister Khin Nyunt outlined a seven-point roadmap for a transition to multiparty democracy. Reviving the moribund National Convention, the new leader aimed to redraft the constitution. The move drew some interest, as Khin Nyunt, the former head of the military's intelligence service, began to broker discussions with Aung San Suu Kyi. Burmese diplomats paraded the reforms at the United Nations. Still, very few inside or outside Burma viewed the process as legitimate. A year later, Senior General Than Shwe forcibly removed the former Ne Win protégé from office and placed him under detention. A purge of officials tied to Khin Nyunt followed.

In 2006, the SPDC announced a surprise relocation of the country's capital to an undeveloped rural area four hundred kilometers north of Rangoon. The decision is believed to have derived from consultations with the junta's favored astrologists. Naypyidaw, the new capital, required a massive construction effort and the relocation of government offices and residences. By literally distancing ministers and administrators from the population, the paranoid Tatmadaw resurrected the age-old court practice of isolating officials.

If intended to decrease the likelihood of antigovernment activism in Rangoon, relocating the capital to Naypyidaw failed. In August 2007, the government imposed a drastic 500 percent hike in fuel prices. Protests followed, led by saffron-robed Buddhist monks and veteran leaders from the 8888 Uprising. The government reacted violently, using plainclothes goons at first and then uniformed soldiers later. Protesters, including monks, were brutally beaten and arrested. The Buddhist clergy demanded an apology from the government, which never came. What followed became Burma's most significant mass protests since 1988, similarly drawing global attention.

On September 28, 2007, throughout the country thousands of monks went to the streets under the banner of the All Burma Monks Alliance, a hitherto-unknown group. As ordinary Burmese joined the monks, demonstrations grew massive in many parts of the country. In Rangoon, some protesters

headed for the famous Shwedagon Pagoda; others flocked to Aung San Suu
Kyi's residence near Inya Lake. Still under house arrest, the Nobel laureate
appeared at her gate, engaging with monks and others. The blessing of the
movement by Burma's leading dissident served as yet another catalyst.
Within a few days, over 100,000 monks and their followers had paralyzed the
country's major cities. Predictably, the Tatmadaw stepped up its brutality in
return. At least thirty-one protesters were killed and many others were
wounded. Pictures and video sent from digital cameras and cell phones
flooded newswires worldwide; images of unarmed, shaven-headed monks
and students lying dead and bloodied on Rangoon streets produced shock
and dismay. Despite an international outcry from Western governments,
ASEAN ministers, and sympathetic international celebrities, the thuggish
junta retained the upper hand.

By October, the "Saffron Revolution" had been suppressed. Temples were
raided by security forces and many monks were detained; others simply disappeared and remain missing. To reduce tensions, a UN envoy arrived to
meet with junta leaders and Aung San Suu Kyi. The protests affirmed widespread discontent among Burma's population, but they also exposed the
weakened state of Burma's opposition to effect political change.

Undeterred by unrest, the SPDC announced plans for a May 2008 referendum on a new constitution, a document drafted exclusively by regime insiders to ensure the military's continued dominance. National League for
Democracy leaders organized a massive "No!" campaign that distributed
leaflets throughout the country.

On May 2, 2008, eight days before the scheduled referendum, Cyclone
Nargis hit Burma's densely populated delta region with devastating consequences; it was the worst natural disaster in the country's history. With
massive force, Nargis caused over 138,000 deaths and left 2.4 million survivors stranded and desperate, according to UN figures. Most disturbing
was Than Shwe's initial reluctance to allow foreign aid and disaster relief to
the cyclone's victims. Injured, homeless, and hungry, millions of Burmese
suffered unnecessarily in the days and weeks that followed. Foreign journalists, restricted by the regime, produced underground reports offering the
world a glimpse of the disaster's massive scale.[7]

While Myanmar's leaders allowed millions to suffer by denying visas to
aid workers and entry to supply ships, the SPDC audaciously went forward
with its constitutional referendum, postponing voting in affected areas.
State-controlled media announced weeks later that voters had approved the
new charter with a 92.4 percent vote. International condemnation for mishandling the disaster and staging a farcical referendum on constitutional
reform was nearly universal.

Then, ten days after Nargis, a new event gripped the world's attention: a 7.9 earthquake in southwest China that killed 90,000 people and left 5 million homeless. Following the Sichuan earthquake, Burmese officials allowed some international aid to trickle in (via Thailand) but kept tight restrictions on foreign aid workers. As the world watched the contrasting relief efforts in China and Burma, the true incompetence and paranoia of Myanmar's military junta was laid bare. For their quick action, Chinese officials won praise from UN secretary-general Ban Ki-moon. Wen Jiabao, China's prime minister, earned the title of "Uncle Wen" from an affectionate Chinese public for his unrelenting work to coordinate earthquake relief efforts. China welcomed international aid from any source. By contrast, Than Shwe became the object of anger and bewilderment from inside and outside Burma. French diplomats called for the military junta to be charged with crimes against humanity and even raised the prospect of the UN Security Council authorizing humanitarian intervention under the emerging principle of "R2P," or Responsibility to Protect. Only following a face-to-face meeting with the UN secretary-general did Than Shwe relax entry restrictions on aid workers, although United States Aid for International Development (USAID) workers were never allowed in. Burma's worst natural disaster was thus exacerbated by a tragic man-made catastrophe.

In 2008, ASEAN leaders took the opportunity to chide Myanmar's leaders, a rare event due to the regional body's commitment to noninterference. In a report at its ministerial meeting, it was announced that $1 billion would be needed for reconstruction. The cyclone had destroyed 450,000 homes, damaged 350,000 others, flooded 600,000 hectares of farmland, and severely damaged or destroyed 75 percent of hospitals and clinics in the region. For their part, Myanmar's leaders played down the document's conclusions. They also claimed that critical reports by survivors had been faked and falsely portrayed government aid efforts. Gradually, the junta allowed more and more aid to trickle in to the worst-hit areas.

In the aftermath of Cyclone Nargis, government repression of political opponents continued. In late 2008, sixty-five-year prison sentences were handed down to fourteen prodemocracy activists, including veterans of the 8888 Uprising. Months later Aung San Suu Kyi's house arrest was extended after the Tatmadaw discovered she had briefly sheltered a fifty-three-year-old American civilian who, in a bizarre nighttime rescue attempt, surreptitiously swam to her home on Inya Lake, believing he alone could miraculously free her. John Yettaw, the Vietnam War veteran and PTSD sufferer at the center of the incident, was later deported after intervention by U.S. senator Jim Webb, a fellow veteran and longtime critic of the effectiveness of Western sanctions.

As 2009 closed, Burma remained in political and economic misery, seemingly stuck on an endless path of repression, poverty, and failed governance. Because of its trajectory, few observers predicted that 2010 would inaugurate a new era of political reform at the behest of the regime itself. The reform program—deliberate, democracy-oriented, and very incomplete—has since transformed the regime in an arguably irreversible fashion. Following decades of tragic and failed military rule, the promise of democracy has emerged once again in Burma. Remarkably, its instigation did not come through a revolutionary change of regime, but from reformist change within the regime.

Under the authority of the new 2008 constitution, Myanmar's leaders began a series of surprising reforms that pivoted around scheduled elections in November 2010. At the beginning of that year, regime leaders released a number of political prisoners, including prominent NLD leader Tin Oo. Tatmadaw representatives then started formal conversations with Aung San Suu Kyi, who remained under house arrest. In preparation for the elections, Prime Minister Thein Sein and a group of moderate SPDC leaders resigned from their military posts and formed the United Solidarity and Development Party (USDP) out of an existing progovernment social organization, the United Solidarity Development Association (USDA). Most analysts saw the USDP as a proxy party for the military.

Then, in another unexpected move weeks before the elections, military leaders unilaterally announced changes to the country's flag, its national anthem, and its official name (from the Union of Myanmar to the Republic of the Union of Myanmar). Skeptical critics, understandably, viewed all of these preelection changes as cosmetic; in hindsight, the SPDC's moves demonstrated its intention to recreate Myanmar's governing institutions after the election was complete.

The 2010 election, boycotted by the NLD because Aung San Suu Kyi remained under house arrest, was predictably won by the USDP and internationally condemned for being fraudulent. Another reason the NLD boycotted the election was that its participation would have meant an end to its long-standing claims to rightful power stemming from the overturned 1990 elections. Shortly after the election, the SPDC announced the formation of a civilian government and the end of military rule. In an event formalizing this action, strongman Than Shwe officially dissolved the SPDC and announced his retirement. The USDP's Thein Sein, the majority party leader in Parliament, was installed as president of Myanmar—technically the first civilian leader of the first nonmilitary government in five decades. Myanmar's generals, ostensibly, had just handed the reins of power to an elected government. What followed was even more astonishing.

President Thein Sein reorganized the government's cabinet, installed proreform ministers, and retired hard-liners. He also began to release political prisoners by the hundreds. From 2010 on, Thein Sein also removed hundreds of blacklisted names from Tatmadaw records and invited exiled Burmese to return with amnesty. In 2011, the government shockingly ended all prepublication censorship, allowed formerly verboten images of Aung San Suu Kyi to appear in public, and announced that unions could freely organize. In the economic sphere, Thein Sein sold off over 300 state-owned enterprises (without public auction), reformed the country's exchange rate regime, liberalized foreign investment rules, and imprudently announced a goal of tripling Myanmar's GDP per capita by 2016 (a feat the Asian Development Bank forecasted as possible by 2030 at the earliest).[8] In another surprising move, especially to Beijing, Thein Sein suspended construction of a Chinese-funded dam in Kachin State after fierce local protest. In the social realm, the new government relaxed cultural controls as well, symbolized by permitting movie theaters to screen once-forbidden Western films. In August 2012, *Titanic 3D* became the first Hollywood film to be legally viewed by Burmese audiences in a generation.

Diplomatically, Thein Sein was also active. He eagerly held meetings with ambassadors and foreign guests to tout his reform program, including high-profile face-to-face meetings with U.S. secretary of state Hillary Clinton and British prime minister David Cameron. Engaging regional leaders, he sought to secure Myanmar's chairmanship of ASEAN, scheduled for 2014—a once controversial prospect because of ASEAN's open criticism over the junta's handling of Cyclone Nargis. At each event, President Thein Sein appeared in public donning civilian clothing rather than the military garb that defined the Myanmar led by his predecessors. In a matter of months, he adeptly began to change the international image of Myanmar's government. A sense that the country was finally embracing the new international era permeated the global community. Western governments, which once isolated Myanmar as a pariah state, began to ease sanctions. By July 2012, the United States had reestablished diplomatic relations with Myanmar to the full-ambassadorial level.

Most dramatically, one week after the 2010 election, Aung San Suu Kyi was suddenly released from house arrest. She soon held direct meetings with Thein Sein and made public statements extending confidence that his government's reform program was genuine. After she was freed, the NLD reregistered as a political party and named Aung San Suu Kyi as a candidate for the Pyithu Hluttaw, Myanmar's lower house.

In by-elections held in April 2012, the NLD won all but one of the forty-four seats it contested. Daw (Aunt) Aung San Suu Kyi—whose 1990 party was denied power after winning 81 percent of the national vote; the international human rights icon and Nobel Laureate; the daughter of the country's slain independence hero; the admiring subject of countless news articles, books, documentaries, films, and a critically acclaimed rock anthem; the graceful woman with flowers in her hair who suffered fifteen total years under house arrest as a prisoner of conscience—finally, at last, took her rightful seat in Burma's Parliament on May 2, 2012.

It remains to be seen whether Aung San Suu Kyi or one of her NLD colleagues will ever lead Myanmar. The ultimate goals of Thein Sein and USDP reformers remain a subject of intense speculation and debate. Some deduce that Myanmar is attempting to wean itself from economic dependence on China. Others view the reforms cynically, as the junta's last-ditch attempt to depoliticize the opposition, or to usher in a dominant-party state under USDP hegemony. Given the military's past, it is difficult to imagine Tatmadaw generals gleefully allowing the NLD to assume control of state institutions as the result of another 1990-style landslide election victory. Myanmar's political future remains daunting.

For her part, the intrepid Aung San Suu Kyi remains cautiously cooperative in her dealings with the regime since her election. Agreeing to stay within constitutional bounds, she has pushed Thein Sein's government for greater reform but avoided overt attempts to delegitimize his authority. With a Mandela-esque aura, she remains wildly beloved at home and abroad, a figure of immense significance in the history of Southeast Asia.

Since being named president, Thein Sein has also sought new deals with restive minorities and allowed for constitutionally mandated elections of local assemblies (albeit with 25 percent quotas for military seats). Nevertheless, Burma's fundamental ethnic tensions persist, and questions over federalism remain unresolved. Even as Naypyitaw's officials sought to keep pace with Thein Sein's reforms, horrific sectarian violence between stateless Rohingya Muslims and Rakhine Buddhists rocked Myanmar throughout 2012. In Rakhine State homes and mosques were burned, vigilante gangs roamed the streets, and desperate Rohingya refugees fled in boats to neighboring Bangladesh. Fearing for the safety of its staff, the United Nations pulled its workers out of the region. The ethnic tensions that persist throughout Burma's borderlands ominously remind Burmese and outsiders alike that the twin ideals of republicanism and union—which now share a place alongside "Myanmar" in the country's official name—remain more aspirational than real.

INSTITUTIONS AND SOCIAL GROUPS

The Military

Since independence, the Burmese military has played the central role in governmental affairs. No other institutions or social classes have even been allowed to legitimately compete with the military. This fact highlights the risks of overly optimistic assessments of Thein Sein's democratic reform program.

With the exception of Brunei, where the monarchy controls every aspect of society, no Southeast Asian nation has been ruled by a single institution to the same degree as Burma.

The Tatmadaw, which began as a popular proindependence force under Aung San, was the only credibly unified force in the country during its early years of self-governance. In 1958, U Nu asked the army to step in temporarily, and in 1962 it took power without an invitation. Ne Win, its undisputed leader for decades, took over state power as a guardian who was above party politics. He ran the government by assigning leading governmental positions to military comrades.

In 1988, facing a social revolution, the military reasserted itself again by shuffling top leaders and engaging in a brutal crackdown on protesters. Yet another major episode of military suppression occurred in 2007 and targeted monks, students, and ordinary citizens engaged in antigovernment protests. Throughout these events, very little was known about how decisions were made among the ruling generals. Whether controlled by Ne Win, SLORC generals, or Than Shwe's SPDC, meetings remained subject to secrecy among the dozen-plus generals who comprised the junta.

The Tatmadaw grew rapidly from a force of 190,000 in the early 1990s to an estimated 400,000 by 2008. The joint U.S.-U.K. invasions of Afghanistan and Iraq confirmed the junta's belief that outside powers can and will team up to invade weak countries. Forever obsessed with security concerns, Than Shwe expanded the country's armed forces to a size second only to Vietnam in Southeast Asia. Nevertheless, the quality of most new recruits was as sketchy as the outdated military hardware that Than Shwe eagerly sought to replace through new arms purchases.

Under the SPDC, arms deals with China, India, Israel, and other countries upgraded Myanmar's weapons systems and doubled the size of its naval fleet. Now two hundred vessels strong, the naval fleet has developed a newfound mission in recent years to protect the country's untapped offshore oil and natural gas resources.[9] Arms trade with North Korea during Than Shwe's tenure raised concerns over the possible exchange of nuclear technology and of a nuclearized Myanmar. In 2012, reformist president Thein Sein publicly vowed to end all arms trade with North Korea and to limit any dealings with Kim Jong Un's regime within the framework of Security Council resolutions.

At the time it was disbanded in 2011, the SPDC retained only two generals from SLORC. Ongoing cease-fires with a number of ethnic insurgencies brokered during the 1990s had ameliorated the Tatmadaw's most serious domestic security concerns. Yet Burma's ongoing civil wars remain the longest-running in the world. Accelerated efforts to reach peaceful settlement with ethnic rebels under Thein Sein's USDP government, including a strategy to fold armed ethnic insurgents into the state military, indicate a more conciliatory approach to ethnic security concerns.

Going forward, the extent to which the Tatmadaw remains a praetorian king-maker or develops a new role as a professionalized military remains an open question. Constitutional arrangements assure it a role in politics, but for the time being, past comparisons of Myanmar's generals with the martial state xenophobes who rule North Korea have begun to disappear under Thein Sein's leadership.

Aung San Suu Kyi

Aung San Suu Kyi was schooled in Burma, where she spent her first fifteen years. A member of a prominent family, she was then sent to India, where her mother was ambassador, and then to England to study politics, philosophy, and economics at Oxford University. She later published books on Burmese history and literature. Prior to 1988, she had no direct political experience and was known primarily as the daughter of Aung San.

Shortly before the 8888 Uprising, she returned to Burma from England to care for her ailing mother. She joined the opposition and, because of her name and superb oratorical ability, began to draw large crowds to her speeches. Burmese women imitated her hair and clothing style. She was cheered for her straightforward attacks against the government and against Ne Win. Her military adversaries, frightened by her mounting popularity, suggested that she was manipulated by communists. On July 20, 1989, the military placed her under house arrest and cut off all communications between her followers and the outside world.

While still under arrest, she was awarded (in absentia) the Nobel Peace Prize in December 1991 for her courageous struggle against the military dictatorship. As a political prisoner, she has suffered three detentions for a total of fifteen years following her return to her homeland. Her last detention followed the 2003 clash at Depayin, where she and her supporters were brutally attacked by over 1,000 plainclothes thugs, who held ties with the USDA. Her 2010 release came shortly after Myanmar's first national elections in over twenty years. In 2012 by-elections, in which she was permitted to run, she won 55,902 votes of 65,471 votes cast in her Rangoon township, or 85 percent of the vote. Known affectionately by supporters as "Daw Suu" (Aunt Suu) or "The Lady," Aung San Suu Kyi remains unparalleled as a popular political figure in modern Burma.

Legislature

Prior to 2010, Burma's legislature experienced only two periods of extended life: as a multiparty bicameral body during the contentious U Nu era (1951–1962); and as a rubber-stamp unicameral body during period under the Ne

Win–controlled BSPP era (1974 to 1988). After the 1990 elections were over-turned, military leaders under SLORC and the SPDC removed all vestiges of legislative power and ruled as a military dictatorship. Constitutional reform revived the legislature in 2010.

As a means to outmaneuver the NLD, and annul any claims to the electoral results of the 1990 election, the SPDC began to engage in constitutional re-form in 2003. The new charter, approved by voters during the immediate af-termath of Cyclone Nargis in 2008, established a new bicameral Parliament, the Pyidaungsu Hluttaw. Currently, the lower house, the Pyithu Hluttaw (House of Representatives), seats 440 representatives: 330 elected from con-stituencies, and 110 appointed military delegates. The upper chamber, the Amytha Hluttaw (House of Nationalities), seats 224 representatives: 168 elected and equally divided between Myanmar's regions and states, and 56 appointed military delegates. Thus, by constitutional mandate, 25 percent of both houses are designated for the Tatmadaw, a convenient number since any constitutional amendment requires over 75 percent approval in both houses.

In spite of recent reforms and the inclusion of opposition parties, the Pyidaungsu Hluttaw remains firmly under the control of the regime author-ities. Even after the 2012 by-elections, swept by the NLD, the proregime USDP retained control of 212 of 330 elected seats. Combined with USDP's seats in the Amytha Hluttaw and the military-proportioned seats in both houses, proregime delegates currently outnumber the NLD 513 to 47 and thus occupy 77 percent of all seats of the bicameral Pyidaungsu Hluttaw. Even so, with legislative term limits constitutionally mandated for five years, the election year of 2015 will undoubtedly prove significant to the country's future and the fate of its long-beleaguered legislature.

Political Parties

In 1993, Than Shwe founded the Union Solidarity and Development Associ-ation (USDA). Organized as a "social welfare organization," the USDA was considered the political arm of the SPDC but was not a political party. With branches in major cities and towns throughout Burma, its grassroots pres-ence rose rapidly, fronting for the regime's cooperative efforts with nascent civil society groups. Its followers appeared in public wearing white long-sleeved shirts and dark green sarongs. The regime dispatched USDA mem-bers for rehabilitation efforts following Cyclone Nargis, its activities prominently displayed on a digital-savvy Web site. From its creation, mem-bers of the USDA held privileged access to state resources. They also consti-tuted the bulk of representatives at the constitutional convention and its local bodies organized the May 2008 charter referendum.[10]

Prior to the 2010 elections, the USDA formalized itself as political party, the Union and Solidarity Development Party (USDP). Echoing the strategies of Golkar, Suharto's pro–New Order quasi-party, which forcibly co-opted Indonesian bureaucrats and interest groups for three decades, the USDP now stands as the largest projunta organization in the country.[11] The USDP's potential to serve as a public counterweight to the NLD is significant. Leery of the organization's veracity, prodemocracy advocates do not view it as a legitimate political party, pointing to the paramilitary thugs it deployed at the Depayin massacre and the crackdown on the 2007 Saffron Revolution.

The most important opposition party in Myanmar remains the National League for Democracy. The party was founded in the wake of the 8888 Uprising by Aung Gyi, U Thura, Tin Oo, and Aung San Suu Kyi. Both Aung Gyi and Tin Oo were dissident generals forcibly removed from the Tatmadaw for turning on the regime. Aung Gyi later turned on the NLD itself, resigning after accusing it of being infiltrated by communists. Tin Oo, after a falling out with Ne Win in 1976, spent years in prison and endured long stints under house arrest, much like Aung San Suu Kyi. After a decade of continuous detention, his most recent release came in 2009. Many NLD supporters remain in detention.

That the NLD has survived in spite of being denied power in 1990 by military fiat and suffering subsequent persecution from antidemocracy SLORC and SPDC governments stands as a remarkable testament to its strength and durability. Its victorious reemergence in 2012 (winning 43 of 44 seats it contested in legislative by-elections) indicates its popularity remains and assures it will continue as a feature of Burmese party politics whether reform trends hold or not.

Myanmar's party system, as revealed by the 2010 general elections and 2012 by-elections, is characterized by two types of parties: national parties and ethnic minority parties. National parties, which run candidates across districts throughout the country, include the proregime USDP, the now smaller promilitary National Union Party, and Aung San Suu Kyi's NLD. Ethnic minority parties coalesce around the regional aspirations of larger minority groups such as the Rakhine, Chin, Shan, Mon, and Wa. Some ethnic groups have yet to embrace party politics or are too small to organize their own. At the present time, ethnic parties lie on the periphery of national legislative significance, but if future elections were to see a plurality victory by the NLD over the USDP, ethnic parties would likely become important partners in a new era of coalition governments.

Monks

Burma's 400,000 Buddhist monks number nearly the same as today's military. Monks are highly respected as teachers and religious leaders, and in the past their predecessors have toppled kings. Burma's Buddhist *sangha*, or monastic order, has been more politically active than the *sangha* in neighboring Thailand. Keeping the monks from rebellion was a key goal of SPDC policy. The SPDC even tried to infiltrate the monkhood with its own agents, who reported to the junta any dissident activity.[12]

The power of the monks to put political pressure on the junta was demonstrated in 2007. Led by the All Burma Monks Alliance and other groups, the monks brought a moral legitimacy to the demonstrations greater than that of Aung San Suu Kyi. At her gate, monks blessed Suu Kyi. In 2007, they also engaged in the rare practice of *thabeik hmauk*, or overturning of the offering bowls, by denying opportunity to immoral leaders to make spiritual merit. When Than Shwe and the military refused to apologize for mistreatment at protests, leading monks led several hundred monks on marches around Rangoon's Shwedagon Pagoda with offering bowls turned symbolically upside-down, a nonviolent affront to regime leaders.

Internationally, images of monks bloodied and beaten drew unique attention to what otherwise may have been lost as everyday third-world unrest. Past events render the military's co-optation of Burma's monks unlikely, but Burma's monks are not necessarily a unified force either. As an opposition group that could threaten regime change, however, Buddhist monks do not seek to capture state power and remain destined to play only a supportive role in a broader movement. They also are not immune to sectarian politics. In 2012, they marched in support of Thein Sein's proposal to deport the country's 800,000 Muslim Rohingya minorities to other countries.

Ethnic Minority Groups

During the postindependence period, Burma's ethnic minority groups have continued to view themselves primarily in terms of ethnic nationalism. The Karens, Karenni, Shans, Kachins, and other groups that fought for state autonomy do not trust the government. In their struggle for minority rights, these groups joined the National Democratic Front (NDF) in revolt. The NDF assumed that the peoples of Burma were members of ethnic-linguistic communities who voluntarily came together in 1947 to form the Union of Burma.[13] In this union, equality of communities was to be reflected in their organization as political units, each having power to govern itself, claim to a reasonable share of the nation's resources, an equal right to develop its land and society, and equal representation in the national government.[14] The states were to be strong and the central government weak. In reality, however, and despite promises to state leaders at the time of independence, the central government became strong and the separate states weak.

To achieve their goals, the minority ethnic groups organized armed insurgencies to protect their territories and to pressure the central government to accept a federated Burma, with ethnic states having autonomy under a federal umbrella government. The most infamous such ethnic warlord was the opium-trading Khun Sa, a Shan figure of Golden Triangle lore who eluded Burmese troops, Thai rangers, and U.S. drug enforcement authorities for over two decades.

Opium itself has a long history in Burma and Southeast Asia. The British, of course, profited from the opium trade and introduced opium poppies for production in upland minority areas. Later, ethnic insurgents such as Khun Sa, as well as the Burmese Communist Party, relied on opium profits to finance their guerrilla activities. At its height, Khun Sa's Shan United Army commanded 20,000 men. The United States set a $2 million bounty for his capture and estimated that he was responsible for 45 percent of the global heroin trade and sourced 80 percent of heroin trafficked on New York City streets. Ethnic Chinese brokers and Thai traffickers also became players in a drug-dependent civil war. In the late 1980s and 1990s, Burma's generals got into the action through cease-fire deals where, in exchange for loyalty, they granted rebels autonomy and basic freedom to pursue narcotics. After U.S. agents thoroughly disrupted his network, Khun Sa finally surrendered to Burmese authorities in exchange for immunity from extradition to the United States. He died in 2007, idling away in Rangoon with four wives and making sundry ruby deals.[15]

In 2001, the NDF and the United Nationalities League for Democracy–Liberated Areas (UNLD-LA) cofounded the Ethnic Nationalities Council (ENC). Moving the fight from armed insurgency to political diplomacy, the ENC's mandate has been to engage in a "tripartite dialogue" between Burma's ethnic minorities, the SPDC, and the NLD. With some exceptions, armed conflict has largely given way to negotiation in recent years, a trend continued under Thein Sein. Still, as recently as 2011, firefights between Burmese soldiers and the Kachin Independence Army erupted in spite of a long-standing truce.

Deals between ethnic groups and Myanmar's government, combined with rising Thai demand for methamphetamines, put Burma's legendary opium production in decline and into the hands of smaller criminal elements. To service Thailand's insatiable sex industry, criminal syndicates also engage in human trafficking of Burmese women, often poorer minorities. Ever vulnerable to power, guns, and the mechanisms of exploitation, many of Burma's ethnic minorities, with long-held goals of state autonomy in a federalized system, await a full conclusion to the world's longest ongoing civil wars.

STATE-SOCIETY RELATIONS AND DEMOCRACY

For almost all of its history, the Burmese state has been dominated by a small number of rulers and institutions. Absolute monarchs, British administrators, and now military generals have made the authoritative decisions that have affected the entire Burmese citizenry. Outside the military, Burma has poorly developed state institutions. Junta leaders have attempted to institutionalize proregime support through its first subsidiary party, the NUP, and more recently through the cultivation of the USDA and USDP. External institutions, such as a parliament, established political parties, and interest groups, have had little influence over the state's policy decisions. In this sense, the Burmese state has been autonomous—independent of societal organizations.

Recent moves by leaders to remove military titles, govern as civilians, and permit opposition parties to compete in elections signal progress, but primarily in relation to Burma's repressive past. Any assessment of political reform in Thein Sein's Myanmar demands caution until there is genuine civilian rule independent of a praetorian military, civilian leaders emerge without roots in the military, or opposition parties acquire state power through free elections.

In contrast to Thailand's mixed-market economy, state authorities in Burma have endlessly intervened in every aspect of the economy—nationalizing public utilities, industries, and agribusinesses and placing numerous obstacles in the path of entrepreneurs. Until 2010, the Burmese state demonstrated little adaptability to changes in the international and regional spheres, and to the worldwide movement toward democratization. This lack of adaptability has undermined the legitimacy once enjoyed by the Tatmadaw. The military is no longer the respected unifier of the nation; instead, it is viewed as a tool for opportunism by supporters and a symbol of stagnation and oppression by its detractors. In this regard, the Burmese state has been weak. It has been a patronage operation with low capacity and legitimacy levels. The closed management of economic reform by Thein Sein, including the sell-off of state-owned enterprises to cronies, suggests state authorities prefer oligopolistic control of liberalized markets rather than the encouragement of societal innovation or entrepreneurship.

Tatmadaw leaders continue to harbor deep fears over challenges to their legitimacy. Military leaders justify centralized authority on the grounds of national unity (threatened by ethnic separatism) and national sovereignty (threatened by foreign meddling and intervention). In Myanmar, civil society groups have been viewed with suspicion. Following Cyclone Nargis, for example, Than Shwe equated the presence of foreign aid workers to an erosion of state sovereignty. Unlike elites in Thailand, Myanmar's rulers have not invited technocrats, politicians, intellectuals, or socioeconomic elites to participate in state affairs. The few outsiders brought into the polity have no autonomous political base or constituency.

Burma's only experience with democracy was a brief period under the 1947 constitution after independence, when U Nu supported representative institutions, free elections, and civil liberties. The ineffectiveness of U Nu's rule was used to rationalize the military takeover of the government in both

1958 and 1962. The military leaders viewed democratic institutions and behavior as "foreign to the traditions" of the Burmese and a rejected legacy of Western imperialism. Than Shwe's roadmap to democracy bore the much-touted and oxymoronic label "discipline-flourishing democracy," a term reformist Thein Sein continues to use.

Even with recent political reform, and a sitting parliament that is partially elected, state-society relations remain balanced in the state's favor. Thein Sein's open embrace of "democracy" in rhetoric and in actual reform notwithstanding, it is difficult to argue that Myanmar has begun a genuine democratic transition. To date reform has been dictated from the top and not through societal institutions. Burma remains a politically closed regime or, at best, a regime transitioning to a hegemonic electoral authoritarian regime (similar to Cambodia or Singapore). Even if fully realized, provisions under the 2008 constitution idealize state-society relations in the context of state-managed illiberal democracy rather than popular sovereignty.

ECONOMY AND DEVELOPMENT

The historical similarities between Burma and Thailand are striking. Both nations have had histories of absolute monarchy; both have practiced Theravada Buddhism; and both have comparable natural resources and fertile soils for agriculture. In the 1950s, Burma and Thailand also shared a similar size of GNP. In view of these similarities, why has Thailand had success in its quest for economic development while Burma has failed?

One answer stems from the most obvious difference between the two nations: The Burmese were colonized by the British, whereas the Thais have been independent throughout their history. The Thais, who did not develop an inferiority complex toward the West or antipathy toward Western ways, were therefore more flexible about adopting and adapting westernization. In contrast, the Burmese consciously eschewed Western ways, including the materialism and commercialism of Western culture, which the Burmese generals believe have ruined Thai society.

Another answer is that the postindependence governments of Burma chose to isolate their nation from the global economic system, relying on government-controlled socialistic economics and autarky. Thailand, on the other hand, opened its economy through a policy of greater market freedom and export-driven growth. The results are dramatic: Thailand's per capita GDP rose from $100 in the 1950s to almost $3,000 in 2006, whereas in the same period Burma's rose from $100 to less than $300. Even when calculated in terms of purchasing power parity, Burma's per capita income in 2011 had reached a meager $1,300, the lowest in Southeast Asia.

"The Burmese Way to Socialism," a nationalist ideology that sought the marriage of Marxism and Buddhism, proved to be an economic failure; it led to neither socialism nor development. In addition to weaknesses inherent to state-controlled production, policies associated with the ideology repressed the Chinese and Indian minorities who served as the core of business and entrepreneurship in other Southeast Asian countries. It also led to a dual economy with a large unofficial black market. Black market prices in Burma have often been higher than official prices, creating incentives for those with access to state resources or imported goods to participate. On the other hand, sellers in the black market ironically benefit by increasing their incomes and by expanding supply, thus lessening consumer frustration. For example, telephones, gasoline, and entertainment products, in short supply, are often made available through the black market. But no country achieves overall development based on black market activity. Combined with weak educational and rural development programs, isolation has kept Burma poor.

Burma's economy reached its nadir in 1987 when the United Nations granted the once-prosperous nation the ignoble status of least-developed country, placing Burma in the same category as Chad, Ethiopia, and Haiti. Whereas Burma once controlled 28 percent of the world's rice trade, it controlled only 2 percent by 1970.[16] Years later, the brutal suppression of demonstrators in 1988 ended the few ongoing Western development projects, reducing the external capital that had been available to the government.

To counter this cessation of aid, Burma opened border trade with Thailand and China and promulgated more liberal foreign investment laws in the 1990s. Foreign investors were permitted to form either wholly owned enterprises or joint ventures in which the foreign partner was required to hold a minimum 35 percent stake. However, little investment was induced by the government's policy because of the country's political instability. What did arrive left quickly. Multinational firms such as PepsiCo, Wal-Mart, Levi Strauss & Co., Tommy Hilfiger, and Liz Claiborne pulled out after short stints. Unfavorable business conditions, pressure from human rights activists, and a 1998 U.S. government ban on new American investment in Burma further inhibited Western investment. In 2004, even more restrictive U.S. laws targeted Burmese imports and prohibited any payments into the country. China, Japan, and ASEAN governments, however, increased economic dealings with junta leaders through policies of "constructive engagement." Burma was permitted to join ASEAN in 1997.

Unable to compete with Southeast Asia's newly industrialized countries and China in textiles, manufacturing, and foreign direct investment, Burma's leaders shifted attention to natural resources. Extractive industries and the energy sector, they realized, were in high demand, and sector revenues often went directly to the state. Burma now exports natural gas and sells offshore exploration rights to Asian and Western partners. China, for its part, became Burma's most interdependent trading partner under the SPDC. Seeking to change the route of its Middle East oil shipments, bypassing the Malacca Strait, China is financing a pipeline from Burma's western coast to Yunnan, in China's southwest. Burmese leaders are also expanding biodiesel production, coercing some farmers to plant biofuel-friendly physic nut trees. One program, with a goal to convert 8 million acres of farmland to physic nut production, resulted in forced land allocation and production quotas nationwide.[17]

It is difficult to be precise about economic growth in Burma because government figures are unreliable. Even so, confidence in the overall picture is possible. In the early 1990s, Burma's annual economic growth rate hovered around 1 percent to 2 percent, and the overall standard of living, especially among rural people dependent on agriculture, had fallen. Only the presence of a black market made the economy tolerable. In the mid-1990s, economic growth rates improved to the 4 percent to 6 percent level, as foreign firms flirted with in-country investments. Following its shift to the energy sector and natural gas exports, state revenues rose and civil servants received large pay raises. The country's trade surplus also grew. Since 2000, Burmese government officials commonly report double-digit growth rates, though many analysts estimate actual rates in the 5 percent to 6 percent range. Economic policies under President Thein Sein have triggered increased foreign investment, but at the expense of farmers, who remain largely excluded from investment benefits. A rising local currency has also made agricultural exports less profitable and created downward pressure on prices.[18]

Whatever claims regime leaders make, Burma's overall socioeconomic picture remains bleak. Ordinary citizens struggle mightily through a chaotic maze of dual prices, inflation, shortages, bribery, and uncertainty. Periods of high inflation, caused in part by sundry salary increases for state employees, have plagued the economy. To finance its chronic budget deficit, the government often resorts to printing money needed to cover imports of military matériel and luxury goods. At the street level, Burma's informal sector rivals its formal economy in size, and a black market persists. The country's basic infrastructure is poor or nonexistent, especially in the countryside. Wasteful construction projects, such as rebuilding the country's administrative capital, impose unnecessary opportunity costs on public funds. Corruption at all levels remains rampant. In its 2011 rankings of 183 countries, Transparency International ranked Myanmar 180. By this measure Myanmar is home to the world's third-most-corrupt government (on par with Somalia and North Korea and well below the rankings of Nigeria and Zimbabwe).

Years of economic autarky and isolation have left the Burmese far worse off than almost all of their Southeast Asian neighbors. The 2011 Human Development Index, which measures income, life expectancy, and education, now ranks Burma the lowest of the countries of Southeast Asia. Even the neophyte nation-state of Timor-Leste ranks higher. If, as expected, economic growth picks up in Myanmar because of Thein Sein's reforms, it will take decades before the country develops the required administrative experience to manage market-based growth on par with Southeast Asia's economic tigers. Thein Sein's economic ambitions are ahead of the country's capacity to realize them.

Foreign Relations

There are many good reasons why the Burmese have emphasized the importance of national security. Their colonial heritage and the Japanese occupation are reminders that Burma has been a victim of both imperialism and aggression. Burma is surrounded by nations with far greater populations and military strength, sharing an 800-mile border with India and greater than 1,000-mile borders with China and Thailand. At times, Burma's ethnic minorities have been supported by outsiders, linked with the drug trade, and associated with elements of the Burmese Communist Party. Moreover, the nation's Indian and Chinese minorities have an influence in the Burmese economy disproportionate to their numbers. Finally, military governments have viewed westernization as a threat to Burmese traditional culture.

The government's response to this insecurity has been a policy of non-alignment. Earlier, Burma attempted to maintain an isolationist foreign policy by refusing to participate in the Indochina conflict, eschewing aid from various nations, and, until the late 1990s, forgoing membership in ASEAN. However, isolationism did not foster economic growth and, under the SPDC, Burma moved to a policy of modified isolationism. Under Thein Sein, modified isolation gave way to a new strategy to open the country. For the first time since 1962, Burmese leaders have begun to prioritize economic imperatives over security concerns and paranoia.

Relations with Thailand have often been tense because of the history of conflict between the two nations. However, relations improved following the 8888 Uprising when Burma, desperate for foreign capital, agreed to Thai requests to exploit its teak forests. Burmese concessions to Thai companies, prohibited from logging in Thailand due to new environmental laws, permitted the extraction of 1.2 million tons of logs annually.[19] Since the 1990s, several Thai politicians and military leaders have visited Burma to coordinate trade, drug eradication, and offshore oil exploration. Unsurprisingly, Thailand was the first country Burmese generals permitted (belatedly) to offer relief aid for cyclone victims. After her 2010 release Aung San Suu Kyi's first visit was to Thailand, and to Burmese refugees on the Thai-Burma border. In 2012, President Thein Sein and Prime Minister Yingluck signed a Memorandum of Understanding to jointly establish Myanmar's first economic zone, the Dawei Deep Seaport and Special Economic Zone.

Relations with Burma's other major neighbors, India and China, have warmed up as well. Earlier, following the 8888 Uprising, the Indian government expressed support for the Burmese people's resolve to achieve democracy. The two countries now trade in arms and share interests in Burma's offshore gas and oil. China, even more aggressively than India, cultivated relations with Burma during the SPDC period of modified isolationism. Border trade, energy interests, the prospect of a trans-Burma oil pipeline to Yunnan, and common interpretations of state sovereignty bring the two countries together; concern over ongoing minority unrest along the China-Myanmar border, and Kachin refugees fleeing into China, have not. Moreover, leery of President Barack Obama's strategic "pivot" to Asia, China is less sanguine about improved U.S.-Myanmar relations and is following Thein Sein's political reforms with caution.

In 1990, the United States downgraded its representation in Burma from an ambassador to a chargé d'affaires but did not sever relations following antigovernment protests. To the extent that any cooperation between the two governments followed, it was primarily to address narcotics trafficking in the region. Otherwise, since abrogating 1990 election results, Burma has faced one tough U.S. sanction measure followed by another. The Clinton administration condemned Burma's oppressive system, imposing visa restrictions on junta members and their families. These acts were followed by increased restrictions on trade and imports and, in 2007, executive orders from George W. Bush directed at blocking the assets of twenty-five top Burmese officials. In a rare foreign policy venture, First Lady Laura Bush publicly chided junta leaders following Cyclone Nargis in a speech to an international audience.

On her first trip to Asia as President Obama's secretary of state, Hillary Clinton announced that the U.S. policy on Burma was under review in hopes of encouraging "more effective" political and economic reform to "help the Burmese people." The combination of post-2010 reforms in Myanmar and Obama administration engagement resulted in the easing of sanctions and restoration of full diplomatic relations. In November 2011, Thein Sein's reform program received its biggest international endorsement to date when Secretary of State Hillary Clinton paid a visit to Naypyidaw, as well as to the released Aung San Suu Kyi at her home in Rangoon. Clinton later arranged for a U.S. business delegation to meet with Thein Sein at the 2012 ASEAN meeting in Phnom Penh. In 2012, Thein Sein was granted a U.S. visa to visit the United States, unthinkable for junta leaders just a few years earlier. He addressed the United Nations General Assembly in New York, where he pledged that he would not backtrack on reforms, drawing comparisons to Soviet reformer Mikhail Gorbachev.

ASEAN, a body normally committed to noninterference, struggled with the junta's ongoing repression since it admitted Burma into the organization. No single country in the organization has put ASEAN's aversion to political interference to the test as much as has Myanmar. Following the violent events of 2007, one caucus of ASEAN state parliamentarians even proposed Myanmar's expulsion from the body. The 2007 crackdown, and the dreadful mishandling of Cyclone Nargis, caused parliaments and legislatures in the region to put serious pressure on foreign ministers to abandon policies of noninterference. ASEAN leaders have long argued that international sanctions isolate Myanmar and that constructive engagement was more likely to produce democratic reform.[20] Myanmar's new trajectory may be evidence of the fruits of engagement. Than Shwe's government declined its turn to chair ASEAN in 2006, but Thein Sein views the same opportunity in 2014 as an opportunity for further endorsement of his reform program and his new-found foreign policy independence.

CONCLUSION

However condemned the regime's 2008 constitutional referendum was by the NLD and international critics, to the ruling generals it marked the beginning of a new era of political and economic reform. In a series of unexpected but welcome moves, Myanmar's ruling generals have now become responsible for transforming their own regime in a seemingly irreversible direction. Such a change within regime, rather than of regime, may eventually prove to be the least disruptive path for Burmese society to enjoy some of the political, economic, and social opportunities common elsewhere in the region. Overall human development in Myanmar, currently the lowest in Southeast Asia, is likely to improve going forward if current trends persist.

The political changes underway in Myanmar are the most promising political developments the Burmese have experienced in decades. Cautious optimism that reforms are genuine pervades Burmese society and the international community. Domestically, political reform derives legitimacy from endorsements by Aung San Suu Kyi and the Burmese people collectively. Internationally, they have received validation by major Western governments, including the United Kingdom, Burma's former colonizer, and the United States, the major force behind long-standing sanctions.

Because the consequences to the regime of yet another democratic reversal would be so severe politically and economically, it is difficult to imagine a 1990-style about-face by regime leaders at this point. Undeniably, the country experienced political disappointment and tragedy before, such as with the 1947 assassination of Aung San and the 1990 nullification of election results by the military. In these cases and others, the promise of visionary leadership was unexpectedly ripped from the Burmese people. One must not rule out the possibility that the Tatmadaw leadership, or some faction within it, may engineer yet another political reversal.

Yet even if Myanmar stays on Thein Sein's course of reform, the country's future remains unclear because of the unprecedented nature of the transition. Moreover, as is constitutionally mandated, the military maintains a direct role in politics by controlling one-quarter of all legislative seats in every assembly of the country. Thus, without further constitutional reform, it seems unlikely that a liberal democracy—where the military serves the people rather than represents them—will fully emerge. One possible scenario is the development of a hegemonic electoral dictatorship, or illiberal democracy, under an increasingly powerful and military-backed USDP. The extent to which military and USDP elites use reforms to enrich themselves may be the first indicator of this trajectory.

Performance legitimization could also buy time for the development of a USDP-hegemonic regime. As witnessed elsewhere in Asia, people tend to leave their governments alone if their own standard of living steadily rises. Throughout the region, illiberal democracy is more the norm than not. Of course, Aung San Suu Kyi and her NLD supporters, who have patiently waited for their opportunity to govern, may nevertheless stand for nothing less than a transition to full-fledged liberal democracy.

Lastly, the biggest threat any future Burmese government will face— whether liberal, illiberal, or authoritarian—lies in the yet-to-be-discovered formula of federalism that keeps ethnic tensions at bay and equitably allocates the powers and benefits of state and market across Burma's disparate populations. Only then will the Republic and Union of Myanmar live up to the promise of its newest name.

NOTES

1. The *r* in *Burma* is not pronounced but serves to lengthen the "ah" sound. The word is pronounced approximately as "Bamah" (as if the "me" and "be" sounds were fairly indistinct). This chapter uses the names Burma and Myanmar interchangeably, with some preference for using *Burma* for historical, cultural, and social contexts and for continuity with previous editions. Written prior to recent political reforms, previous editions of this book used only *Burma*. Most governments, scholars, and media outlets have now adopted the use of *Myanmar*, although *Burma* is still widely acceptable.

2. Burma's population is predominantly Theravada Buddhist (89 percent), a religion found particularly among Burmans, Shan, Mon, and Karens. Christianity (4 percent) is widespread among some Karen groups, Chins, and other upland groups in northern Burma. Islam (4 percent) exists in pockets among lowland Burmans, Indians, Bengalis, and the predominantly Muslim Rohingya minority of western Burma. Many upland groups along Burma's borders practice traditional indigenous religions and share common transnational ethnic relations with similar groups scattered throughout Southeast Asia and southwest China.

3. Burma Watcher, "Burma in 1988," *Asian Survey* 29, no. 2 (February 1989): 174.

4. Thant Myint U, *The River of Lost Footsteps: A Personal History of Burma* (New York: Farrar, Straus and Giroux, 2006), 32–34.

5. Ibid., 35.

6. Kyaw Yin Hlaing, "Myanmar in 2003: Frustration or Despair?" *Asian Survey* 44, no. 1 (January/February 2004): 88.

7. For an excellent account of Cyclone Nargis, see Emma Larkin, *No Bad News for the King: The True Story of Cyclone Nargis and Its Aftermath in Burma* (New York: Penguin, 2010).

8. David Steinberg, "Myanmar in 2010: The Elections Year and Beyond," in *Southeast Asian Affairs 2011*, ed. Daljit Singh (Singapore: Institute of Southeast Asian Studies, 2011), 173–189; Michael Schuman, "Will Burma Become Asia's Next Economic Tiger?" *Time*, August 22, 2012, http://business.time.com/2012/08/22/will-burma-become-asias-next-economic-tiger.

9. Aung Zaw, "A Growing Tatmadaw," *The Irrawaddy* 14, no. 6 (March 2006): www2.irrawaddy.org/article.php?art_id=5537.

10. Wai Moe, "USDA to Organize Referendum, Election," *The Irrawaddy* (11 February 2008), http://www2.irrawaddy.org/article.php?art_id=10260.

11. See chapter 8 of this book for a full account of Indonesia's Golkar party under Suharto.

12. Larkin, *No Bad News for the King*, 138.

13. Josef Silverstein, "National Unity in Burma: Is It Possible?" in *Durable Stability in Southeast Asia*, ed. Kusuma Snitwongse and Sukhumbhand Paribatra (Singapore: Institute of Southeast Asian Studies, 1987), 80.

14. Ibid., 80–81.

15. "Obituary: Khun Sa," *The Economist*, November 8, 2007, www.economist.com /node/10097596/.

16. Maureen Aung-Thwin, "Burmese Days," *Foreign Affairs* 68, no. 2 (February 1989): 150.

17. Ardeth Maung Thawnghmung and Maung Aung Myoe, "Myanmar in 2006: Another Year of Housekeeping?" *Asian Survey* 47, no. 1 (January/February 2007): 197.

18. Jayshree Bajoria, "Understanding Myanmar," Council on Foreign Relations, www.cfr.org/human-rights/understanding-myanmar/p14385.

19. James F. Guyot and John Badgley, "Myanmar in 1989," *Asian Survey* 30, no. 2 (February 1990): 191.

20. For an excellent treatment of ASEAN and the dilemmas that shape the organization, see Donald K. Emmerson, "Introduction," in *Hard Choices: Security, Democracy, and Regionalism in Southeast Asia* (Stanford: The Walter H. Shorenstein Asia-Pacific Research Center, 2008), 3–56.

RESOURCE GUIDE

A useful tool for bibliographic and other information on Burma is available from Australia National University's WWW Virtual Library: www.gksoft.com/govt/en/mm.html.

The University of California–Berkeley maintains a useful portal for digital and print resources on Burma: www.lib.berkeley.edu/SSEAL/SoutheastAsia/seaelec.html. Northern Illinois University's Southeast Asia Digital Library includes a range of useful links that cover government, academic, and research institutions specific to Burma: http://sea.lib .niu.edu. The University of Wisconsin–Madison Libraries maintains a list of digital and print resources on Burma: www.library.wisc.edu/guides/SEAsia/resarea.html.

The government-controlled newspaper of Myanmar, the *New Light of Myanmar*, is available online at www.myanmar.com/newspaper/nlm/index.html. Myanmar's Ministry of Foreign Affairs also maintains a Web site in English with new releases and reports of government activity at http://www.mofa.gov.mm/.

A number of Internet news sources are also available from Burmese in exile and human rights organizations, including *The Irrawaddy* at www.irrawaddy.org; *Mizzima News* at www.mizzima.com; and *Burma Digest* at http://burmadigest.wordpress.com. The Democratic Voice of Burma at www.dvb.no provides original articles and video news stories in English about human rights and political issues in Burma. Aung San Suu Kyi's own site is www.dassk.com. Sites devoted to ethnic minority groups include the Ethnic Nationalities Council at www.encburma.net and the Karen Human Rights group at www.khrg.org.

4

VIETNAM

S TRETCHING SOME 1,200 MILES FROM ITS BORDER WITH CHINA TO its southernmost point in the South China Sea, Vietnam is shaped like two rice baskets at either end of a pole. The bulk of the population lives in the two baskets: the Red River Delta in the north and the Mekong River Delta in the south. The pole is the mountainous stretch of territory in the central, sparsely populated part of the country.

Vietnam, with more people than France, Germany, or Egypt, is the world's thirteenth-most-populous country. The majority of Vietnam's 88 million people work in agriculture. Formerly, most Vietnamese practiced Mahayana Buddhism, but Vietnamese society has been secularized since independence and now most residents do not actively practice or pursue religious beliefs. Among those who do, Buddhism still predominates, although about 7 percent are Roman Catholics, a religion brought to Vietnam during the French colonial period. Confucianist principles from the nation's Chinese heritage remain widespread across society and stress centralized political authority, duty, and subordination to superiors: ruled to ruler, son to father, and pupil to teacher. Many minority religions also exist in Vietnam, including the indigenous Cao Dai and Hoa Hao sects, with over 1 million adherents each.[1]

Nationalism has been the key concept for understanding Vietnamese politics. Indeed, Vietnam's search for a national identity received its greatest impetus during the thousand-year Chinese domination (111 BCE–939 CE). The ability of the Vietnamese to emerge from that period with many of their traditions intact is a clear indication of the nationalist urge that has pervaded the country's history. Similarly, the struggle against French colonialism, Japanese occupation, and U.S. intervention reflects the importance of that nationalism.

Vietnam has not always been united. During the era of French colonialism, the country was divided into three areas: Tonkin in the north, with

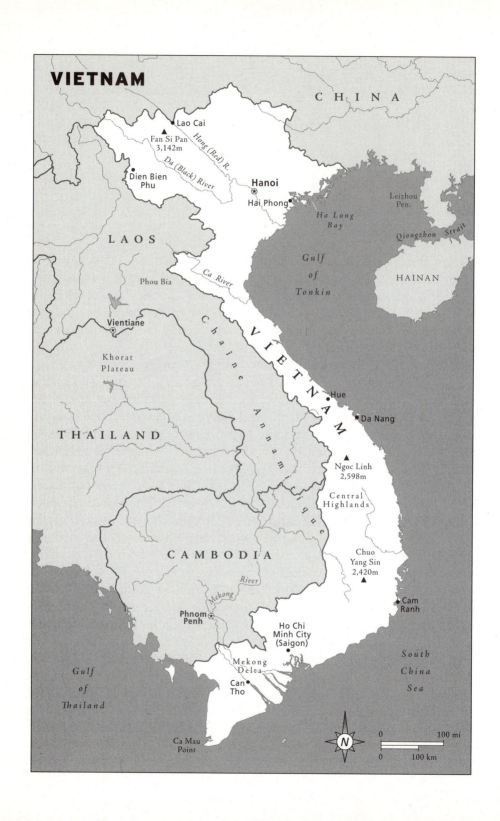

Hanoi as the capital; Annam in the middle, with Hue as the capital; and in the south, Cochin China, whose capital was Saigon. Traditionally, the northerners have seen themselves as modern, progressive, and efficient, and they have viewed the southerners as lazy. The Annamese have seen themselves as highly cultured, the northerners as grasping, and the southerners as rustic. Southerners have regarded themselves as pacifistic and their northern neighbors as aggressive and violent.

In addition to these differing regional perceptions, national unification had to overcome the cultural and political dichotomy between the rural areas and the cities. Such interaction as there was consisted largely of the exploitation of the peasantry by the mandarin class. Moreover, Vietnam is populated by minority groups that have traditionally been treated with disdain by the Vietnamese majority. Many of these fifty-four official minority groups, which comprise about 14 percent of the total population, are upland dwellers in the central and northern mountains.

Despite the divisiveness that has characterized much of Vietnamese history, a nationalist continuity has remained in the form of anticolonialism and antineoimperialism. Following the Japanese defeat in 1945, Ho Chi Minh—the leader of the League for the Independence of Vietnam, known as the Vietminh—proclaimed the country's independence and set up a provisional government that he headed. The first lines of Ho's historic speech on Vietnamese freedom were lifted directly from the U.S. Declaration of Independence. The French and representatives of the newly established Democratic Republic of Vietnam, led by Ho, initially agreed that a new independent state existed and that the French would not move to reclaim their former colony. However, the agreement broke down, and a series of clashes ignited the First Indochina War, which lasted eight years and became an object of U.S. Cold War interests.

The military defeat of the French led to the Geneva Conference of 1954, which sought to separate the rival French and Vietminh forces by setting up a temporary military demarcation line at the seventeenth parallel. This line was not intended to be a political or territorial boundary. In addition, the Geneva agreements called for eventual national elections to establish a single administration throughout the country. During the Geneva Conference, an anti-Vietminh administration emerged below the seventeenth parallel, led initially by the former Annamese emperor Bao Dai and subsequently by the strongly anticommunist Catholic mandarin Ngo Dinh Diem. On October 26, 1955, Diem proclaimed the Republic of Vietnam, better known as South Vietnam, with its capital in Saigon and himself as the first president; he had the support of the United States. He repudiated the Geneva agreements, specifically the provision for national elections.

Ho Chi Minh had agreed to the Geneva agreements at least partly because he believed that national elections would ensure reunification under communist Vietminh leadership. Ho, who was both a nationalist and a communist, saw the two ideologies as inseparable. His goal of a united Vietnam was scuttled when it became clear that Diem had no intention of merging with the north.

During Diem's increasingly repressive rule in the late 1950s, South Vietnam became the site of a guerrilla insurgency against his government. The political arm of the guerrilla activity was the National Liberation Front (NLF), which was initially an autonomous, southern-based movement. The military arm was known as the Viet Cong (Vietnamese Communist). A large number of northerners who had moved to the south following the Geneva Conference joined these guerrillas. In the early 1960s, the North Vietnamese provided increasing military support to the NLF. The People's Revolutionary Party—South Vietnam's communist party, which was controlled by the north—gradually came to dominate the NLF until ultimately the two organizations were indistinguishable.

To counteract the insurgency, Diem relied on U.S. advisers, weaponry, money, and soldiers. U.S. support began in 1954 with 1,000 advisers, which increased to 12,000 by 1962. Despite this support, Diem's own position deteriorated until U.S. President John Kennedy acquiesced to a coup d'état against Diem by South Vietnamese generals. The coup, which took place in October 1963, and Diem's concurrent death, paved the way for a dozen ineffective and unstable military governments, which were less interested in economic or social reforms than in a military victory over the Viet Cong and the North Vietnamese.

U.S. involvement continued to escalate. In February 1965, the United States began massive bombing of the north to interdict North Vietnamese supply lines, erode morale, and provide time for the south to strengthen its forces. None of these purposes was achieved. By 1968, half a million U.S. military personnel were in Vietnam, but the Tet offensive by the north, which involved coordinated attacks on all major cities and towns in the south, demonstrated the ineffectiveness of the U.S. bombing policy, demoralized American troops, and fully revealed the communists' unyielding will to suffer mass casualties for their cause. Opposition to the war in the United States intensified, and President Lyndon Johnson announced he would not seek reelection.

Ho Chi Minh's death in 1969, meanwhile, hardened his followers' resolve to realize the vision of a unified country. A collective leadership arose in Ho's absence with Le Duan the first among equals. No one could replace Ho, for his stature was too vast to be inherited by a single person. The leadership transition proceeded smoothly, without major shifts in war strategy or destabilizing factional purges. The Soviet Union, China, and other countries of the communist bloc continued giving the north material support. The guerrilla warfare tactics of General Vo Nguyen Giap thoroughly frustrated U.S. troops and commanders. U.S. losses mounted from month to month.

South Vietnam had increasingly become a client state of the United States. To reduce this dependency and to blunt rising U.S. protests against the war, in the early 1970s President Richard Nixon began a policy of "Vietnamization"—the gradual withdrawal of U.S. troops from Vietnam—while escalating the bombing against the north. In May 1970, U.S. and South Vietnamese troops invaded Cambodia, ostensibly to halt Viet Cong use of Cambodian sanctuaries. The result, however, was a massive escalation of the war to all of Indochina, unparalleled demonstrations in the United States against the war, and the unification of insurgent forces in Cambodia known as the Khmer Rouge.

Following Nixon's historic 1972 visit to China and the Christmas bombing of Hanoi later that same year (in which 40,000 tons of bombs were dropped), the Paris Peace Accords were signed by the contending powers in January 1973. North Vietnam agreed to a cease-fire, while the United States agreed not only to a cessation of bombing in the north but also to withdrawal of its troops. The Paris Peace Accords were essentially a victory for the north because North Vietnamese troops were able to stay in place. Without U.S. bombing support and financial aid (the United States had spent over $112 billion in Vietnam since the 1950s), South Vietnam could not withstand the pressure from the North.

The rationale for U.S. intervention in Vietnam had several foundations. The first concern was the perceived national interest of the United States itself. Most U.S. policymakers saw the fall of Vietnam to communism as one more stage in the growth of a cancer that could eventually spread to America itself. Thus, South Vietnam became a testing ground for communist wars of national liberation. It was believed that anything less than a committed stand against communist aggression would be tantamount to an invitation for further aggression in other parts of the world. American policymakers also cited the commitment of five presidents, the terms of the Southeast Asia Treaty Organization (SEATO), and agreements with South Vietnam as justification for U.S. involvement; they believed that American credibility as a world power was at stake.

Finally, decisions regarding Vietnam were also a function of internal pressure. Each president feared a political backlash if he were seen as soft on communism or responsible for the defeat of South Vietnam. Therefore, Vietnam became the test of presidential strength, especially for Johnson and Nixon, both of whom articulated the need for total victory.

The U.S. rationale for intervention was in part a function of the ignorance and arrogance of American policymakers at the time. A lack of appreciation for Vietnamese history, society, and culture, combined with a blind belief in faulty theories of democracy and mistaken assessments of U.S. power, doomed U.S. policymakers from the start. U.S. policy in Vietnam was the unfortunate result of several small steps, gradual escalatory moves that by themselves seemed to strategists to be restrained but that in sum committed American blood and treasure to an unwinnable war. Policy decisions resulted in a war in which over 2 million American soldiers fought and 58,000 died.

In April 1975, North Vietnamese troops moved swiftly through the south, conquering province after province and eventually capturing Saigon. A war for Vietnamese independence that had endured for three decades came to a swift close. The cost of victory was over 2 million Vietnamese dead, with millions more injured and displaced. Cities, towns, and rural villages were left devastated from years of conflict. More bombs were dropped during "the American War"—as the Vietnamese refer to it—than were dropped in all past wars combined. About 4 million Vietnamese (as well as thousands of U.S. veterans) would also become long-term sufferers of the crippling effects of Agent Orange, a toxic defoliant dropped from U.S. planes to clear forests for war.

The immediate causes of the communist victory included the corruption of the South Vietnamese army and the end of its U.S. support. Longer-term reasons for the communist success included the artificiality of South Vietnam's political system. The South Vietnamese government, which did not meet the needs of the people, was viewed by northerners as well as many southerners as a lackey of the United States. Also, the war was never fully understood by U.S. policymakers, who underestimated the importance of nationalism and the tenacity of the Vietnamese people to withstand great pressure. Moreover, the war never received the wholehearted support of the American public or of even a large element of the government. As the war continued, more and more Americans became convinced that the means used by the U.S. government were disproportionate to the stated goals.

The North Vietnamese moved swiftly to consolidate their power. Not since the 1860s, when the French began appropriating Vietnamese territory, had Vietnam been fully unified and absent foreign occupation. The newly united nation was named the Socialist Republic of Vietnam. Ho Chi Minh's goal of a united Vietnam under communist rule was reached, and in his honor Saigon was renamed Ho Chi Minh City. Hanoi became the nation's capital. Plans were carried out to transform the south's economy from capitalism to socialism, and "reeducation camps" were established to indoctrinate former partisans of the South Vietnamese government with socialist values. An estimated 2.5 million Vietnamese were sent to these camps, which lasted into the mid-1990s.

The southerners did not take well to the economic programs of their new rulers, and many fled the country in a first wave of refugees. They resisted efforts to collectivize and redistribute the land. Moreover, the Vietnamese economy deteriorated, worsened by drought and the diversion of resources to its military in Cambodia and along the Chinese border. Poor management and planning by the central authorities were also responsible for the economic catastrophe the new revolutionary government faced.

As the Vietnamese government ended the traditional free-market system in the south, the indigenous Chinese, long the mainstay of entrepreneurship in Saigon (now Ho Chi Minh City), fled the country. The government's reform of the monetary system had wiped out the savings of these shop owners. The result was a second wave of refugees, this time ethnic Chinese who fled by sea and thus became known as "boat people." During 1978 and 1979, 75,000 refugees per month fled Vietnam, arriving on the shores of Thailand, Malaysia, Singapore, Indonesia, the Philippines, and Hong Kong, overwhelming those countries' humanitarian resources.[2] Nearly 2 million Vietnamese, representing all ethnic backgrounds, left the country in the years following the communist takeover.

On December 25, 1978, with the concurrence of the Soviet Union, Vietnamese troops invaded Cambodia and within a month captured Phnom Penh and established a new government led by an unknown Vietnamese-trained Cambodian named Heng Samrin. The Vietnamese claimed that they launched their invasion to restore order and security in border areas by punishing Cambodia for a long series of border incursions and for intransigence in negotiations. The Vietnamese also insisted that they were liberating Cambodians from the genocide and repression of the Pol Pot regime. The invasion acted as an impetus for the subsequent Chinese invasion of Vietnam in February 1979. The Chinese hoped their own offensive would force Vietnam to withdraw its occupation force of 200,000 troops from Cambodia. China desired to "teach Vietnam a lesson," to convince the Vietnamese that China was not a paper tiger, to punish the country for its harsh treatment of overseas Chinese, and to send a signal to the Soviet Union that China would not acquiesce to growing Soviet influence in Southeast Asia. Although neither country was able to claim clear-cut victory, Vietnamese forces remained in Cambodia.

Vietnamese expectations that independence from foreign exploitation for the first time in over a hundred years would bring them a better life were dashed by the continued deterioration of the economy. In the 1980s, a decade after their defeat of the United States—the world's mightiest and most technologically sophisticated nation—the Vietnamese people's standard of living was worse than before the war. Indeed, the economy had advanced little since the French colonization of Vietnam in the late nineteenth century.[3]

The Sixth Congress of the Communist Party of Vietnam (CPV) realized the seriousness of the economic malaise and met in December 1986 to implement a plan to remedy the problems. Nguyen Van Linh, a prominent reformer, was named CPV general secretary. His appointment and the retirement of such old-guard communist revolutionary leaders as President Truong Chinh, Premier Pham Van Dong, and Foreign Minister Le Duc Tho signaled a significant turn in Vietnamese politics. The leadership shift to the more pragmatic, economically oriented, reform-minded younger officials from the ideologically conservative, security-minded party leaders was the first major break in leadership patterns since Ho Chi Minh came to power after World War II.

At the December 1986 party congress, Linh set forth a policy of *doi moi* (renovation), a plan publicly approved by the CPV leaders, all of whom agreed that the policies of the previous eleven years—since the end of the war—should not be continued. *Doi moi* called for major economic and political changes with the proviso that the party-led dictatorship of the proletariat remain sacrosanct. The move was timed, not coincidentally, with Mikhail Gorbachev's decision that the Soviet Union would reduce support for client states and move domestically toward perestroika, or economic restructuring.

Nevertheless, despite past failures, reform was difficult because a strong coalition of conservative party leaders felt threatened by the changes. CPV leaders feared that the party's dominance would be lost, and military leaders—who played an important role in the Politburo—believed that *doi moi* threatened national security because it diminished the importance of military strength in favor of economic development.[4]

The changes included rapid movement away from the centrally planned economy and development of a more market-oriented model. The shift built upon the economic reforms that had begun in the late 1970s when a contract system was introduced and decentralization of various sectors of the economy was carried out. The contract system had allowed peasants to sell a small portion of their crops after meeting their obligations to the government. That system had stagnated when peasants refused to cooperate because their profits were so small that they had no incentive to produce more. The new plan provided greater incentives, including the leasing (and later purchasing) of land formerly nationalized by the government.

Renovation also called for more public debate and more power for the National Assembly, the main legislative branch of the government. Many political prisoners were released and corrupt officials ousted from their positions. The press was allowed to criticize government policies more aggressively, at least until the Seventh Party Congress in 1991. The destabilizing protests in Burma (1988) and China (1989) that preceded the CPV's five-year congress, and the collapse of the Soviet Union that followed, cemented party resolve: *Doi moi* would go forward but open political expression would not.

Although popular, renovation met with sharp criticism when new policies initially failed to improve the economy. In 1988, for example, famine was barely averted in the northern provinces, and inflation increased to almost 1,000 percent. Vietnam's reformers increasingly found themselves on the defensive.

As Vietnam entered the 1990s, the government was in transition from the old-guard revolutionary forces, who had held power in the north since independence, to younger (although still elderly) reform-minded communists, who were more willing to try new means to achieve their aims. Dramatic and far-reaching changes in Vietnam occurred in 1995, when the country normalized diplomatic relations with Washington and became a member of ASEAN, an alliance originally formed to oppose "Vietnamese intervention." Vietnam's Southeast Asian neighbors, eyeing Vietnam's large market, had accepted Vietnam's economic rebirth.

Economic ties were also the impetus for reconciliation with the United States. Conservative American politicians and business leaders, having seen the advantages to American business from the 1994 lifting of the U.S. embargo against Vietnam, threw support behind plans to support new ties. There was virtually no negative reaction by Americans to the new policy, except for minor complaints against President Bill Clinton himself for not having participated in the war thirty years earlier. The first U.S. ambassador to the Socialist Republic of Vietnam, Douglas "Pete" Peterson, had spent six years in Hanoi as a prisoner of war. Reconciliation, not recrimination, became the new standard in U.S.-Vietnam relations.

Doi moi has created new challenges for the CPV, but from the mid-1980s to the present, the effects of new policies, on balance, have been positive for the Vietnamese. A major challenge has been reform's disproportional benefits. Vietnam's northern and southern regions, once divided and at war, soon found themselves competing under *doi moi* policies for foreign investment, largesse from the state, and political influence. Whereas the north had followed communist economic policies since the 1950s, the south had experienced communist planning for only ten years, from 1975 to 1986. These differences meant many southerners were better equipped with entrepreneurial skills and business acumen when *doi moi* began. Foreign investors, sensitive to business climate and government meddling, also preferred the expansive Ho Chi Minh City and its more hands-off investment zones to smaller and more bureaucratic Hanoi. By 2004, Ho Chi Minh City, with 5 percent of the country's total population, was producing over 20 percent of Vietnam's GDP. The party's top positions increasingly began to favor southerners with track records of reform success.

After a decade of fits and starts and many frustrations on the part of foreign investors, Vietnam's policy shift began to produce dramatic results. Following the south's lead, the Red River Delta region in the north, including many rural provinces, began to experience rapid economic growth. Remarkably, between 1993 and 2004, overall poverty rates in Vietnam fell from 59 percent to 20 percent.[5] Political life remained circumscribed, but individual freedoms were expanded. Socially, a new youth culture emerged, symbolized by rock music, fast motorbikes, and high levels of material consumption. The country's first generation raised in a unified, postwar Vietnam found common ground not in Uncle Ho's vision of simple living but in pop culture, music videos, and designer logos.[6]

Beyond strong economic growth, ASEAN membership, and normal relations with the United States, Vietnam's final mark of *doi moi* success came in 2007 when it achieved membership in the WTO. At the CPV's Tenth Party Congress, held in the year prior to WTO ascension, party business was confined largely to reshuffling leadership positions and staid pledges to enhance government efficiency. Nevertheless, indicating a measured shift toward greater rule of law, the party allowed unprecedented preconference openness and increased transparency of party business.[7] Vietnam's party of reform-minded communists was now more concerned with growth-related official corruption than with corrupt policies unable to produce growth. Vietnam's track record of economic success and poverty alleviation was in fact drawing praise from the international community.

On April 8, 2006, 118 signatories led by a bank official and former army officer published the *Manifesto for Freedom and Democracy* two weeks before the Tenth Party Congress. It called for "a separation of powers" and a "pluralistic and multiparty system." Some members of the group, known as Bloc 8406 (the date of the manifesto's release) subsequently attempted to form opposition political parties, introduce new publications, and form workers' associations. A swift state crackdown followed, and Bloc 8406's leaders were imprisoned. Other members were harassed and their organizations were forcibly dismantled.[8] The group generated only 2,000 open members and proved unable to replicate mass movements such as those witnessed in Eastern Europe in 1989. The episode also affirmed the party's intolerance for oppositional politics.

Post-1986 economic growth in Vietnam has produced inequality, but at lower levels than in Thailand, Indonesia, and China. Although 70 percent of Vietnamese still reside in rural areas, it is not uncommon for particular provinces to report double-digit economic growth, driven by food production and agriculture exports. Changes to budgeting procedures have also permitted local authorities more autonomy to allocate expenditures to suit local needs.[9] Improvements in rural development are also credited to Vietnam's collaborative programs with the World Bank and international agencies tied to the United Nations. Vietnam, unlike many of its globalizing neighbors, has not achieved economic growth by abandoning its rural majority.

Unfortunately, Vietnamese leaders have not heeded all the lessons of their neighbors' experiences with boom and bust capital markets. Vietnam's young stock markets in Ho Chi Minh City and Hanoi reached new heights only to collapse precipitously. Between January and June 2008, Vietnamese stocks lost 60 percent of their value. Ho Chi Minh City's market, catering to foreign money, dropped every day it traded in May. Inflation soared over 25 percent, and angry consumers reacted by hoarding goods and abandoning the Vietnamese currency. The experience began to raise new questions about the sustainability of *doi moi*–driven growth and CPV governance of the economy. The economic turbulence did not begin to subside until 2012, after a series of macroeconomic policy adjustments.

Overall, however, the picture remains positive. In the more than twenty-five years since reforms began, Vietnam's economic achievements remain noteworthy. Vietnam today is a different country than it was in the decade following "the American War." Before *doi moi*, 60 percent of Vietnamese lived in poverty, forced to suffer in a hopeless economy and with a government unable to provide basic services. Today, only 15 percent of Vietnam's large population lives below the poverty line, and almost everyone has access to basic education, health care, decent employment, and economic opportunity. In comparative terms, over 80 percent of Vietnamese enjoy a standard of living currently unknown to a third of all Burmese, Cambodians, Filipinos, Laotians, and East Timorese. Vietnam today is a Southeast Asian success story—one qualified nonetheless by the cost single-party rule imposes on civil liberties, political freedom, and official justice.

INSTITUTIONS AND SOCIAL GROUPS

Ho Chi Minh

As the founding father of independent, communist Vietnam; the victorious leader over the Japanese, French, and Americans; and the founder of the CPV, Ho is the most important Vietnamese of contemporary times and perhaps the most important leader in recent Southeast Asian history. He was and remains a central institution—the symbol of united, nationalist, communist Vietnam. Pictures of "Uncle Ho" are ubiquitous in Vietnam, statues and busts of the leader adorn public places, and millions of people have viewed his embalmed body in the Soviet-built mausoleum in Hanoi.

Ho's father was a Confucian scholar who was active in anticolonial activities; his mother died when he was ten. Throughout his life he used numerous pseudonyms (the name Ho Chi Minh means "he who enlightens"). He spent thirty years abroad, living in and traveling to the Soviet Union, China, New

York, London, and Paris. He became a committed communist and founded the forerunner parties of the CPV, including the Indo-Chinese Communist Party in 1930 and the Vietminh in 1941. His tastes were simple, even ascetic, yet he was tenacious and sometimes ruthless in the means he used to achieve his goals.

Ho died six years before the nation was reunited. His last testament requested that at his death there be a one-year moratorium on farm taxes and that his ashes be placed in urns in the three parts of Vietnam: Cochin China, Annam, and Tonkin. However, these requests were not heeded by Ho's successors. Instead, taxes were raised, and his body was embalmed and put on display in a massive building similar to Lenin's mausoleum in Moscow. No Vietnamese leader has subsequently received the adulation Ho received during his life, although every leader has attempted to wrap himself in Ho's mantle. "Ho Chi Minh Thought" is the party's guiding philosophy.

Communist Party of Vietnam

Although the communist party rule in postwar Eastern Europe was imposed from without by Soviet arms, the Communist Party is indigenous to the Vietnamese and was the vehicle for the independence struggle against the French colonialists and, later, the Americans. In modern Vietnamese history, the CPV has had an almost exclusive claim to represent the broader ideals of nationalism and patriotism. For many Vietnamese, the CPV and nationalist struggle are identical.

Party membership numbers around 3 million, more than 3 percent of the population. After stagnating membership in the 1990s, the party quickly expanded membership, raising questions by some about whether quantity has reduced quality. For many youth, party membership is not attractive. A recent decision to allow party members to engage in business—something many were already doing—rankled revolutionary party purists, in particular.

Vietnamese politics as practiced in the Politburo is best understood by an analogy to the great game of *bung-di*, or faction bashing.[10] Party factions, long prevalent in the communist party, form around individuals but traffic in issues. They are enduring but not permanent, and they can divide and reform to meet changing needs. Despite attempts to contain factionalism, they remain ubiquitous. In the early *doi moi* period, Vietnam's Politburo divided into four major factions: reformers, neoconservatives, bureaucrats, and the military.[11] Today, the divide between reformers and neoconservatives has softened with successful economic growth. Political liberalization, to the extent it is discussed at all, excludes any suggestions of radical reform to multiparty democracy. In Vietnam, no opposition parties are allowed to form and challenge the CPV for state power.

Nationalism remains the glue that binds the CPV's generations, factions, and regional interests together while underpinning the party's ongoing legitimacy to govern. The party's elevation of Ho Chi Minh thought to official ideology in 1989 was designed to buttress this legitimacy amidst policy reforms. At that time the party claimed that its *doi moi* policies were consistent with Ho's views about how socialism could be built in Vietnam—views that, they qualified, had been previously kept from the public. Citing rediscovered "original" documents, the CPV used Ho's "view of socialism" to justify market-oriented *doi moi* and to "delegitimize the policies of the leadership from 1975 to 1986."[12]

Since Ho's death, collective leadership has characterized Communist Party rule in Vietnam. Today, the party Politburo is made up of younger members. These leaders are better educated and concern themselves more with Vietnam's economic productivity and technological improvement than with revolution and ideology.

In a system where party and state overlap extensively, top party leaders hold all significant offices of state government. Out of the Eleventh Party Congress in 2011 emerged an all-powerful fourteen-member Politburo, inclusive of Vietnam's current ruling triumvirate: (1) Party Secretary Nguyen Phu Trong, a conservative and former Chair of the National Assembly; (2) President Truong Tan Sang, a southerner and pragmatist who functions as head of state; and (3) Prime Minister Nguyen Tan Dung, a southerner known for his anticorruption agenda now serving a second five-year term. Northerner Nguyen Sinh Hung, a former finance minister, is currently chairman of the National Assembly. This position wields less power than the other three but plays an important role in Vietnam's party-controlled rule.

The National Assembly

Formerly insignificant, the National Assembly of the Socialist Republic of Vietnam is beginning to perform functions similar to legislatures elsewhere in Southeast Asia. The CPV revamped the National Assembly's role at its Seventh Party Congress in 2001. Increased attention to the rule of law in the Vietnamese system is requiring the National Assembly to do more than simply rubber-stamp party dictates. Changes have included greater participation in law-based policy formation and new constitutional powers that permit votes of no-confidence in ministers and officials appointed by the assembly.[13] With recent changes the "role of the National Assembly is not to let the people rule but to widen the range of voices heard in the political mainstream."[14] In 2010, for the first time in its history, the National Assembly blocked a government spending package and all of its related projects.

National Assembly delegates are chosen through national elections. These elections involve more candidates than available seats. Nonparty candidates may run for office, and many do win seats, but all candidates must first be vetted by the Vietnam Fatherland Front (VFF). No parties opposed to the CPV or Ho Chi Minh ideology are free to compete in assembly elections. In 2011, Vietnamese voters elected delegates to the Thirteenth National Assembly. A total of 827 candidates competed for 500 seats; almost 9 percent of delegate winners were nonparty, but VFF-approved, candidates.[15]

Vietnam Fatherland Front

The Vietnam Fatherland Front is a constitutionally mandated corporatist-style umbrella organization. Under its aegis are all state-sanctioned mass organizations, including all unions (e.g. Women's Union, Farmer's Union, Lawyers' Association), all religious organizations, and all NGOs that are local or internationally based. Civil society in Vietnam is thus thoroughly monitored through the VFF, which acts as gatekeeper, rulemaker, and enforcer of permissible activity. Its stated goal is to unify the country in all "political and spiritual matters." The VFF forcibly co-opts civil society organizations to provide services to society that the state fails or chooses not to provide. No foreign NGOs legally operate in Vietnam without VFF sanction. Officially, the CPV itself is under the authority of the VFF, but the reality is exactly opposite.

Military

The Vietnamese army is the CPV's creation, and the leading generals are members of the party leadership. The 4.4 million–member People's Army of Vietnam (PAVN) is the largest in Southeast Asia and includes one of the world's largest reserve forces. After 1975, the PAVN, initially given the mission of reunifying the nation, was charged with defending Vietnam from external attack, such as when the Chinese crossed Vietnam's northern border in 1979. In contrast to armies elsewhere in Southeast Asia, the Vietnamese army has not threatened a coup against the communist leadership. Its role remains subordinate to that of the party.

STATE-SOCIETY RELATIONS AND DEMOCRACY

According to Article 4 of the Constitution of the Socialist Republic of Vietnam, the Communist Party of Vietnam is "the force assuming leadership of state and society." In its first few decades, the CPV and the Vietnamese state were virtually synonymous, and society remained wholly subordinate. As a single-party dictatorship, all authoritative decisions were made by the party and then disseminated to the populace through a tightly controlled state organization that allowed no dissent. Since reunification, and especially since 1986, a more complex array of forces has emerged within both state and society.

With *doi moi*, the CPV-led state lost dictatorial control over economic and social life. Factions, alliances, and debates within the party grew and increasingly began to mirror those emerging in Vietnam's rapidly changing society. The state remains Leninist, but the scope of political debate has broadened. The distinctions between party, state, and society have blurred as market activity, personal choice, and party-business networks have replaced centralized planning.

The legitimacy of the Vietnamese state is rooted in its communist revolution, which expelled foreign occupiers, unified the country, and established the socialist republic. This legitimacy has not been seriously challenged by the Vietnamese since 1975. Channels through which the people could mount such a challenge have been limited by strict, single-party rule.

As for the party's own legitimacy to govern (distinct from the legitimacy of the socialist republic itself), disastrous economic results of the 1975–1986 period resulted in a growing domestic legitimacy crisis. *Doi moi* policies breathed new life into the party. Today, the CPV leans on performance legitimization, combined with official interpretations of Ho Chi Minh Thought, as the bulwark against a possible domestic challenge to its legitimacy. It is important to note that the party has never delegitimized its authority through any traumatic, Tiananmen-style crackdowns where the military turns on its own people.[16]

The party formerly ruled through dictates generated by its own governmental apparatus. Today, Vietnam is home to a more complex state apparatus attempting to institutionalize procedures, processes, and laws for a mixed economy. Many demands on the state today are more technical than political; others remain purely political. External demands to comply with UN programs, World Bank projects, and WTO membership, for example, differentiate the technical nature of the state's role today from its prereform past. Even with these changes, Vietnam remains closer to "rule by law" than to the "rule of law."

In the economic domain, where performance legitimacy is largely established, democratic ideals such as decentralization and accountability are accepted as necessary for an effective economy. Economic principles such as "the market" and "competition," once viewed as decadent bourgeois concepts, have become the centerpieces of renovation.

Somewhat ironically, *doi moi* has in many ways expanded the state's role vis-à-vis society. A form of "state capitalism" has replaced a Soviet-style planning system. Vietnam's unprofitable state-owned enterprises (SOEs), for example, are gradually being divested, but many with potential remain under state ownership. The biggest SOEs, known as "General Corporations," monopolize major sectors (e.g., cement, coal, rubber, and shipbuilding), engage international markets, and often own their finance companies. The risks of these South Korean chaebol-style arrangements lie in the obvious hazards of self-financing and unethical or criminal behavior by corporate and party elites.[17]

The Vietnamese state, after transferring over 100 military-owned enterprises to civilian rule, has also created a sovereign wealth fund, the State Capital Investment Company, along the lines of Singapore's Temesek and Malaysia's Khazanah Nasional. The party uses the fund to influence strategic investments in key Vietnamese industries and to ensure that new wealth generated in the private sector comes back to the state. The state bailed out businesses and banks in the wake of the 2008–2009 global financial crisis, provided massive funds for economic stimulus, and created a national asset-management company to deal with spiraling bad debts. Of course, none of these recent initiatives, which expand the state's market role, have been subject to public accountability through elected representative institutions.

Vietnam has no history of democracy. State-society relations have been Confucianist, stressing hierarchy and order, and more recently communist, emphasizing the party's unquestioned supremacy. The movement of the Eastern European communist governments toward democracy has not impelled the Vietnamese leadership or the Vietnamese people to initiate a similar transformation of their own government. Indeed, in 1989, the central committee of the CPV, alarmed by developments in Eastern Europe, Burma, and China, rejected appeals for political pluralism in Vietnam. President Nguyen Van Linh stated that the party rejected calls for "bourgeois liberalization, pluralism, political plurality, and multiopposition parties aimed at denying Marxism-Leninism, socialism, and the party's leadership."[18] Since that time, sporadic attempts inside and outside the state to test the party's commitment to these principles have resulted in failure. In spite of expanding economic and social freedom, the party "seems absolutely determined to maintain its political monopoly."[19]

In contrast to elected leaders in open, pluralistic democracies, Vietnam's governors have fewer constituencies to satisfy. Bureaucratic loyalties lie primarily with the state rather than with autonomous religious, ethnic, or class interests. Intellectuals and academics have largely been depoliticized, co-opted, or otherwise silenced, as typified by the treatment of dissidents associated with Bloc 8406. In Vietnam, the highest government leaders are generally one and the same as top party leaders. Intertwined networks of party leaders and business entrepreneurs dominate the state and private sectors. Entanglements between private and public, state and market run thick.

With respect to progress in civil liberties, the government's record is at best mixed. Conflict over religious freedom occurs, for example, between dissident Buddhist monks and communist government officials. Many Buddhists wish to establish the Unified Buddhist Church in place of the Vietnam Buddhist Church, long under the dominance of the CPV. The exiled Vietnamese monk Thich Nhat Hanh (once nominated for a Nobel Peace Prize by Martin Luther King Jr.) has been permitted to return for visits to Vietnam in recent years, but tensions between CPV leaders and Vietnam's Buddhist community remain. On the other hand, Vietnamese Catholics, initially persecuted by communists, practice with less fear than in the past. Unlike in China, where allegiance to the pope in Rome is disallowed, Catholics in Vietnam are permitted to engage with the Roman Church.

Labor rights, a major target of the international rights community, are slowly improving. In the early 2000s, the government entered programs with the International Labor Organization to reform labor laws and practices. New laws have made it easier for migrant workers from rural areas to obtain benefits once denied them.[20] Collaboration has yet to produce labor protection in line with global standards—union organizing, for example, is still limited by party approval. Recent economic troubles have produced greater labor discontent, challenging the regime. According to Vietnam's Labor Ministry, nearly 1,000 labor strikes erupted in 2011—twice as many as in 2010 and four times as many as in 1997.[21]

Freedom of the press does not fully exist in Vietnam, but the Internet, which functions more freely here than in China, is transforming bloggers into reporters and activists. Facebook has nearly 4 million users in the country, and bad news travels faster than ever outside of state control. This activity creates a dilemma for party officials who fear the demonstrable capability of social networking to coalesce public opinion against them. In 2011, Vietnamese bloggers organized large protests in the wake of Chinese provocations in the Spratly Islands, in the South China Sea (see the discussion below). The protesters, angry at China, also expressed derision of their own government's "weak response."[22] Press accounts exposing government corruption are increasingly permitted, but they also permit top leaders to showcase "anticorruption" campaigns.

ECONOMY AND DEVELOPMENT

After the end of the war in 1975, the Vietnamese economy declined for a full fifteen years. Inflation rates were astronomical, and unemployment hovered at about 20 percent. Infrastructure essentials such as ports, roads, and electricity were primitive, and housing abysmal. Vietnam's banking system was barely viable, partly because there was so little managerial expertise. Annual per capita income was estimated to be $200, making Vietnam one of the poorest nations in the world. Famine, which threatened the northern provinces in the 1980s, affecting 10 million farmers, forced Vietnam—a country once self-sufficient in rice—to appeal for international food aid. Ho Chi Minh's favorite aphorism, emblazoned on red banners strung across streets throughout Vietnam—"Nothing is more precious than independence and freedom"—was interpreted in an ironic and sardonic sense. In unguarded moments, Vietnamese stated that "nothing" was exactly what they had.

Given Vietnam's superb natural resources, the country's poverty was all the more shocking and embarrassing to Vietnamese leaders. However, there were important reasons why the country was unable to develop in parallel fashion to the neighboring ASEAN countries. A major reason is the extensive war damage, which required tremendous resources to repair. In the south alone, the war produced 20,000 bomb craters, 10 million refugees, 362,000 invalids, 1 million widows, 880,000 orphans, 250,000 drug addicts, 300,000 prostitutes, and 3 million unemployed. Two-thirds of the villages and 5 million hectares of forests were destroyed.[23]

The U.S. involvement in South Vietnam created a dependent economy, and the billions of dollars spent on the war brought a surfeit of capital that disappeared abruptly when the United States disengaged. Hanoi had expected to receive some $3 billion in reparations aid, which had been promised by U.S. Secretary of State Henry Kissinger but was later refused when the United States maintained that North Vietnam had not carried out the terms of the Paris Peace Accords. Soviet aid did not make up for the loss of Western aid and trade because of the U.S.-sponsored trade embargo. Moreover, the Soviet Union's technological aid was insufficient in many ways.

Adding to Vietnam's woes was mismanagement by its leadership. Alternating between reform and orthodoxy, Vietnam's leaders "displayed a paranoid world view, a low adaptability level, perfidy consistently perceived in the motives of others and perpetuation of a cult-type leadership capable of believing the illogical, the irrational, even the absurd."[24] Nationalization and collectivization, thrust upon the south after reunification, failed miserably because southerners would not adhere to socialist policies. Peasants refused to meet their obligations to the state when the state's prices for their crops did not cover even the costs of production.

To overcome the crisis, the CPV's Sixth Congress, in December 1986, proposed major reforms under *doi moi*. Rice output in 1986 was far below 1942 levels, and northern farmers, as members of state-organized cooperatives, produced 52 percent less than farmers from the south who resisted collectivization. To alleviate this situation, land laws were modified to guarantee farmers a ten- to fifteen-year tenure on land they cultivated, although the expectation was that land could henceforth be owned in perpetuity and be inherited. This policy change signaled the end of efforts to collectivize agriculture in the south.

The 1986 reforms gave farmers the legal right to sell their produce on the free market after each paid a tax based on his or her output. Approximately 10 percent to 20 percent of the tax went to the state for the farmers' use of cooperatively owned machinery and for fertilizer and other necessities. Under the new system, farmers could keep a far larger percentage of their output than under the former contract system. Although it took several years for the policy to have a positive impact, Vietnam reemerged in 1989 as a major rice exporter for the first time since the 1950s. It became one of the world's three largest rice exporters, along with Thailand and the United States; most of its rice is exported to West Africa, the Philippines, India, Sri Lanka, and China.

Vietnam's foreign investment code was also revised to attract more foreign investors. To draw joint ventures, the government liberalized tax policies and extended guarantees that investment capital would not be expropriated or joint ventures nationalized.[25] The 1987 investment law offered a two-year tax moratorium for joint ventures and established export processing zones in which foreign companies could import materials, use low-cost local labor for assembly, and export final products. A large proportion of the new investors were overseas Vietnamese.[26] The new code increased trade with Japan, Singapore, Hong Kong, France, Indonesia, and India but did not bring in the amount of capital hoped for because of the continuing U.S. trade embargo. More and more countries, however, broke the embargo to take advantage of the liberalized trade and investment opportunities, especially regarding offshore oil exploration.

The reforms made a dramatic difference in Vietnam's everyday economy. Construction of homes, office buildings, bridges, roads, and schools, for example, burgeoned throughout the country, even in the north, where the economy had been stagnant for many decades. Privately run restaurants and shops opened and flourished. Inflation dropped to more manageable levels as a result of the devaluation of Vietnam's currency, the dong, to the free-market rate, and government austerity measures—recommended by the IMF, with which Vietnam hoped to restore relations—were adopted to attract investment, credit, and technology from the West. Vietnam also reformed its meager, Russian-based tourist industry by investing in new hotels and encouraging more air traffic from Western countries.

Vietnam remained impoverished, but for the first time since the end of the war there was economic development. In a sense, however, the country remained divided because development was more rapid in the south than in the north (partly as a result of the millions of dollars sent back to relatives from the 2 million southern Vietnamese living abroad). Unemployment remained high, especially among those considered "unreliable" because of their involvement with the former Saigon regime.

It was initially believed that the loss of the Soviet Union as a major financial supporter would undermine the Vietnamese economy irrevocably. However, by 1992 the economy had improved, with increased rice production and controlled inflation. Both exports and imports increased dramatically, and trade with Japan as well as Singapore and the other ASEAN countries more than made up for the Soviet loss.

The ending of constraints on the IMF's assistance to Vietnam in 1993 and the lifting of the American embargo in 1994 were responsible for a huge increase in foreign direct investment. These openings represented the breakdown of the last external barriers to Vietnam's goal of becoming an Asian tiger. GNP growth rose to an annual 8.2 percent, with progress in all economic sectors. The politicians remained committed to *doi moi*, so the mid-1990s became an era of fundamental economic change. Ho Chi Minh City's economy grew by an astonishing 15 percent, and the new free-market system inexorably affected every sector of the economy. Vietnam was increasingly viewed as the new economic frontier, capable of achieving extraordinary growth rates because of its disciplined workforce, cheap labor and materials, and zealous goal to join the global capitalist system.

In 1995 and 1996, annual economic growth rates stood at 9.5 percent—among the highest in the world. Given the country's remarkable growth and the enthusiasm of the world community for the new Vietnam, the subsequent difficulties of 1997 were surprising. In the wake of regional crisis, the economic boom suddenly hit a plateau and growth rates declined. The number of tourists also plunged rapidly. Confidence in reform dropped. Foreign entrepreneurs, citing additional frustration with Vietnam's byzantine bureaucracy, reduced their investment.

Added to these problems were underdeveloped economic institutions and government corruption. The banking system remained primitive, virtually incapable of making or collecting on loans. The dong was overvalued, and Vietnamese exports were becoming more expensive even though the products were often of low quality. Foreign companies shut down their factories in the absence of legal contracts and to protest the emphasis on under-the-table payments demanded by both private business elites and public officials.

Vietnam's late 1990s economic decline was driven by the regional financial crisis, underdeveloped institutions, corruption, and policies that failed to improve its business climate. Emphasizing stability over growth, Vietnamese leaders saw a domestic slowdown continue through 2002, but GDP rates never dropped below 5 percent. Relative to some of the established economic tigers, Vietnam fared well. In fact, during the early 2000s global recession, Vietnam's growth was actually among the strongest in the world, even amidst its own domestic slowdown.

Part of Vietnam's success at the time was due to a U.S.-Vietnam bilateral trade agreement signed in 2000 that enhanced manufactured exports and invited new investment. Growth rates pushed upward to nearly 7.5 percent by 2003, and export growth again reached double digits. Observers noted, however, that much of this new growth was taking place in the state sector, driven by heavy state investments of "low quality" and tainted by official corruption.[27] Questions also persisted about how Vietnam could again handle continued rapid growth without quickly upgrading the country's infrastructure and educational system. Low-quality investment and structural limits notwithstanding, Vietnam's GDP climbed higher still, into the 8 percent range, by 2005.

WTO membership starting in 2007 further accelerated Vietnamese exports to the United States, Japan, South Korea, and Singapore. Investment growth improved as well. Intel Corp., for example, selected Vietnam for its new $300 million chip-testing facility. Vietnam's economic performance seemed to be moving from strength to strength. "Securities fever," as it was called, hit local and foreign investors. For a couple of years, Vietnam's stock market was among the world's most promising. Ordinary Vietnamese, many for the first time in their lives, began to float money on new exchanges in Ho Chi Minh City and Hanoi. However, poor government regulation made the fledgling Asian bourses vulnerable to manipulation, misinformation, and fraud. The government, with many state enterprises listed on the Hanoi exchange, grew increasingly nervous and hastily passed securities laws it had little capacity to actually enforce.

By 2007, the two-decade-old reform movement produced one of the country's highest GDP growth rates under *doi moi*: 8.5 percent. Crude oil, textiles, seafood, coffee, rubber, and rice were pouring out of the country. The United States became Vietnam's largest export trading partner. Vietnam's economic winners looked for places to both spend and multiply their new earnings. Consumption of import luxuries ballooned due to lower import taxes. Vietnam's insatiable class of super-rich gobbled up European luxury cars, designer cosmetics, and high-priced mobile phones. Winners also poured money into land. Commercial real estate in Hanoi and Ho Chi Minh City soared, fetching higher prices per square meter than in New York, Singapore, and Tokyo. By the end of 2007, the economy was racing. Vietnam's two stock exchanges reached a combined value of $29 billion, about $28 billion more than just three years earlier.

This peak of investor exuberance was followed, as many predicted, by a spectacular collapse of Vietnam's stock markets in 2008. Vietnam's rapid growth had generated a growing trade imbalance and rising inflation. In a matter of weeks, the world's hottest stock markets became the world's worst performing. Consumers, many with memories of hyperinflation in the past, began to hoard commodities and buy gold, exacerbating inflationary pressures. Vietnam's currency also fell under pressure. Ominously, observers pointed to parallels with Thailand and Indonesia in 1997.

Vietnam's shell-shocked government, facing its first real capital market crisis, tightened the reins on the economy. Officials moved quickly to raise interest rates and announce a total ban on the importation of gold. Import taxes on luxury goods also were adjusted upward. Also, hoping to ward off black-marketeers and currency speculators, officials quietly devalued the dong by 2 percent against the dollar. International investors took the devaluation as a bad sign—as the beginning of much larger devaluations accompanied by a serious economic crisis. State and foreign enterprises faced new uncertainties. Vietnam's twenty-year, *doi moi*–driven ride of rapid growth began shifting into lower gear.

Since 2008, Vietnamese officials have battled inflation and twice devalued Vietnam's currency while trying not to cripple growth or incite social unrest. Hovering near 15,600 dong per U.S. dollar in early in 2008, devaluations left the currency two years later at rates above 20,800 dong per U.S. dollar. GDP growth in 2009 dropped to 5.3 percent and has averaged just over 6 percent since. With one of the world's weakest currencies, and rising trade and fiscal deficits, Vietnam's economy came to a near standstill in 2011. The excesses of lending to SOEs and bad loans in the real estate market caught up with Vietnam, and foreign investors began, once again, to question the sustainability of Vietnam's economic successes. The outcome of the Eleventh Party Congress did little to assuage critics and investors. The party affirmed its strategy of supporting SOEs in the short term and chose not to pursue a path of sudden austerity. Economic turbulence aside, Vietnam remains on track to meet all of its UN Millennium Development Goals by 2015, an admirable accomplishment unique to few countries in the developing world.

FOREIGN RELATIONS

In the post-1975 period, Vietnamese foreign policy was framed by fundamental Marxist-Leninist principles. The nation's reliance on socialist solidarity versus the interventionist, exploitative capitalist world narrowed its options and reduced the flexibility that the conduct of foreign relations requires in a world of rapid change. Foreign policy was carried out in *dau tranh* (struggle) terms, in which diplomacy was treated strategically—like protracted military conflicts—over an extended period of time.[28] This approach made negotiations with allies and adversaries difficult because Vietnam's arguments were presented as statements of superior virtue, not as expressions of national interest.

Before 1986, the major goal of Vietnamese foreign policy had been to secure the sovereignty of the nation against all aggressors. To meet this goal, Vietnamese foreign policy sought to ensure a cooperative, nonthreatening

Indochina firmly allied with Vietnam; prevent an anticommunist front from threatening Vietnamese interests; limit the role of the United States, China, and the Soviet Union in Vietnam's sphere of influence; and establish working relations with neighboring ASEAN countries. These latter, more specific goals were met with varying degrees of success. Vietnam's ongoing occupation of Cambodia, which began in 1979, complicated its relations with major powers and regional neighbors.

After 1986, ideological fundamentalism decreased, and policymakers stressed the need for Vietnam to play a greater role in the global economic system. Vietnam's leaders saw that communist governments were failing around the world, that Vietnam was economically isolated, and that the nation had become too dependent on the Soviet Union; thus, they moved in fundamentally new directions in foreign policy.

Politburo liberals argued that keeping Cambodia as a friendly neighbor was important but not to the point of threatening Vietnam's economic collapse. These reformers argued that a withdrawal from Cambodia would end Vietnam's international isolation by leading to the normalization of ties with the United States, halting the multilateral trade embargo against Vietnam, and inviting Western aid.[29] Adding to pressure to withdraw was the restiveness of Vietnam's armed forces, demoralized by the military stalemate in Cambodia that had cost some 55,000 Vietnamese lives.

However, withdrawal from Cambodia, begun in September 1989, did not bring the expected international gratitude. Instead, ASEAN and the United States faulted the troop withdrawal for not being part of a comprehensive peace plan for Cambodia and for not allowing monitoring by an international control mechanism. It was not until July 1990, when U.S. secretary of state James Baker announced that his government would begin direct negotiations with Vietnam relating to the Cambodian situation, that the withdrawal elicited a positive response from the United States. Meanwhile, no moves were made toward normalizing relations, and the trade embargo continued.

Vietnam also moved to improve relations with Asian and Western nations interested in developing economic ties. Hundreds of trade and investment delegations from Japan, Taiwan, South Korea, Thailand, and various European countries arrived to set up business ventures. Relations with China also improved, partly because of the vast border trade between the two nations.

For the United States, Vietnam had been a low foreign policy priority since the end of the war. The American foreign policy establishment was no longer concerned about Vietnam or its fate. The noncommunist countries of Southeast Asia, for their part, were flourishing in the 1980s and no longer viewed themselves as potential victims of Vietnamese aggression. Many agreed with the sentiment of a Thai prime minister that the time had arrived to turn Southeast Asia "from a battlefield to a marketplace."

In the United States, memories of the war were fading, and Vietnam soon became more cooperative on the issue of unaccounted-for American prisoners of war. Hanoi accepted a standing U.S. offer to conduct U.S.-funded joint searches in provincial areas where the remains of those listed as missing in action were thought to be located. It was during this period that the question of normalizing relations between the United States and Vietnam was brought to the fore.

From a Vietnamese perspective, normalization was desirable, notwithstanding the government's negative view of past U.S. involvement in Indochina. Soviet aid to Vietnam had decreased, and Soviet president Gorbachev confirmed his country's intention to give up its military bases in Vietnam. Russians were not liked in Vietnam, and there was a surprising feeling of warmth for Americans in both the northern and southern areas. Vietnam was still very poor, and normalization with the United States could open doors to international aid from the West.

On the U.S. side, one argument for normalization viewed Vietnam as the next economic frontier. Japan, South Korea, Taiwan, and Thailand were already investing heavily in the country, taking advantage of its inexpensive labor and disciplined workforce. With its liberal new foreign investment code, Vietnam had become more enticing to business ventures. The Washington business lobby became increasingly supportive of normalization so the trade embargo could be lifted. Political arguments followed economic ones. It was believed that closer economic relations with the Vietnamese (the so-called engagement thesis) would help spur political liberalization and even democracy in Vietnam. Military arguments for normalization stressed U.S. strategic interests. The need to deepen U.S. ties in the region seemed timely, given the uncertain status of bases in the Philippines and China's ambitions now that the U.S.S.R. was withdrawing from the region.

Arguments against normalization stressed that diplomatic relations with Vietnam would legitimize a repressive government. Indeed, many Vietnamese refugees in the United States opposed normalization for that reason. In their view, the North Vietnamese had brutally and illegally taken control of the south, and they should not be rewarded for that action. Many U.S. veterans' groups were also embittered by talks of normalization, emphasizing the unresolved POW/MIA issue.

Because Vietnam had withdrawn its troops from Cambodia, supported the Cambodian peace process, and begun to cooperate on POW/MIA issues, George H. W. Bush began the process of normalization but did not complete it before leaving office. Bush softened the terms of the embargo by allowing telephone links with Vietnam to resume, a welcome event for the 1.5 million

Viet Kieu (overseas Vietnamese) living in the United States. He also permitted U.S. firms to sign contracts, which could quickly be executed once the trade embargo was lifted.

Early in his presidency, Bill Clinton announced that diplomatic relations would not be restored until "every MIA and POW is accounted for." This impossible condition discouraged supporters of improved ties between the two nations. Meanwhile, virtually every other Western nation was involved in various economic relationships with the Vietnamese. It was not until 1994 and 1995 that the Clinton administration lifted the embargo and diplomatic relations were established.

The demise of the world's socialist nations undercut Vietnamese foreign policy, which was based on solidarity with the Soviet Union and its allies. This dramatic change made improving Vietnam's ties with the Western capitalist world the best means of future economic aid and trade. At the same time, Vietnam mended fences with its traditional adversary, China; leaders of the two nations attended a summit and restored many crucial ties. Although these improved relations were damaged by Chinese claims of sovereignty over the Spratly Islands (see below), the positive aspects largely outweighed the negative ones. The two communist neighbors, once enemies battling over the fate of Cambodia, normalized relations in 1991. Cooperation and noninterference increasingly defined their relationship in the 1990s. By the early 2000s, a mature stage of normalcy came to characterize Sino-Vietnamese trade relations, symbolized most importantly by Vietnam's lucrative exports of crude oil to China. Although the relationship is asymmetrical, Vietnam is merely deferential, not subordinate, to rising China.[30]

In 1995, Vietnam basked in its status as ASEAN's newest member. The country's foreign policy has since demonstrated how the development of economic ties and cordial relations now outweighs the CPV's previous suspicions and worries over the country's security. Symbolic of this transformation was a major diplomatic event in 2006 when twenty heads of state gathered in Hanoi for the Asia-Pacific Economic Cooperation (APEC) meeting. Following that meeting, Vietnam, once a war-torn pariah state to Western countries, achieved a string of diplomatic successes and firmly established itself as a cooperative partner in the community of nations. First, it was permitted to join the WTO as a full member in 2007. Then, one year later, Vietnam's member peers in the United Nations elected it (on a vote of 190 to 183) to a two-year spot on the UN Security Council. In rotation, Vietnam served two successful stints as president of the world's most powerful body, leading it through debates over sanctions on North Korea and Iran, among other matters.

Subsequently, Vietnam has chaired ASEAN and served as country host for annual meetings of ASEAN, ASEAN +3, the Asian Regional Forum, and the East Asian Summit. Vietnam's rising credibility as a solid diplomatic partner has enhanced its global image as a stable, forward-looking nation, supportive of multilateralism and the broad objectives of the international community, a rarity among similarly politically closed regimes.

The Spratly Islands Dispute

Without question, the most important security issues for Vietnam involve disputes over the Spratly Islands. The island group, located in the South China Sea (called the "East Sea" by Vietnamese), is believed to hold vast untapped oil and natural gas resources. The Spratlys are variously claimed by six countries: Vietnam, China, Taiwan, the Philippines, Malaysia, and Brunei. No native inhabitants reside on the islands, but all claimants, except Brunei, have military outposts and often station ships in the archipelago. When added together, the exposed land of the islands and the atolls, reefs and outcroppings in the disputed area equals about 5 square miles. Nonetheless, potential underwater oil and natural gas resources, as well as mineral extraction and fishing rights, have become the high-stakes prizes for competing claimants. More broadly, the South China Sea is a vital strategic waterway linking the Persian Gulf with Japan, Taiwan, and South Korea, all of which rely on free passage for their oil imports. It is a sea-lane of immense importance to every Asian country, to Middle East oil exporters, and to the United States.

With respect to claimants, both China and Vietnam make competing "historical" claims over the Spratlys, as well as the nearby Paracel Islands. In the 1970s and 1980s, China and Vietnam went to blows over the islands, and a 1974 clash left the Paracels in Chinese hands. Forty years of skirmishes and conflicts between the two rivals have cost over 100 Vietnamese lives. The Philippines, another major claimant, argues its own history, its own geographic proximity to the Spratlys, and the provisions of the 1982 United Nations Law of the Sea Convention (UNCLOS) justify its legal claims to the territory (see chapter 7).

Malaysia, also citing UNCLOS, makes a claim on a small number of islands. Brunei makes no claims of territory but seeks to protect its UNCLOS rights of economically controlling waters that are within 200 nautical miles of its shoreline. Taiwan, or the Republic of China, makes the same claims over the area as the People's Republic of China. Though it is active in the area and controls a landing strip on the largest island in the Spratlys, Taiwan's ambiguous diplomatic status inhibits its ability to maneuver on the issue, and it does not coordinate with Beijing on the matter whatsoever.

A diplomatic solution to competing claims remains elusive. Even the language used to describe islands is disputed. Many islets, outcroppings, and reefs share three or four names: in Vietnamese, Tagalog, Chinese, or often in English, Spanish, or Portuguese. In 2002, at annual ASEAN meetings, a major agreement was struck between interested parties to lessen tensions. All countries agreed to a code of diplomatic conduct stating that no party would use force or the threat of force in resolving the matter. In 2004, state-supported oil companies from China, the Philippines, and Vietnam agreed to seismic exploration of the area. Over time, however, cooperation has broken down and new tensions and skirmishes have erupted, including a widely broadcasted showdown between a Vietnamese ship and a Chinese patrol boat in 2011 that fully reignited the row.

China, which has a "talk and take" reputation—talk peace, but take islands forcibly—openly prefers bilateral talks as a means to resolve the dispute. Other claimants prefer regional talks and a multilateral resolution. Honoring boundaries demarcated by UNCLOS is unacceptable to China unless all parties recognize Beijing's territorial claims (all of the islands). UNCLOS, designed to demarcate territorial waters based on sovereign land boundaries, is ill-equipped to solve rival claims of above-ground territory. In effect, UNCLOS causes claimants use their own maps to justify their interpretation of international boundaries. The result is overlapping claims of sovereignty that each party bases on international law. Exacerbating the issue is the fact that the United States—which actually views the convention as the best viable avenue for conflict resolution—has yet to ratify UNCLOS itself. Without credibility as a full signatory, the U.S. push for a multilateral, UNCLOS-based agreement smacks of hypocrisy, particularly as viewed by China.

Domestically, the issue makes great political hay for leaders eager to cultivate nationalist sentiment and to win local support, including in Vietnam. Diplomatic and military posturing, including live-fire exercises or the dispatching of "combat ready" patrols, can lead to favorable op-eds in home papers and spark street protests in opposing capitals. In recent years, Spratlys-related anti-Chinese protests have become more frequent in both Hanoi and Manila. Vietnam has loudly accused the Chinese of cutting and damaging its cables in the area and recently sent Buddhist monks to renovate and reside in old temples found on some of the islands. The issue has even inspired low-grade cyber-attacks: In 2011, Vietnamese nationalists accessed Chinese government web portals and defaced them with Vietnamese symbols and content. Chinese hackers reciprocated.

Beyond the passions generated by public protests, cyber-violence, and sea-lane stare-downs, it is the changing structural forces at work that prove just how volatile the Spratly dispute could become for Vietnam and the region. Strategic activities by both China and the United States, and inter-ASEAN disagreements, have produced new geopolitical dynamics and dangers. After conciliatory talks in the early 2000s, Beijing has since delivered multiple policy statements warning governments in the region against pursuing any oil exploration or mineral surveys of the disputed areas. Chinese "law enforcement" ships have regularly patrolled waters in intimidating fashion. Accusations of sovereign interference have been volleyed back and forth publically between claimants.

Perhaps most significantly, a new strategic context developed around the Spratly Islands dispute when U.S. President Barack Obama announced in 2011 a "strategic pivot" to rebalance diplomatic attention and U.S. forces from the Middle East to Asia. A year later, ASEAN held its annual meeting in Phnom Penh with China and the United States present. The United States, represented by Secretary of State Hillary Clinton, pushed for multilateral progress on a Spratly Islands agreement beyond the 2002 code of conduct, but the conference ended without an agreement on the matter. Vietnam and the Philippines welcomed the U.S. effort, but Cambodia, siding with China, refused to address the issue. The meeting regrettably produced only vague statements affirming that ASEAN members will continue to respect UNCLOS and the 1976 Treaty of Amity and Cooperation of Southeast Asia.

One of the reasons an agreement failed to emerge at the 2012 ASEAN summit was an emphatic declaration by Vietnam just weeks prior to the conference. After a year of repeated statements by Prime Minister Nguyen Tan Dung that Vietnam had "indisputable sovereignty" over the Paracels and Spratly territories, the National Assembly codified the claim by passing the Vietnamese Maritime Law. China responded with "resolute and vehement opposition" to the law and emphatically restated its own sovereign claims.[31] These acrimonious events suggest that the dispute is further from resolution than ever.

CONCLUSION

Vietnam's future is linked to the ability of the Vietnamese Communist Party to balance economic reform with strict one-party rule. With rich natural resources, a large, disciplined workforce, and a long tradition of entrepreneurial activity, Vietnam has become one of Asia's newest economic frontiers. Although its communist government undermined Vietnam's advantages with oppressive policies and mismanagement before 1986, the regime's economic reforms have since produced impressive developmental gains. Vietnamese today enjoy a blend of opportunity, wealth, and personal freedom that their ancestors never knew. In spite of the CPV's monopoly on political life, constraints on civil society, and endemic corruption among its elites, the balance sheet for Vietnam today is solidly positive, especially in comparison to its poorer Indochinese neighbors.

The outstanding question remains, nevertheless, of whether growing inequality, economic crisis, or greater demands for political liberalization by future generations will eventually destabilize the country. For the foreseeable future, Vietnam's Leninist party structure seems poised to remain one of the lone survivors of the collapse of global communism.

At home, Vietnam's new international status as an emerging market and diplomatic leader has added to the CPV's performance legitimacy. In 2006, when Hanoi hosted the APEC meetings, visiting state leaders took time for a photo dressed in the traditional local attire of the host country, as is customary at annual APEC meetings. For the Vietnamese people—recent survivors of European colonialism, Japanese occupation, a U.S.-U.S.S.R. proxy war, and a dreadful border war with another former occupier, China—the image of George W. Bush, Vladimir Putin, Shinzo Abe, and Hu Jintao adorned in colorful, silk-woven *ao dai* tunics and standing side by side with Vietnamese president Nguyen Minh Triet, symbolized more than cordial relations. The image stood as evidence of the sovereignty and respect the Vietnamese had finally won from decades of struggle. As Uncle Ho had promised, nothing would be more precious than to realize freedom and independence from foreign control.

NOTES

1. The Cao Dai religion, founded in the 1920s and located in South Vietnam, eclectically blends Buddhism, Taoism, Confucianism, Christianity, and other beliefs into a single, monotheistic religious system. Hoa Hao, founded in the 1930s and also located in the Mekong Delta region, is a variant of Buddhism that deemphasizes monastic temple worship in favor of lay practice.

2. Frederick Z. Brown, *Second Chance: The United States and Indochina in the 1990s* (New York: Council on Foreign Relations, 1989), 39.

3. David G. Marr and Christine P. White, eds., *Postwar Vietnam: Dilemmas in Socialist Development* (Ithaca, NY: Southeast Asia Program, Cornell University, 1988), 2.

4. Ronald J. Cima, "Vietnam's Economic Reform," *Asian Survey* 29, no. 8 (August 1989): 789.

5. *Vietnam Country Brief*, World Bank, February 2007, www.worldbank.org.

6. For an excellent account of social change related to Vietnam's youth in the 1990s, see Robert Templer, *Shadows and Wind: A View of Modern Vietnam* (New York: Penguin Books, 1998).

7. Vo X. Han, "Vietnam in 2007," *Asian Survey* 48, no. 1 (January/February 2008): 33–34.

8. For an excellent account that reviews the dissident activity of Bloc 8406, see Bill Hayton, *Vietnam: Rising Dragon* (New Haven: Yale, 2010).

9. *Vietnam Development Report 2005: Governance*, joint donor report to the Vietnam Consultative Group Meeting, December 2004 (Hanoi: Vietnam Development Information Center, 2004), i.

10. Douglas Pike, "Political Institutionalization in Vietnam," in *Asian Political Institutionalization*, ed. Robert A. Scalapino, Seizaburo Sato, and Jusuf Wanandi (Berkeley: Institute of East Asian Studies, University of California, 1986), 49–51.

11. Douglas Pike, "Change and Continuity in Vietnam," *Current History* 89, no. 545 (March 1990): 118.

12. Thaveeporn Vasavakul, "Vietnam: The Changing Models of Legitimation," in *Political Legitimacy in Southeast Asia: The Quest for Moral Authority*, ed. Muthiah Alagappa (Stanford, CA: Stanford University Press, 1995), 277.

13. *Vietnam Development Report 2005: Governance*, i.

14. Hayton, *Vietnam: Rising Dragon*, 96.

15. Vo, "Vietnam in 2007," 34.

16. "Vietnam: Country Report," Transformation Index BTI 2012, http://www.bti -project.org/countryreports/aso/vnm/.

17. Ibid., 18–19.

18. *Asia Yearbook, 1990* (Hong Kong: Far Eastern Economic Review, 1990), 241.

19. Hayton, *Vietnam: Rising Dragon*, 114–115.

20. Hy V. Long, "Vietnam in 2006," *Asian Survey* 47, no. 1 (January/February 2008): 170.

21. David Brown, "Vietnam's Not-So-Rare-Protests," *Asia Sentinel*, July 30, 2012, www.asiasentinel.com.

22. Ibid.

23. Marr and White, *Postwar Vietnam*, 3.

24. Pike, "Political Institutionalization in Vietnam," 43.

25. Ronald J. Cima, "Vietnam in 1988: The Brink of Renewal," *Asian Survey* 29, no. 1 (January 1989): 67.

26. Cima, "Vietnam's Economic Reform," 797.

27. Adam Forde, "Vietnam in 2003: The Road to Ungovernability," *Asian Survey* 44, no. 1 (January/February 2004): 124.

28. Douglas Pike, "Vietnam and Its Neighbors: Internal Influences on External Relations," in *ASEAN in Regional and Global Context*, ed. Karl D. Jackson, Sukhumbhand Paribatra, and J. Soedjati Djiwandono (Berkeley: Institute of East Asian Studies, University of California, 1986), 240.

29. Ronald J. Cima, "Vietnam in 1989: Initiating the Post-Cambodia Period," *Asian Survey* 30, no. 10 (January 1990): 89.

30. Brantley Womack, *China and Vietnam: The Politics of Asymmetry* (Cambridge, UK: Cambridge University Press, 2006), 29.

31. Jane Perlez, "Vietnam Law on Contested Islands Draws China's Ire," *New York Times*, June 21, 2012, A8.

RESOURCE GUIDE

A useful tool for bibliographic and other information on Vietnam is available from Australia National University's WWW Virtual Library: www.gksoft.com/govt/en/vn .html. The University of California–Berkeley maintains a useful portal for digital and print resources on Vietnam: www.lib.berkeley.edu/SSEAL/SoutheastAsia/seaelec.html. Northern Illinois University's Southeast Asia Digital Library includes a range of useful links that cover government, academic, and research institutions specific to Vietnam: http://sea.lib.niu.edu. The University of Wisconsin–Madison Libraries similarly maintains a list of digital and print resources on Vietnam: www.library.wisc.edu/guides/SEAsia /resarea.html.

The government Web portal of the Socialist Republic of Vietnam is available in English at www.chinhphu.vn/portal/page/portal/English. The Communist Party of Vietnam is at www.cpv.org.vn/cpv/index_E.html. A list of member organizations falling under the Vietnam Fatherland Front is available at www.ngocentre.org.vn/node/46. A list of active international agencies, NGOs, and organizations operating in Vietnam is available at www.devdir.org/files/Vietnam.PDF. As Vietnam is a pilot country for the UN One Program, a useful site is www.un.org.vn.

Readers can supplement this chapter with figures and publication information found in the country profile pages of data.UN.org and ADB.org. Recent and archived news articles are maintained on specific country profile pages by BBC.com and NYTimes.com. Useful country reports produced by the Bertelsmann Foundation are at www.bti-project .org/home/index.nc. The United Nations maintains a useful page tracking the Millennium Development Goals progress of all countries at http://mdgs.un.org/unsd/mdg /Data.aspx. Radio Free Asia provides uncensored news reports on Vietnam at www .rfa.org/english/news/vietnam.

For daily news in English, see *Vietnam News* at http://vietnamnews.vnagency.com .vn/ and VietNamNet Bridge at http://english.vietnamnet.vn. Nhan Dan provides news directly from the Vietnam Communist Party at www.nhandan.com.vn/cmlink/nhandan -online/homepage.

5

CAMBODIA

THE MANY NAMES UNDER WHICH CAMBODIA HAS LIVED IN THE past few decades reflect the turmoil its people have experienced. Cambodia was once known as the Kingdom of Cambodia, but the country became the Khmer Republic when the military came to power in 1970. From 1975 to 1979, the period of tyrannical Khmer Rouge leadership, the country's name was changed to Democratic Kampuchea, followed by the People's Republic of Kampuchea when the Khmer Rouge was replaced by a Vietnamese-backed government. In 1989, the country became the State of Cambodia only to return to its former name, the Kingdom of Cambodia, when the country restored royal institutions under a constitutional monarchy in 1993.

Cambodians trace their heritage to the great Khmer civilization, which culminated in the twelfth century when the Khmers ruled over most of modern-day Cambodia, Laos, Thailand, and the Mekong Delta in Vietnam. This magnificent civilization, symbolized by the great temples at Angkor, lasted over five hundred years and reached a level of military, technological, political, and philosophical achievement that was unmatched in Southeast Asian history. The "hydraulic city" of Angkor was sustained by an impressive system of earthen *baray* (massive rectangular reservoirs), moats, ponds, and irrigation canals. Over the centuries, Hinduism (following Vishnu and Shiva) and Buddhism (for the most part Mahayana but eventually Theravada) guided *deva-raja* (god-king) rulers and the estimated 1 million people who lived in the world's largest preindustrial settlement. The excessive demands created by uneconomic activities such as monument building and war, decades-long drought, and hydroclimate variability contributed to Angkor's fall in the fifteenth century to Ayutthaya.[1] Subsequent kingdoms suffered from instability and external pressure until 1864, when the French took over a weak Cambodia as a protectorate.

The great Khmer civilization has now become the Kingdom of Cambodia, with 14.3 million residents. Most Cambodians are rural farmers who live in

CAMBODIA

THAILAND

LAOS

Mekong R.

Sreng River

Preah
Vihear

Kong River

Srepok River

Angkor
Wat

Steung
Treng

Siem Reap

Battambang

Tonle
Sap

C A M B O D I A

Kratie

Mekong R.

Phnom Aural
1,813m ▲

Kampong
Cham

Phnom
Penh

V I E T N A M

Sihanoukville

Gulf of
Thailand

Mekong
Delta

South
China
Sea

N

| 0 | | 50 mi |
0   50 km

poverty. At 77 percent, the country retains the highest percentage of rural population in the entire region. Religiously, Theravada Buddhism predominates among the populace. As a nation, Cambodia personifies tragedy, its people having suffered unspeakable horrors during the Khmer Rouge era, from 1975 to the beginning of 1979. Indeed, neither the people nor the nation has fully recovered from these horrors. Signs of improvement are emerging, but progress remains inhibited by corrupt leadership, a plundering of the country's natural resources, and a deep dependence on foreign assistance.

Cambodia's search for identity and nationhood, once the country was freed from French colonialism, was dominated by Prince Norodom Sihanouk, whom the French had placed on the throne in 1941. In 1955, one year after Cambodia's independence was granted, King Sihanouk abdicated, named his father as king, and entered politics directly as Prince Sihanouk. His unrivaled dominance of Cambodian life from the end of World War II to 1970 was due to the way he had achieved leadership, which was by plebiscite, and to the unsurpassed loyalty of rural Cambodians. He was revered as a *deva-raja* in the tradition of the Angkor kings, and his authority rested on charismatic, traditional, repressive, and legal foundations.

Sihanouk, who controlled all important policymaking institutions, exhibited a remarkable capacity to keep each major sector of society in check, thereby maintaining political stability. His overthrow, on March 18, 1970, was therefore a surprise to most analysts of Cambodian politics. On that date, while Sihanouk was in the Soviet Union, the Cambodian National Assembly—charging Sihanouk with abuses of office—unanimously condemned him to death for treason and corruption. His position was assumed by General Lon Nol, the premier in Sihanouk's government.

Sihanouk's downfall stemmed from the presence of North Vietnamese and Viet Cong forces in so-called Cambodian sanctuaries. Against his army's wishes, Sihanouk had allowed the Vietnamese to use this territory, although his trip to Moscow was to request Soviet aid in ousting the Vietnamese. The Vietnamese had become so entrenched in Cambodia that by mid-1969 they had built a base of support in a region that encompassed nearly one-fourth of Cambodia's total area. Sihanouk had also allowed shipments of Chinese arms across the country from the Cambodian port of Sihanoukville.

Sihanouk's relations with the United States during this time were both acrimonious and supportive. He opposed U.S. involvement in Vietnam, although as the North Vietnamese established themselves in Cambodian territory, he reversed policy and argued the need for an American force in Asia to provide a balance of power to the communist nations. From the U.S. perspective, Sihanouk was mercurial and untrustworthy; thus, his ouster was welcome. Although it remains the subject of much speculation, no definitive evidence has yet proven that Sihanouk's overthrow was supported by covert U.S. government assistance.

From Sihanouk's perspective, his frequently changing policies were consistent with his overall objective of keeping his country neutral and sovereign. His vacillation, nevertheless, cost him the loyalty of elite groups in Cambodia. The army united around General Lon Nol, sharing the view that Sihanouk was not moving strongly enough to remove the Vietnamese from Cambodian territory. Bureaucrats resented Sihanouk's total control over policymaking and personnel decisions; intellectuals opposed his policies of press and speech censorship; and young graduates were frustrated by the lack of job opportunities. Although Sihanouk retained the loyalty of the rural masses, that group wielded little influence in Cambodian politics. The Cambodian National Assembly deemed Sihanouk's inconsistent policies regarding the Vietnamese intrusion as an act of treason. It also charged that the prince had engaged in corruption and had ruined the economy by nationalizing Cambodia's few industries.

Sihanouk's major failure was his inability to institutionalize a political system in which power relations were not exclusively a function of his own desires and whims. Initially his charisma was the country's primary integrating force; subsequently, however, his total dominance of Cambodian political life undermined the nation's major institutions. The army became the dominant institution in Cambodian politics in March 1970, and for a short time Lon Nol had the support of many Cambodians. However, after a few months it became clear that the new government was not only inefficient but corrupt.

At the end of April 1970, U.S. President Richard Nixon, without first informing Lon Nol's government, announced an American invasion of Cambodia to protect the lives of U.S. soldiers, to ensure the success of his "Vietnamization" program, and to gain a decent interval for U.S. withdrawal from Vietnam. He announced that the intervention would clear Cambodia of all major enemy sanctuaries, including the headquarters of the communist military operation in South Vietnam.

In fact, the Nixon administration had been secretly bombing Cambodia since 1969, without the knowledge or authorization of the U.S. Congress. U.S. forces dropped an estimated 550,000 tons of bombs on Cambodia, about twenty-five times the explosive force of the atomic bomb that devastated Hiroshima, Japan, and three and a half times as many bombs as were dropped on Japan during World War II. Nearly half the population was uprooted, and Cambodians became refugees in their own country.[2] The bombing had no substantive effect on the protection of South Vietnam, serving only to create chaos and panic in the Cambodian countryside.

Five years of total war on Cambodian soil followed. The U.S.-backed Lon Nol government proved incapable of coping with either international or domestic crises. The regime was corrupt, food shortages occurred, inflation was out of control, and hundreds of thousands of Cambodians were displaced—the population of Phnom Penh, Cambodia's capital and largest city, swelled from 600,000 to 2 million. One out of ten Cambodians was killed in the war—most from U.S. bombings and suicide missions sent by Lon Nol to repel the Vietnamese. From his exile in Beijing, Prince Sihanouk announced his support for the radical rebels, the Khmer Rouge, who opposed the Lon Nol regime. The country fell into a civil war that did not end until April 1975, when the Khmer Rouge took control of the countryside and forced Phnom Penh into submission.

The massive U.S. bombings, the social dislocation, and the corruption of the Lon Nol government attracted support to the formerly weak Khmer Rouge, which many believed was made up of nationalist "peasant reformers."[3] That myth was quickly dispelled when the Khmer Rouge ordered the complete evacuation of Phnom Penh within hours of the takeover.

Pol Pot, the leader of one of several Khmer Rouge factions who eventually became the dominant individual in the new government, headed a tightly disciplined party vanguard called Angka (the organization), which ruthlessly ran the country. Angka represented itself as the leader of oppressed workers, farmers, and peasants against the "feudal, imperialistic, capitalist, reactionary, and oppressor classes" of the former regimes. The name Cambodia was changed to Democratic Kampuchea, and Prince Sihanouk was brought back as the nominal head of state but in reality lived day-to-day under house arrest.

Angka used draconian measures to silence even potential voices of opposition and to reduce to impotency every person believed to be allied with the former ruling groups. The means to this end included strict discipline, total control, terror, and isolation from "impure" societies. The new regime's first undertaking, carried out immediately after the fall of Phnom Penh, was the evacuation of every person from Cambodia's major cities to the countryside. At first it was believed the evacuation was to last for only three days because the new government feared mass starvation in Phnom Penh and other cities, which had very limited supplies of rice. The evacuation, however, was meant to be permanent, to "purify" Cambodian society of decadent urban ways and to ensure internal security by ridding the country of "spies, imperialists, and enemies." The evacuations led to thousands of deaths and the separations of countless families.

Angka also purged persons who were in any way connected to the Lon Nol regime or were believed to harbor the slightest "bourgeois" values. Former residents of Phnom Penh were treated especially harshly by the regime. Cambodians with Chinese or Vietnamese ethnicity, considered impure and untrustworthy, were imprisoned and killed. Temples were closed, and Buddhist monks were forcibly disrobed or murdered. The country's entire intelligentsia was executed, often in hideous ways. In places where displaced people were resettled, high death rates resulted from starvation, illness, and forced labor. An estimated 1.7 million people were executed or worked to death between 1975 and 1979, an act of genocide that has few parallels in history.

Further "enhancing" the Khmer Rouge's rule was the policy of forced labor through collectivization and the total restructuring of the economy. All Cambodian entrepreneurs lost their money when the regime halted the use of currency and nationalized private businesses. The family unit was replaced by collectives of up to a thousand households, which ate and worked together. "New people," so labeled in contrast to the "old people" already living in the countryside, were beaten and humiliated to serve Angka no differently than draft animals. Khmer Rouge troops enforced these harsh new policies and made sure that no one resorted to the bourgeois values of privatism, hierarchy, individualism, and the nuclear family. For over three years, agrarian idealism in the form of forced labor defined the sum total of economic production. Unlike communist-led countries elsewhere, the Khmer Rouge made little attempt to develop industry, education, or technology. They sought to create an autarkic agrarian utopia that rejected not only capital and markets but also Soviet-style heavy industrialization.

Survivors reported that Cambodian society was rigidly organized into separate groups of men, women, the elderly, children six to fifteen years of age, and older teenagers. Only small quantities of food were available for communal workers. No schools were open, and no money was in circulation. Buddhist temples were converted into granaries for storing rice, and 80 percent of all books in Cambodia were thrown into rivers. Recalibrating history, the Khmer Rouge declared it "Year Zero"; nothing from the past would be tolerated. Under Pol Pot, Cambodia became one of the most closed societies on earth. During his three-year rule, only a few diplomats and reporters were allowed to enter the country, under tightly controlled conditions for propaganda purposes. The extent of economic hardship and the regime's brutality was foggy to outsiders. Horrific stories retold by traumatized refugees became one of the few windows into Democratic Kampuchea.

The xenophobic ideology that underpinned Khmer Rouge policies included elements of Marxism-Leninism and Maoism, mixed with Khmer nationalism, which romanticized agrarian utopianism. Some of this ideology was informed by 1950s doctoral theses submitted to French universities written by Hou Yuon and Khieu Samphan. These theses argued that the exploitation of Cambodia's peasants was the source of the country's problems; that only by recapturing the peasantry's agrarian potential could the country achieve self-reliance. Hou Yuon, known to be critical of Khmer Rouge methods, died of uncertain causes in the early period of Pol Pot's rule. Khieu Samphan eventually served as state president of Democratic Kampuchea.

Following the communist victory in Vietnam in the spring of 1975, the Khmer Rouge began raiding Vietnam's border towns, thereby threatening Vietnam's important Mekong Delta region and causing thousands to lose their homes. An estimated 30,000 Vietnamese civilians were killed during these attacks. Pol Pot may have intended to reclaim the territory of the ancient Khmer Empire, which once included most of southern Vietnam—home to a sizable Cambodian minority. By 1978, however, it was clear the Khmer Rouge was also fighting a civil war against Vietnamese-backed Cambodians antagonistic toward Pol Pot.[4]

On Christmas Day 1978, a Vietnamese-led invasion overthrew Pol Pot's regime and installed Heng Samrin as president. Heng Samrin was an unknown former Khmer Rouge division commander who had sought refuge in Vietnam when his faction was overpowered by Pol Pot. He was soon replaced by Foreign Minister Hun Sen, who became the nation's most important leader for the next thirty-five years. Democratic Kampuchea became the People's Republic of Kampuchea (PRK). Vietnamese troops took Phnom Penh after less than two weeks of fighting and forced the Khmer Rouge to flee to the mountains in the western part of the country near the Thai border. Many Cambodians took advantage of the Vietnamese invasion to flee the country. Refugee camps in Thailand became overwhelmed with new arrivals. From these camps, over a million Cambodians would find resettlement in third countries; almost a quarter of a million resettled in the United States.

Vietnam announced that the purpose of its invasion was to end the constant border clashes, which jeopardized Vietnamese citizens, and to expel the hated Pol Pot regime. Vietnam also desired a friendly government, rather than an ally of China, on its doorstep. The Khmer Rouge was Maoist and supportive of China, Vietnam's principal enemy. Because China provided aid to the Khmer Rouge, and the Soviet Union supported Vietnam, the invasion has been interpreted as a Sino-Soviet proxy war. Historical precedents suggest that more was at issue in this conflict than competition between the major communist powers, but it is impossible to discount what Moscow and Beijing had at stake in the region.

The new Vietnamese-installed government moved to undo the most onerous policies of the Khmer Rouge, and Phnom Penh was slowly repopulated. The Vietnamese helped to revive piped water and electricity systems but did not impose economic planning or controls. Marriage and family restrictions were ended, forced collectives were abolished, and the practice of Buddhism was again allowed, though monitored. Schools were reopened, and primary school education was reinstituted. After four years of the "killing fields," a semblance of normality appeared in Cambodian society.

Despite reforms, the new government faced severe problems. The Cambodians disliked and distrusted the Vietnamese officials and occupation soldiers (who numbered almost 200,000) but nevertheless realized that the Vietnamese were all that stood between them and the return of the Khmer Rouge. In addition, Pol Pot's annihilation of virtually all skilled and educated Cambodians had caused an administrative vacuum. For example, there were only forty-five doctors in the entire country. Few trained administrators had survived, and the country had no currency, no markets, no financial institutions, and no industry.[5] Due to the remnant mines placed throughout Cambodia during the war years, even routine rice planting became a dangerous activity. Over time, more than one in three hundred Cambodians would fall victim to land mines. To this day, Cambodia retains the highest number of amputees per capita in the world.

The new government also faced a famine from 1978 to 1980, in which hundreds of thousands starved to death; to compound the problem, continued fighting between the Heng Samrin and Khmer Rouge forces disrupted the harvest of what little rice had been planted. Farmers were so physically weakened that they could not adequately care for their crops. International agencies were mobilized to provide food, and although thousands of people were saved from starvation, the rescue was only partially successful. As evidence of hoarding, favoritism, and corruption came to light, aid agencies were discouraged, but an even greater problem was the lack of qualified administrative personnel. In general, there was altogether too little food, and it arrived too late.

Affecting poor production, in part, was Cambodia's depleted labor force. If Cambodia had not been drawn into the Vietnam War and had not suffered subsequently from the devastation of U.S. bombing; if Cambodia had not been depleted by genocide under a tyrannical regime, by famine, and by the flight of hundreds of thousands seeking food and freedom, the country's population in 1980 would have been over 10 million. Instead, the total population in 1980 was about half that. Few societies have ever sustained such tremendous losses.

Vietnam's 1979 invasion was not welcomed by Asian countries or the international community at large. Although it freed Cambodians from Khmer Rouge rule, Vietnam's aggression was considered a violation of international law. Cold War politics influenced the positions of countries in the region. China began a border war with Vietnam as punishment for overtaking their Khmer Rouge allies. Thailand's military grew nervous about the presence of Soviet-backed Vietnamese troops along its eastern border and became patrons of remnant Khmer Rouge. The United Nations refused to recognize Heng Samrin's regime and instead gave Cambodia's seat to the Coalition Government of Democratic Kampuchea (CGDK), a government-in-exile formed in 1982 and composed of three disparate factions united solely in their opposition to the Vietnamese-sponsored regime in Phnom Penh.

The CGDK factions consisted of Sihanoukists, led by Sihanouk's son Prince Norodom Ranariddh; the Khmer People's National Liberation Front (KPNLF), an anticommunist group led by Son Sann, a former prime minister; and, remarkably, the ousted Khmer Rouge. Coordinating their work from held territory and camps along the Thai-Cambodian border, the CGDK drew the blessing of the international community as an anti-Vietnamese alliance. Although the Sihanoukists and KPNLF had no affection for the Khmer Rouge, their common goal of ousting the Vietnamese from power produced the uneasy alliance.

Prince Sihanouk was named coalition president largely because he was recognized internationally. The Sihanoukists included a military arm, the Armée Nationale Sihanoukiste, of about 3,000. The KPNLF, with about 5,000 troops, was supported by the noncommunist ASEAN states and the United States. The KPNLF and Sihanoukists enjoyed annual funding of about $7 million from the United States. The Khmer Rouge, fronted by Khieu Samphan, was clearly the largest and most powerful of the three factions, with 35,000 troops loyal to Pol Pot. Supported by China with infantry weapons, rocket-propelled grenades, and mortars, the Khmer Rouge was the best-equipped, most capable, and best-organized fighting force in the country. By virtue of the CGDK's recognition by the United Nations, the Khmer Rouge, astonishingly, was represented in New York throughout the 1980s.

Years of infighting, resignations, and scheming among the three factions did not come to an end until Vietnam, facing declining Soviet support in the late 1980s, and focused on *doi moi* reforms that required foreign investment, announced plans to withdraw its troops from Cambodia. In an effort to resolve the Cambodian situation, the three coalition partners met with Hun Sen's government in 1991 and agreed to a UN-brokered peace plan signed in Paris.

The historic agreement—established with the concurrence of permanent members of the UN Security Council now operating in a post–Cold War world—created a four-party Supreme National Council (SNC) headed by Sihanouk, who would serve as Cambodia's head of state. The agreement also planned for a multinational force of UN peacekeepers and administrators to be stationed in Cambodia: the UN Transitional Authority in Cambodia (UNTAC). UNTAC's purpose would be to manage a cease-fire, disarm factions, conduct free elections, begin the repatriation of refugees, and administer the country's foreign affairs, national defense, and finance. The success of the peacekeeping mission thus depended upon the remarkable notion that foreign troops, unable to able to speak Khmer (the Cambodian language) and ignorant of Cambodian culture, could demilitarize all rebel factions, including the Khmer Rouge.

When Prince Sihanouk returned triumphantly to Phnom Penh in November 1991 to become the Cambodian head of state, Cambodians had hopes that the UNTAC experiment could succeed. Shortly thereafter, Khieu Samphan, the Khmer Rouge representative on the SNC, returned as well but was met by a mob that came close to tearing him apart limb from limb. Khieu Samphan was rescued and later returned to participate in the coalition, but the mob action clearly indicated the strong hatred Cambodians still felt toward the Khmer Rouge.

In executing the agreement, UNTAC essentially governed Cambodia from March 1992 to September 1993. About 16,000 blue-helmeted UN peacekeepers blanketed the country, and over 3,300 civilian administrators took control of Phnom Penh. For a time, Cambodia (a sovereign country) was governed by foreign experts: A Japanese served as UNTAC's chief officer, an American ran the finance ministry, a Pole controlled the foreign ministry, and an Australian oversaw all military forces in the country. Before the mission was completed, one hundred UN member states had contributed peacekeepers, civil administrators, and election monitors to UNTAC. The bizarre makeup of the UN program indicated the desperate nature of the Cambodian imbroglio after years of civil war, genocidal rule, foreign aggression, and societal chaos.

It soon became clear that the tasks UNTAC had set for itself were too great to be accomplished in only eighteen months. To run a government, oversee the repatriation of 350,000 refugees, supervise a cease-fire among factions that hated and distrusted one another, and conduct the first Cambodian election in decades were impossible goals even for an organization provided with $2.8 billion, the most expensive and far-reaching plan of this type in world history.

UNTAC, alas, was not able to pacify the nation because numerous violations of the cease-fire occurred, mostly by the Khmer Rouge. Disregarding the Paris agreement, the Khmer Rouge sought actively to expand its zones of influence and thereby control as many people as possible before the elections. The Hun Sen administration in Phnom Penh, which had turned over much of its power to UNTAC, engaged in its own violations and corruption, raising the question of whether any of the factions could run the government once elections had been held.

Despite cease-fire violations, popular support for the National Assembly elections was strong. Hun Sen organized the Cambodian People's Party (CPP), while Prince Ranariddh mobilized the United National Front for an Independent, Peaceful, and Cooperative Cambodia (FUNCINPEC). Both the CPP and FUNCINPEC campaigned on anti–Khmer Rouge platforms. The CPP argued that only the Hun Sen administration was strong enough to prevent a return of the Khmer Rouge. Prince Ranariddh's Sihanoukists, on the other hand, campaigned on the claim that the prince was the only Cambodian alive who had sufficient prestige to reconcile the murderous factions. FUNCINPEC candidates reminded voters that Hun Sen had once been a member of the Khmer Rouge and had been installed in power by the Vietnamese, who were detested by most Cambodians. FUNCINPEC candidates also pointed out the CPP's blatant corruption, noting that Phnom Penh had become a boomtown catering to the whims of UN troops and foreign advisers.

The Khmer Rouge refused to disarm or demobilize its area. Weeks before the polls, Khieu Samphan unsurprisingly announced that the Khmer Rouge would boycott the election and, effectively, the entire peace process. The stated reasons for the boycott were accusations that Vietnamese troops and citizens had remained in Cambodia and would take over the country once elections had been completed, and that UNTAC was biased in favor of the Hun Sen administration in Phnom Penh. No evidence was presented to substantiate these accusations.

The chances for a free and fair election were bleak because of Khmer Rouge intransigence, the absence of Cambodian experience with open elections, reluctance on the part of the ruling Hun Sen administration to give up authority, and the populace's fear of the UNTAC foreigners who were essentially administering their country. Nevertheless, between May 23 and 27, 1993, 90 percent of the eligible voters cast ballots for members of a legislative assembly with powers to draft a new constitution. Although the Khmer Rouge did not participate in the elections, they did not sabotage them after it became clear that the overwhelming majority of Cambodians had rejected Khmer Rouge pressure. The largest plurality (45 percent) was won by Prince Ranariddh's FUNCINPEC; Hun Sen's CPP trailed with 38.6 percent of the vote.

The UNTAC authorities declared the elections free and fair, and the United Nations evacuated its peacekeepers in November 1993, leaving the government entirely in the hands of Cambodians for the first time since 1979. Prince Ranariddh and Hun Sen were designated co-prime ministers after Hun Sen threatened civil war if left out of the top position. (The prince was designated first prime minister and Hun Sen second prime minister.) The elderly Norodom Sihanouk was again named king, but he soon left the country for cancer treatment. The Khmer Rouge was kept out of the assembly and the executive branch. A new era of modern Cambodian politics had begun.

By 1994, Cambodia had achieved a semifunctioning government, and life in the rural areas as well as in the cities had returned to some degree of normality. There was hope that the standard of living would improve with increasing foreign investment and political stability. However, underneath this appearance of normality were deep problems that included ubiquitous corruption, crime, and patronage. Factional struggles between the two prime ministers and their respective parties bogged down the government. The Khmer Rouge continued its terrorist attacks, which placed an immense financial burden on the national budget. The government could not maintain law and order; dissidents were regularly assassinated, and the government was widely blamed for being incapable of stopping the carnage.

The political rivalry between FUNCINPEC and the CPP was ongoing and involved the frequent ouster of prominent ministers; unsuccessful attempts at power sharing at the district levels, a bizarre situation in which all cabinet ministries were run by top officials from both of the rival parties; disagreements over policy issues such as how to deal with the Khmer Rouge; and general anger on the part of Ranariddh's contingent over Hun Sen's forced entry into the government leadership. The rivalry culminated in Hun Sen's coup against First Prime Minister Ranariddh on July 6, 1997—a coup inspired by intrigue occurring within Khmer Rouge holdouts in Cambodia's hinterlands.

Hoping to resolve the outstanding problem of the Khmer Rouge presence in the country, both prime ministers attempted to court dissident Khmer Rouge leaders, the most notorious being Ieng Sary and Khieu Samphan. These men, and a few other top Khmer Rouge leaders, sought amnesty and reintegration into Cambodia's new system by announcing they had formed separate political parties. Ieng Sary also pledged to integrate his 3,000 troops (about one-third of the entire remaining Khmer Rouge force) into the national army. Hun Sen feared a Khmer Rouge–FUNCINPEC alliance, which could isolate his CPP and create a formidable force.

The open split among Khmer Rouge factions proved destabilizing. Fighting erupted in Anlong Veng, a Khmer Rouge stronghold along Cambodia's northern border. Rumors swirled about Pol Pot's fate: that he had ordered the killing of one of his longtime cadres, had been captured, was on the run or hiding in exile or already dead. Determining what was factual proved difficult. Since the Vietnamese invasion in late 1979, Pol Pot had not been seen or photographed at all. Meanwhile, Hun Sen agreed to amnesty for the defector Ieng Sary, hoping to woo him away from the prince's camp. Prince Ranariddh, in a power play against Hun Sen, began to engage Khieu Samphan, hinting that a deal with Khmer Rouge remnants was on the horizon.

In a sense, the relative stability of post-1993 Cambodia had put the Khmer Rouge in a bind. Any real hope they harbored for a return to power had dissipated. Lacking international patrons (due to the end of the Cold War), and unable to hold on to their shrinking territory (due to government troop advances), Khmer Rouge leaders increasingly realized their days were numbered. Hemmed in and desperate, they began to turn on each other. Cambodia's co–prime ministers faced uncertainty as well, due to the imminent dissolution of the Khmer Rouge. Neither could agree on terms of amnesty, participation, or criminal prosecution for the scheming Khmer Rouge leaders. Competing for influence, the co–prime ministers turned on each other, and Hun Sen made a bold grab for power.

Prince Ranariddh was out of the country when Hun Sen's coup took place. He charged Ranariddh with a variety of traitorous acts, including unauthorized negotiations with Khmer Rouge hard-liners. King Sihanouk, still ill and out of the country, refused to endorse the new government, but he did nothing to stop the coup and its aftermath. Because Hun Sen promised to arrest him upon reentry, Ranariddh remained in exile.

The coup reportedly was financed by alleged drug baron Theng Bunma, president of the Cambodian Chamber of Commerce, who publicly stated that he had given Hun Sen $1 million to stabilize the country's political situation. Following the coup, a number of FUNCINPEC supporters were assassinated; others were imprisoned while their homes were ransacked. Although Hun Sen apologized for the breakdown in law and order, the chaos continued for several months; the precarious balance that had emerged through Cambodia's joint leadership had been destroyed.

Twenty days after Hun Sen's coup, Pol Pot was affirmed to be alive and had been brought before a Khmer Rouge "people's tribunal" in Anlong Veng. The trial was held in an open-air, thatched-roof pavilion with dirt floors and bamboo furniture—symbolic of Khmer Rouge achievements. In a stunning turnaround, Pol Pot, the architect and perpetrator of the "killing fields," sat as an anguished old man, accused of murdering a top Khmer Rouge comrade and his family. He was denounced by the crowd, who screamed "Crush! Crush! Crush!" when his prosecutor identified him. Pol Pot was found guilty and placed under house arrest for life by his erstwhile Khmer Rouge captors.

Pictures of Pol Pot and video of his show trial (taken by the intrepid *Far Eastern Economic Review* correspondent Nate Thayer) were broadcast internationally. It was the first time the outside world had seen Pol Pot since his murderous rule.

The world reacted strongly to Pol Pot's one-day trial. Responsible for the torture and death of millions of people, he appeared like an elderly grandfather. His public statements to Nate Thayer were unrepentant; he asserted that he had a clear conscience. Pol Pot talked about his modesty, his lack of interest in leadership, his unobtrusive style of politics. He claimed his opponents had been executed by the Vietnamese and that the skulls of those tortured and killed at Tuol Sleng prison could not have been Cambodian because they were too small. He seemed most eager to talk about his poor health (he was seventy-two in 1997) and his enjoyment of his new wife and twelve-year-old daughter, the apple of his eye. Pol Pot epitomized the fabled banality of the truly evil person.

Pol Pot's final days were spent under house arrest with government troops closing in on his jungle redoubt. He died of an apparent heart attack on April 15, 1998, supposedly two hours after listening to a Voice of America broadcast that announced his captors were negotiating his handover to international authorities. Some observers suspected suicide, or assisted suicide by his young wife. The truth will remain unclear since his body was immediately cremated in a disgraceful funeral pyre that included automobile tires, old furniture, and debris.

With his death, Pol Pot, one of history's mass murderers, escaped retribution and legal accountability for his crimes. After years of uneasy negotiations involving the United Nations and representatives of multiple countries, Hun Sen finally agreed in 2006 to set up a hybrid court with both domestic and international judges for Pol Pot's living colleagues: the Extraordinary Chambers in the Courts of Cambodia (ECCC). Prosecution in the tribunal would fall under Cambodian law, inclusive of international crimes.

Twenty-seven years after the Khmer Rouge was expelled from power, the first Khmer Rouge leader appeared before the court on July 31, 2007. In a pretrial hearing, the onetime director of the notorious S-21 torture center, Kang Kek Ieu, or "Comrade Duch" (pronounced "Doik"), faced the Cambodian people on the following charges: crimes against humanity, mass killings, forced movements, forced labor, inhumane living conditions, and torture. Months of testimony and evidence were presented against Duch, who was baptized as an evangelical Christian under a false identity during his years in hiding. Generally cooperative with the tribunal, he was sentenced by the ECCC to life imprisonment. Trials began in mid-2011 for three other leading figures of Democratic Kampuchea: Khieu Samphan, Noun Chea, and Ieng Sary. A fourth leader, Ieng Sary's wife, Ieng Thirith, also remains charged and in detention, but her trial has been delayed due to her increasing symptoms of dementia.

The chaotic departure of the Khmer Rouge from Cambodian politics in the 1990s complicated the country's effort to restore order and develop economically. Hun Sen's 1997 coup was followed by elections for the National Assembly in July 1998, primarily to please donor countries that had withheld funds due to the coup (Cambodia's government's budget is largely dependent on foreign aid monies). The postcoup elections were marred by corruption, intimidation, and candidate assassinations. The CPP received 41 percent of the votes cast, FUNCINPEC 32 percent, and the Sam Rainsy Party 14 percent. Minor parties won the rest of the vote but did not receive seats in the 122-seat National Assembly. Hun Sen was renamed prime minister, and Prince Ranariddh was allowed to return from exile to be the president of the National Assembly under a reborn CPP-FUNCINPEC coalition. Supporters of Sam Rainsy became the opposition in the assembly.

As the new millennium began, the hope for cooperation among political parties and politicians was real. No major war was being fought, and the Khmer Rouge was no longer a threat. Nevertheless, Hun Sen's grip on power began to focus on his role as the gatekeeper to the Cambodian economy, and he thwarted any serious attempt at opposition politics. Networks of patronage rather than democratic institutions and civil society increasingly defined Hun Sen's Cambodia. FUNICPEC and other political parties began to suffocate under the CPP-dominated government apparatus.

Beginning with his power grab in 1997, Hun Sen's control over political and economic life has become more complete and corrupt. With a growing economy, new Cambodian tycoons have emerged in the country, all of whom are linked to Hun Sen. Foreign investors, primarily from Asia, have likewise sought Hun Sen's partnership. Much of the investment has centered on forest resources, tourism, and entertainment. Karaoke bars, casinos, and massage parlors have popped up all over Cambodia, especially along the Thai border to the west. Garment manufacturers too have discovered Cambodia's eager and inexpensive labor force. International aid organizations, wielding hundreds of millions of dollars, indirectly control part of the government's agenda, but Hun Sen continues to harass any that attempt oppositional politics. Cambodia's economy has grown, but it has not experienced genuine development. The majority of Cambodians still living in the countryside remain poor and left to fend for themselves, conditions exacerbated by negative economic growth in 2008 and a meager economic recovery since.

The dramatic drop in economic growth in 2008 predictably caused unemployment, factory closures, and societal distress, but this caused Hun Sen to grasp the reins of power even more tightly. To intimidate and silence those who criticized his indifference to growing problems, he discharged the bureaucratic, judicial, and security apparatuses at his disposal. His only major concession to opponents in recent years was a "temporary suspension" of land grants to private companies who were forcibly evicting residents from their homes. This move was, predictably, too little, too late. His July 2012 announcement was years overdue, made only after tens of thousands of urban and rural Cambodians had already suffered legal evictions and had been forced to resettle in inadequate housing. It also came three weeks too late to save the life of Chut Wutty, a prominent environmental activist who was killed by police when traveling with journalists while investigating the land grant issue.

Hun Sen's CPP predictably took 90 of 123 seats of the National Assembly in Cambodia's 2008 general elections. In 2012 Senate elections (where only elected members of Parliament and commune leaders cast ballots), 46 of 57 seats went to the CPP. With opposition politicians and parties thoroughly boxed in, the electoral system remains far from free and fair. There is little doubt that national elections scheduled for 2013 will produce similar results, affirming CPP dominance. Hun Sen effectively controls all Khmer security forces, Khmer courts, and all of the Khmer language print and broadcast media. With a constitution pledged to principles of liberal democracy and pluralism, Cambodia annually holds the dubious distinction as the only country in Southeast Asia with a democratic constitution that is rated "not free" by Freedom House.

Current political trends in Cambodia move in one direction: toward Hun Sen. Newly drafted CPP laws enforced by courts and backed by security forces leave labor unions facing prosecution, peaceful protestors jailed for dissent, and villagers defenseless against land developers.[6] Meanwhile, businesses and corporations enjoy ever more freedom to maneuver in the CPP-dominated system. Ominously within Hun Sen's grasp is the holy grail of state revenue and control: black gold. Currently negotiating with Cambodia's government are Japanese, South Korean, and U.S. oil and gas firms eager to exploit the country's maritime rights in the Gulf of Siam. The treasure of untapped resources under Cambodian land and water is valued at over $1.7 billion annually, an amount that would double the regime's current budget revenues.[7]

INSTITUTIONS AND SOCIAL GROUPS

Prince Sihanouk

After the 1940s, Prince Norodom Sihanouk dominated all aspects of Cambodian society. Although placed on the throne by the French in 1941 (when he was nineteen) and thought by the French to be pliable, Sihanouk became the symbol of Cambodian independence. With his shrill voice, he rallied his people during an era when Cambodia was known as "an island of tranquility in a sea of chaos." Conversant in ten languages, the author of five books, and a stage and movie actor and director, he was the country's most cosmopolitan citizen. Dogmatic about the value of neutrality, and willing to play any side to survive politically, he was described by observers as temperamental, duplicitous, and inscrutable.

Although Sihanouk ruled autocratically, exercising dominance over the National Assembly, his government was supported by the overwhelming majority of the people. Sihanouk maintained the support of the rural population but eventually lost that of Cambodia's urban elites, who opposed his foreign and economic policies. After he was overthrown by his own premier in 1970, he allied himself with the Khmer Rouge rebels while in exile and, when the Khmer Rouge took power, returned to Phnom Penh as a ceremonial leader. Subsequently, he cooperated with the Khmer Rouge, even though it had murdered five of his sons and daughters, fourteen of his grandchildren, and more than a million of his former subjects. Sihanouk was an egotist who was willing to prolong the civil war to maximize his own authority.

Sihanouk denounced the Vietnamese-backed Hun Sen administration; he lived in exile in Beijing and Pyongyang for much of this period, receiving medical treatment for his numerous maladies. His movement in and out of Cambodia solidified his reputation as a mercurial figure. Sihanouk lost much popular support by being out of power for over twenty years and allying himself with the Khmer Rouge. Nevertheless, he remained one of the country's major institutions, eventually returning to Cambodia to become king following the UNTAC-sponsored elections in 1993.

While king, Sihanouk held little formal power and showed regret for some of his actions. He said that if he were not a Buddhist he would kill himself, believing his life to be filled with shame, humiliation, and despair over Cambodia's past and future.

In 2004, King Sihanouk abdicated in favor of his son Norodom Sihamoni. A bachelor, and a classical dancer by training, Sihamoni lived most of his life in Prague, Pyongyang, and Paris. As a relatively unknown figure to most Cambodians, his appointment came as a welcome move and dampened rumors that Hun Sen planned to abolish the monarchy upon Sihanouk's death. Before his coronation, the apolitical Sihamoni had served as Cambodia's cultural ambassador to the United Nations but otherwise was uninvolved in national life.

King Sihamoni is gradually winning the affection of his subjects but is not as revered as his father was. His state visits to China and neighboring countries have served Cambodia's interests. Given the short life of the resurrected monarchy, it remains to be seen whether the institution will endure in coming years. In 2008, Sihanouk, ever erratic, publicly raised the possibility of his son's own abdication only to recant the comments later. Hun Sen's own behavior has taken on more and more regal tones as he increasingly eclipses Sihamoni's role as head of state.

At eighty-nine, Norodom Sihanouk died in a Beijing hospital on October 15, 2012. Days later, his body was returned to Cambodia and a procession in his honor drew hundreds of thousands of mourners. After lying in state for three months, the remains of Cambodia's most beloved cultural figure were publically cremated by Buddhist monks at Cambodia's Royal Palace.

Hun Sen

The opposite of Sihanouk in many ways, Prime Minister Hun Sen has been Cambodia's most important leader in the post–Khmer Rouge period. He was born into a peasant family and did not finish high school. Hun Sen was twenty-four when the Khmer Rouge came to power under Pol Pot. The Khmer Rouge evacuated his family from its rural home, killed his eldest son, and imprisoned his wife. Blinded in one eye by a U.S. cluster bomb, Hun Sen joined the Khmer Rouge as a senior commander and may have become party to its genocidal fanaticism. He defected in 1977, as Pol Pot began his systematic executions of dissident Khmer Rouge members, and escaped to Vietnam.

In 1986, Cambodia was being administered by a Vietnamese-installed government. Hun Sen, the prime minister and foreign minister, had become the most influential figure in the People's Republic of Kampuchea, although Heng Samrin, the head of state, held the highest position. Hun Sen's regime controlled the cities and most of the countryside with the aid of Vietnamese soldiers and advisers. However, few nations recognized this regime as Cambodia's legitimate government despite its control over virtually all aspects of the country's life.

As leader of the Vietnamese-backed PRK, Hun Sen traveled abroad to win foreign aid and support; he was known more as a pragmatist than as an ideologist. His attempts to position his government as being more independent of Vietnam improved his popularity in Cambodia. This popularity, however, was not matched internationally, where he was still viewed as a leader who had come to power from aggression. These global assessments of Hun Sen's aggressive and self-serving nature were reinforced when he demanded a share of the prime ministership in 1993 and when he grabbed power in 1997. Where analysts found Sihanouk to be enigmatic, Hun Sen remains predictably Machiavellian.

Hun Sen, who prefers to be called "*somdech*" (prince), shrewdly uses his Cambodian People's Party to maintain his hold on power. Employing elections and the trappings of democracy on one hand, and methods of intimidation, harassment, and fear on the other, Hun Sen perpetuates rule best described as electoral authoritarianism. Hoping to challenge the cultural appeal of his royalist rivals, Hun Sen has sought to soften his image by building clinics and schools and by providing special funds for families with triplets. (Some Cambodians believe the lost souls of Khmer Rouge victims find their way into already pregnant women for rebirth.)[8] Hun Sen also craftily engineers Cambodian nationalism to his political advantage, as witnessed in recent controversies with Thailand over Angkor-era temples.

Hun Sen's tough image in domestic and foreign policy remains as fixed as his grip on power. As the country's most powerful leader and one of the world's longest ruling executives, "*somdech*" Hun Sen sits atop Cambodia lacking any serious rivals.

Political Parties

The Cambodian People's Party is by far the largest and most broad-based party in Cambodia. With access to government coffers and bureaucratic connections spread through Cambodia's local areas, the CPP is organized as if it were a grassroots structure; functionally, it is anything but a bottom-up people's party. The CPP is a centralized, patronage-based, hegemonic party that persistently blurs the lines between itself and the state.

Hun Sen and fellow party leader Chea Sim cultivate the CPP's image as a party of stability. Trumpeting fear, the CPP tells the electorate that it stands as the lone bulwark between social stability and a return to disorder. The party operates in the absence of ideology or a coherent political platform. It prefers to paint its opponents as dangerous to Cambodia's future.

To ward off perceptions that the CPP's claims may be true, FUNCINPEC, the party built by Prince Ranariddh, has strategically joined in coalition governments with the CPP. FUNCINPEC, an acronym for its French name, Front Uninational pour un Cambodge Indépendant Neutre, Pacifique, et Coopératif, grew out of the Sihanoukists' tripartite opposition to the Vietnamese-backed Hun Sen in the 1980s. In the 1990s, it existed as a partner, but potential challenger, to Hun Sen. In the 2000s, FUNCINPEC has struggled to find its place in the political milieu. In 2006, the party, alleging corruption, sued its own founder and expelled him from the party. The prince formed a new party, the Norodom Ranariddh Party, awkwardly managed from Malaysia, where he remained in exile until his brother, King Sihamoni, granted him a pardon from the charges against him. Ranariddh subsequently retired from politics. FUNCINPEC lost all nine of its seats during the 2012 Senate elections, and the Norodom Ranariddh Party, under new leadership, barely hangs on to the few seats it won in 2006 Parliament elections.

In the midst of the Preah Vihear temple controversy with Thailand, Cambodia held an election in July 2008. Fewer parties competed than did in 2003, and Hun Sen's CPP won 58 percent of the vote, which translated into 72 seats. The Norodom Ranariddh Party won only 7 seats. FUNCINPEC, a shell of its former self, produced a similar meager result with only 6 seats. The Sam Rainsy Party took 27 seats. Other parties occupied the remaining 11 seats.

Cambodia's only genuine opposition party since 1993 has been the Sam Rainsy Party (SRP), formerly the Khmer National Party (KNP). Sam Rainsy served as a finance minister and a member of FUNCINPEC until he was forced out of his position in 1994. His party draws support from liberal segments of society, but it struggles to develop a functional apparatus due to harassment from Hun Sen and government officials. Numerous candidates and activists affiliated with the SRP have been anonymously persecuted, shot at, and murdered. For his antigovernment statements, Sam Rainsy has faced defamation lawsuits, stints in exile, a royal pardon, and politically costly deals with Hun Sen. As of late 2012, he remained in exile in Australia.

International Aid Community

The Kingdom of Cambodia, in its most recent incarnation, was born from international assistance. Few countries have such an intimate history with the broad constellation of the global community's official and private foreign aid organizations. Cambodia, the object of much international sympathy, remains relatively open to government and nongovernmental organizations that provide myriad services: resettlement, education, health care, construction of infrastructure, rural development, technical assistance, and even human rights promotion. Thousands of foreigners and local Cambodians are employed in 450-plus NGOs and dozens of UN-affiliated agencies and bilateral aid programs, such as USAID, the Japanese International Cooperation Agency, and the Australian Government Overseas Aid Program.[9]

So pervasive is the aid community that everyday life for many Cambodians is currently interwoven with the many schools, clinics, and infrastructure projects that mushroomed in recent years due to foreign support. A sudden departure of aid flows and aid workers would have a crippling effect on the economy and on Cambodian society in general. Fifteen years following UNTAC, around 10 percent to 15 percent of GDP was still derived annually from international assistance, leading to worries about "aid addiction." Much of the annual government budget depends on cash flows from Japan and the European Union, creating opportunities for official corruption. Donor countries often express concerns over bureaucratic corruption, but many Cambodians believe the wide salary gaps between foreign aid workers and local employees is just as morally repugnant.

With a few exceptions, individuals in the foreign aid community steer clear of direct involvement in Cambodia's political life. Indirectly, Hun Sen's government benefits from the incremental improvements to Cambodian life made possible by aid workers and their programs. The large flows of official development assistance, channeled through Cambodia's government, serve somewhat as a check on government behavior, keeping open repression fairly rare.[10] Unlike Burma, where the military regime functions with relatively little foreign presence in the country to worry about, Cambodia's leaders must remain more conscious of who is watching.

STATE-SOCIETY RELATIONS AND DEMOCRACY

Since its independence, modern Cambodia has proven to be among the world's weakest states. Viewed from the outside, this weakness is indicated by repeated episodes of foreign occupation as well as penetration of the state by domestic elite interests. Invaded by both Vietnamese and U.S. forces, Sihanouk's state was unable to enforce its own policy of neutrality. Civil war and the threat of civil war also impeded state development before, during, and after Khmer Rouge rule. In 1979, foreign occupation turned Cambodia into a Vietnamese puppet state until 1992, when the United Nations literally took over all state functions. Following UNTAC's departure, the fundamental weakness of the Cambodian state has continued due in large part to Hun

Sen's expanding network apparatus, which has displaced the development of autonomous state institutions. Even today, Cambodia has few experienced technocrats whose loyalty is primarily to the state; its army is weak and undependable, and its judges and courts are compromised. Virtually all state officials are beholden to Hun Sen's inner circle and largesse.

As viewed from the inside, in the context of Cambodia's own experience, a weak state is nonetheless preferable to a failed state. Cambodia, a failed state in the late 1980s, recovered due to tremendous international support and Cambodians' willingness to demilitarize warring factions and start over. Brought to its knees, and desperate for peace and order, the state allowed foreigners to reoccupy the ministries the colonial French once controlled. Although the state's capacity remains weak and the state is too often fused with CPP rule itself, Cambodia's viability looks somewhat promising. Whether the country can produce (or endure) a shift in power from one set of rulers to another, without succumbing to the impulses of violence and militarism, remains an open question.

Thus, in spite of being a weak state, the greatest challenges to the legitimacy and viability of the Cambodian state are likely in the past. Internationally, world leaders and donor countries have shown patience with Hun Sen, allowing him the political space—too much perhaps—to restore a state formerly subject to foreign control. Hun Sen's political legitimacy has been derived from three sources: (1) his experience as a Cambodian leader who initially guided Cambodia through the post–Khmer Rouge period; (2) his leadership of a party elected multiple times to take the reins of government; and (3) his public popularity, which is far from unanimous but draws support from beneficiaries of the government and Cambodia's widest patronage network: local-level officials.

Although relative political stability has been established since 1993, Cambodia is not transitioning to democracy. Unfortunately, the Paris Peace Agreement and UNTAC's rapid efforts to secure peace through cease-fire agreements and popular elections set a low baseline for democratic expectations. By using a strategy emphasizing peace building and national elections, the Paris Agreement actually put Cambodia on a course toward electoral autocracy, not institutionalized democracy. In hindsight, the expectations for democratic transition in the 1990s were naively optimistic. Most Cambodians, bewildered by UNTAC's complex mission, were too inexperienced with popular politics to demand much from representative government. Largely poor, rural, and uneducated, the people had a scope of political expectations at the time that ranged little beyond keeping the Khmer Rouge out of power and receiving help with basic needs. Collective action, public opinion, and exercising individual civil liberties were foreign notions to most Cambodians. The 1993 election unintentionally launched a pattern where electioneering came to reinforce patronage-based authoritarianism at the expense of developing interest representation, oppositional politics, and civil liberties.

Cambodia's democratic transition, if showing movement at all, is reversing itself. Over its history, Cambodia has never experienced genuine democratic rule. Since the days of ancient Angkor, autocratic rulers have led governments with scarcely any accountability to the ruled. Cambodians have a long history of Hindu-Buddhist notions of the *deva-raja* (god-king) and deference to those in authority. The principles of absolutism, hierarchy, and status, introduced centuries ago, resurfaced after Pol Pot and remain important influences on Cambodian politics. In the words of one prominent scholar of Cambodia, the majority of the population today sees Hun Sen "as a *fait accompli*, rather like a monarch, rather than an elected and responsive leader. Hun Sen presides in a regal manner over everything that happens in Cambodia; like many kings, he has no respect for pluralism, an independent judiciary, or the separation of powers."[11]

Ironically, reinforcing Hun Sen's rule, and the rise of patronage politics over democratization, are not only local and foreign business tycoons negotiating contracts and kickbacks with Hun Sen's inner circle, but also international donors and NGOs that set the policy agenda and help fund the CPP-managed coffers of patronage (i.e., the budgets of government ministries and departmental programs). With so many foreign actors influencing affairs, the domestic interest groups, associations, and mass organizations that should be applying pressure on elected representatives have little opportunity to evolve and shape the agenda. The donor communities, many of whom openly balk at demanding serious political reform to stay in operation, have become apathetically tolerant of rampant government corruption and ineptitude.[12] With donors providing resources to both state and nonstate actors, the Cambodian people have yet to wrest democracy from a system of top-down resource allocation.[13]

Cambodia's 123-seat National Assembly, an object of tremendous political attention during national elections, also falls well short of its democratic function to represent societal interests. The assembly's very design virtually ensures CPP's dominance in the body for the foreseeable future. As it functions today, the National Assembly is deliberately designed to support Hun Sen's hegemonic electoral authoritarian regime. For example, the proportional voting system used to elect the Parliament disproportionately rewards larger parties with a greater number of seats. In 2003, for example, the CPP won only 47 percent of the vote but still occupied 59 percent of assembly seats. Similarly, in 2008, the CPP won 58 percent of all votes but occupied 73 percent of assembly seats. In 1995, Hun Sen also engineered change in the constitutional threshold of assembly seats needed to form a coalition government from 66 percent to a simple majority. When the charter reform went through the Assembly, Hun Sen threatened to imprison opposition leader Sam Rainsy if his party voted against the amendment.[14] Declining voter turnout, evident with each passing election, indicates the collective resignation among Cambodians that elections fail to provide any check on Hun Sen's power.

Lastly, although Cambodia's constitution calls for adherence to human rights, a disturbing degree of lawlessness still characterizes state-society relations. Those who champion civil society and human rights often risk their personal safety to advance their cause. The politically motivated murders of political radio host Chour Chetharith (2003), prominent labor rights activist Chea Vichea (2004), opposition newspaper journalist Khim Sambor (2008), and environmental activist Chut Wutty (2012)—as well as a dozen other activists since the early 1990s—offer chilling reminders of means employed by those in power to silence critics who openly challenge them. Official investigations of political murders distressingly flounder in courts where government judges, using no witnesses, extend guilty verdicts to defendants with no known political ties. Honest judges, seeking truthful verdicts, often find themselves removed from the bench.

ECONOMY AND DEVELOPMENT

When the Vietnamese-sponsored regime took control in 1979, the government restored a currency system, trade, and wage labor but favored a planned economy based on the Vietnamese model. Private enterprise and private property were not officially allowed but informally tolerated. Beginning in the mid-1980s, the PRK regime instituted its own version of Vietnamese-style *doi moi* by liberalizing foreign investment laws, allowing private industries, increasing international trade, returning land to peasant ownership, permitting private transportation enterprises, guaranteeing the end of the nationalization of private enterprises, and legalizing the private sector.[15] This opening of the economy immediately improved the output of the industrial, agricultural, and private sectors.

Initially, about two dozen NGOs from Australia, Europe, and the United States provided approximately $10 million per year in relief and development assistance. These NGOs, which supported nutrition centers, hospitals, and artificial limb factories, also oversaw water supply, animal welfare, sanitation, irrigation, and educational projects.[16] Under the Vietnamese, only certain UN agencies that provided emergency relief, such as UNICEF and the World Food Programme, were allowed to operate inside Cambodia, whereas the UN Development Program, the World Health Organization, and other development-oriented UN agencies were not.[17] Even so, Cambodia's needs were far greater than what the NGOs provided.

In Phnom Penh, the economy changed dramatically following UNTAC's departure, with a boom in consumer goods, mostly from Thailand and China; increased car traffic; out-of-control land speculation; and inflation, driven by a huge supply of money, mostly from the high per diem payments made to foreign aid personnel, whose daily income was often equivalent to Cambodians' average *yearly* income.

By 1997, there were still only about sixty small industries in Cambodia, operating at half capacity. The major investments for foreign exchange at the time were rubber, timber, and tourism. Manufacturing focused on apparel factories that benefited from the Multi Fibre Arrangement, a globally negotiated country export quota scheme to assist developing countries. By the early 2000s, the number of factories grew to well over one hundred, with many operating at full capacity.

Tourism also began to grow. Academic delegations and adventure travelers were joined by big-ticket travelers on group tours. The magnificent ruins of Angkor, at one time a popular tourist attraction, were unavailable for most of the 1970s and 1980s. By the early 1990s, Cambodia was not attracting significant numbers of visitors due to poor roads, rail service, and air transport, and because the Khmer Rouge still controlled nearby land. That changed rapidly after 1992 when Angkor Wat was designated a UNESCO World Heritage Site, and especially when direct air service became available in 1998. Siem Reap, a once-small town near Angkor-era temples, now finds itself inundated with large resort-style hotels and busloads of wealthy seniors from Europe, North America, and Asia on package tours. The growth of Chinese tourism in particular contributes substantially to Angkor Wat's 4,000 daily visitors and its $50 million in annual receipts. By 2020 a predicted 6 million total visitors are expected to tour the temple complex annually.[18]

Under CPP-FUNCINPEC coalition governments, Cambodia experienced modest to low growth rates in the 1990s. Since 2000, however, Cambodia's economic growth has taken a rapid turn upward. Cambodia averaged 10.9 percent annual GDP growth between 2000 and 2006; over the same period, per capita income increased from $288 to $513, doubling in only six years.[19] Due to the global financial crisis, and an anemic growth rate of 0.1 percent in 2009, Cambodia's economy has since averaged GDP growth around only 6 percent annually. Per capita income still rose to $830 in 2011, but nearly one in three Cambodians remains in poverty in 2012. Compared to the region's other poor countries, Cambodia suffers the highest degree of income inequality, suggesting that recent economic gains benefit primarily those who already have wealth.

From a domestic perspective, some encouragement can be derived from Cambodia's overall economic activity in spite of income disparities and vulnerability to fluctuating global markets. Tourism, light industry, and manufacturing are growing rapidly. The apparel industry, in particular, plays an important role in Cambodia's new economy. At its peak, it employed 300,000 workers in more than five hundred factories producing for global brands such as Polo, the Gap, and Banana Republic. Somewhat surprisingly, Cambodia consented to implementing higher international standards for textile workers and has won praise from the International Labor Organization. Cambodia enjoys a positive reputation among socially minded clothing buyers in Paris, New York, and London. For a time, the success of the apparel industry continued despite the expiration of Multi Fibre Arrangement in 2005, which many observers predicted would cripple Cambodia's competitiveness. However, it was a drop in global demand in 2009 that painfully reversed the industry's expansion. Over 130 factories closed or suspended production and, in turn, 60,000 workers saw their jobs terminated or suspended.[20]

From a comparative perspective, however, the reality is more daunting. Cambodia's economy may be growing, but it is so far behind its neighbors that even years of sustained growth will not raise it to regional averages. About four in five Cambodians still live as poor farmers in rural areas and barely four in ten have access to improved water. Deficient irrigation works limit Cambodia's agricultural potential, demonstrated by record surpluses of rice in 2006, a particularly good rain year. Where Thai and Vietnamese farmers lead the world in rice exports, Cambodian farmers are only beginning to produce beyond domestic needs. Cambodia is on track to meet only two of eight UN Millennium Development Goals. In spite of aggregate economic growth, progress has stagnated on key development indicators, including poverty reduction, maternal health, and secondary education participation.[21] Cambodians share a level of substandard development similar to most people in Burma, Laos, and Timor-Leste.

The Kingdom of Cambodia's economic future is now linked to its WTO membership, secured in 2004. Cambodia will not improve economically if it does not diversify and improve the quality of its export products. Its economy is still too dependent on foreign aid and NGO activity. The new frontier in oil exploration being charted—with projections estimating peak oil revenues above three times the country's current international aid receipts— could help, but it raises concerns that Cambodia may substitute one form of revenue addiction for another. Moreover, oil revenues could simply act to replenish current CPP slush funds currently derived from Cambodia's rapidly depleting forests and other natural resources.[22]

FOREIGN RELATIONS

Throughout its modern history, Cambodia has been the target of aggression by its larger neighbors and by Western and communist imperialists. The French, Americans, Soviets, Chinese, Vietnamese, and Thais have all attempted at various times to control Cambodian affairs. During the Cold War, Cambodia was the victim of direct U.S. and Vietnamese intervention as well as Chinese support for antigovernment rebels. The Vietnamese intervention of December 1978 occurred with significant support from the Soviets, who funded the operation and provided much of the weaponry.

After the Vietnamese invasion, the United Nations continued to recognize the Pol Pot regime despite the fact that the Khmer Rouge controlled only about 2 percent of the population and that Pol Pot had been branded as one of history's worst violators of human rights. The United States, playing Cold War politics under Jimmy Carter, simplistically viewed the PRK as a puppet of Vietnam and, thus, a surrogate of the Soviet Union.

The end of the Cold War brought new opportunities for a comprehensive peace settlement after a decade of factional conflict. Warmer relations between the United States and the Soviet Union influenced a new U.S. policy toward Cambodia. For many years, U.S. goals in Cambodia included the withdrawal of Vietnamese military forces; the repudiation of the Khmer Rouge; a political settlement that would permit Cambodians to choose their form of government; and an independent, neutral, and nonaligned Cambodia, protected from outside interference by international guarantees.[23]

As the Cold War came to a close, ASEAN was not united on the best means by which to deal with Cambodia. Whereas Singapore took a hardline stance against the Hun Sen government, Thailand wished to convert Indochina "from a battlefield to a marketplace," with the Thais themselves taking the leading economic role in mainland Southeast Asia. Thai Prime Minister Chatichai Choonhavan met with Prime Minister Hun Sen on numerous occasions to negotiate trade programs and a settlement of the Cambodian imbroglio.

After the October 1991 peace accords were signed, the Supreme National Council under Sihanouk became Cambodia's legitimate government. Although part of the SNC, the Khmer Rouge lost Chinese aid when China and Vietnam moved to a rapprochement in 1992 and when China attempted to improve its international reputation following the 1989 Tiananmen Square tragedy. In addition, UN-imposed sanctions against the Khmer Rouge undermined an important source of funding: Thai investors who had engaged the border rebels in deals for timber and gems. To support the peace process, the United States ended its economic embargo against Cambodia. In a matter of a little more than a decade, Cambodia transformed itself from Khmer Rouge pariah state, into a Vietnamese puppet state, into an international experiment, and then into a weakling state, dependent on international patrons.

Cambodia's international relations evolved further in 1999 when it became a member of ASEAN, only two years after Hun Sen's power grab via coup d'état. Since that time, relations with Vietnam became more balanced than in the past, but Cambodia has turned actively toward China, the regional power Cambodia views to be its main protector, patron, and strategic partner. China has provided military aid to Cambodia and agreed to a "comprehensive cooperative partnership," with Beijing's consultation on "issues of regional peace, stability, and development" as well as economic matters.[24] The ASEAN–China Free Trade Agreement, signed in Phnom Penh in 2002, included a zero tariff classification on certain imports from Cambodia.[25] Cambodian trade with China is expected to climb to $5 billion by 2020.

In terms of foreign assistance, China provided over $1 billion annually in loans and aid to Cambodia in 2010 and 2011, more than any other bilateral or multilateral donor. In 2011, at a ceremonial opening with Hun Sen presiding, the Chinese state-run company Sinohydro activated China's largest hydroelectric dam in Kampot Province. By 2015, four more Chinese-built dams, worth some $1.6 billion, will go online through build-operate-transfer schemes and provide a total 915 megawatts for Cambodia's electricity grid.[26] Unlike foreign assistance from Western sources, Chinese aid does not come with any requirements for democratic performance, rule of law, environmental impact statement, or property compensation. While China has its eye on Cambodia's oil and gas resources, the massive aid packages have also bought China a needed ASEAN ally in the Spratlys dispute. In 2012, when Cambodia hosted annual ASEAN meetings with China and the United States present, progress on a regional solution failed largely due to Cambodian objections.

Cambodia's biggest foreign relations concerns in recent years have been with its Thai neighbors to the west. In 2003, after a Thai actress supposedly commented that she would not perform in Cambodia until Angkor Wat was returned to Thailand, anti-Thai riots erupted on Phnom Penh streets. Rioters attacked several Thai-owned businesses, causing $50 million worth of damages. No Thais were injured or killed, but the incident troubled relations between the two countries, partly because of Hun Sen's poor handling of the situation. Tensions over the matter reverberated for a time, but eventually economic interests triumphed again and the two governments found themselves signing border trade deals and cooperating on oil exploration in the years that followed.[27]

Relations with Thailand subsequently deteriorated in 2007 when Cambodia submitted a celebrated border temple for UNESCO World Heritage Site status. Nestled on a cliff overlooking Cambodia's northern plains, the dramatically set Preah Vihear temple was the subject of a 1962 International Court of Justice case that ruled the temple was in Cambodian territory in spite of Thai claims otherwise. Thai authorities unsuccessfully demanded postponement of the UNESCO proposal. With much chest-pounding by Hun Sen (reciprocated by his Thai counterparts), Cambodian and Thai border troops engaged in deadly skirmishes near the temple in

2008 and again in 2011. The incident drew the attention of the UN Security Council, which feared a full-scale border war. UNESCO later approved the designation, and the dispute festered until another ruling by the International Court of Justice forced both sides to withdraw their troops beyond a newly demarcated demilitarized zone.

Internationally, the long-awaited tribunal for Khmer Rouge leaders at last became a reality in 2007. Although the Khmer Rouge is no longer an organized force, its legacy, alas, continues to define international perceptions of Cambodia and its people. Cambodia's biggest foreign policy challenge going forward is to transcend this image—to create for itself a truly post–Khmer Rouge international identity, much in the same way Vietnam is shedding its "Vietnam War" image by redefining itself as one of Asia's emerging economies. Sympathetic governments and aid organizations have afforded Hun Sen a generous degree of political space to engineer this feat, but his regime's reputation for corruption, exploitation, and failed democracy is doing little to improve the country's image or standing.

CONCLUSION

Regime instability, indicated by the country's many name changes, has dictated Cambodia's recent past. No people in Southeast Asia have undergone the magnitude of horrific trauma that Cambodians suffered from the 1960s to the present. War, genocide, famine, and oppression have devastated the society once known as an oasis of tranquility. With virtually its entire educated class decimated, Cambodia is attempting to rebuild. However, it is still buffeted by the world's great powers, by its neighbors, and by internal political despotism. The phenomenal resilience of the Cambodians is the most hopeful sign that the "killing fields" will never return and that Cambodia can develop and remain independent.

Nevertheless, for the foreseeable future Cambodia will continue to have weak state institutions, to be led by a strongman, and to be threatened by internal political conflict. Without better-trained administrators, an improved infrastructure, and continued external aid, the outlook for political development is bleak. Hun Sen, proven capable of employing any means to ensure power, is unlikely to permit electoral politics, or any other process, to remove him from the apex of power. Patronage, corruption, and disregard for civil liberties are likely to characterize the Cambodian political system for many years to come. Champions of democracy face an uphill battle.

NOTES

1. Factors contributing to the decline of Angkor remain a subject of intense study. The role of monument building and war is emphasized, for example, in D. R. Sardesai's *Southeast Asia Past and Present*, 6th edition (Boulder: Westview Press, 2009). The signifi-

cant role of climate change as a factor in the decline of the "hydraulic city" of Angkor is a relatively recent archeological discovery; see Brenda M. Buckley et al., "Climate as a Contributing Factor in the Demise of Angkor, Cambodia," *Proceedings of the National Academy of Sciences* 107, no. 15, April 13, 2010: 6,748–6,752.

2. Eva Mysliwiec, *Punishing the Poor: The International Isolation of Kampuchea* (Oxford, U.K.: Oxfam, 1988), 2.

3. The most comprehensive account of the effect U.S. bombing had in bringing the Khmer Rouge to power is found in William Shawcross, *Sideshow: Kissinger, Nixon, and the Destruction of Cambodia* (New York: Simon and Schuster, 1979)

4. David P. Chandler et al., *In Search of Southeast Asia: A Modern History*, ed. David Joel Steinberg (Honolulu: University of Hawaii Press, 1987), 381–382.

5. Ibid., 11.

6. Steven Heder, "Cambodia in 2010: Hun Sen's Further Consolidation," *Asian Survey* 51, no. 1 (January/February 2011): 211–212.

7. Khlem Chanreatrey, "Big Questions over Black Gold," *Economics Today*, July 23, 2012, http://etmcambodia.com/viewarticles.php?articlesid=201.

8. Duncan McCargo, "Cambodia: Getting Away with Authoritarianism?" *Journal of Democracy* 16, no. 4 (2005): 103.

9. Information about Cambodia's vast NGO community can be found at a Web site maintained by the Cooperation Committee for Cambodia: http://ccc-cambodia.org /home.html.

10. McCargo, "Cambodia: Getting Away with Authoritarianism?" 108.

11. David Chandler, "Cambodia in 2009: Plus C'est la Meme Chose," *Asian Survey* 50, no. 1 (January/February 2010): 229.

12. McCargo, "Cambodia: Getting Away with Authoritarianism?" 110.

13. Melanie Beresford, "Cambodia in 2004: An Artificial Democratization Process," *Asian Survey* 45, no. 1 (January/February 2005): 137.

14. Caroline Hughes, "Cambodia in 2007: Development and Dispossession," *Asian Survey* 48, no. 1 (January/February 2008): 74.

15. Robert J. Muscat, *Cambodia: Post-Settlement Reconstruction and Development* (New York: East Asian Institute, Columbia University, 1989), 88–89.

16. Mysliwiec, *Punishing the Poor*, 66.

17. Muscat, *Cambodia: Post-Settlement Reconstruction and Development*, 2.

18. "Angkor Wat Plagued by Mass Tourism, Insufficient Management," Global Heritage Fund, July 19, 2011, http://globalheritagefund.org/onthewire/blog/angkor_wat.

19. Figures are from the Royal Government of Cambodia, Ministry of Economy and Finance. UN Development Program figures for 2007 show a gross national income per capita of $540.

20. Chandler, "Cambodia in 2009," 230.

21. See the United Nations Development Programme-Cambodia, www.un.org.kh /undp.

22. Hughes, "Cambodia in 2007," 72–73.

23. Frederick Z. Brown, *Second Chance: The United States and Indochina in the 1990s* (New York: Council on Foreign Relations, 1989), 11.

24. Oskar Weggel, "Cambodia in 2006: Self-Promotion and Self-Deception," *Asian Survey* 47, no. 1 (January/February 2007): 146.

25. Robert Sutter, *Chinese Foreign Relations: Power and Policy since the Cold War* (Lanham, MD: Rowman & Littlefield, 2008), 268.

26. "Cambodia's Largest Hydroelectric Dam Begins Operation," *Xinhua News*, December 7, 2012, http://news.xinhuanet.com/english/world/2011-12/07/c_131293571.htm.

27. Weggel, "Cambodia in 2006," 146.

RESOURCE GUIDE

A useful tool for bibliographic and other information on Cambodia is available from Australia National University's WWW Virtual Library: www.gksoft.com/govt/en/kh.html. The University of California–Berkeley maintains a useful portal for digital and print resources on Cambodia: www.lib.berkeley.edu/SSEAL/SoutheastAsia/seaelec.html. Northern Illinois University's Southeast Asia Digital Library includes a range of useful links that cover government, academic, and research institutions specific to Cambodia: http://sea.lib.niu.edu. The University of Wisconsin–Madison Libraries similarly maintains a list of digital and print resources on Cambodia: www.library.wisc.edu/guides/SEAsia/resarea.html.

Readers can supplement this chapter with figures and publication information found in the country profile pages of data.UN.org. and ADB.org. Recent and archived news articles are maintained on specific country profile pages by BBC.com and NYTimes.com. Useful country reports are also produced by the Bertelsmann Foundation at www.bti-project.org/home/index.nc.

The official site of the Cambodian government is www.cambodia.gov.kh. For the party line of the CPP and Hun Sen, visit "Cambodia New Vision" at www.cnv.org.kh. The official Web site of King Norodom Sihamoni is at www.norodomsihamoni.org. An independent organization, the Cambodia Development Research Institute, focuses on development policy analysis: www.cdri.org.kh.

UNTAC provides details on its mission at www.un.org/Depts/dpko/dpko/co_mission/untac.htm. For information on the vast NGO community operating in Cambodia, visit www.ngoforum.org.kh/eng/ and www.devdir.org/files/Cambodia.PDF.

The Cambodian Genocide Program at Yale University, www.yale.edu/cgp, maintains research tools and databases on the Khmer Rouge period. The Web site of the Extraordinary Chambers in the Courts of Cambodia provides information on ongoing judicial action at www.eccc.gov.kh/en, as does Genocide Watch at www.genocidewatch.org/cambodiaproject.html. Students may be interested to know that Khieu Samphan's 1959 thesis, "Cambodia's Economy and Industrial Development," is available through interlibrary loan.

6

LAOS

LAOS MIGHT BEST BE DESCRIBED AS A QUASI NATION. IT EMERGED from maps drawn by European colonialists rather than from a sense of territory and nationhood among a united people. The history of Laos is riddled with constant warfare among contending forces within its borders and the meddling of external powers from without—mainly Thailand, Vietnam, China, France, and the United States.

Since it seized power in 1975, the present communist government has faced ongoing problems with few signs of genuine progress: uniting ethnic groups that have fought with each other for decades, resettling large groups of refugees, promoting development in an overwhelmingly rural population, educating a citizenry with minimal educational institutions, and protecting the nation's sovereignty against encroachment by neighbors and outside powers.

Laos is landlocked, but uniquely so. Its isolation is exacerbated by the physiographic borders it shares with each of its neighbors. Remote mountains lie along Laos' northern borders with China and Vietnam, and the rugged Annam Cordillera defines its long eastern border with Vietnam (inhibiting overland routes to the South China Sea). To its west, the broad and meandering Mekong River separates Laos from Burma and most of Thailand. Culturally, the Mekong supported Lao peoples on both sides of the river, but the first modern bridge appeared only in the mid-1990s. Laos' river access to the Mekong Delta is inhibited by the unnavigable Khong Falls on its southern border. Thus, lowland Laos, inclusive of the Plain of Jars, sits as a land island, disadvantaged in the new international era by the lack of highways, railways, and port access.[1] Given the relative economic dynamism of its neighbors, Laos' full economic potential as a modern crossroads for trade and transport is yet unmet.

Contemporary Laos has changed little over the decades. It remains a largely rural, subsistence, agrarian society of some 6.2 million people divided

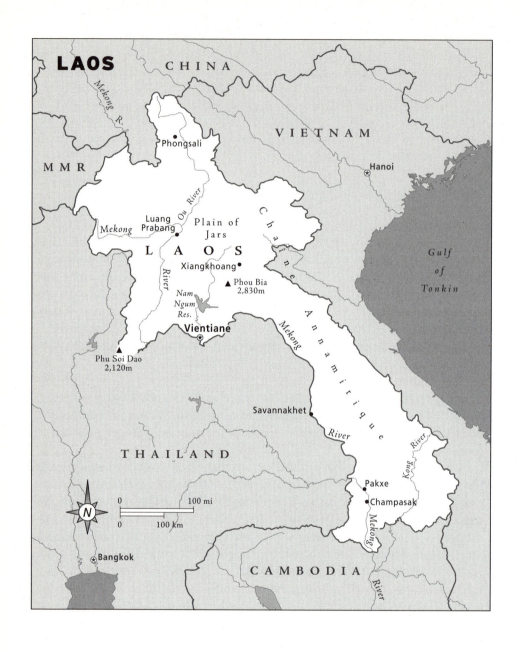

LAOS

CHINA

Mekong R.

MMR

VIETNAM

Phongsali

Hanoi

Ou River

Luang
Prabang

Plain of
Jars

Mekong

L A O S

River

Xiangkhoang

▲ Phou Bia
2,830m

Nam
Ngum
Res.

Gulf
of
Tonkin

A
n
n
a
m
i
t
i
q
u
e

Mekong

Vientiane

▲
Phu Soi Dao
2,120m

Savannakhet

River

THAILAND

Kong River

N

0   100 mi

0   100 km

Pakxe
Champasak

Mekong

Bangkok

CAMBODIA

River

among over forty ethnic groups, with the dominant lowland Lao consisting of just over 4 million people. The population density of Laos is the lowest of all Asian countries. Theravada Buddhism, variably blended with local spirit beliefs, predominates among the Lao and among many upland groups. Most ethnic Lao are isolated from both their regional neighbors and the world, as well as from upland ethnic minorities within Laos itself.

Almost all Lao are poor. The household economy is based on rice and still relies on water buffalo—with over 1,200,000 head, there is roughly one water buffalo for every five persons in Laos.[2] Modern farming techniques and equipment have been slow to reach Lao farmers. Amazingly, less than 5 percent of the country is suitable for agriculture, yet 80 percent of Lao work in the sector. In spite of recent economic gains from economic reforms, Laos' per capita gross national income in 2011 was only $1,130.

Contemporary problems in Laos originate from centuries-old conflicts, when ancient Lan Xang—"the Kingdom of a Million Elephants"—was a battleground for the expansionism of neighboring states. It was not until the fourteenth century that a semblance of national unity emerged. However, dynastic quarrels in the eighteenth century undermined this unity, and the area was divided into the kingdoms of Luang Prabang in the north, Champasak in the south, and Vientiane in the central region.

Vietnam and Thailand periodically plundered Lao kingdoms until the French colonized the area beginning in the late 1880s. In 1899, the French claim of suzerainty consolidated Laos into a single political unit, but French rule did little to modernize or integrate the nation. On the contrary, a small group of elite Lao families was allowed to consolidate its power; thus, the Lao emerged from colonial rule (after World War II) more divided, isolated, and backward than ever.

From 1941 to 1945, the Japanese ruled Laos, although the collaborating Vichy French administered many governmental affairs. At the end of the war, the Gaullist French recaptured Vientiane, the administrative capital, and fought a group called the Lao-Issara (Free Lao), which established a government-in-exile in Bangkok. This group became the forerunner and nucleus of the separate procommunist, anti-French Neo Lao Hak Sat (NLHS)—the Lao Patriotic Front. Lao-Issara was led by Prince Souvanna Phouma and his half-brother, Prince Souphanouvong, who later broke off and joined the NLHS, which was operating in areas held by the Vietminh. By 1953, the NLHS's military force, known as the Pathet Lao, had seized control of the nation's northeastern provinces.

In 1954, France accorded self-government to Laos at the Geneva Conference, which effectively gave Laos complete independence. The aftermath of the Geneva Conference was a period of disarray for Laos, as the competing sides vied for control of the populace and the countryside. Also in 1954, when the Pathet Lao was making significant military gains in large areas of the countryside, the United States sponsored a coup by anticommunists against Souvanna Phouma, who had become premier of the new nation but was considered too much of a neutralist by the U.S. government. The coup failed, but Souvanna Phouma was given notice that even neutralist policies were considered intolerable by the United States. When a right-wing government appeared in 1955, the United States immediately began a $45 million annual aid program.

In 1957, the neutralists, led by Souvanna—this time with backing from the United States—set up a government emphasizing national unity, with cabinet posts for leftists and rightists. In special elections called for in the Geneva agreements, NLHS candidates won the majority of seats, an outcome deemed intolerable by Souvanna's government and by U.S. diplomats. To overturn the results of the election and reverse the apparent popular trend toward a communist government, the United States—principally through the CIA—extended massive support to right-wing regimes that excluded NLHS representation. There were numerous coups d'état during this period as anticommunist leaders jockeyed for power. However, the major beneficiary of governmental chaos was the NLHS movement, which continued to expand its control as it received increasing amounts of military supplies and support from the Soviet Union.

At the second Geneva Conference, in 1961, neutralist Souvanna, leftist Souphanouvong, and rightist Boun Oum agreed on coalition rule. The United States reversed its policy and supported Souvanna Phouma's appointment as prime minister (after he gave secret permission to the United States to bomb Pathet Lao areas). The coalition collapsed almost immediately, however, as factions maneuvered for power. The NLHS broke from the coalition, and Souvanna Phouma's Royal Lao government, a constitutional monarchy, became a virtual client of the United States.

Escalation of the Vietnam War changed the nature of the struggle between the NLHS and Royal Lao government forces. Hanoi's interest in Laos increased as its need for sanctuaries from U.S. bombing became paramount. Vietnam, in violation of the Geneva agreements, escalated its presence in the northeastern provinces of Laos as the United States, also in violation of the agreements, began secret bombing missions to Laos in 1964. In the following years, the landlocked nation became one of the most heavily bombed countries in history; some 2.1 million tons of bombs were dropped between 1964 and 1972 (about two-thirds of a ton per Lao).[3] Despite this ferocity, the strategic effect of the bombing was minimal, prompting the CIA to train and supply Hmong and other upland peoples, introduce military advisers, and use the U.S. Agency for International Development as a front for intelligence and training purposes. Laos became the battleground for a neighboring war fought by surrogate powers.

The Laos Peace Accords came in 1973 as the American withdrawal from Vietnam was completed. The accords called for stopping the bombing, disbanding foreign-supported forces, removing all foreign troops, and instituting the coalition Provisional Government of National Unity (PGNU). The new ministries were divided between the Royalists and the Pathet Lao. At the time of the signing of the accords, the NLHS controlled about three-fourths of all Lao territory and one-half of the population. Both sides were allowed to keep their zones of control until elections could be arranged.

The well-organized Pathet Lao (now called the Lao People's Liberation Army) prevailed over the Royal Lao faction in the coalition government, which lacked discipline, was enervated by family feuds, and was considered a puppet of the United States. The Pathet Lao spoke convincingly to the rural people of Laos, who had seen their agricultural base destroyed, their population dislocated, and their villages destroyed.[4] No family had been left unscathed by the civil war and the U.S. bombing.

In December 1975, the Pathet Lao dissolved the PGNU, abolished the 622-year-old monarchy, and established the Lao People's Democratic Republic (PDR). The change in government was preceded by communist victories in Vietnam and Cambodia and by procommunist demonstrations throughout Laos. The rightist ministers fled, and all power was eventually assumed by the communists. Souvanna Phouma resigned, and Kaysone Phomvihane, general secretary of the newly formed Lao People's Revolutionary Party (LPRP), became the new prime minister. A Supreme People's Council was set up with Prince Souphanouvong as president and chief of state, while Kaysone Phomvihane—virtually unknown to all but a handful of communist leaders before 1975—assumed political and administrative control of the country. In contrast to Vietnam and Cambodia, where communists came to power as a result of military victory, the change of government in Laos came about relatively peacefully.

The communist victory changed Lao politics fundamentally. For centuries the region had been dominated by a small group of wealthy families that wielded great political and economic influence. Most of those families fled to Thailand, Europe, or the United States, and those that remained underwent "reeducation" programs to cleanse them of their "bourgeois mentality." An estimated 300,000 persons, many of them the most educated in Laos, fled to Thailand following the change in government. The flight of educated Lao and the systematic expunging of civil servants of the former administration created a leadership vacuum that seriously impaired the government's ability to administer and implement new programs.

The new government moved quickly to eradicate the worst vestiges of what they considered bourgeois society by banning nightclubs, massage parlors, and dance halls. Private enterprise was stifled, and the government attempted, rather feebly, to collectivize farms. Most farmers resisted collectivization and continued subsistence production.[5] The government's reeducation programs, affecting thousands of Lao, made the populace wary of the new regime. Refugees reported arrogant bureaucrats and repressive rules and regulations.

Another major change was the withdrawal of the United States as a principal player in Lao politics. Most Western aid, which had funded over 90 percent of the Royal Lao government budget, ended when the communists took power, although the countryside was still devastated from the war. Although the United States did not break diplomatic relations with Laos after the communist takeover, U.S. involvement became peripheral, and the Soviet Union and Vietnam filled the vacuum. In 1979, the leaders of Laos and Vietnam signed a joint revolutionary declaration, the Treaty of Friendship and Cooperation, granting Vietnam the right to maintain some 40,000 troops in Laos. China soon accused Vietnam of working to create an Indo-Chinese federation dominated by the Vietnamese and withdrew the aid it had given to Laos for numerous development projects. The Soviet Union, supplying some 2,000 advisers and $50 million in annual aid, was Laos' superpower patron until 1991, when the U.S.S.R. collapsed.

The Lao PDR was ruled from 1975 to 1991 without a constitution. When one was finally adopted, it strengthened the presidency (at that time held by Kaysone), although the LPRP retained its position as the primary institution. Civil liberties were allowed "as prescribed by law," but the major advantage of the document was to provide a semblance of stability and predictability with regard to governmental affairs.

President Kaysone's death in November 1992 provided an opportunity for Laos to usher in a new generation of leaders more in tune with the international movement away from communism and toward democracy. However, Prime Minister (and former defense minister) Khamtay Siphandone, who was nearly seventy years old, was named leader of the LPRP, and National Assembly chairman Nouhak Phoumsavanh, who was nearly eighty, was named president. Their hard-line conservatism and provincial outlook frustrated those who wanted Laos to look more toward the West for direction.

In the late 1980s, Laos, like China and Vietnam before it, opened its economy by pursuing a "new thinking," or a market-based approach. Under the "New Economic Mechanism," the government jettisoned failed collectivization policies and centralized economic allocation. By 1995, the twentieth anniversary of LPRP rule in Laos, market economics was in command and party rule was far less doctrinaire. The LPRP also gave new life to

Buddhism by restoring temples and encouraging the *sangha*, or Buddhist monastic order, to play a role in development. In what was surely a communist-world first, the funeral service for the regime's first president, the "Red Prince" Souphanouvong, was an entirely traditional Buddhist ceremony, with no ideological overtones.

In 1996, the Sixth Congress of the LPRP further moved Laos toward comprehensive but slow economic reforms. Personalism, conservatism, and nationalism remained the dominant characteristics of the leading party. Military generals held six of the nine positions in the Politburo; party leaders viewed the continuation of their unity (in a nation made up of numerous ethnic groups) as the primary national goal. This goal has been difficult to achieve because the economic reforms have made the urban areas wealthier, whereas the rural areas, populated by minorities, have remained poor.

Since the new millennium began, the Lao government has continued to liberalize the economy but retained its centralized monopoly on political life. Signs of Asian-style economic dynamism have emerged, mainly in urban areas, but economic reform has yet to modernize or transform the economy to the degree it has in neighboring Vietnam. Laos continues to be both Buddhist and authoritarian, both Marxist and capitalist. Regime leaders, now portraying themselves as the protectors of Theravada Buddhism, build monuments to legendary Buddhist monarchs of fourteenth-century Lan Xang to prop up their legitimacy.

Khamtay, at eighty-three years of age, was replaced as state president in 2006 by Choummaly Sayasone, yet another old-line conservative. He has yet to be replaced. Other leadership changes produced by the Eighth Party Congress did little to dislodge political hard-liners from the Politburo. The post–revolutionary generation leaders who did emerge from the Congress celebrate ties to Laos' communist past. Among the party's most notable new insiders are the sons of Kaysone and Khamtay, suggesting hints of dynastic rule.[6]

Buoasone Bouphavanh, a younger official who became the regime's fifth prime minister in 2006, surprisingly resigned in late 2010 claiming "family problems" as the cause. Speculations abounded as to the real reason, but one seasoned observer believes that loss of support by party bosses only months before the Ninth Party Congress of 2011 was the result of Buoasone's attempt to crack down on the "negative phenomena" of corruption.[7] Whatever the reason, his replacement, former Pathet Lao guerrilla Thongsing Thammavong, ten years Buoasone's senior, represents a return of the old guard.

INSTITUTIONS AND SOCIAL GROUPS

Lao People's Revolutionary Party

Since 1975, the country's dominant institution has been the LPRP, the communist party that emerged from the Pathet Lao leadership. Led by elderly revolutionaries who fought against the French, Japanese, and Americans, the party has practiced democratic centralism, requiring party leaders' unanimous support in all decisions. Policy was formulated and implemented by the party Politburo, led by Kaysone Phomvihane. Kaysone had emerged in December 1975 from the caves of a northern province where he and his Pathet Lao colleagues had hidden to escape U.S. bombing. Outside the inner circle of the Pathet Lao, few Lao knew him or knew about him, and Kaysone eschewed a cult of personality, living quietly and making himself available to very few visitors except communist allies. Little was known about his past except for his close association with Vietnam, where he had studied at the University of Hanoi.

Kaysone held the positions of prime minister and then president, as well as general secretary of the LPRP. Surrounded by colleagues from his revolutionary days in the 1950s, he changed his rule little after 1975. Continuity and stability were the themes of governmental leadership until 1979, when reforms were instituted that significantly changed the government's hard-line policies.[8] After that time, and especially after 1986, when the "new thinking" reforms were instituted, Kaysone visited noncommunist countries, and his activities were even reported in the press. Nevertheless, he remained one of the world's least-known leaders up to his death in 1992.

The LPRP, having failed to achieve popular support for its socialist policies, launched a series of reform policies in 1986 to decentralize economic decision-making and to liberalize, both economically and politically. In 1989—for the first time—the LPRP allowed elections for the National Assembly, Laos' nominal legislative body. Some 121 government-approved candidates ran for 79 seats, and 65 of the victors were party members.[9] Since the 2006 elections, all but 2 of the now-115 seats are held by members of the party. Assembly elections, little more than Soviet-style plebiscites for preselected LPRP candidates, mean little in a system where the assembly institution enjoys little independence from the party apparatus. In spite of cosmetic changes, the locus of all power in the system remains the 11-member Politburo, itself the product of a 61-member Party Central Committee.

To a certain degree, mass organizations that assemble youth, women, labor, or minority groups to follow party directives are more connected to the grass roots of Lao society than the LPRP itself. The Lao Front for National Construction (LFNC), for example, is charged with the daunting task of unifying Laos' disparate ethnic groups. Created in 1979, the LFNC's organizational reach extends to every administrative level of government in an effort to co-opt local leaders into the state apparatus.

The LPRP is corrupt. "Corruption is the ogre in the woodpile of Lao politics," according to one scholar, who adds, "Members of the Politburo and their families have become excessively rich."[10] Skimming off of concessions in mining, timber, and hydropower projects is standard practice. Even as aggregate economic growth raises per capita averages, it is members of the party and their close associates who are experiencing the most gains.

Unlike Vietnam and China, where the military is increasingly separate from party leadership, military leadership remains integrated with the LPRP. After a focused recruitment effort, party membership now stands above 190,000, more than double the party's size in 1995. It remains to be seen whether a younger generation of leaders will emerge to replace the "revolutionary generation" of the LPRP. Buoasone's sudden resignation in 2010 doesn't bode well for such a possibility.

International Aid Community

The Lao PDR government collaborates extensively with the international aid community in pursuing its development policies. International agencies, regional bodies, and bilateral aid programs do not directly control policy but do much to set the policy agenda in Vientiane. A principal international partner, for example, is the United Nations Development Program (UNDP). It ties its current efforts in Laos to achieving UN Millennium Development Goals. Focusing on programs to reduce Laos' poverty rate by half and move the country out of least developed country (LDC) status, the UNDP guides a formalized roundtable process of aid coordination with various UN agencies and the network of embryonic civil society organizations now operating in the country.[11]

Other principal partners with the Lao government include the Asian Development Bank, through its Greater Mekong Sub-Regional Program, the IMF and World Bank, and over fifty bilateral agencies of OECD countries that help prop up the Lao state. The Asian Development Bank alone is responsible for 75 loans worth over $1.7 billion since 1968. The World Bank is particularly influential in supporting the massive hydropower projects the Lao government is undertaking. Antiglobalization critics angrily indict the World Bank for manipulating Lao authorities and the policy agenda.[12]

Lao Abroad

Since 1975, over 300,000 refugees, mostly lowland Lao, have left the country. Ethnic Hmong, Mien, Lahu, and other upland groups recruited by the CIA for its secret war in Laos also compose a large segment of this migrant population. Without U.S. "allies" to protect them, many Hmong and others were subject to genocidal recrimination in the form of chemical-biological toxins falling from Vientiane aircraft in the late 1970s and 1980s. As reported by droves of refugees fleeing into Thailand, whole villages suffered illness and fatal hemorrhaging from "red, yellow, and green gases" dropped from the sky. Disastrous living conditions forced others, including many lowland Lao, to seek refuge as well. Refugees reported forced labor, torture, "seminar camps," and starvation.[13]

After years in Thai border camps, most refugees were resettled in third countries such as the United States, France, and Australia. A vocal segment of the overseas refugee community now actively lobbies foreign governments to exert greater pressure on the LPRP communist regime. Lao refugees regularly target their protests against the governments of the United States and Thailand for failing to address the refugee problem as well as ongoing human rights abuses by Vientiane. The plight of upland minority groups within Laos and the forcible repatriation of refugees from border camps draw the attention of Amnesty International and other human rights groups.

Among the Lao abroad is exiled crown prince Soulivong Savang, grandson of King Vattana. Laos' last king died in a reeducation camp following his overthrow in 1975. Soulivong has held meetings with U.S. government officials and pushed for a more aggressive international isolation of Vientiane. Residing in France, the crown prince remains a dim symbol of hope for Lao seeking regime change and restoration of a constitutional monarchy.

In 2007, Hmong community leader Vang Pao, a former CIA ally, was arrested at his home in California on evidence of plotting to overthrow the Lao government—an act in violation of U.S. law prohibiting Americans from acting violently against foreign governments that have peaceful relations with the United States. In support of the legendary leader, hundreds of Hmong-Americans flocked to the Los Angeles courthouse where Vang stood accused. Vang was eventually released on a $1.5 million bond. The alleged plot of Vang Pao and his coconspirators included smuggling Stinger missiles into rebel areas and hiring U.S. mercenary forces to launch an offensive on Lao government forces. Hmong rebels have in fact organized attacks within Laos in recent years, producing some fatalities. At the age of eighty-one, Vang Pao died in 2011. With him perhaps died any future rebellion activity from the Hmong abroad.

An increasing number of economic migrants from Laos, often undocumented, now work in Thailand as laborers. The wages earned and wealth created by these workers, together with the earnings of overseas Lao in third countries, often find their way back to relatives in Laos. In recent years, remittances from abroad, according to Lao government reports, accounted for as much as 28 percent of household earnings in many parts of Laos.[14] The Lao government has also sought, without great success, to entice wealthy and capable overseas Lao back to the country by offering them government jobs, new homes, and other perks.

State-Society Relations and Democracy

Laos, like its neighbors Cambodia and Myanmar, is an example of a state with little capacity to meet the needs of its citizenry or to mobilize its collective strength. Laos does not have a societal group that is independent of social controls and designs of state leaders. The LPRP dominates every aspect of Lao political life, having co-opted virtually the entire administrative class and local leadership. In Laos there is no independent intellectual class capable of competing with the state leaders. The long tradition of student activism seen in Thailand, Indonesia, and Burma is almost nonexistent. A 2009 attempt of antigovernment protest by a group of student activists led to arrests and exile in Thailand. Internet activism, to the extent it exists, is dominated by second-generation overseas Lao who indicate little desire to return to a country they technically never left.

Additionally weakening the Lao state is the absence of skillful or charismatic leaders. Kaysone Phomvihane's leadership resulted more from his control of the LPRP and from repression than from his capacity to gain the respect and approbation of the Lao people. Subsequent leaders function more as party managers than as mobilizers of popular sentiment or political will.

Political institutions beyond the LPRP are feeble or nonexistent. Whereas Thailand enjoys the symbolic importance of a king to provide overall state legitimacy, Laos has had no parallel institution since 1975. Buddhism is receiving renewed government support, but the institutionalization of the *sangha* as a political actor is weak compared to the role of the monastic order in Thailand and Myanmar. Moreover, increasing dependency on financial and technical assistance from international aid agencies and wealthy Asian entrepreneurs fosters patronage and corruption—phenomena of state weakness, not strength.

There is no semblance of democracy in Laos, nor has there ever been. The country's communist leadership has not instituted reforms permitting a representative system or civil liberties. It can be classified as a politically closed regime. Testimony to the Lao people's view that their government is not legitimate is the fact that since it came into power, about one in ten residents have left the country. Indeed, the regime's insecurity regarding its legitimacy is shown by its refusal to allow any kind of opposition or free elections. Civil society is closely monitored, although a 2008 law put in motion at the behest of the UNDP permits civil society organizations greater autonomy to operate. The government has also experimented with village-level elections.

The fall of communist governments in Eastern Europe as the new international era began did not affect the Lao people because they did not have access to information about these changes at the time. Greater exposure to the world since, due to increased tourism, new bridges to Thailand, and increased contact with China and Vietnam, is a notable change. The Lao government does not censor the Internet, according to Freedom House. Television broadcasts from Thailand are the public's main external link to the outside world. Nevertheless, the dearth of education in the country inhibits opportunities for a civic consciousness to develop. The country's first university was finally opened in 1996. Soochow University of China announced in 2012 plans to establish a branch campus in Vientiane.

Political liberalization, let alone democratization, is a distant prospect for Laos. Strong economic growth since 2000 is creating a fledgling urban middle class, but those benefiting most are those closest to the regime and least likely to pressure it to reform. Laos' LPRP rulers maintain a monolithic hold on political power and face no overt political opposition.[15] With regime change an unlikely prospect, greater political transformation depends on a generational shift in leadership.

ECONOMY AND DEVELOPMENT

Laos is one of the world's poorest countries. With a gross national income per capita of $1,130, and a poverty rate of nearly 26 percent, the standard of living is low. In Laos, only 20 percent of births are attended by a skilled professional compared to 99 percent in neighboring Thailand and 88 percent in neighboring Vietnam. About 80 percent of the labor force in Laos remains in agriculture, typically as rice farmers inhibited by poor distribution systems and market coordination. In rural areas, less than four out of ten residents have access to improved sanitation. The spread of HIV/AIDS is growing rapidly, and malaria, tuberculosis, and chronic diarrhea are widespread.

Although such extreme poverty is not new to Laos, the contrast with economic standards in the other ASEAN countries is obvious. Over the past decade, Laos has experienced limited progress in reducing the incidence of disease and improving basic living conditions. Yet, in measures of overall development, Laos annually joins Cambodia, Myanmar, and Timor-Leste among the bottom third of annual world rankings of the Human Development Index.

In terms of economic policy, LPRP leaders realized after only four years of rule that their agricultural and industrial policies were failing to revive the economy. In 1979, therefore, a process of decentralization was begun. By the early 1980s, pragmatic policies were formally set forth at the Third Congress of the LPRP. The government's control over the economy was loosened; agriculture began decollectivization; and new technology was introduced, resulting in larger crop output and self-sufficiency in rice for the first time since the revolution. These reforms were called *chin tanakan may* (new thinking), Laos' version of the Soviet Union's perestroika or Vietnam's *doi moi*.

The most fundamental changes, however, did not begin until 1986 at the Fourth Congress of the LPRP. These changes, called the "New Economic Mechanism," allowed family farms to completely replace the unpopular agricultural cooperatives. Also, market mechanisms generally replaced centralized planning. In 1988, Kaysone admitted that the party's policy of putting private traders out of business, collectivizing farmers, and nationalizing industry had caused the production and circulation of goods to come to a halt, grievously affecting the people's livelihood.[16] The World Bank had been critical of the government's policy and cited Laos' agricultural inefficiency, declining industrial output, dependency on loans from socialist nations (on poor terms), stagnant exports, and huge balance of payment deficits, all of which acted to perpetuate underdevelopment.[17]

The reforms emphasized grassroots economic units including factories, merchants' shops, and construction projects.[18] Rather than move directly from subsistence to large-scale collective farming, peasant families were encouraged to join the barter economy, trading their surplus production for commodities. State land was distributed to individual families on a long-term basis, and consideration was given to making such land inheritable.[19]

The reforms also included a new foreign investment code designed to attract outside investment to finance the Lao infrastructure, but the results were initially disappointing. Laos did not have a constitution or a civil code, a fact that frightened off many potential participants. Corruption also discouraged foreign investors reluctant to pay "tea money" to officials. An equally important problem was administrative capacity: Laos demonstrated little absorptive capability that would allow follow-through on investment and aid projects. Following its neighbors embroiled in the 1997 Asian economic crisis, Laos experienced triple-digit inflation and a currency collapse during the late 1990s. Laos' currency, the kip, fell 87 percent, from 1,080 to over 10,000 per dollar, greater than any other drop in the region.

Since 2000, however, Laos' economy has experienced rapid GDP growth, averaging above 7 percent from 2005 to 2011. Inflation has been moderate, and the kip has stabilized, although Thai baht and U.S. dollars remain in wide use. Foreign investment by Asian companies in textiles, food processing, and low-tech assembly is expanding Laos' once-pathetic industrial sector. Only 6 percent of GDP in 1990, industry now accounts for nearly 30 percent of economic activity. Drawing from financial and technical support from South Korea and Thailand, Laos opened a stock exchange in 2011.

Tourism, another recent arrival to the struggling Lao economy, now generates over $130 million per year with over a million annual tourist arrivals.[20] Laos' former royal capital of Luang Prabang, nestled along the Mekong River in the country's northern mountains, was declared a UNESCO World Heritage Site in 1995. Tourism, combined with international aid, creates strong incentives for the Lao government to keep the country open. Contrasting with Burma's military junta, the LPRP-led Laos depends mightily on international aid in its growth strategy.

Though amounts are not publicly disclosed by the government, most estimates put foreign aid at about 40 percent of Laos' GDP. Since 1989, when the United States granted its first assistance to Laos since the communist takeover, by supporting a $1 million antinarcotics project, international aid to Laos has gradually expanded to a diverse array of intergovernmental, bilateral, and nongovernmental sources. In addition to rural development, communications, and community health projects, the major focus of foreign assistance is on overcoming Laos' unfortunate landlocked geography. Thus, the construction of trans-Mekong bridges and hydroelectric dams gains much attention.

In 1994, Australia financed the construction of a bridge to Thailand near Vientiane, the first along the six hundred miles of river that form much of the Thai border. A second bridge to Thailand, in southern Laos, opened in 2006 and was financed by Japan. A third link across the Mekong is planned to connect northern Thailand and Laos with overland routes to Kunming, China, and plans for a fourth bridge—to Burma—exist. An on-again, off-again proposal for a high-speed train to link Laos (and the rest of Southeast Asia) with Yunnan Province, China, is reportedly back on track. Both countries view the project as critical to their future. The new bridges, along with improved land routes to Vietnam, function as globalization lifelines to landlocked Laos. Thai food processing and manufacturing companies, for example, are busily relocating factories to Laos due to the improved infrastructure. Mining, a transport-intensive industry, is also experiencing new private investment from Australian companies, much to the dismay of environmentalists.

Through assistance from the World Bank and the Asian Development Bank, the Lao government now pursues an economic growth strategy built on massive hydroelectric projects, aimed to feed the insatiable power grids of Thailand, China, and Vietnam. Twenty-five-year purchase agreements tied to the projects were a welcome arrival to Laos' cash-strapped government. Controversy surrounding resettlement of displaced villagers, environmental destruction, and the distribution of benefits tied to hydropower draws serious international attention. The current construction of the $1.3 billion, 1,070-megawatt Nam Theun 2 Dam, for example, will displace 100,000 people, or nearly one in sixty Lao citizens. At least ten other hydropower dams are in the construction or planning stage. Rumors abound that the government's goal is to construct seventy total dams. In 2012, somewhat remarkably, the government suspended plans to build the Xayaburi hydroelectric project on the Mekong after strident complaints from downstream neighbors.[21]

At current growth rates, Laos could graduate from LDC status by 2020. This achievement would meet a joint Lao government–UNDP goal. Notwithstanding income gains, poverty reduction faces significant challenges. Eight in ten Lao residents are still in rural areas far removed from Vientiane's fledgling factories and Luang Prabang's tourist trade. They remain even more distant from export revenues from mining and hydropower that are absorbed by government accounts. Economic opportunity for most rural and upland Lao remains sorely limited.

FOREIGN RELATIONS

As a landlocked nation, Laos has always had to rely on its neighbors for security. Traditionally, Thailand, China, and Vietnam have had the greatest impact on Lao political affairs because these nations share long borders with Laos and control its access to the oceans. After World War II, however, the United States became the paramount power, with almost total control over every aspect of Lao political and economic life.

Until 1975, the United States played the leading institutional role in Laos. By dominating the policies of the Vientiane administrations and financing the Lao military, the United States became the patron and the Lao government became a client of U.S. interests. To secure the continuation in power of pro-U.S. forces, the United States engaged in a secret war in Laos in the 1960s, which cost $2 billion annually. Covert operations and massive bombing raids over Laos were designed to strengthen the anticommunist government in Vientiane, demolish the Pathet Lao infrastructure, and interdict soldiers from North Vietnam. In the long run, however, none of these goals were achieved.

After 1975, the United States no longer had influence over the Lao government, and CIA-supported allies such as the Hmong were left to defend themselves. Not until 1987 did relations with the United States change, when the two governments signed agreements for crop substitution programs. Laos had agreed to make a "maximum effort" to stop opium trafficking, and in return, the United States removed Laos from its "decertification list" and reopened its aid program. The irony of these events was the previous tacit U.S. support of upland drug running as a means for upland groups to finance their war efforts.

A major source of tension between the United States and Laos concerned some five hundred U.S. troops from the Vietnam War classified as missing in action in Laos. The Lao government was bitter about U.S. demands to conduct excavations because it offered no compensation for the thousands of Lao continuing to die every year from miniature land mine bomblets (called "bombies"), full-size land mines, and other unexploded ordnance (UXO) still scattered throughout the Lao countryside. The lasting presence of UXO, the legacy of 580,000 U.S. bombing missions, continues to hinder rural development, rendering thousands of acres of arable land too dangerous to use.

In 2012, U.S. Secretary of State Hillary Clinton became the highest-ranking U.S. official to visit Laos since Secretary of State John Foster Dulles in 1955. Secretary Clinton visited an artificial limb center and met with UXO victims, but the United States has yet to sign the International Convention on Cluster Bombs. The visit, ostensibly to note the scheduled 2013 entry of Laos into the WTO, was viewed as yet another signal to China that it will not be the only superpower active in the region going forward.

Until recently, Vietnam was the country with the greatest influence on Laos' foreign and domestic policies. In 1975, Vietnam placed approximately 50,000 troops in the country. Although there was fear in the 1980s that Laos and Cambodia would be assimilated into a greater Indochina federation under Vietnamese dominance, such a confederation never occurred. All Vietnamese troops were withdrawn by 1990, and Laos began to assert a more independent policy by strengthening its relations with Thailand, ASEAN, and China.

Laos' relations with Thailand have been tense since the Pathet Lao took power, because the Thais viewed Laos as a base of support for insurgency and because the hundreds of thousands of Lao (and Cambodian) refugees who have crossed into Thailand are viewed as an economic burden. In 1987–1988, Laos and Thailand fought a bloody three-month war over a disputed border area. Later, as relations warmed, Thai businesspeople took advantage of the economic reforms in Laos to set up businesses, and border towns became market centers for Thailand. Thai companies are primary investors in the growing sectors of Laos' new economy.

Improved relations have not resolved the centuries-old problem of a strong Thailand versus a weak Laos. As reform began, sentiment from Laos emerged that Thailand, having failed to destroy Laos with its military power, was employing a new domination strategy: attacking Laos with economic power. Although the Lao government later distanced itself from this view, many Lao continued to fear that Thailand—with more than ten times the population of Laos and a history of aggression against its smaller neighbor—might once again intervene. Since the country joined ASEAN, with its strong principle of noninterference, many such fears in Laos have abated in the past decade.

In the new international era, no longer able to rely on Soviet aid, Laos has moved to improve relations with China, which remains an important trade ally and a major supplier of weaponry. Since 1990, China has invested over $1 billion in Laos, and two-way trade has risen rapidly. More important to China, however, are needed overland links through Laos to Thailand and its growing markets. In the Golden Triangle region, increased river trade on the Mekong has created greater incentives for improved overland highways and train routes linking China and Thailand via Laos. With support from the Asian Development Bank and the six countries of the Greater Mekong Sub-region, a project to complete a 1,800-kilometer (1,110-mile) international road from Kunming, China, to Bangkok, Thailand, was recently launched. Vientiane's government hosted the third Greater Mekong Subregion meeting in 2008.

After a fifteen-year process, Laos was formally offered WTO membership in late 2012. Classified as a least developed country, Laos' ascension to the global trading body followed special guidelines. The process required thirty-seven new laws, over fifty decrees, and nine new bilateral treaties before it could qualify. Gaining WTO membership is far more than a symbolic event because it creates easier access to export markets for the landlocked country. Aside from newly independent Timor-Leste, all other Southeast Asian countries were already WTO members when Laos was accepted.

CONCLUSION

Laos is the "forgotten country" of Southeast Asia because it is small and is no longer strategically important to the world's major powers. Its total population is far smaller than that of the city of Bangkok. Laos' leadership is un-known to the world, and its military capacity is practically nonexistent. In contrast to Thailand and Vietnam, Laos has changed little over the past several decades. Though the current mini–economic boom is altering Vientiane, and tourists now dot the streets of Luang Prabang, development in most of the country's towns and hill areas has remained largely static. Meeting its stated goal to exit LDC status by 2020 would be a major achievement for Laos. Such a feat, however, will require China-like growth rates and development efforts that reach Laos' diverse and largely rural populace.

NOTES

1. The Plain of Jars is a common name for the Xiangkhoang Plateau, where in certain areas hundreds of thick, three-meter-tall stone jars lie strewn across the plain. With the jars dating back to 500 BCE, their source and purpose remains a subject of Lao legend and of considerable archaeological debate.

2. Takai Yasuhiro and Thanongsone Sibounheuang, "Conflict between Water Buffalo and Market-Oriented Agriculture: A Case Study from Northern Laos," *Southeast Asian Studies* 47, no. 4 (March 2010): 452.

3. W. Randall Ireson and Carol J. Ireson, "Laos," in *Coming to Terms: Indochina, the United States, and the War*, ed. Douglas Allen and Ngo Vinh Long (Boulder, CO: West-view Press, 1991), 66.

4. Ibid.

5. The most seminal work documenting the difficulties of collectivizing agriculture in Laos is Grant Evans, *Lao Peasants Under Socialism* (New Haven: Yale University Press, 1990).

6. Geoffrey C. Gunn, "Laos in 2006: Changing of the Guard," *Asian Survey* 47, no. 1 (January/February 2007): 184–185.

7. Martin Stuart-Fox, "Family Problems," *Inside Story*, January 19, 2011, http://inside .org.au/family-problems.

8. Macalister Brown and Joseph J. Zasloff, *Apprentice Revolutionaries: The Communist Movement in Laos, 1930–1985* (Stanford, CA: Hoover Institution Press, 1986), 165.

9. Geoffrey C. Gunn, "Laos in 1989: Quiet Revolution in the Marketplace," *Asian Survey* 30, no. 1 (January 1990): 84.

10. Fox, "Family Problems," inside.org.au/family-problems.

11. Geoffrey Gunn, "Laos in 2007: Regional Integration and International Fallout," *Asian Survey* 48, no. 1 (January/February 2008): 64.

12. Merial Goldman, *Imperial Nature: The World Bank and Struggles for Social Justice in the Age of Globalization* (New Haven, CT: Yale University Press, 2005).

13. Jane Hamilton-Merritt, *Tragic Mountains: The Hmong, the Americans, and Secret Wars for Laos, 1942–1992* (Bloomington: Indiana University Press, 1993).

14. Bertil Lintner, "Laggard Laos Turns Economic Corner," *Asia Times Online*, January 10, 2008, www.atimes.com/atimes/Southeast_Asia/JA10Ae01.html.

15. Bertil Lintner, "Political Dissent in Laos," *The Irawaddy* 8, no. 6 (June 2000): http://www2.irrawaddy.org/article.php?art_id=1903&page=1.

16. *Asia Yearbook, 1990* (Hong Kong: Far Eastern Economic Review, 1990), 161.

17. Charles A. Joiner, "Laos in 1987," *Asian Survey* 28, no. 1 (January 1988), 104.

18. Ibid., 96.

19. Martin Stuart-Fox, "Laos in 1988," *Asian Survey* 29, no. 1 (January 1989): 81–82.

20. Gunn, "Laos in 2007," 66.

21. Jane Perlez, "Vietnam War's Legacy Is Vivid as Clinton Visits Laos," *New York Times*, July 11, 2012, http://www.nytimes.com/2012/07/12/world/asia/on-visit-to-laos -clinton-is-reminded-of-vietnam-war.html?_r=0.

RESOURCE GUIDE

A useful tool for bibliographic and other information on Laos is available from Australia National University's WWW Virtual Library: www.gksoft.com/govt/en/la.html. The University of California–Berkeley maintains a useful portal for digital and print resources on Laos: www.lib.berkeley.edu/SSEAL/SoutheastAsia/seaelec.html. Northern Illinois University's Southeast Asia Digital Library includes a range of useful links that cover government, academic, and research institutions specific to Laos: http://sea.lib.niu .edu. The University of Wisconsin–Madison Libraries similarly maintains a list of digital and print resources on Laos: www.library.wisc.edu/guides/SEAsia/resarea.html.

Readers can supplement this chapter with figures and publication information found in the country profile pages of data.UN.org. and ADB.org. Recent and archived news articles are maintained on specific country profile pages by BBC.com and NYTimes.com. Radio Free Asia maintains an active news site for Laos: www.rfa.org/english/news/laos. Useful country reports are also produced by the Bertelsmann Foundation at www .bti-project.org/home/index.nc.

Under the direction of the Ministry of Culture and Information, the *Vientiane Times* offers English-language news: www.vientianetimes.org.la. A similar news agency with closer connections to the LPRP is the Lao News Agency, at http://www.kpl.net.la/. The UNDP Lao provides useful economic development information: www.undplao.org. To appreciate the significance of hydroelectric power and its rising effects on Laos and the region, visit the Nam Theun 2 Dam Web site at www.namtheun2.com. Radio Free Asia created a useful multimedia site on the Xayaburi Dam project at www.rfa.org/english /multimedia/xayaburi-interactive-06062012130031.html. The Hmong International Human Rights Watch is found at www.hmongihrw.org. Students interested in Lao language and culture should visit Northern Illinois University's SEAsite at www.seasite.niu.edu/.

7

THE PHILIPPINES

IN THE QUEST FOR POLITICAL AND ECONOMIC DEVELOPMENT, THE experience of the Philippines is unique in Southeast Asia. The Philippines experienced a longer colonization and greater influence from the West than any country in the region. In many respects, foreign culture was thrust upon Filipinos through four hundred years under Spanish colonization and forty-eight years of American occupation—"four hundred years in a convent, and fifty years in Hollywood" Filipinos sometime joke. In fact, many legacies from these formative periods persist. The Philippines today faces difficulties that first arose during colonialism: oligarchic politics, personalism, chronic economic inequality, church-state tensions, and a fascination with celebrity. In the Philippines, development and democratization are stymied by the diminished capacity of the political system to cope with the people's demands. The result is more often institutional decay rather than development, and authoritarianism rather than accountability.[1]

The Philippines, with over 94 million people, recently overtook Vietnam as Southeast Asia's second most populous country. The archipelago includes 7,107 islands. Nine of these islands—including Luzon, the largest and most politically significant—contain 90 percent of the population. Over 170 languages are spoken across the islands, with Tagalog serving as the lingua franca. The religious makeup of the Philippines reflects Spanish and U.S. colonial influences, as well as the country's proximity to Muslim neighbors Malaysia and Indonesia. Officially, over 81 percent of the current population is Catholic; Protestant and evangelical groups account for another 12 percent; Islam, at 5 percent, prevails across many of the southern islands.

The Philippines is largely poor, with a gross national income of $2,210. One in three Filipinos lives below the national poverty line. Pockets of wealth and modernity do exist in urban areas of Manila and other principal cities. Despite political dysfunction, lawlessness, and endemic corruption, the country's economy has experienced modest aggregate growth in recent decades,

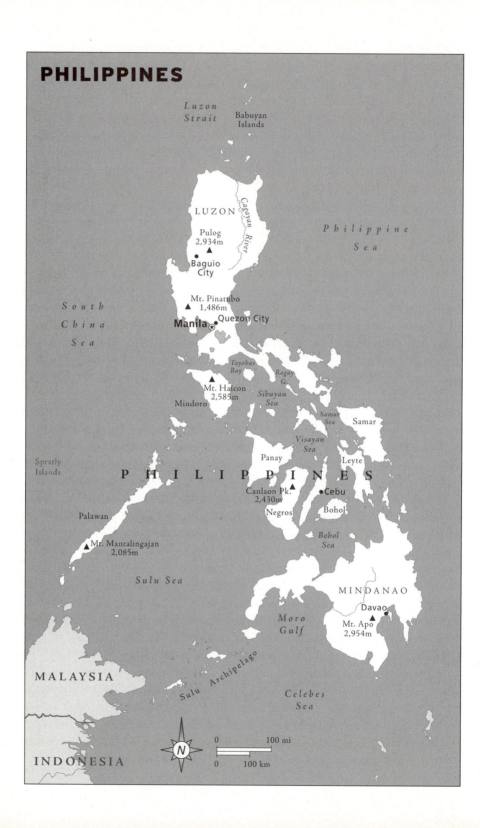

PHILIPPINES

Luzon Strait

Babuyan Islands

LUZON

Cagayan River

Pulog
2,934m ▲

● Baguio City

Philippine Sea

South China Sea

Mt. Pinatubo
▲ 1,486m

Manila ● ⊛ ● Quezon City

Tayabas Bay

Ragay G.

▲ Mt. Halcon
2,585m

Mindoro

Sibuyan Sea

Samar Sea

Samar

Visayan Sea

P H I L I P P I N E S

Panay

Leyte

Spratly Islands

Canlaon Pk. ▲
2,430m

● Cebu

Negros

Bohol

Palawan

▲ Mt. Mantalingajan
2,085m

Bohol Sea

Sulu Sea

MINDANAO

Davao ●
▲
Mt. Apo
2,954m

Moro Gulf

MALAYSIA

Sulu Archipelago

Celebes Sea

INDONESIA

N

0   100 mi

0   100 km

and a middle class is emerging. A national audience favoring authority grounded in formal institutions rather than personalism exists, but "violence and guile" have tragically operated as the currency of social mobility.[2]

In many respects the experience of the Philippines parallels a Latin American trajectory more than it does Asian political history. The long Spanish and shorter (but also influential) U.S. domination of the Philippines left a mixed legacy. From the Spanish, the Filipinos inherited not only Catholicism but a highly inequitable system of land tenure dominated by a powerful land-owning class. The landed families and the hierarchical society, still powerful in Filipino politics, were rooted in clan warfare and Spanish feudalism. U.S. rule nudged the country's political structures toward competitive democracy, introduced a system of public education that vastly improved literacy rates (along with incorporating English as a national language), and fostered the rise of technocrats, bureaucrats, and entrepreneurs.

The U.S. presence from 1898 to 1946 (a consequence of the Spanish-American War) provoked Filipinos to wage an unsuccessful war against their new occupiers. Politically, occupation helped nurture provincial leaders and a nascent oligarchy at the expense of the masses.[3] It also integrated the Philippine economy into the U.S. economy along colonial lines. The economic relationship between the Philippines and the United States was built on the primary goods produced for the American market, such as tobacco, sugar, and tropical fibers. In fact, the U.S. administration of the Philippines wasn't declared temporary until sixteen years after the initial occupation, when President Woodrow Wilson pushed the Philippine Autonomy Act through the U.S. Congress. The act supported a transition to free, democratic government—an event delayed by further squabbling among American politicians, the Great Depression, commonwealth status in 1935, and Japanese occupation during World War II.

Philippine independence, proclaimed on July 4, 1946, began a period of semidemocratic rule within the context of a continuing oligarchy. A series of democratically elected presidents ruled over a society still pervaded by personalism and *compadrazgo* (godfather-based ritual kinship). The greatest democratic gains, however, were during the four years the country had under President Ramon Magsaysay, who died in a tragic plane crash in 1957. The magnetic Magsaysay, elected on the basis of his successful crushing of the communist Huk rebellion and his clean image, promoted civil liberties and enhanced Philippine democracy. His legacy remains larger than his successes in government, since he struggled to manage the young postcolonial democracy. Violence perpetrated by the private armies surrounding the nation's elite families continued during his tenure and long afterward.

When Ferdinand Marcos was first elected president in 1965, the Philippines was experiencing economic growth and political stability. The vital

Liberal and Nacionalista Parties, despite their fluid, nonideological nature, ensured a lively competition for public office. At the same time, Philippine society suffered from problems that originated during the colonial era, the most salient of which were social and economic inequality, corruption, food shortages, and widespread violence.

In 1969, Marcos became the first president in the postindependence Philippines to be reelected. His reelection was bought in the sense that he gave government funds to local officials who manipulated the vote in his favor. A constitutional provision precluded a third term, so Marcos planned to stay in power by abrogating the constitution and asserting that national crises demanded extraordinary measures. His proclamation of martial law in September 1972 ended formal democratic rule and began a fourteen-year period of authoritarian rule.

A majority of Filipino citizens supported Marcos's initial steps to end the breakdown of law and order, his promise of land reform, and his strengthening of the army against insurrections by communists throughout the archipelago and by Muslim dissidents in the southern islands. This support dissipated as it became clear that Marcos's achievements did not match his rhetoric and that the "temporary" period of martial law was merely a pretext to perpetuate his personal power.

Acting with the wholehearted support of the U.S. government and using his martial law powers, Marcos was both executive and legislator. To give legitimacy to his regime, he instituted referenda, all of which turned out a 90 percent vote in favor of his continued tenure. There were no checks on his self-appointed powers. Press censorship of antigovernment criticism, jailing of dissidents, lack of basic civil liberties, absence of a secret ballot, and control of ballot counting were the methods Marcos used to secure his rule.

By the mid-1970s, Marcos's so-named New Society initiatives under martial law began to disintegrate with the rise of lawlessness in the countryside; the realization that the "constitutional authoritarian" government was more authoritarian than constitutional; the imprisonment of respected political leaders such as Marcos's rival, Senator Benigno Aquino Jr.; and the growing awareness of a mismanaged economy. Unemployment rose to over 20 percent and underemployment to 40 percent, real income shrank as inflation increased, and corruption reached an intolerable state under crony capitalism, whereby Marcos's friends were placed in charge of business conglomerates despite their lack of business acumen.

The "lifting" of martial law in 1981 temporarily improved the image of the New Society but did not significantly change the authoritarian political order. The government continued to be based on personalism, with no legitimacy granted to governmental institutions. Compared to the period before martial law and to conditions in neighboring countries, Philippine politics during the Marcos era were increasingly characterized by decay rather than by development. As the regime lost its legitimacy, the Armed Forces of the Philippines became less professional, the economy worsened, and the Communist Party of the Philippines and its military arm, the New People's Army (NPA), strengthened, thereby undermining the original rationale for martial law. Economically, Marcos created monopolies for himself, his family, and political cronies. The country's most profitable exports, such as sugar, coconuts, and tobacco, were thoroughly under his control, with profits syphoned off to offshore accounts.

In August 1983, after the hierarchy of the Philippine Catholic Church and business leaders had turned against Marcos, and when Marcos's health was known to be precarious, Senator Aquino returned to the Philippines after several years of exile in the United States. Aquino, the single greatest challenger to President Marcos, was dramatically assassinated the moment he stepped out of the airplane that had flown him back to his country. The almost universal belief of Filipinos in the government's complicity in this assassination released long-suppressed grievances. The Marcos regime would no doubt have fallen even without Aquino's martyrdom, for Filipinos already knew that Marcos and his associates were responsible for the country's low vitality, whereas other noncommunist Southeast Asian nations were flourishing.[4]

After Aquino was assassinated, the Philippines suffered disastrous declines in industrial and agricultural production and in wages and employment as well as capital flight, high inflation, severe undernourishment for children in rural areas, and a rich-poor gap wider than in any other nation in the region. While the other noncommunist Southeast Asian nations boasted high growth, it posted negative growth rates.

A momentous event in contemporary Philippine politics took place during three remarkable months, from December 1985 through February 1986. Bowing to intense pressure from the United States, wishing to take advantage of his improved health during a remission of his illness, desiring to end opposition attacks on him, sensing the disarray of potential opposition candidates, and confident about his capacity to engineer a mandate, Marcos called for snap elections to be held on February 7, 1986.

From the moment Marcos announced the elections, the key question was whether the opposition could unite around a single candidate, and the answer was unclear until the final filing day. Previously, the opposition had been able to unite only in its disdain for Marcos. Because of the highly personal nature of Philippine politics, the competing ambitions of potential leaders, and Marcos's ability to manipulate and co-opt rival forces, the opposition had a difficult time presenting a serious alternative.

Structurally, the opposition suffered from the disintegration of the two-party system during martial law. Instead, there were now many parties and organizations, each with an ambitious leader who wanted to be the candidate to run against Marcos. Corazon Aquino, the widow of the martyred Senator Benigno Aquino Jr., emerged as the person around whom all the opposition-ists could coalesce.

Her genuine reluctance to lead added to her appearance as a sincere, honest, and incorruptible candidate, precisely the antithesis of the president. A grassroots groundswell of support culminated in a petition with over a million signatures from Filipinos urging her to run for the presidency. Aquino fashioned an eleventh-hour agreement to run, with a rival presidential candidate, Salvador H. Laurel, as her vice president. For the first time since 1972, when martial law was declared, the opposition had achieved unity.

Candidate Aquino proclaimed a "people's campaign," realizing that she could not match the president in financial or organizational strength. Marcos and his campaign had easy access to government money, which allowed him to raise officials' salaries, decrease taxes, and lower fuel and utility rates. By the end of the campaign, some $500 million from the government treasury had been spent to reelect the president. In contrast, the opposition spent $10 million, all of it raised from donations.

Aquino's campaign speeches stressed her sincerity and honesty while vilifying the president for his corruption and immorality. She cited evidence that the president had lied both about his role as a hero in World War II and about his fortune of several billion dollars in real estate around the world. Aquino's major theme was that Marcos had brought economic ruin and political dictatorship to the nation and that she would restore integrity.

Marcos's campaign focused on his experience, including his wartime record, in contrast to his opponent's "naïveté." He stressed the need for strong male leadership rather than weak female leadership, suggesting that a woman's place was in the bedroom rather than in the political arena. Marcos, a staunch ally of U.S. President Ronald Reagan, accused Aquino of planning to cancel the Military Bases Agreement with the United States and that communists had taken over Aquino's campaign.

The voting was marred by fraud committed by Marcos supporters. When the "official" count gave Marcos 54 percent of the vote, the National Assembly—the final arbiter for voting controversies—proclaimed Marcos the winner, but the opposition launched a peaceful crusade of civil disobedience to bring down Marcos and allow the real winner, Aquino, to assume office. The U.S. State Department, official observers, journalists from dozens of nations, the Catholic Church, and most Filipinos agreed that Aquino had actually won the election by a large margin. In an embarrassing statement, Reagan indicated that Marcos's claim of fraud on the Aquino side deserved equal attention.[5]

As Aquino's civil disobedience campaign took hold, a series of high-profile defections from the president began. Defense Minister Juan Ponce Enrile and Lieutenant General Fidel Ramos, vice chief of the armed forces, defected from the Marcos camp and called for Aquino's ascension to the presidency.

When Marcos threatened to retaliate by bombing the headquarters of Enrile and Ramos, thousands of Filipinos—urged on by the archbishop of Manila, Cardinal Jaime Sin—surrounded the building, some even lying in the streets to keep the tanks from approaching. This display by students, farmers, nuns, and shop owners became known as "People Power." The tank commanders eventually retreated, and many defected to the opposition. The United States signaled its support of the rebellion, thereby undermining Marcos's claim that only he enjoyed the confidence of the superpowers. On February 25, 1986, Aquino and Laurel proclaimed the people's victory and were sworn in as president and vice president. The next day, Marcos fled the country with his family to live in exile in Hawaii, where he died on September 28, 1989, at the age of seventy-two.

With little bloodshed, People Power had triumphed over a regime that had dominated the political, social, and economic life of the Philippines for twenty-one years. The republic was awash with optimism that a new era in Philippine politics had arrived. The EDSA revolution, named after the avenue at the core of the demonstrations, transformed the political life of the country. In both political and economic realms, President Aquino's administration achieved notable gains. Filipinos again could express pride in their country's government after years of corrupt and demeaning leadership. Governmental institutions were rejuvenated under a president whose commitment to democratic values and procedures was irrevocable. Even during Aquino's first year as president, when she had virtually unlimited powers, she focused on restoring the democratic process. Civil liberties were reinstated, political prisoners were released, and free elections were regularized. These gains and others came about through the promulgation of a new democratic constitution approved by over 75 percent of the Filipino people in a February 1987 referendum.

Aquino had raised the people's expectations with promises of reform in all areas of life. She promised the end of the politics of personalism and the beginning of the politics of principle. Compared to the recent past in the Philippines, the Aquino administration earned high marks, but judged against higher standards, such as those of its Asian neighbors, its record was weak. Although the level of corruption and privilege decreased significantly under her administration, Aquino failed to change the system in a fundamental way. As with all Philippine presidencies during the country's postindependence period, the Aquino administration was also characterized by oligarchic rule, economic and social inequality, desperate poverty, and the politics of personalism. Within four years of assuming the presidency, Aquino survived six coup attempts.

Aquino's initial and unsuccessful attempts to end communist insurgency were based on reconciliation, a policy the armed forces vigorously fought against, claiming the NPA insurgents were taking advantage of the military's soft line by strengthening their positions. To keep the military from rebelling, Aquino's counterinsurgency policy eventually moved toward a more conservative, hard-line approach, including support for community vigilante groups established to repulse the rebels. These localized anticommunist self-defense organizations proliferated with the failure of ongoing peace negotiations between the Aquino government and the NPA. Aquino's endorsement of vigilantism was a sign that the communist movement was still extremely active, despite her administration's reforms. It also invited international criticism that her government was prone to "serious and unjustifiable" violations of human rights and had "turned the whole of the Philippines into a battlefield pitting civilian against civilian."[6]

Contending with a desperately sick economy resulting from mismanagement by the previous regime, the Aquino administration achieved modest aggregate growth. In development policy, however, Aquino failed to pursue meaningful land reform and ineffectively dealt with corruption allegations against her own family members. Her Comprehensive Agrarian Reform Program was compromised by loopholes allowing her family to retain longheld family land. At the time it was passed, 169 of the 200 elected members of Congress were leaders of established landowning families or otherwise related to landed elites. Aquino's six-thousand-hectare hacienda on Luzon, named "Luisita," remained farmed by tenants and untouched by her own agrarian reform plan.

In short, Aquino failed to institutionalize the overwhelming personal support she received from the populace. She did not develop a political party that could carry on her reform policies when she was no longer in office. Her followers, who affectionately called her "Tita Cory" (Aunt Cory), expected that she would solve the nation's problems single-handedly. The proliferation of political parties during her administration weakened administrative discipline, as the leaders of various organizations vied for power rather than cooperated for the common good. Personalism once again triumphed over institutional legitimacy.

The post-Marcos period soon began to breed new disillusionment. Public opinion surveys showed that President Aquino's initial, almost universal support decreased steadily as her tenure in office lengthened. Beginning in December 1989 with a failed military coup attempt that temporarily destabilized the government, a series of dreadful events occurred that many Filipinos saw as ominous indications that the government's mandate was tenuous. A horrendous earthquake in July 1990, which devastated much of northern Luzon, was followed by the Iraqi invasion of Kuwait, which raised the price of oil in the Philippines, undermining the fragile economy. These events were followed by a series of destructive typhoons and floods that killed hundreds and created thousands of homeless, while also lowering crop yields across the country.

Then, in June 1991, Luzon's Mount Pinatubo erupted after having been dormant for five hundred years. In the most devastating volcanic eruption in modern Asian history, eight hundred Filipinos died from volcanic destruction and related diseases. Clark Air Force Base, which was situated only about twenty miles from Mount Pinatubo, was buried beneath several feet of ash and subsequently closed down by the United States. The immediate effect was the loss of 70,000 jobs and $500 million in U.S. foreign aid.

After intense public speculation, Tita Cory decided not to seek a second term. (The constitutionality of a second term was part of the debate.) Seven candidates declared their intention to become president, all but one of whom represented traditional interests. The most notorious of the *trapos*, or traditional politicians (*trapos* is also a Tagalog word for "rags"), was former first lady Imelda Marcos, known worldwide for her 1,200 pairs of shoes. Aquino endorsed her minister of defense, Fidel V. Ramos, who was subsequently elected in May 1992 by plurality with only 23.4 percent of the popular vote. Ramos was known for his heroism in turning against his former boss, Ferdinand Marcos, in 1986 and for his competent leadership in defending Aquino against army-initiated coups. Nevertheless, he was laconic and careful to a fault.

Ramos faced many of the same crises Aquino had been unable to solve: chronic crime; ransom kidnappings; continuing insurgencies by communists, rightist soldiers, and Muslim separatists; a debilitated economy with the lowest growth rate among the ASEAN countries; and daily electrical brownouts. Ramos appointed commissions and directed his vice president to head up committees to solve these extraordinary problems. He also engaged in intensive visits to ASEAN member countries to discover which policies the Philippines could most effectively emulate. His economic program, implemented under the slogan "Philippines 2000," indicated the target year he believed the country could join the ranks of the newly industrialized countries.

During his six-year term (1992–1998), Ramos became known as the nation's most effective president of the postindependence period. In aggregate terms, his success is shown by record growth rates approaching 7 percent, overall growth in exports, and declining rates of absolute poverty. More specifically, he transformed the former U.S. naval base on Subic Bay into an enterprise zone with foreign investment; privatized certain state enterprises, including Philippine Airlines; and pushed through a fast-track mechanism for privatizing power companies, a decision that helped solve the ubiquitous problem of electrical shortages.

Critics pointed out that Ramos's privatization schemes often benefitted associates and that he favored foreign over local capital, as typified by his decision to allow foreign investors the right to 100 percent ownership in Philippine companies. Ramos, like Aquino before him, hewed closely to the neoliberal policy prescriptions of the World Bank and the IMF during his tenure. Leftists in the country accused him of creating a neocolonial state. Nevertheless, by the time he left office, the country was on more solid footing for market-based growth than when he began and his overall popularity was high.

Because the constitution allows for only a single term in office, Ramos's friends began campaigning for a constitutional amendment that would allow him to run for a second term. This attempt was strongly opposed by numerous opposition groups and by Cardinal Sin, who viewed the effort as a throwback to the days of the Marcos dictatorship. Finally, in the face of massive protest demonstrations, Ramos was forced to announce publicly and straightforwardly that he would not seek a second term. Even many of his supporters believed that enacting a constitutional amendment to allow a second presidential term would set a bad precedent.

Winning a landslide victory in the next election was his vice president, Joseph Estrada (nicknamed "Erap"—the Tagalog word for "friend," spelled backward), a garrulous populist known for his playboy lifestyle, which included womanizing and gambling, and for his starring roles in over 100 action films. He was favored overwhelmingly by the rural poor and opposed vociferously by the urban intellectuals who viewed him as rude, crude, and boorish.

Estrada began his six-year term of office auspiciously, with a majority in both houses of the Philippine Congress. The 1997 economic crisis had not affected the Philippines as strongly as it had Thailand, Malaysia, and Indonesia, at least partially because the economy was relatively weak. As the new millennium began, the Philippines boasted positive economic growth rates, a significant change from negative growth rates caused by recent financial contagion. Estrada's rhetoric favored the poor during his first two years as president, but he did not succeed in producing policies that alleviated the difficulties of the poorer classes.

In 2000, Estrada was accused of gross corruption, and an impeachment trial began in the Senate. Evidence showed that Estrada had been involved in illegal gambling activities and that he had accepted public monies for his private gain. His personal life was condemned, especially regarding his lavish gifts to his minor wives and mistresses. For many in the poorer classes, the trial was viewed as the elite's attempt to undermine and overthrow their champion. Nevertheless, the evidence grew and mass demonstrations against him took place.

In January 2001, the impeachment trial collapsed when the Senate voted 11 to 10 to disallow prosecutors from using bank documents as evidence proving Estrada's ill-gotten wealth. This act was viewed as a virtual exoneration of Estrada. Hundreds of thousands of Filipinos demonstrated against Estrada, and the military and most government officials rose against him until he was forced to leave Malacañang Palace, the traditional home of the president. The Supreme Court declared that the office of president was vacant and that the vice president could legally assume the presidency. Although Vice President Gloria Macapagal Arroyo had resigned her cabinet post months before to protest the Estrada administration, she nevertheless replaced Estrada.

Estrada was later arrested and tried on charges of plundering $300 million in state funds. He was eventually found guilty and sentenced to life in prison. An official pardon in 2007 by Arroyo kept Estrada from serving his sentence. The pardon was made on the condition that the former president stay out of politics permanently.

Under Arroyo, the Philippines continued to reverse the political stability won by Ramos but destroyed by Estrada. President Arroyo, often referred to as "GMA" by the media, was the daughter of Diosdado Macapagal, former president and doyen of the Filipino establishment. She was a classmate of Bill Clinton's at Georgetown University and holds a doctorate in economics from the University of the Philippines. She entered office facing a citizenry split over the constitutionality of the overthrow of Estrada. She also faced an economic malaise lingering from the Asian economic crisis and a refurbished military capable of attempting a coup d'état against her.

In July 2003, a rebel faction of the Armed Forces of the Philippines seized a shopping mall and the Oakwood luxury apartment complex in Manila's financial district. They demanded that Arroyo and others in her administration resign, claiming that corruption threatened the country. They also alleged that top military brass had staged bombing incidents on the island of Mindano to attract more U.S. military aid in the aftermath of the 9/11 attacks. The "Oakwood Mutiny," as it became known, ended hours later and resulted in the arrests of perpetrators and the resignations of officials who had mishandled the affair.

While completing the remainder of Estrada's presidential term, Arroyo publicly declared her desire to stay out of the 2004 presidential elections. Later reversing her decision, Arroyo ran and won against a field of weak candidates that included an Estrada ally, an anticorruption icon, and a broadcaster-cum-evangelist gadfly. The elections were marred by allegations of rigging and, later, the leak of an explosive election-time conversation between Arroyo and an election commissioner. Pollsters found that most Filipinos believed the elections were tainted. Calls for Arroyo's impeachment followed, and her unpopularity grew over the course of her presidency.

In 2006, upon the twentieth anniversary of the People Power movement to oust Marcos, Arroyo, citing coup rumors, made the unpopular move of declaring a state of emergency. She deployed the military to Manila streets and barricaded Malacañang Palace with barbed wire. Scheduled marches were canceled, and what was to be a celebration of Philippine democracy actually echoed Marcos's own 1972 imposition of martial law.[7] Arroyo lifted martial law three weeks later and then arrested suspected political enemies on specious charges.

A year later, the leader of the Oakwood Mutiny, Senator Antonio Trillanes, audaciously attempted yet another coup during his own court proceeding. A disorganized band of armed rebels stormed the courtroom and a nearby hotel and declared a new government. Following gunfire, the rebels were forced to give up hours later, and the coup was viewed as a publicity stunt as much as a serious attempt to seize power. Trillanes, who had only recently run for Senate from prison and won, waited in vain during the fiasco for a People Power uprising that never emerged.

Throughout her presidency, Arroyo maintained power via patronage to politicos, provincial bosses, and the military brass. It is a familiar but dangerous formula in Philippine politics. The hidden dealings of the country's top leaders often surface publically to reveal cronyism and family corruption. One corruption scandal involving government communications contracts, for example, even drew in Arroyo's husband, the "First Gentleman," who left the country for a year in self-exile. Also revealed during Arroyo's tenure was a secret meeting at the presidential place where bags of cash were handed to House of Representatives members who had been told to first support then later derail a "sham" presidential impeachment proceeding to thwart the possibility of a genuine attempt.[8]

Then, on November 23, 2009, an appalling episode of political violence occurred under Arroyo's watch. A prominent political family in Maguindano Province brazenly engineered the massacre of fifty-eight people in election-related violence. Members and associates of the Ampatuan family, who dominate the province and who share membership in Arroyo's political party, forcibly stopped a large convoy of political rivals en route to the election office. The group was on its way to file candidacy papers for their own nominee, Esmael Mangudadatu, who sought to challenge an Ampatuan family member for the provincial governorship. The perpetrators used high-powered firearms in the assault and then crushed and buried the victims in mass graves using an earthmover. Gruesome images of the incident were widely broadcast. Among the dead were Mangudadatu's wife, his sister, and numerous aides and supporters (including a pregnant woman), as well as thirty accompanying journalists who had come to document the candidacy filing.

In a public move, Arroyo immediately distanced herself from the Ampatuans. She quickly engineered their expulsion from her party and declared a state of emergency in the province. Nevertheless, the Ampatuan political clan—virtual warlords in Maguindano with a private army of 3,000—had helped GMA secure votes in her previous elections. Her known political ties to the family raised questions and fueled more doubts about her own integrity.[9] Domestically and internationally, the incident stood as a reminder of just how dirty Filipino politics remained under Arroyo's nine-year tenure. Over time, seventy-nine people faced charges in relation to the incident, but prosecution was slow. As cases have gone to court, a half dozen potential witnesses have been mysteriously killed and others intimidated.

In 2010, new elections were held for president and Congress. Constitutionally restricted from running for presidential office for a third term, Arroyo endorsed Gilbert Teodoro, her secretary of national defense, for the country's top spot. Teodoro, a young and rising politician, left his party and joined hers in 2009 to cement ties. The other presidential candidates included a prominent billionaire real estate developer and longtime politician, Senator Manuel Villar, and the former president Joseph Estrada. Remarkably, Erap returned to electoral politics after having been ousted by mass protests for corruption, criminally convicted, pardoned by his successor, and then politically rehabilitated by a constitutional court. For many of the poor, Estrada still symbolized their aspirations better than the alternative choices of family elites.

Another high-profile candidate was Benigno S. Aquino III, the only son of assassinated politician Benigno "Ninoy" Aquino and former president Corazon Aquino. Known as "Noynoy," Benigno Aquino's pedigree, résumé, and life story combined to produce electoral gold. Forced into exile under Marcos with his parents, he later saw his father dramatically assassinated, watched his mother lead a revolution, and took bullets himself during a failed coup attempt against her (one bullet remains lodged in his neck). He studied economics at Ateneo de Manila University and even took courses from Arroyo prior to her presidency. He worked for private businesses (including Nike Philippines) and served as a congressman for multiple terms. He announced his candidacy barely a month after his mother, the hero of anti-Marcos People Power, died of cancer. His campaign slogan was "If no one is corrupt, no one will be poor."

Victory came easy to Noynoy in a plurality vote of 41 percent (among nine candidates). Estrada amazingly came in second, with just over a quarter of the vote.[10] The billionaire Villar, who won the support of communist leaders during his campaign for his pro-poor platform, came in a distant third. Teodoro, Arroyo's candidate, garnered the support of barely 10 percent of Filipino voters, further cementing the failed legacy of Arroyo's presidency. GMA, not finished with politics herself, ran for a congressional seat in Pampanga, winning easily after having lavished her home district with special projects during her presidency.

After his victory, Aquino's supporters quickly updated his nickname to "PNoy" by combining the words "president" and "Noynoy." Among PNoy's first acts was an executive order to establish a truth commission to investigate his predecessor for graft, human rights violations, and other political mischief. The Supreme Court ruled the commission unconstitutional and it never formally emerged. Undeterred, the corruption allegations by PNoy against Arroyo persisted in public and eventually found their way into the criminal justice system. In classic Filipino-style politics, where political expediency trumps all, PNoy welcomed allegations against Arroyo by a member of the murderous Ampatuan clan, now in custody, that Arroyo had indeed engineered vote rigging and project kickbacks in their province.[11]

In late 2011, while hospitalized for a bone ailment, former president Arroyo was arrested and then detained at a military hospital for eight months before being released on bail. She currently faces separate charges of vote tampering, plunder, and graft. The latter two charges allege she and nine other officials siphoned $8.7 million from a state charity lottery for personal use and that she also took a $30 million bribe to abort a $327 million telecom deal with a Chinese company. If the charges are proven in court, the former president and her allies face sentences of life imprisonment.

As president, Noynoy Aquino put the country on a more positive track, though chronic problems persist. To address the country's protracted fiscal deficit, he revamped fiscal management and brought the debt-to-GDP ratio to a thirteen-year low. He also ordered officials to aggressively go after white-collar criminals and tax evaders. In 2012, the first person in Philippine history to be sentenced for tax evasion was imprisoned. That same year PNoy's reputation as a corruption fighter grew after a successful, high-profile impeachment of the country's Supreme Court chief justice, Renato Corona, who was found guilty of graft. Aquino also took on the Catholic Church over reproductive rights and won respect for his handling of the ongoing Spratly Islands dispute with China. International perceptions of the Philippines have improved under Aquino, and investors have cautiously increased investment. GDP growth has increased to an average of over 5 percent during his presidency, and the country's credit rating has improved to its highest level in a decade.

PNoy's high public approval ratings began to slip in 2012, however, due to rising inflation, ineffective antipoverty initiatives, and a growing reputation for indecisiveness. Somewhat predictably, the longer Noynoy is in power the more familiar the Filipino-style story sounds. Chronic problems remain, and most of them center around corruption. The country's corruption ranking sits between that of Syria and Iran, it is considered the third-most-dangerous country in the world for journalists, and its poverty levels remain on par with Myanmar, Uganda, and Tanzania. Its poverty rate of one in three people stands in stark contrast to those of its tiger economy neighbors, Thailand, Malaysia, and Indonesia, whose combined average is less than one in ten people.

It will take much more than a hero's pedigree and high-profile corruption cases for Noynoy Aquino to help the country overcome the structural forces and political culture that inhibit human development. Ever endemic to Filipino politics, personalism, subornment, and guile continue to shape events and define the oligarchic tendencies of Philippine democratic rule. Poverty of the many amidst the plenty of the privileged persists.

INSTITUTIONS AND SOCIAL GROUPS

Patron-Client Relations

The Philippine government can be described as clientelist, a form of societal organization in which political life centers on relationships that are largely person to person, informal, hierarchical, reciprocal, and based on *utang na loob*, an obligation of indebtedness. Because they are too weak, interest groups, political parties, the legislature, and other government institutions have been supplanted by clientelist relationships. Thus, political life in the Philippines has consisted of constantly changing coalitions of clientele groups that serve both to articulate mass interests and to ensure government control over the people. At the top, these patron networks create a type of predatory oligarchy that engages in "booty capitalism" and suffers from a "guns, goons, and gold mentality."[12]

Overreliance on patron-client networks undermines the importance and legitimacy of democratic institutions, resulting in the continued decay rather than development of Philippine politics. Under President Marcos, the clientelist nature of Philippine society was most evident in the president's grant of monopoly privileges to selected followers. Marcos put the control of numerous industries in the hands of his clients and assured them of immunity from loss; when the economy began to collapse and his authority lost legitimacy (after the assassination of Senator Aquino), Marcos lost control, first over the resources he used to reward his clients and eventually over the entire society.

During the rise of President Corazon Aquino, Marcos's clientele lost its source of favors, and new patronage groups emerged. This same pattern followed with subsequent presidents, albeit in a less corrupt manner than with Marcos. The biggest departure from cronyism was perhaps Fidel Ramos.

Even so, most Philippine politicians find it difficult to ignore these relationships and thus rely on their own clientele. The tenures of both Estrada and
Arroyo illustrate this fact well. It is still too early in Benigno Aquino's presidency to judge if he will stray from this pattern.

Constitutions

The Malolos constitution of 1899, promulgated by Filipino nationalists under the leadership of Emilio Aguinaldo and the first democratic constitution
in Asia, was based on South American and Spanish models and embodied
the ideas of liberal democracy, representative government, separation of
powers, and a system of checks and balances. This constitution endured only
a short time before the United States ended the republic.

The U.S.-sponsored constitution of 1935 provided for a representative democracy based on the U.S. presidential model. Japanese occupiers set up their
own constitution in 1943 for the Philippines, but it was viewed as illegitimate
and collapsed with the end of World War II. The 1935 constitution was subsequently restored and served the Philippines until 1973. In 1972, Marcos
convened a constitutional convention to draft a new constitution based on a
parliamentary rather than a presidential model. However, Marcos's declaration of martial law silenced debate on his proposed constitution; a few
months later, a constitutional convention approved the new document,
which called for a parliamentary form of government led by a prime minister
and allowed the interim president (Marcos) to decide when to convene the
interim national assembly and, further, to make and execute all laws until he
convened the assembly. The constitution was then approved by *barangay*
(people's assemblies) and went into effect on January 17, 1973.

Corazon Aquino's People Power victory led to a "Freedom constitution,"
a provisional document issued by presidential proclamation. It provided for
presidential appointment of a constitutional commission to draft a new, permanent constitution. Meanwhile, until the commission presented a new
constitution, which resembled the one of 1935, President Aquino held executive and legislative powers. A plebiscite on February 2, 1987, supported the
new document, with 75 percent of the voters approving.

Under the 1987 Constitution, the powers of the president are more circumscribed than under previous Philippine constitutions. The presidential
term is six years, with no reelection permitted. To curb the familial patronage of the Marcos years, the president's spouse and all close relatives are
barred from appointment as public officials. Martial law powers are also circumscribed, providing both the legislative and judicial branches the power
to review legal bases for the imposition of martial law.

Challenges to the 1987 Constitution have persisted through various pre-
texts. In clear violation of the constitution, multiple coup attempts by rebel

elements within the military have sought to overthrow chief executives. All have failed. Estrada's removal is sometimes referred to as a "coup" but represents an ambiguous departure from constitutional practice. It was not the result of a military seizure of power. The removal of the president by the military, during a botched impeachment trial, was an act endorsed by the Supreme Court. Following the constitution, the court certified as legal the ascension of Vice President Arroyo to the presidency.

Attempts for major constitutional reform have been proposed at times by past governments, including those of Ramos, Estrada, and Arroyo. In many cases, proposals favor the adoption of parliamentary-style government, and unicameral legislature, to reduce congressional gridlock and enhance the policymaking of the executive. "Charter change," commonly referred to as "cha-cha" by Filipinos, is a difficult prospect for sitting governments that are likely to benefit from the changes. President Arroyo campaigned on a pledge of charter change, but Benigno Aquino, whose mother initiated the now twenty-five-year-old 1987 Constitution, has publically announced his reservations about any "cha-cha" under his watch.

The Legislature

In the postindependence period, the Philippine legislature has been both a bulwark protecting freedom and a tool for legitimizing presidential decrees. The 1987 Constitution gives numerous prerogatives to the Congress, including the sole power to declare war, to withdraw presidential emergency powers, and to determine revenue origination and appropriation. Whereas the Marcos constitution of 1973 allowed President Marcos to exercise both legislative and executive powers, in contrast the 1987 Constitution clearly separates these powers. It includes a bicameral Congress, consisting of a twenty-four-member Senate, elected at large for six years and for not more than two consecutive terms, and a House of Representatives of not more than 250 members, most of whom are elected from legislative districts apportioned on the basis of population.

The remaining members of the House, 20 percent, are elected through an at-large party list system with a 2 percent threshold for seat placement. Designed as a functional representation system, the party lists system is organized around "sectors," or parties that represent labor, women, minority communities, and similar groups (excluding religion). Accusations are common that leading parties manipulate the sector party list system to gain more support in the House.

Political Parties

The Philippines had a two-party system for most of its early democratic period (1946–1972), when the Liberal and Nacionalista Parties alternately held power, with neither party ever able to get its presidential nominee re-elected.[13] The ideological differences between the two parties were negligible. For the most part, the two parties functioned as mobilizers of votes for specific candidates.

Under Marcos, one party dominated the political scene. Marcos's Kilusang Bagong Lipunan (KBL; New Society Movement) was a noncompetitive, authoritarian party devoted to keeping Marcos in power and maintaining the support of the U.S. government. Through his magnetic personality, his dominance of the bureaucracy and the legislative and executive branches, his fraudulent plebiscites and referenda, and his manipulation of nationalist symbols, Marcos controlled every aspect of the party and its program.

In the post–martial law era after 1981, the KBL continued to dominate politics. However, as Marcos's support deteriorated, opposition parties began to emerge. The most important of these were organized under the United Nationalist Democratic Organization, or UNIDO, a coalition of parties formed in 1979 by Salvador Laurel, who had broken from the KBL. UNIDO, largely an alliance of establishment politicians who had lost out when Marcos took control, was united primarily in its opposition to his domination of the political scene. Thus, it became an umbrella organization encompassing a number of smaller parties under the leadership of Senator Benigno Aquino Jr. and his party LABAN! (Fight!), which he formed as a political prisoner of Marcos. UNIDO coalition parties later formed the core of support for Corazon Aquino during her 1986 presidential run.

Since the early 1990s, the most successful political parties have included (1) the Lakas-Christian Muslim Democrats, the party of Fidel Ramos launched after the EDSA revolution; (2) the center-left Liberal Party, the country's second oldest and the party of both the late Benigno Aquino Jr. before his imprisonment and his son, Benigno Aquino III; (3) the populist-oriented Pwersa ng Masang Pilipino, the party vehicle used by Estrada; and (4) a revived Nacionalista Party, which today bears a reputation of being a probusiness, conservative party. These "mainstream" parties in the Philippines are generic catch-all parties that serve as patron-client political machines for those at the top. Smaller parties tend to be more ideological and issue oriented. In 2009, the center-right Lakas-Christian Muslim Democrats merged with Arroyo's Kampi Party and so remained the largest party in the House following 2010 elections, occupying 37 percent of seats.

At the national and local levels, party politics remains an elite-establishment activity based on patronage and personalism. Wealthy founders and politicians fund parties, and party switching does occur on occasion. The need for coalitions to pass legislation forces alliances and empowers party bosses who wheel and deal for votes. The easiest path to Congress is as a member of an entrenched political family, typically one with a regional presence somewhere in the archipelago. For most Filipinos, party activity matters only during elections. Even then, political parties play little role in presidential elections, which are determined primarily by the general public's attitudes toward individual candidates.

The Military

Although long involved with supporting particular candidates for office, the military has never played the dominant role in Philippine politics. In contrast to Thailand's, the Philippine military has been subordinated to civilian leaders and given the orthodox task of providing external defense and security against domestic subversion. (Marcos exploited this second task to protect his personal interests.) Fidel Ramos is the only president to have been a military general.

The Armed Forces of the Philippines (AFP) had total personnel of 37,000 in the 1940s. Between 1975 and 1976, the number jumped from 90,000 to 142,000. Marcos expanded the army to three-and-a-half times its former strength during his tenure, which increased military involvement in civilian life, including the militarization of internal security forces.[14] Under Marcos, the military was deprofessionalized through his appointments of cronies and fellow ethnic Ilocanos (from northern Luzon) to the commanding positions. The clearest such example was Marcos's appointment of his cousin Fabian Ver as armed forces chief of staff. Ver, who was subsequently determined by a government-appointed investigatory commission to have helped plan the assassination of Senator Aquino, politicized the military, turning it into a security force for Marcos and the enforcer of his martial law.

A group of reform-minded soldiers who reacted against the politicization of the military and its diminished professionalism organized into the Reform the Armed Forces Movement (RAM) and led the army rebellion against Marcos after the 1986 elections. Juan Ponce Enrile, a RAM leader, was awarded the position of minister of defense in Corazon Aquino's government for his role in ousting Marcos and supporting Aquino. Along with other RAM officers, he eventually turned against Aquino and led coup attempts against her government.

Despite attempts to reprofessionalize the military, or because of them, Aquino was constantly threatened by elements within the AFP. On December 1, 1989, members of the elite Scout Rangers captured air bases, the Fort Bonifacio army camp, and two television stations and attacked the presidential Malacañang Palace. Except for a call for President Aquino's resignation, no specific demands were made by the rebel forces. To repulse the attack, Aquino asked the United States to provide air support to forces loyal to the government. U.S. F-4 Phantom jets, flying from Clark Air Force Base, immobilized the rebel forces, which had occupied hotels and office buildings in Manila; the rebels agreed to a negotiated settlement. Seventy-nine people were killed and over six hundred were wounded during the episode. Politically, Aquino lost face because of her decision to request U.S. support. The event exacerbated nationalist and anti-U.S. sentiments and complicated later negotiations on the removal of American bases.

During the Ramos and Estrada presidencies, no military coups were attempted. Ramos was the first Philippine president since Ramon Magsaysay to view security in broad terms, taking into account military, political, economic, societal, and environmental factors. Coup rumors persisted under Arroyo's rule and came to life with the weak attempt by a rebel AFP faction tied to the Oakwood Mutiny.

The AFP currently boasts 125,000 troops but has suffered from an enduring "institutional rot" due to poor organization and equipment, factionalism, and uncontrolled elements.[15] Regionally, the Philippine army is considered weak. Depending on the direction that the Spratly Islands dispute takes in the future (see below), the AFP could face the most serious test of its military capacity yet. Rising tensions in the South China Sea have led President Benigno Aquino III and top generals to pursue a "Capability Upgrade Program" and the purchase of new helicopters and weapons, and potentially submarines and new aircraft from the United States.

Women

Traditionally, women have played only minor roles in Philippine politics. Women never held key positions of power in the legislature, cabinet, military, or bureaucracy. The rise of Imelda Marcos, Corazon Aquino, and Gloria Macapagal Arroyo to positions of immense power is anomalous rather than a pattern, as all are related to powerful male politicians. Imelda Marcos, who was governor of Metropolitan Manila and minister of human settlements until her husband was overthrown in 1986, owed her claim to leadership to her husband's authoritarian rule. Aquino was the saintly widow of Senator Benigno Aquino Jr. Arroyo, the daughter of a president, spent her teen years in the halls of Malacañang Palace. The rise to power of these women, and others in Filipino political and business circles, is often as much a function of their family name as it is the successful surmounting of the formidable barriers that have traditionally kept women out of power.[16] Comparatively, however, it is worth noting that the Philippines ranks better than other countries in the region in terms of the United Nation's Gender Empowerment Measure. Twenty-two percent of legislative seats won in the 2010 elections are occupied by women, a number twice as high as other elected legislatures in the region.

The Catholic Church

As citizens of the only predominantly Christian country in Asia, Filipinos have felt themselves to be different from and even superior to their Asian neighbors. With over 12,000 priests and nuns throughout the archipelago, the largest land holdings in the nation, and control over thousands of parishes, schools, and hospitals, the Catholic Church is a significant political, economic, and social institution. Factionalized among conservative, centrist, and progressive forces, the church has played a crucial role in all areas of Philippine life.

The most politically active leader of the church in the Philippines in the new international era has been Jaime Cardinal Sin, archbishop of Manila and head of the centrist faction. Cardinal Sin, who jokingly called his residence "The House of Sin," was a Filipino of Chinese decent with a reputation for good humor. In conjunction with church bishops and clergy, Sin played an important role in undermining President Marcos's administration and in fashioning the compromise that unified the opposition under Corazon Aquino.

In policy matters, church leaders have been outspoken in condemning corruption and other dishonest practices and in supporting programs that favor the poor and greater social justice. The church's condemnation of family planning, specifically the use of contraceptives, has kept successive governments from implementing a comprehensive plan designed to improve health standards and reduce poverty. The church's stand against homosexuality and artificial contraception has also made it difficult for condoms and sex education to be made available to those most in need. When Ramos, a protestant, and the first non-Catholic president in Philippine history, set forth an anti-AIDS program that included the distribution of condoms, Cardinal Sin denounced both the plan and the president himself. President Arroyo, alternatively, championed "natural family planning" and cited the nation's declining birth rate as supportive evidence. Noynoy Aquino, facing an open threat of excommunication by church leaders, chose to bypass a reproductive rights bill that had been stalled for fifteen years and directly fund the Department of Health to procure family planning supplies.

Notwithstanding controversies, the church has emerged as a primary symbol of peaceful change, warning against political excesses by government and opposition groups alike. Cardinal Sin retired in 2003 and died two years later. His replacement, Gaudencio Rosales, has proven more politically moderate than his predecessor but remains willing to speak out against birth control legislation.

Papal visits play a significant role in shaping the Filipino Catholic church, its direction, and the standing of its local leaders. Pope John Paul II's second visit to the Philippines, for World Youth Day in Manila in 1995, for example, produced a crowd of 4 million, the largest papal crowd to gather in world history. Filipino Catholics and Cardinal Rosales eagerly await Pope Benedict XVI's first Asian trip, although he has declined three formal invitations.

Communist Insurgents

With origins in the Soviet-supported Huk rebellion, the revolutionary opposition in the Philippines gained strength in the 1960s but became a meaningful threat to the nation's security during Marcos's rule. The Communist Party of the Philippines, the central organizational unit of the revolutionary opposition, is the largest communist party in ASEAN and oversees the New People's Army (NPA), the region's last remaining communist insurgency. The Maoist NPA controls about 5,000 troops spread throughout the archipelago's provinces. At its peak in the 1980s, the NPA had 20,000 loyalists who controlled some 20 percent of the country's territory.

The NPA's strength has come from disillusioned peasants, especially tenant farmers and day laborers, whose hopes for a better life were lifted by Marcos's announcement of a "New Society" and then dashed by unfulfilled promises and expectations. Similarly, the rise of Corazon Aquino initially weakened the NPA until her promises of meaningful land reform and improvement in the standard of living went unmet. Many students, intellectuals, and leftists in the Catholic Church, inspired by Peruvian Gustavo Gutierrez and Latin American liberation theology, supported the NPA's nationalist struggle against imperialism and poverty as "just violence." Other citizens supported the NPA as the only viable force against the corruption and abuses of rights perpetrated by local dynastic politicians and military units.

Thailand's success in countering insurgency stemmed from combining a policy of reconciliation and amnesty with economic development. In the Philippines, however, reconciliation policies by Corazon Aquino, Ramos, and Arroyo were not matched with a concomitant improvement in the standard of living. Although very little outside support is provided to the NPA, it was able to capitalize on the negative growth of the national economy and on the consequent extreme poverty suffered by nearly half of the population. The nation's interminable economic difficulties make it difficult to resolve the protracted, forty-year guerrilla war.

The NPA's political arm, based in the Netherlands, expressed a willingness to meet with the new Benigno Aquino government after years of rejecting negotiations. Peace talks later began in 2011, held in Oslo with Norway acting as a broker. They quickly stalled as the objectives of both sides remain worlds apart. In four decades, the numbers of deaths linked to the conflict range between 35,000 and 40,000 people.

Moro Islamic Separatists

Fighting primarily for an independent state for Muslims in the southern islands of the Philippines, Moro nationalists launched an armed campaign in 1972. In 1975, the Moro National Liberation Front (MNLF) was formally recognized by the Organization of the Islamic Conference (OIC). Engaging in armed warfare, sabotage, and political violence, the MNLF struck agreements for autonomy under Marcos and Corazon Aquino that were never fully implemented. In 1984, a leadership struggle led to the creation of a second group, the Moro Islamic Liberation Front (MILF).[17] Also in the 1980s, a third group, Abu Sayyaf, formed with the assistance of a brother-in-law of Osama bin Laden.[18]

In 1996, the Philippine government established the Autonomous Region in Muslim Mindano (ARMM) as part of a historic peace agreement with the MNLF. Implementation, however, struggled and produced lingering resentment. The conflict with the MILF waged on but conditions changed following the 9/11 attacks and subsequent U.S. war on terrorism, which drew attention to all the groups in the area, their activities, and their affiliations. Abu Sayyaf's alleged connections with al-Qaeda and Jemaah Islamiyah (based in Indonesia) came under great suspicion as the group adopted strategies of kidnapping tourists for ransom to finance their rebellion, risky activities belying evidence that Abu Sayyaf acted as a tentacle of the well-financed al-Qaeda.

Eventually, over 7,500 U.S. troops were stationed in Mindano related to a military offensive to weaken the remaining Moro separatists and Abu Sayyaf Islamists. The use of military pressure was combined with political efforts led by Mahathir bin Mohamad of Malaysia, the OIC, and USAID programs to help reintegrate Moro fighters into civilian life. A reduction in fighting occurred, but local bombings still plagued the area.

In December 2007, an agreement between the MILF and MNLF to put aside their decades-old animosity gave new hope that a political resolution with the Arroyo government was possible.[19] The Arroyo administration signed a controversial memorandum of understanding with the MILF to expand the ARMM into an ancestral homeland with wide-ranging self-government for the Moros. Drawing the ire of many Filipinos, the agreement was viewed by nationalist critics as a violation of the constitution and a threat to the republic. Fighting continued after the memorandum was signed, and Philippine courts eventually nullified the deal. Under Benigno Aquino III, however, a new framework for peace brokered by Malaysia's prime minister Najib Razak was agreed to in 2012 by Aquino and MILF leader Murad Ebrahim. The agreement will phase in regional autonomy for the Moros by 2016, inclusive of control over local law enforcement and a revenue-sharing arrangement with the central government over natural resources in the area.[20]

One of the sticking points inhibiting prior agreement was the MILF's supposed ties to the more radical Islamist group Abu Sayyaf, an allegation that MILF leaders deny. Aquino, like others before him, refuses to recognize Abu Sayyaf as anything but a terrorist group and has vowed to crush its estimated 250 remaining members. Approximately 2,000 Islamist terrorists have been captured or killed by Philippine forces since a 2006 offensive was launched with the assistance of U.S. counterinsurgency advisors. In 2010, two of Abu Sayyaf's top leaders were killed, further weakening the terrorist organization. Abu Sayyaf, concentrated on Jolo, an island in the southernmost Sulu Archipelago, did not participate in 2012 peace talks and is unlikely to ever compromise with government leaders. Its stated goal is to establish its own Islamic state.

STATE-SOCIETY RELATIONS AND DEMOCRACY

The Philippines was once known as Southeast Asia's "showcase of democracy." In terms of the formal institutions of government, that description was accurate. In the postindependence period, up to the time of martial law, the Philippine state appeared strong and the government carried out its functions based on constitutional guidelines, through the separation of powers and adherence to a bill of rights. On the surface, it appeared that the state's capacity was growing and that democratic institutions were consolidating.

Behaviorally, however, the picture was much different. State autonomy and democratic institutions have always been eclipsed by oligarchic inertia in the Philippines. Since the Spanish colonized the Philippines almost five hundred years ago, the nation has been ruled by a small number of family dynasties that have controlled both the economic and political spheres through decidedly undemocratic means. From the great haciendas of the Spaniards to the patronage politics of the U.S. period, these dynasties have ruled in a baronial, feudal manner, each controlling a particular area of the archipelago. Even during the country's "showcase" period of democracy, the fundamental forces that determined allocation never changed: intertwined landed wealth and state power. As characterized by one scholar, evidence from the "the highly mythologized Magsaysay period (1953–1957) bear[s] witness to a familiar and long-standing sense that democracy practiced in the Philippines is not quite, not really, well, democracy."[21]

The country's archipelagic nature is partially responsible for the development of this decentralized, dynastic system. Pervasive poverty also helps explain why the poor learn to rely on their wealthy patrons. In the Philippines, dynastic families sponsor the weddings of their laborers and tenants, pay for children's education, and care for the sick, thereby forming a tie of dependency that keeps the poor deferential and loyal. Without strong government institutions, patron-client relations develop to meet the needs of the majority poor.

The dynastic nature of Philippine politics is also due to cultural factors. A Filipino's loyalty is directed first to family, then to close friends, then to the local community, then to personally known political leaders, and finally to distant, impersonal governmental agencies. Although all of these concentric circles of allegiance place emphasis on the personal nature of loyalty, an individual's family and patron family demand the deepest loyalties.[22] In the *compadre* (godfather) system, reciprocity is formed in which the higher-status *compadre* renders material benefits and prestige and the lower-status family provides loyalty, deference, and support. Thus, a candidate for office may be asked to sponsor a marriage or a newborn baby in return for a family's electoral support, and the family then has the right to seek political patronage from its new *compadre*.[23] Politicians are equally desirous of becoming sponsors to ensure a wide base of electoral support.

For democratic consolidation to take root in the Philippines, the formal institutions of government must become more than facades for oligarchic rule. The overwhelming majority of newly elected senators and representatives are members of families who have dominated Philippine politics for centuries. Although the people in charge of the government have changed, and despite various efforts to reform the system, there have been too few fundamental changes in the character of the Philippine political system.

Under Arroyo, a deepened sense of political malaise persisted throughout the Philippines. Benigno S. Aquino III's election restored some optimism, but the overall system of oligarchy remains entrenched, a sort of dysfunctional democracy. Public cynicism extends itself especially to oppositional politics. People Power, once the essence of democratic spirit, is slowly becoming delegitimized as a useful political tool. Each time a popular revolt or elections overthrows a corrupt president (e.g., Marcos, Estrada, Arroyo) a new set of elites take the reins of power only to extend oligarchic rule and, consequently, disillusionment.[24] This revolving door of elites is referred to as *pulitika*, the "jockeying for position among the old political oligarchy."[25]

The most recent elections, in 2010, illustrate just how shallow formal democracy has become in the Philippines. In a country where democracy has become synonymous with elections, election races often resemble cheap reality show contests and public evaluations of celebrity popularity. Pop culture icons and infamous figures now commonly join the usual array of *trapos* candidates as representatives of the Filipino people. The dubious list of celebrities elected to prominent offices in 2010 included multiple TV stars and pop icons; world champion boxer Manny Pacquio (who formed his own party, the People's Champ Movement); former First

Lady Imelda Marcos and her presidential-wannabe son; a convicted rapist; a notorious gangster-warlord and his son, who is a self-identified cocaine and gambling addict facing drug charges in Hong Kong; and fifteen members of the mafia-like Ampatuan clan.[26]

Civil society in the Philippines has grown in the face of oligarchy, but it is overwhelmed by a disturbing degree of violence and lawlessness at the local level. Weak state and democratic institutions contribute to a culture of violence and impunity. From year to year, Reporters Without Borders ranks the Philippines as one of the most dangerous countries in which to practice journalism. Since 1991, over seventy journalists have been killed and only a handful of cases have been brought to conviction. Political violence in the form of bombings, assassinations, and voter intimidation chronically haunts elections. Over 275 people were killed during the 2004 and 2007 elections, and the 2010 elections were declared by officials as the most violent yet, with one in three municipalities experiencing "ERVIs," or election-related violent incidents. Moreover, in spite of government pledges to neutralize them, there exist an estimated 112 private armies in the Philippines employed by politicians to harass and intimidate opponents and their supporters.[27] Some argue that recent decentralization of fiscal authority has raised the stakes of local government, compounding the trend toward election violence.[28] Regardless, after sixty years of attempting democratic transition, rather than developing quality democratic institutions, the Philippines appears closer to consolidating *pulitika* and the wretched practices of political violence, gangsterism, and judicial impunity.

ECONOMY AND DEVELOPMENT

If Thailand has been a favorite case study for market-led development of agricultural societies in the past several decades, the Philippines has became the model for what not to do. On a par with Thailand in the mid-1970s, each nation had an annual per capita GNP of just over $300. Since that time, the Philippines has slipped well behind, achieving in 2011 a $4,100 per capita GDP in terms of purchasing power parity in contrast to Thailand's $9,700. Despite abundant natural resources, strong ties to the United States, and an English-speaking workforce, the Philippines has failed to realize its economic potential. Inequality remains the constant theme of the Philippine economy, even during periods of growth.

The Philippine economy has been skewed since the days of Spanish colonialism, which thrust a feudal economic system upon the Filipinos. When Americans refined the Philippines with their neocolonial system, the Philippine economy fell under the control of outside forces, including multinational corporations and a group of fabulously wealthy Filipino families (mostly with Spanish or Chinese backgrounds). Neocolonial relations between Americans and Filipinos were characterized by exploitation rather than cooperation for the mutual good, with the bulk of the profits gained by businesses in the Philippines going to Americans.

The Philippine economy at the end of World War II was in a shambles because of the widespread destruction in Manila and of basic infrastructure throughout the archipelago. As with most Southeast Asian nations in the 1950s, the Philippines adopted an import-substitution industrialization (ISI) strategy to develop its economy. In essence, the ISI strategy restricted imports of foreign goods to improve the balance of payments and to generate new industries to make the nation more self-sufficient. The United States had already penetrated the domestic Philippine economy, so Americans did not oppose this policy.

Initially, ISI policies worked well in terms of benefiting domestic manufacturing industries, and between 1950 and 1980 the share of manufacturing in the total economy rose from 8 percent to 25 percent, whereas the share of agriculture declined from 42 percent to 23 percent.[29] Manufacturing accounted for more than half the value of Philippine exports in the 1970s, just a decade after accounting for only 6 percent. At the same time, however, every economic indicator showed the Philippines to have the least effective economy in the region. Moreover, only a small group of Marcos-centered industrialists and financiers benefited from this new form of state capitalism, while small businesses and labor groups were weakened.

In the agricultural and commodities sector, where most Filipinos were employed, the economy suffered ongoing maldevelopment. In the postindependence era, the concentration of wealth and land has been more pervasive in the Philippines than in any other Southeast Asian nation. Weak democratic institutions have proven unable to redistribute income or to create new opportunities for Philippine voters.

The mixed success of ISI led international agencies such as the World Bank to change their advice and to recommend an export-oriented industrialization strategy for economic development. However, interference by Marcos cronies kept protectionist measures and monopoly controls intact, so the new strategy never worked effectively. In the commodities sector, reform was largely ignored. Marcos had given his best friends monopoly control over the sugar and coconut sectors, which led to their amassing fabulous riches. These riches ended up in Swiss and U.S. bank accounts and in real estate investments throughout the world, a capital flight that subverted the economy into an incurable state.

In the 1970s, Marcos and his sugar barons made a costly bet on global markets by hoarding the commodity, only to see the price bubble burst by the end of the decade and render the country's sugar stock worthless. In the early 1980s, rising oil prices and the collapse of other commodities resulted in economic recession and acute economic hardship for many Filipinos. Farm prices had dropped so low that starvation became a real threat in the major sugar areas.[30]

Marcos's poor economic performance occurred simultaneously with the people's growing disenchantment with the New Society's authoritarian ways and gross corruption. Urban laborers grew increasingly angry about the erosion of their wages and the deterioration of working conditions, while employers found themselves losing profits because of the increased costs of energy and pressure from the Marcos administration to raise wages. Both of these groups, as well as the farmers, could see that President Marcos's family and cronies were living in ostentatious luxury.

All these factors so undermined the economy that only a spark was needed to bring Filipinos to the streets to demand change. That spark turned out to be the return home and assassination of Senator Aquino in August 1983. For Filipinos, the regime was a disaster not only economically but morally as well.

Economic growth rates since Marcos reflect participation in Asia's economic dynamism but at a slower pace due to chronic challenges in the Philippine economy. Corazon Aquino and Ramos helped economic growth return to the Philippines only to see it thwarted by dependence on oil imports, inflation, and the Asian economic crisis of the late 1990s. High population growth rates, which persisted well above 2 percent until the new millennium, combined with inefficient use of educational resources, have exacerbated the country's economic woes. Unemployment and underemployment have caused many Filipinos to travel abroad as guest workers in the Middle East, Hong Kong, Japan, and even fellow ASEAN states. Remittances topped $14 billion in 2007, about 10 percent of the Philippines' GDP. Only the overseas workers from China, India, and Mexico send home more money than do Filipino expatriates and guest workers.

For his part, Fidel Ramos focused his presidency on improving the Philippine economy by liberalizing virtually every facet of the economy, allowing technocrats and the market system to prevail. He did not address land reform. By 1994, the economic growth rate had reached 5.1 percent—not outstanding by Southeast Asian standards but high compared to previous performance in the Philippines. By 1996, growth had reached 6.8 percent, an unprecedentedly high figure, helped by the lack of any major natural calamities during the year. The 1997 economic debacle that began in Thailand caused a devaluation of the Philippine peso, and the first signs in several years of an end to the growth period.

Arroyo came into the presidency when investor confidence was low. Estrada's cronyism before her had undermined the confidence of domestic business executives and foreign investors. He had coped incompetently with privatizing unproductive industries (mostly run by his cronies). The stock market was in tatters, and the peso continued to lose value. Despite Arroyo's political difficulties, her economic policies produced improved results initially, but their success plummeted after the 2008 global financial crisis. Outsourced international customer service (call centers) has recently joined microchip processing and automotive manufacturing as promising areas for economic growth. Under Benigno Aquino III, who is an economist, the Philippines' economic growth and its stock market have recovered well, the latter reaching record highs.

Close to thirty years have now passed since Marcos's ouster, yet the problems besetting the Philippines today remain those familiar to the past: economic inequality, land disputes, monopolistic industries, corrupt leadership, and an elite class more concerned with self-interest than with the public good. These are problems that can be resolved only by fundamental changes in all areas of Filipino life, including the social, economic, cultural, and political realms. For most Filipinos, the standard of living remains lower than what most people experience in Southeast Asia. With respect to progress on Millennium Development Goals (MDGs), economic growth in the Philippines has not produced development results on par with its neighbors, such as Vietnam. A 2006 report by the United Nations and Asian Development Bank identified the Philippines and Myanmar as Asia's worst laggards in making progress toward MDG targets.[31] Since 2000, the child mortality rate has barely declined and the poverty rate has actually worsened. Goals to improve maternal health and education have also fallen far short. In fact, between 2009 and 2011 the country's maternal mortality rate actually rose (alarmingly) from 162 to 221 (per 100,000 live births). At current rates, the Philippines will not meet its MDG goal of 52 until after 2050.

FOREIGN RELATIONS

The United States, the Philippines' closest ally, also represents the republic's biggest foreign policy problem. Since the colonial period, the United States and the Philippines have had a "special relationship," a term that aptly describes the close and complex ties shared by the two nations for almost a hundred years. The countries are party to a bilateral mutual defense treaty signed in 1951.

The Philippines, as Asia's most Americanized country, shares a common Christian heritage and the widespread use of the English language. In fashion, music, art, education, and politics, Filipinos often emulate Americans rather than their Asian neighbors. The result has been a love-hate relationship. Many Filipinos look to the United States as their hope and even their future home at the same time that they demonstrate against U.S. interference in their affairs. While under Marcos, a 1972 Gallup Poll of 2,000 Filipinos revealed that 60 percent favored making the Philippines the fifty-first American state; only 28 percent were opposed to the idea.[32] U.S. support of President Marcos, which sustained and prolonged his rule, was applauded by some and denounced by others. The last-minute U.S. endorsement of President Aquino, which came after it became clear that Marcos was finished, together with help in persuading Marcos to leave the country (for safe exile in Hawaii), only partially helped to undo the damage.

The presence of U.S. military bases on Philippine territory, which continued following Marcos's departure, intensified the conflicting emotions Filipinos felt toward the United States. Though most Filipinos were eager to shed their dependence on U.S. protection, an estimated 3 percent of the Philippine GNP was generated, directly or indirectly, by the bases: by the 30,000 U.S. personnel, by the 45,000 Filipinos who worked on the bases, and by Filipino businesses established near the bases, as well as by taxes paid by all these employees. An estimated $500 million, a huge amount in a poor country, was generated by the bases each year and fed into the local economy.

Negotiations commenced in 1990 to determine the future of both Subic Bay Naval Base and Clark Air Force Base. For U.S. negotiators, the issue was the continuation of the military's forward defense strategy in the Pacific. For the Filipino negotiators, the crucial points did not involve strategic advantage but rather issues of nationalism, constitutional principles, compensation, and social problems. Indeed, many Filipinos viewed Olongapo (near Subic) and Angeles City (adjacent to Clark) as "moral cesspools"—in Olongapo alone, some 16,000 prostitutes serviced sailors on leave. Around the bases, HIV and other sexually transmitted diseases were rampant.

After months of negotiations, the Philippine Senate rejected the bases agreement and requested that the Americans leave Subic. Prior to this decision, the United States had already begun withdrawal from Clark Air Force Base as a result of the destruction from the 1991 eruption of Mount Pinatubo. Internationally, the decision lowered confidence in Philippine stability and worsened the image of an already desperate economy. However, for many Filipinos, the long-term gain for the country's psyche was thought to be worth the short-term costs. Shouldering sole responsibility for security and foreign affairs would oblige Filipinos to look more creatively and determinedly for appropriate solutions to their problems. By 1998, the Philippines invited U.S. troops back for a new round of recurring training exercises with Philippine forces.

Post-9/11 agreements between Gloria Macapagal Arroyo and U.S. President George W. Bush resurrected some of the mixed feelings Filipinos had toward the United States. Many Filipinos did not want to turn to the U.S. umbrella yet again, but evidence from the 9/11 Commission Report revealed that al-Qaeda hijackers had met in the Philippines before the attacks. The troubled south took on international dimensions with new fears of international Islamists operating amidst Moro separatists, namely the al-Qaeda-linked groups of Abu Sayyaf and Jemaah Islamiyah.

Arroyo offered the Philippines' full support for Bush's war on terrorism, and the United States gradually dispatched over 7,500 troops to assist with fighting rebellion and terrorism in the separatist Muslim south. By 2006, the U.S. State Department had officially declared certain areas of the south as "safe havens for terrorists." Months later, echoing the U.S. PATRIOT Act, the Philippine House of Representatives and Senate passed the Human Security Act to allow wiretapping of suspected terrorists.

Joint exercises are now commonplace between U.S. and Philippine troops, as are sporadic bomb blasts (and kidnappings) claimed by Abu Sayyaf and Jemaah Islamiyah. The Joint Special Operations Task Force-Philippines (JSOTF-P) remains the primary vehicle for U.S. involvement in the area. Operating with a counterinsurgency mission, the JSOTF-P emphasizes technical and humanitarian assistance to the AFP and local populations. U.S. military activity, some of it outsourced to U.S. defense contractors, includes arms sales to the AFP and cash rewards for local informants. Rumors of plans to reestablish a permanent U.S. base in the Philippines located in the south (expectedly) sparked new controversy. In the new international era, the Philippines remains wedded to U.S. protection and patronage, much as it did during the Cold War, World War II, and the Spanish-American War.

The Spratly Islands Dispute

For Philippine leaders, the Spratly Islands imbroglio is the security flash point of greatest concern (see chapter 4 for more context on the Spratlys dispute). Philippine interest in the South China Sea—called the "West Philippine Sea" by Filipinos—involves particular territorial claims to several islands and to maritime jurisdiction over a wide expanse of the sea's resources. Philippine officials define the problem in terms of respect for Philippine territorial rights and sovereignty. For the military the Spratlys are a matter of national prestige and overall security. The Philippine military is much weaker than its Chinese and Vietnamese counterparts, and diplomatic concessions by past Philippine presidents on the matter have caused the issue to fester in Philippine politics. Chinese claims and actions create a formidable threat to Philippine interests in the South China Sea.

In 2011, during the same year that President Barack Obama announced his "strategic pivot" to build a U.S. presence in Asia, U.S. Ambassador to the Philippines Harry Thomas publically stated in Manila, "I assure you, in all subjects, we the United States, are with the Philippines."[33] Philippine leaders interpreted Thomas's remarks as a coded assurance that any Chinese belligerence will be met with a U.S. response. Reaction to this and similar U.S. policy statements, not to mention subsequent diplomatic activity by Secretary of State Hillary Clinton across the region, provoked negative reactions in Beijing and agitated the Chinese public. Officially, however, the United States has stated no position on sovereignty claims in the South China Sea, only that the resolution of the dispute be peaceful.

In 2012, an incident involving the Philippine Navy and Chinese patrol boats (ostensibly protecting Chinese fishing boats) near Scarborough Shoal created a tense two-month standoff between the two countries. Subsequent diplomatic tension, public protest, and military brinksmanship proved just how potentially volatile the Spratlys dispute had become. Both sides saved face by withdrawing due to rough seas and the coming typhoon season. ASEAN's failed meeting in Phnom Penh that same year only embittered all sides further. The Philippines prefers a multilateral and regional approach, whereas the Chinese prefer a bilateral approach to reconcile the conflict.

Manila later contracted a private company and announced it would soon begin to drill for oil and natural gas at Reed Bank (80 nautical miles from the Philippines and 578 nautical miles from China). How China and other interested parties react to this activity may be telling about how the dispute over the Spratlys will evolve, or devolve.

CONCLUSION

The contemporary Philippine political system is formally democratic, with structures and procedures conducive to an open polity. Informally, however, the system remains oligarchic, ruled by a self-perpetuating elite of landed families that has commanded the political and economic scene for centuries. Figuratively and literally, President Corazon Aquino symbolized this grand contradiction even in the wake of People Power: commitment to democracy versus loyalty to her wealthy family. All subsequent presidents except one have unsurprisingly sprung from elite families. Unfortunately, the lone exception (Estrada) sadly represents the celebrity-driven alternative to the usual slate of elite family candidates Filipino voters see on their ballots. The fact that ex-president Arroyo—who pardoned her own corrupt predecessor from a life sentence—now stands in judgment of plundering state funds is at once a sad and encouraging sign. One can only hope that legal and institutional accountability is beginning to trump the usual personalism, patronage, and impunity of Filipino politics.

For "PNoy," the new Aquino in power, the challenge to develop the country's democratic institutions—rather than a Malacañang Palace client base—is all too real. Truly neutralizing the graft, gangsters, and goons dominating the system is perhaps an impossible task for a single leader; it may have to be the project of the rising generation. Filipino civil society carries the heavy task of helping the country's citizens to demand and realize a better system.

The Philippines has not assimilated modern democratic values with traditional ways in a coherent or harmonious manner. Although nominally democratic, its leaders face constant challenges of legitimacy, allegations of corruption, and threats from the country's military. More tragically, Philippine leaders have rarely met the people's needs. Poverty rates have barely dropped, and the standard of living has deteriorated because of mismanagement and the greed of the country's oligarchic families. The Philippine polity has yet to develop an effective capacity to cope with changing demands and to assert the nation's destiny.

NOTES

1. David Wurfel, *Filipino Politics: Development and Decay* (Ithaca, NY: Cornell University Press, 1988).

2. John T. Sidel, "The Philippines: The Languages of Legitimation," in *Political Legitimacy in Southeast Asia: The Quest for Moral Authority*, ed. Muthiah Alagappa (Stanford, CA: Stanford University Press, 1995), 165–168.

3. Paul Hutchcroft, "The Arroyo Imbroglio in the Philippines," *Journal of Democracy* 19. no. 1 (2008): 142.

4. William Overholt persuasively argues that, contrary to the established view that the assassination caused the collapse of the regime or even accelerated Marcos's decline, the assassination was a successful stratagem by Marcos to delay the consequences of his regime's political, moral, and financial bankruptcy. See William Overholt, "The Rise and Fall of Ferdinand Marcos," *Asian Survey* 26, no. 11 (November 1986): 1,137–1,163.

5. For a comprehensive look at U.S. Cold War support of Marcos, see Raymond Bonner, *Waltzing with a Dictator: The Marcoses and the Making of American Policy* (New York: Times Books, 1987).

6. Justus M. van der Kroef, "The Philippines: Day of the Vigilantes," *Asian Survey* 28, no. 6 (June 1988): 630.

7. Sheila S. Coronel, "The Philippines in 2006: Democracy and Its Discontents," *Asian Survey* 47, no. 1 (January/February 2007): 175.

8. Allen Hicken, "The Philippines in 2007: Ballots, Budgets, and Bribes," *Asian Survey* 48, no. 1 (January/February 2008): 76–77.

9. "Philippine Massacre Exposes Political Underworld," *BBC News*, January 21, 2010, http://news.bbc.co.uk/2/hi/asia-pacific/8470726.stm.

10. In 2012, at age seventy-five, "Erap" announced new plans to run for mayor of Manila in 2013, a prospect preelection polls show likely to return him to public office.

11. Gil C. Cabacungan Jr., "Lawyers Tell Arroyo: Say Nothing More," *Philippine Daily Enquirer*, July 18, 2011, http://newsinfo.inquirer.net/25035/lawyers-tell-arroyo-say-nothing-more.

12. Patricio Abinales, "The Philippines in 2009: The Blustery Days of August," *Asian Survey* 50, no. 1 (January/February 2010): 218.

13. One of the best overviews of the evolution of political parties in the Philippines is Luzviminda G. Tancangco, "The Electoral System and Political Parties in the Philippines," in *Government and Politics of the Philippines*, ed. Raul P. De Guzman and Mila A. Reforma (Singapore: Oxford University Press, 1988). Part of the following paragraphs are based on her analysis.

14. Felipe B. Miranda and Ruben F. Ciron, "Development and the Military in the Philippines: Military Perceptions in a Time of Continuing Crisis," in *Soldiers and Stability in Southeast Asia,* ed. J. Soedjati Djiwandono and Yong Mun Cheong (Singapore: Institute of Southeast Asian Studies, 1988), 169.

15. Michael J. Montesano, "The Philippines in 2003: Troubles, None of Them New," *Asian Survey* 44, no. 1 (January/February 2004): 96.

16. Raul P. De Guzman, Alex B. Brillantes Jr., and Arturo G. Pacho, "The Bureaucracy," in *Government and Politics of the Philippines,* ed. Raul P. De Guzman and Mila A. Reforma (Singapore: Oxford University Press, 1988), 180.

17. Michael Leifer, *Dictionary of the Modern Politics of South-East Asia* (London: Routledge, 1995), 162.

18. Simon Elegant, "The Return of Abu Sayyaf," *Time*, August 23, 2004, www.time.com/time/magazine/article/0,9171,686107,00.html.

19. Hicken, "The Philippines in 2007," 78.

20. "Philippines and Muslim Rebels Sign Key Peace Plan," *BBC News*, October 15, 2012, http://www.bbc.co.uk/news/world-asia-19944101.

21. Sidel, "The Philippines: Languages of Legitimation," 147.

22. Linda K. Richter, "Exploring Theories of Female Leadership in South and Southeast Asia," paper presented to the Association for Asian Studies, Chicago, April 1990, p. 7.

23. David Joel Steinberg, "The Web of Filipino Allegiance," *Solidarity* 2, no. 6 (March/April 1967): 25.

24. Coronel, "The Philippines in 2006," 178.

25. Sidel, "The Philippines: Languages of Legitimation," 147, n. 44.

26. Patricio N. Abilanes, "The Philippines in 2010: Blood, Ballots, and Beyond," *Asian Survey* 5, no.1 (January/February 2011): 163–172.

27. Kristine L. Alave, "Most Violent Elections Yet, Says Comcon Exec," *Philippine Daily Enquirer*, July 4, 2010, http://newsinfo.inquirer.net/breakingnews/nation/view/20100407-262908/Most-violent-elections-yet-says-Comelec-exec.

28. Carlos H. Conde, "Election Violence Escalating in the Philippines," *International Herald Tribune*, May 6, 2007, http://www.nytimes.com/2007/05/06/world/asia/06iht-phils.1.5583626.html.

29. S. K. Jayasuriya, "The Politics of Economic Policy in the Philippines During the Marcos Era," in *Southeast Asia in the 1980s: The Politics of Economic Crisis*, ed. Richard Robison, Kevin Hewison, and Richard Higgott (Sydney: Allen & Unwin, 1987), 82.

30. Ibid., 83.

31. Coronel, "The Philippines in 2006," 182.

32. "Filipinos Favor U.S. Statehood: Says Poll," *The Age*, May 18, 1972, 6

33. "Spratly Islands Word War: US Will Defend RP," *Philippine News*, May 9, 2011, http://www.philippinenews.com/top-stories/2526-spratly-islands-word-war-us-will -defend-rp.html.

Resource Guide

A useful tool for bibliographic and other information on the Philippines is available from Australia National University's WWW Virtual Library: www.gksoft.com/govt/en /ph.html. The University of California–Berkeley maintains a useful portal for digital and print resources on the Philippines: www.lib.berkeley.edu/SSEAL/SoutheastAsia/sea-elec.html. Northern Illinois University's Southeast Asia Digital Library includes a range of useful links that cover government, academic, and research institutions specific to the Philippines: http://sea.lib.niu.edu. The University of Wisconsin–Madison Libraries similarly maintains a list of digital and print resources on the Philippines: www.library.wisc .edu/guides/seasia/resarea.html.

Readers can supplement this chapter with figures and publication information found in the country profile pages of data.UN.org. and ADB.org. Recent and archived news articles are maintained on specific country profile pages by BBC.com and NYTimes.com. Useful country reports are also produced by the Bertelsmann Foundation at www .bti-project.org/home/index.nc.

A government-sponsored and generic information portal about the Philippines is at www.pia.gov.ph. The official governmental portal is at www.gov.ph. A research institute that devotes itself to development issues with policy reports and scholarly articles is the Philippine Institute for Development Studies: www.pids.gov.ph. The National Economic Development Authority provides similar material: www.neda.gov.ph. A daily news sources is the *Manila Times*, which is over one hundred years old and has searchable archives: www.manilatimes.net. Philippine News, at www.philippinenews.com, is another useful publication for current events. GMA News, at www.gmanews.tv, provides video news clips. News sources especially devoted to the millions of Filipinos living outside the country include www.philippinestoday.net and www.filipinoexpress.com. Moro writers maintain a site dedicated to their cause at www.luwaran.com. Students interested in Tagalog language and Filipino culture should visit Northern Illinois University's SEAsite at http://www.seasite.niu.edu/.

8

INDONESIA

INDONESIA, WITH ITS 242 MILLION INHABITANTS, PRESENTS DIFFERENT challenges in its quest for economic and political development compared to its less-populated neighbors. As an equatorial archipelago stretching as wide as the United States, Indonesia is the fourth-most-populous country in the world. Over one-third of all Southeast Asians live in Indonesia. Eleven major ethnic groups and hundreds of minor ones inhabit 6,000 of the country's 17,000 islands.[1] Amazingly, more than half of all Indonesians live on the island of Java, one of the most densely populated areas of the world. Although 85 percent of the country's population is nominally Muslim, the variety of religious beliefs within this Islamic ambience suggests diversity more than unity. Thus, even as the world's largest Muslim country, Indonesia is continually shaped by geographic, linguistic, ethnic, and social heterogeneity. The population has overcome almost insuperable obstacles in achieving nationhood.

Indonesia experienced a daunting struggle for independence at the end of World War II. Having lived under Dutch control for 350 years and then Japanese occupation during World War II, Indonesians looked for a leader who could forge unity within diversity in the postindependence period. As spokesman for Indonesian independence, leader of the revolutionary struggle against the Dutch from 1945 to 1949, and first president of independent Indonesia, Sukarno became the charismatic "solidarity maker"—destined, it seemed, to forge a "new Indonesian person."

Postindependence Indonesia can be divided into four periods, separated by one- to two-year transition phases: (1) fragile parliamentary governance under Sukarno, 1950–1957; (2) "guided democracy" under Sukarno, 1959–1965; (3) the "New Order" under Suharto, 1967–1998; and (4) liberal democratic reform under multiple presidents, 1999–present. The first period featured numerous political parties, elections, and weak parliamentary government. These Western-style governmental forms—adopted to prove to Indonesians

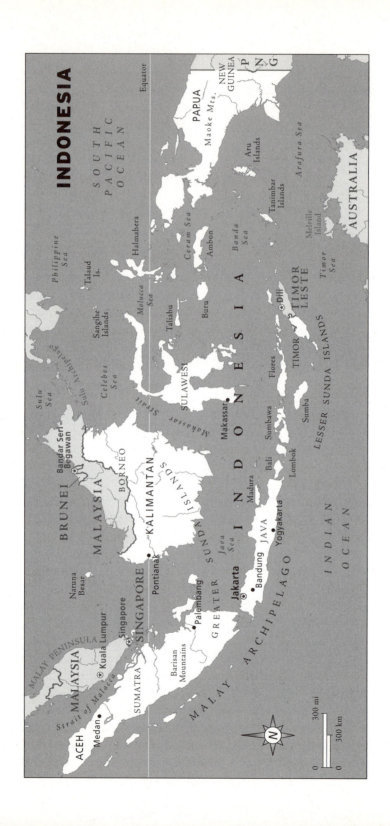

that they could govern themselves in a "modern" democratic manner—did not fit well with traditional Indonesian culture, which placed little value on representation, group formation, and majority rule. Sukarno pejoratively referred to democracy as "50 percent plus one" governance. Eventually, westernized institutions were blamed for the government's inability to meet the people's economic needs.

As liberal democracy floundered, Sukarno moved toward a system based on traditional political concepts, mixed and reformulated to meet goals of nation-building. The essence of "guided democracy" was *gotong royong* (mutual cooperation), where decisions could be arrived at with unanimous approval via collaboration rather than competition. Western-style voting was also replaced by *musyawarah-mufakat*—a traditional method of deliberation-consensus—with Sukarno himself as the ultimate and unchallenged arbiter.

To rally support for guided democracy, Sukarno made nationalism the cornerstone of his new ideology. Nationalism was defined as the submergence of regional and ethnic loyalties in favor of national ones, allegiance to Sukarno, indigenous patterns of governance (free from the mentality of colonialism), and the annihilation of neocolonialism. Loyalty to the greater interest was rooted in *Bhinneka Tunggal Ika*, a Javanese-derived phrase meaning "We are of many kinds, but one" (sometimes translated as "Unity in Diversity" or "*E pluribus unum*").

Fearful of disunity, Sukarno had brilliantly established *Bahasa Indonesia* (a minority Malay-based dialect) as the new national language upon independence. Although the country was home to over three hundred languages, demographic realities rendered Javanese the most commonly used language per capita. Nevertheless, by resisting the temptation to designate Javanese as the national language, and by favoring a minority lingua franca used by coastal traders, Sukarno ameliorated Javanese chauvinism, a force that continually challenges the unity of postcolonial Indonesia.

Sukarno also cultivated the idea of *Pancasila,* a term adopted from Sanskrit meaning "five precepts." *Pancasila*, the declared state philosophy of Indonesia, syncretically embraces the belief in one God, humanitarianism, nationalism, democracy, and social justice. Ambiguously defining each, often in long, fiery speeches, Sukarno's vision of "sociodemocracy" audaciously blended elements of liberalism, Marxism, theism, traditionalism, and modernism. The country's official emblem, the *Garuda Pancasila*, was unfolded by Sukarno as a mythical Hindu bird adorned with a coat of arms symbolizing the principles of *Pancasila*. A decorative ribbon held by the bird's talons declared the state motto.

Where *Pancasila* defined the scope of politics, *Marhaenism* functioned as the centerpiece of Sukarno's economic philosophy. *Marhaenism* targeted the rural experience as a type of subsistence socialism. Deriving its name from an apocryphal Sundanese farmer he supposedly met while cycling, Sukarno used it to emphasize "self-help" as the chief bulwark against "exploitation." By glorifying Indonesia's many small cultivators "who worked for themselves and no one else," *Marhaenism*'s economic ideals thus belied any need for class revolution or organized struggle. It promoted, rather illogically, the development of an atomized but unified rural proletariat of national loyalists—a Sukarnoist dream of content, self-sustaining peasants neither radicalized into class consciousness nor corrupted by individualism or avaricious want.

By embracing *Pancasila*, *Bhinneka Tunggal Ika*, *Bahasa Indonesia*, and *Marhaenism*, Sukarno encircled the new regime with his own ideology, goals, and charisma, indistinguishably fusing his persona with the postcolonial state and regime. Recognized and celebrated across the third world for his postcolonial ideology and vision, Sukarno, similar to many of his contemporaries (Mao, Nasser, and Castro), was a one-man political institution.

After he banned most political parties, reduced the power of Parliament, and suspended civil liberties, Sukarno's political course under guided democracy became erratic. He moved ideologically to the left, embracing the Communist Party of Indonesia (PKI), and then to the right—strengthening the armed forces—when the PKI became too dominant. He tried desperately to balance the demands of numerous groups, including the PKI, Chinese entrepreneurs, students, rural farmers, rightist Muslims, outer-island groups, and the army.

Although guided democracy was initially supported as an Indonesian antidote to failed Western liberalism, deteriorating economic conditions and administrative chaos created disunity rather than erasing it. In practice, *Marhaenism* resulted in rural neglect, a disorganized attempt at state-led nationalization, and a large, informal, free-for-all economy. Conditions of poverty thus worsened. Forever obsessed with foreign exploitation, Sukarno nationalized Dutch and British holdings, expelled 40,000 foreign expatriates, and demanded foreign-held territories in Borneo and New Guinea. As domestic problems deepened, he turned his attention abroad, pursuing a coercive foreign policy known as *Konfrontasi* (confrontation).

Under *Konfrontasi*, Sukarno moved beyond the Dutch and began to target the Federation of Malaysia, Britain, the United States, and the United Nations. Sukarno refused to recognize Malaysia with diplomatic relations upon its 1963 independence from the British and began to engage in guerrilla warfare with the new state over territorial claims. Then in 1964, Sukarno told the U.S. ambassador at a public gathering to "go to hell with your aid," despite Indonesia's dependence on Western military and financial assistance. Thoroughly convinced of a neocolonial plot and irate over international support of Malaysia, Sukarno spitefully withdrew Indonesia from the United Nations, rejecting its aid and antipoverty programs as well.

Sukarno's narcissistic obsession with his own international image exacerbated policy failure on the domestic front—rural neglect in particular. Under guided democracy, Indonesian society deteriorated precipitously. Government corruption turned flagrant, and the cost of living index rose from a base of 100 in 1957 to 36,000 in 1965. Unemployment grew rampant, and hungry peasants migrated en masse, forming a distressed population of urban homeless. Politically, the PKI gained strength, supported by radicalized peasants and stressed urbanites who began to arm themselves with Chinese-made weapons.

Sukarnoism's final ideological piece, *Nasakom*, was perhaps more tactical than visionary. Introduced in the early 1960s, the acronym-slogan embraced a tripod of social values: nationalism, religion, and communism. With *Nasakom*, Sukarno openly embraced the country's communists as part of Indonesia's political future. With this move, the PKI's confidence surged even as revolutionary movements elsewhere in Southeast Asia were gaining strength. Images of the sickle and hammer and pictures of Marx, Lenin, and Mao began to appear proudly in public. Coinciding as it did with rising poverty, a faltering economy, and foreign policy zealousness, Sukarno's shift to the left sparked fear among right-wing military leaders and Western governments, as well as many pious Muslims throughout the archipelago.

On the night of September 30, 1965, in one of the seminal events in contemporary Southeast Asian history, a group of pro-Sukarno dissident army and air force officers launched a purge of their high command, alleging that a CIA-sponsored coup to topple Sukarno was being planned. In a dramatic abduction, six senior generals were murdered and subsequently dumped down a well at "Crocodile Hole" outside of Jakarta. An immediate and successful countercoup then followed, targeting the perpetrators. Within a matter of hours, the coup leaders were captured and the putsch came to an end. *Gestapu,* as it was named, collapsed because the army united against the rebels and the population failed to rise in support of the coup.

The events of 1965 remain surrounded by shadow, rumor, and intrigue. Nebulous circumstantial evidence surrounding the coup suggests possible involvement by American or British intelligence. Some skeptics theorize the whole affair was orchestrated by the CIA and the anticommunist Suharto. Nevertheless, the precise roles of the dissident army rebels, the army generals, the PKI, foreign agents, and President Sukarno himself may never be known; evidence remains inconclusive and contradictory.[2]

What is clear is that *Gestapu* rendered Sukarno politically sterile, tainting his legacy and contributing to the emancipator's ignominious demise. It is also clear that General Suharto, the commander of the Strategic Army Reserve and one of the few surviving generals, assumed command of the army and, within two years, the entire country. The events of 1965 fundamentally changed Indonesia's political structure, decimated the PKI, led to one of the worst bloodbaths in history, and swept into power a military government that ruled Indonesia for thirty years.

In the months following the failed coup, hundreds of thousands of suspected communists and sympathizers were slaughtered by members of the army and anti-communist vigilante groups. This massive slaughter was aimed primarily at Sino-Indonesians, who were despised by many for having a disproportionately large role in the Indonesian economy and who were suspected of being more loyal to their Chinese homeland and communism than to Indonesia. Despite its enormity, the slaughter did not become the focus of international condemnation, perhaps because it occurred during the height of the Cold War and because the new anticommunist government in Indonesia was allied with the United States.

By 1967, Suharto had reduced Sukarno's power, banned the PKI, ended *Konfrontasi* against Malaysia, brought Indonesia back into the United Nations, and taken all power for himself. Suharto proclaimed a "New Order" for Indonesia, ending the twenty-year charismatic, ideological, and ultimately catastrophic postindependence leadership of Sukarno and beginning a period of development-oriented, authoritarian, and stable rule that endured until the Asian economic crisis of the late 1990s. Sukarno, at the age of sixty-nine and under house arrest, died of kidney failure on June 21, 1970.

The first task of Suharto's New Order was to create a stable and legitimate political system with control throughout the archipelago; the second task was to rehabilitate the shattered economy. Suharto used the military to accomplish the first goal, portraying the armed forces as the savior against the communist threat that had existed before the coup. To counter the problems of inflation, corruption, and poor economic growth, Suharto instituted a bureaucratic authoritarian state where power was limited to the state itself, led by the military, his close friends, some Western-trained technocrats, and eventually his family members. Suharto based New Order control primarily on co-optation and bureaucratic repression.

To enhance his nationalist credentials, Suharto mobilized the Indonesian army in 1975 to occupy East Timor, after the territory had declared independence from the Portuguese that same year. He feared that Catholic East Timor would be led by leftists and could become a beachhead for Soviet expansion. In 1976, East Timor became Indonesia's twenty-seventh province, but this was accomplished amid terrible carnage with fully 10 percent of the population killed during the invasion. Over time, Suharto's Indonesia developed East Timor with schools, hospitals, and infrastructure, but most residents continued to reject Indonesian control. Indonesian suppression of East Timorese dissent was brutal and, at times, merciless. In 1996, the Nobel Peace Prize was awarded to two East Timorese leaders, Catholic Bishop

Carlos Filipe Ximenes Belo and exiled freedom fighter José Ramos Horta, for their courageous struggle against Indonesian aggression.

To consolidate power, Suharto also pursued a strategy to depoliticize all potential challengers. He purged the army of pro-Sukarno forces and made it the basis of his own strength. Suharto set up a "political organization" called Golkar (an abbreviated form of *golongan karya*, or functional group), which was administered by officials at every level of government, from national to village. Suharto also restricted political association by forcing four Muslim political parties to merge into one: the United Development Party (PPP). The remaining secular and Christian parties were also forced to merge under the Indonesian Democratic Party (PDI). These two opposition parties, the only ones permitted by law, did not have access to the state resources available to Golkar.

Throughout Suharto's thirty-year rule, political freedom and civil liberties were subject to serious constraint. Journalists self-censored their work or were subject to harassment and detention. Business associations and NGOs operated under close supervision of Golkar's corporatist state. To keep Islamic claims on the state at bay, Suharto embraced *Pancasila* as the New Order's guiding political ideology. Later, as Islam's influence grew outside his control, he sought to co-opt Islam more directly by making a pilgrimage to Mecca and supporting the formation of the Indonesian Association of Muslim Intellectuals (ICMI), an organization loyal to the New Order regime.

Suharto also used elections to prop up his legitimacy for continued rule. Golkar's victories in these elections were guaranteed through institutional arrangements ensuring that Suharto loyalists would maintain control of the People's Consultative Assembly (MPR). The MPR's membership was drawn from elected delegates, the military, and presidential appointees. Serving also as an electoral college, the MPR formally elected the president and vice president for five-year terms. Suharto thus handpicked much of the delegatory body that elected (and reelected) him to office.

Over six general elections from 1971 to 1997, the vote for Golkar never fell below 62 percent and Suharto's claim on the presidency was never challenged. Golkar's electoral success was due to (1) a requirement that all governmental bureaucrats and employees join Golkar, (2) laws that restricted political parties and prohibited a free opposition, and (3) performance legitimacy with respect to improving economic conditions and post-Sukarno political stability.

Suharto was as successful in rehabilitating the economy as he was in stabilizing and legitimizing the political system. Following the advice of a group of Western-educated economic technocrats he had assembled, he cut government and defense spending and reaped revenues from the sale of oil. As a result, inflation was reduced, per capita income was greatly increased, and economic growth maintained a steady pace. Indonesia eventually became self-sufficient in rice, and the availability of food improved. The success of Suharto's economic policy stood in stark contrast to Sukarno's failures. In 1967, when Suharto took full power, per capita GDP stood at $100; at the time of his ouster in 1998, it had risen tenfold, to $1,080. Under Suharto's watch Indonesia became recognized as a Southeast Asian tiger economy, joining the new international era as a contending emerging market.

Economic growth brought Suharto legitimacy and undercut allegations made by his detractors about the authoritarian nature of his regime. These allegations included accusations of nepotism and corruption for allowing his wife and children to control lucrative monopolies. Critics also pointed to a widening gap between rich and poor accompanying the country's tremendous economic growth. Over time, Indonesian students and intellectuals began to carefully criticize the New Order, push for increased democracy, and resist Suharto's autocratic rule. Human rights issues became central as living standards rose, a vibrant middle class emerged, and more and more Indonesians came to believe that military-dominated governments were anachronistic in an age of democratization.

By 1997, an election year, Indonesia's growing population was younger than ever. To a whole generation of Indonesians, Suharto was the only president they had known. Because of his advanced age, much discussion about the shape that post-Suharto Indonesia might take characterized the preelection period. Golkar (unsurprisingly) won a sweeping victory in Indonesia's general elections to seat representatives in the MPR, thus ensuring Suharto's reelection if he desired to stay in power. Suharto announced his availability for a seventh term even as the country confronted a growing regional economic crisis. By late 1997, Indonesia, following Thailand, faced a loss of investor confidence, capital flight, rising debt, and economic uncertainty.

As the economy soured, criticism of Suharto grew proportionally. The major criticism of Suharto's leadership concerned his family's and friends' domination of indigenous business and industrial conglomerates. More and more areas of the industrial economy—television stations, toll roads, telecommunications facilities, oil tankers—had become controlled by Suharto's children during his rule.[3] Because these monopolies arose through personal contacts with the president, the international business community became increasingly cynical about the economy.

Suharto rebuked foreign criticism and responded to detractors by using coercion, force, or denial. Free speech was continually suppressed as local and international journalists confronted restrictions. Many older Indonesians still remembered the dire poverty and chaos of the former regime and were willing to give the New Order much slack. But with a growing middle class, widespread literacy, and access to radio, television, and the printed media, the new generation of Indonesians was quickly growing into a dynamic force for change. The effects of the Asian economic crisis clashed head-on with Suharto's long-standing performance legitimacy.

With the twin pressures of economic collapse and political crisis bearing down, Suharto fretted, teetered, and balked in making needed policy adjustments during the ensuing months. An initial rescue package from the IMF was announced at the end of October 1997. This package stopped the economic slide only temporarily since new concerns over Suharto's ailing health kept investors nervous. The economy worsened, and Indonesia's currency, the rupiah, dropped to 10,000 per dollar, whereas it had been 2,430 prior to the crisis. Inflation skyrocketed. Job losses increased. Pessimism flooded the archipelago nation. Charges of official corruption, collusion, and crony capitalism became common topics for the media and public.

After twice rejecting the conditions of another IMF rescue package, Suharto, still ailing, finally agreed to a second $43 billion bailout package in April 1998. Conditionality on the massive loan, however, not only cut subsidies on crucial goods that affected everyday Indonesians (cooking oil, instant noodles, paper, plywood, and cement) but further exposed the extent to which Suharto's family and tycoon partners controlled the public budget and every major sector of the country's economy. In May, Indonesia erupted when sustained street demonstrations turned violent. Antigovernment protests proliferated, and Sino-Indonesian business owners were attacked, often brutally. The violence drove the rupiah down further, to 16,500 per dollar. Indonesia's thirty-year run of political stability and steady economic growth was over.

Amidst the disarray, on May 20, 1998, following ten days of antigovernment demonstrations led by students, Suharto resigned. B. J. Habibie, then vice president, was sworn in as the country's new leader, receiving the military's support. Because Habibie was viewed as a Suharto protégé, he faced the problem of distancing himself from the former president. The politically powerful in Indonesia viewed Habibie as an unpredictable gadfly unsuited for the presidency. While setting forth economic policies designed to resolve the crises of currency devaluation, inflation, and unemployment, Habibie indicated his support for reform and democratization. He called for new elections, free of the party constraints known under Suharto's rule.

Among Habibie's most significant decisions during his short tenure was to hold a referendum in East Timor offering an option of autonomy or independence. The result was an East Timorese majority of 78 percent favoring independence. The transition to independence was made difficult by the Indonesian military's continued oppression and violence against the East Timorese people. Massive intervention from the international community and the United Nations was eventually needed to assist Timor-Leste into its new era of independence.[4]

On June 7, 1999, democratic elections were held for the first post-Suharto Parliament in Indonesia. Some forty-eight parties competed for 500 seats. Habibie, attempting to lead Golkar, had already lost the confidence of the population and received little support. With Golkar down, the elections resulted in a plurality victory for the Partai Demokrasi Indonesia-Perjuangan (Indonesian Democracy Party-Struggle, or PDI-P), led by Megawati Sukarnoputri, daughter of the founding father and first president of Indonesia. Her party won 34 percent of the vote, or 153 seats in Parliament. Golkar won only 22 percent, or 120 seats, while Partai Kebangkitan Bangsa (National Awakening Party, or PKB) won 12 percent, or 51 seats. The PKB was led by Abdurrahman Wahid, leader of the Nahdlatul Ulama (NU), the nation's largest Islamic organization. Other parties won fewer seats.

Ninety percent of eligible Indonesians voted in this first democratic election since 1955. Because the PDI-P won the greatest number of votes, many believed Sukarnoputri would become president. However, she chose not to campaign for the presidency. Her gender worked against her, since many devout Muslims indicated they could not abide a female leader, and she was viewed as a secularist among the more fundamentalist. Wahid ran for president and won; Sukarnoputri became his vice president.

President Wahid faced overwhelming crises, none of which he successfully resolved. His tenure as president failed to come to grips with any of Indonesia's modern problems. He proved incapable of running an economy and was ill-suited for the task of recovery. His failing health also kept him from being a vibrant leader. Legally blind and enfeebled by strokes, Wahid came across as a very old person who could not cope with the daily stresses of his position. He often dozed during his own speeches, which were presented by his aide.

Under Wahid, the Indonesian archipelago looked as if it might disintegrate. Separatist movements, which had been bottled up by Suharto, hit Aceh on Sumatra, the Dayak region of Kalimantan, and West Irian Jaya (West Papua) on the eastern end of the archipelago. The resulting instability raised the question of whether Indonesia could reform and stabilize simultaneously. In 2001, after just nineteen months of his five-year term, Wahid was twice censured by the MPR as a prelude to full impeachment. The first rebuke was on February 1 and the second was on April 29. Sukarnoputri's party, PDI-P, supported censure. Wahid was asked to give a response to Parliament, which he did, but it was deemed unacceptable when he claimed the Parliament was acting unconstitutionally.

Finally, on July 22, 2001, the MPR met to debate Wahid's impeachment and to name Sukarnoputri president. The vote against Wahid was 591 to 0. Wahid responded by ordering an emergency rule, which he hoped would postpone or end the move against him, but Indonesia's security forces and the legislature defied him and did not follow the orders. Wahid warned that if he were forced from office, many provinces would attempt to separate themselves from Indonesia. But that came to naught, and on July 23, 2001, Megawati Sukarnoputri became president of the world's largest Muslim country. Wahid initially refused to leave the presidential palace but then relented and went to the United States to seek medical treatment.

Megawati Sukarnoputri had not entered politics until the mid-1990s, but rose to prominence after troops attacked her party's headquarters upon Suharto's orders. Raised in a presidential palace, a college dropout, and thrice married (including an annulled two-week elopement to an Egyptian diplomat), she was known to be taciturn, shy, and not particularly savvy regarding politics. She derived much of her support from Sukarno's charismatic aura, but her own style proved far different. "Mega," as she is commonly called, did not share her father's love for theatrical oration or his aptitude for political infighting. Upon assuming the presidency, her task was not to build a new nation but to reform Suharto's corrupt ancien régime. The effort was dubbed "*reformasi*": an agenda to reform institutions, bring corrupt officials to account, and revive the ailing economy.

Immediately dictating the context of Megawati's rule were the events of September 11, which occurred half a world away only weeks after her appointment. She soon found her country caught in the crosshairs of America's war on terrorism. She rejected claims by Washington that terrorists operated in her country until events proved her wrong. In 2002 and 2003, deadly terrorist bombings targeting nightclubs, hotels, and the Australian embassy rocked Bali and Jakarta. The plotters of the bombings, members of the Indonesia-based Jemaah Islamiyah (JI), were known communicants with Osama bin Laden's al-Qaeda. Megawati pledged to quell domestic terrorism but on her own terms, largely independent of the United States' antiterrorism framework, which was tainted by deep resentment among Indonesians, who universally condemned the U.S. occupation of Iraq.

The disconnect between the governments grew. The Bush administration viewed Indonesia as a terrorist haven but Megawati, like many Indonesians, viewed U.S. Middle East policy as responsible for her own society's victimization at the hands of chauvinistic Arab-Islamists and extremists. Alternatively, street-level conspiracy theories claimed that Bush agents had perpetrated the local bombings to bring an anti-Muslim war to Indonesia. U.S.-Indonesian relations became more strained than they had been since the Sukarno era of *Konfrontasi*.

Although attending the UN-sponsored ceremony granting Timor-Leste full independence helped Megawati's standing with Washington and Canberra, cold diplomacy defined relations between Indonesia and its principal Western partners. Unlike leaders in Thailand, the Philippines, Singapore, and even Malaysia, who cautiously supported Western antiterrorism efforts, Megawati pursued a more reticent approach. For example, fearing alienation among Muslims and taking care not to speak too strongly against political Islam, she refused to classify JI and similar groups as illegal organizations. At the same time, she apprehended suspects in the Bali and Jakarta bombings and sent them to court, where some received death sentences—although Abu Bakar Ba'asyir, the suspected mastermind and spiritual head of JI, served what eventually became a shortened prison term.

Beyond security issues and terrorism, Megawati's greatest troubles were in managing the domestic economy, controlling ethnic separatism, and delivering on her anticorruption agenda. Under her watch, foreign investment did not return to Indonesia's beleaguered economy at the rate it did elsewhere in Southeast Asia. Displaced workers continued to move into a growing informal sector, and farmers struggled with drought support. Tourism, an early recovery sector, also fell sharply, due to terrorist fears and the 2003 regional outbreak of SARS (Severe Acute Respiratory Syndrome).[5]

In both Aceh and Irian Jaya, Megawati's unprecedented attempts to establish greater autonomy backfired and resulted in further revolt and military suppression. Violent rioting between Christians and Muslims in the Moluccas islands also erupted in 2004, drawing unwanted international attention. Megawati also failed to bring to justice corrupt officials and military officers of the New Order era, including Suharto himself (deemed too ill to stand trial).

Megawati Sukarnoputri's most significant reform under *reformasi* proved to undermine her own political career. Amidst continued economic and ethnic troubles, the sitting president reversed a previous position and supported a constitutional change for direct presidential elections. Subsequently, in October 2004, she lost the presidency to Susilo Bambang Yudhoyono in the country's first direct election of an executive. Yudhoyono, a minister with a military background and security policy experience, pledged decisiveness on *reformasi* where his predecessor had failed.

Weeks later, on December 26, 2004, a magnitude 9.0 earthquake off the Sumatra coast caused the most deadly tsunami in recorded history.[6] Of the twelve countries affected, Indonesia experienced the greatest devastation: 126,804 dead; 93,458 missing; 474,619 internally displaced; and an estimated $5.4 billion in damage, a figure almost equivalent to Sumatra's entire GDP. International sympathy poured in, propelled by the media age and harrowing images of loss and destruction that were broadcast globally. Rescue aid from Asian, Western, and Muslim sources amassed with unprecedented speed and at record levels for a natural disaster. Former U.S. presidents Bill Clinton and George H. W. Bush became special UN ambassadors, to raise funds for recovery, and visited Sumatra. During the early months of 2005, the entire international community was consumed with addressing relief and recovery from the disaster in Sumatra and elsewhere.

Politically, the tsunami was significant, given that areas partial to Aceh's independence movement were among the hardest hit. Multiple countries dispatched military units to take part in a broadly coordinated aid mission. Images of U.S. troops arriving in Aceh, unthinkable before December 26, symbolized the suspension of political concern in favor of humanitarian necessity. In August 2005, Yudhoyono, less than a year into his presidency, was able to reach a disarmament agreement with Aceh's depleted rebels that offered them greater autonomy—the three-decade-old separatist movement that had produced over 15,000 deaths finally concluded. A year later Aceh held its own direct elections, selecting a former rebel leader to serve as provincial governor.

On the other side of the archipelago, untouched by the tsunami, the story in West Papua followed a different track, and Yudhoyono's efforts were less conclusive. West Papuans had been granted greater autonomy in 2002 by the government, including the shedding of the unwanted administrative name Irian Jaya in favor of West Papua. However, rough implementation of the agreement kept tensions festering and separatists hoping for an independence referendum.[7] Given the revenues West Papua's mining resources produce for the country's economy, the likelihood that Jakarta will allow such an event remains low.

Over the course of his presidency, Susilo Bambang Yudhoyono (popularly known as "SBY") skillfully reversed the direction of ailing Indonesia. Although a member of a minority party when elected (Partai Demokrat), Yudhoyono revived economic growth, quelled ethnic separatism, further depoliticized the military, and won praise from the United States and Australia for effective counterterrorism efforts. Using his specialized Detachment 88 force, funded in part by the U.S. State Department, Yudhoyono won credit for capturing Jemaah Islamiyah's top political leader, its top recruiter of suicide bombers, and its chief bomb-maker.

In spite of relative success, Yudhoyono's popularity took some hits during his first term. Indonesia's open political environment, expanding civil society, and free press held the president accountable for failed promises. Much of the *reformasi* agenda remained elusive, and impunity for corrupt officials remained problematic. Ironically, Megawati Sukarnoputri and her PDI-P colleagues were counted among the biggest critics of Yudhoyono and his inability to execute trials against Suharto and New Order tycoons, something they had also failed to achieve when in power.

On behalf of the country, government prosecutors eventually filed a lawsuit against Suharto for embezzling $440 million and for damages of $1.1 billion—by all estimates a drop in the bucket. In a 2004 report,

Transparency International estimated Suharto's ill-gained wealth at $15–35 billion and listed him as the most corrupt politician of all time; far ahead of the Philippines' Marcos (ranked second at $5–10 billion) and Mobutu of Zaire (ranked third at $5 billion). In January 2008, with his civil suit pending, Suharto died of organ failure. Neither Sukarnoputri nor Yudhoyono (nor anybody else) would ever be able to claim victory in bringing the world's most corrupt chief executive to justice.

In April 2009, SBY's Partai Demokrat swept parliamentary elections in a major defeat of Golkar and PDI-P, previously the largest parties in the assembly. In an endorsement of his leadership, Yudhoyono's party picked up a remarkable 95 new seats and secured a plurality of 150 of the body's 560 total seats. Indonesia also held its second direct presidential election on July 8, 2009. Yudhoyono, as expected, defeated his two primary challengers: Megawati Sukarnoputri (PDI-P) and Jusuf Kalla (Golkar). Both elections (which neighboring Filipinos envied for their lack of violence and controversy) signaled the decline of Suharto-era parties and the inability of Islamic parties to appeal to more than one in four Indonesian voters.[8]

During his second term, aside from some high-profile corruption scandals that created episodic firestorms of online and media activity, and failing to end labor unrest related to weak laws protecting temporary contract laborers, SBY proved skilled in guiding the country. By 2012, Indonesia enjoyed its fifth straight year with a "free" rating from Freedom House, and its consistently strong economy produced new debates about Indonesia's international status. Investors and financial experts began speculating about whether Indonesia should be listed among the so-called BRIC economies (the large producers of Brazil, Russia, India, and China), or that it should perhaps even outright replace weaker-performing Russia or India on the list.[9] Outside of China, no major economy grew more rapidly than SBY's Indonesia since the global financial meltdown of 2008–2009. Even Indonesia's corruption ranking, according to Transparency International, is moving in the right direction, dropping from 143 in 2007 to 100 in 2012.

With the passing of Suharto in 2008, ten years after his regime collapsed, Indonesia has more than symbolically transformed itself into a new political system. Today, constitutionally correct party activity, lawmaking, and peaceful leadership rivalries are encouraging developments of movement toward democratic consolidation. In Indonesia, political power is now gained, wielded, challenged, and transferred legitimately, and the country is developing the concept of loyal opposition in a plural political framework.[10] In everyday Indonesian politics, the electorate concerns itself with the rule of law, party competition, and holding elected leaders accountable, in contrast to past concerns about the legitimacy of the state or its regime. It remains to be seen whether democratic advances will endure, but, on its current trajectory, Indonesia is gradually democratizing.

INSTITUTIONS AND SOCIAL GROUPS

The Constitution

The 1945 Constitution has been the primary legal document guiding contemporary Indonesia since its independence. Although manipulated by both Sukarno and Suharto to suit their respective purposes, the document has retained popular legitimacy. Since the collapse of New Order rule, the constitution has proven pliable to reform and undergone major changes affecting all branches of government. These changes, as part of *reformasi*, have been aimed squarely at addressing past political problems.

Indonesia's current constitution oversees a hybrid presidential and parliamentary form of government. Presidents today are not rulers in the manner of either Sukarno or Suharto. Although it appears to be a presidential system, executive power is now checked by more than just an electorate. The Indonesian legislature is empowered to subject the president to votes of confidence. Elected presidents must also work with elected legislators to formulate policy. Because executives are not necessarily from the largest political party, the legislature may feel no compunction to follow the president's policy agenda. Where the president holds greatest power is in appointing cabinet members, acting as commander in chief of the armed forces, and arbitrating foreign affairs as head of state. As now amended, the constitution states that elected presidents in post-Suharto Indonesia can serve only two five-year terms.

To ensure that a president is elected by a majority rather than a plurality vote, Indonesia's constitutionally mandated electoral law employs a run-off system. In 2004, during its first direct presidential elections, for example, none of the five candidates broke the 50 percent mark to ensure victory. As top vote-getters, Susilo Bambang Yudhoyono and incumbent Megawati Sukarnoputri combined for 60 percent of the vote, forcing a runoff. Yudhoyono subsequently won over 60 percent of the runoff vote to secure the presidency. During the first round of voting in the 2009 election, SBY secured over 60 percent of the vote and a run-off was not necessary. Regardless of later postelection performance, the run-off method enhances the legitimacy of presidential selection and overall regime stability.

The present constitution establishes a 692-member People's Consultative Assembly (MPR) as the highest governmental body in the land. During most of the Sukarno period and all of the Suharto period, the MPR did not function as a free representative legislature. Only since the 1999 legislative elections and subsequent constitutional changes has the MPR begun to serve a democratic function embedded in pluralist, free party competition. Where the MPR formerly elected the president and vice president as an electoral college, a constitutional amendment in 2004 stripped the assembly of such power. Today, the MPR holds powers to pass constitutional amendments and impeach the president (an MPR power Abdurrahman Wahid would attest is indeed functional). Day-to-day legislative activity, however, is handled by the country's recently reformed bicameral legislature, whose combined membership constitutes the MPR itself.

The lower house, the Dewan Perwakilan Rakyat (People's Representative Council, or DPR), seats 560 members through national elections in a mixed system of district and proportional representation. Under the constitution, the DPR is the locus of legislative power. A body with regional representation, the 132-seat Dewan Perwakilan Daerah (Regional Representative Council, DPD), was recently developed. The DPD cannot revise DPR legislation, but it can formulate legislation related to local autonomy, resource management, fiscal matters, and other issues concerning provincial relations with the central government. Though important, the DPD does not carry the standing or authority of an upper house, such as the U.S. Senate.

Pancasila

As the country's national ideology, *Pancasila* underpins the constitution supporting the basis of statehood and the ideals of legitimate government. It includes five principles:

1. Belief in one God (embracing religious belief and tolerance vis-à-vis secularism)
2. Humanitarianism (implying civilized society absent of oppression)
3. Nationalism (implying unity amidst ethnic diversity, or *Bhinneka Tunggal Ika*)
4. Democracy (defined as consensus-oriented decisionmaking, or *musyawarah-mufakat*)
5. Social justice (idealized as the economic welfare of all peoples of Indonesia)

To create a defense against Western liberalism as well as Islamic privilege, Indonesia's founders sought to develop an anticolonial political ideology that embodied republicanism and embraced Indonesian aspirations. Few have since questioned its validity, although its interpretation occupies the ideological center of Indonesian political debate. Islamic groups, in particular, are among those who challenge *Pancasila*'s secular dimensions. One such challenge came in 1980 when Islamic groups, the PPP, and a number of retired military figures submitted a petition known as the "Petisi Kelompok 50" (Group of 50 Petition), criticizing Suharto and his administration for using *Pancasila* to undermine political opposition. Predictably, the government-dominated Parliament ignored the petition.[11]

Open to interpretation with changing conditions, *Pancasila* ideology has retained its legitimacy throughout the country's major political transitions. Although no longer required, most political parties, including SBY's Partai Demokrat, embrace *Pancasila* as their official party ideology. In the post-Suharto era, government manipulation of *Pancasila* has given way to increasing public contestation of its meaning.

Although attempts have been made, no other Southeast Asian country can claim the success Indonesia has had in creating and maintaining its own state philosophy. Among Muslim-predominant countries elsewhere, *Pancasila* has arguably proven less divisive than Turkey's secular-rationalist Kemalism, more internationally and domestically legitimate than Iran's theocratic imperative, and more compatible with modernity than the ultra-conservative Salafism currently animating antimodern Islamist movements throughout the Muslim world. In analyses of the ongoing Arab Spring, many observers vaunt Indonesia as the preeminent model of an Islamic society with functional pluralist democracy. *Pancasila*, which is the often-overlooked ideological core of that model, is among Sukarno's most admirable legacies.

Political Parties

Until the 1999 election, no party was realistically able to compete with Golkar, the official party of the government and the military. Golkar functioned simultaneously as the principal support of the government and as the representative of the Indonesian people. The military originally established Golkar in the 1960s to oppose communist organizations; thus, the party developed a national apparatus down to the village level. The only other permissible parties under New Order rule—the United Development Party (PPP) and the Indonesian Democratic Party (PDI), were destined to oppositional roles and split Golkar's opponents into two controlled camps.

All of this changed in 1999 when Indonesia held open democratic elections with multiple parties. The biggest plurality of votes went to Megawati Sukarnoputri's Indonesian Democracy Party-Struggle (PDI-P), which garnered 34 percent of votes for the DPR. Golkar won only 22 percent, down over 40 percentage points from the previous election. At the time, the MPR still elected the country's executive. Although Megawati had rights to claim the presidency because of her party's plurality victory, Abdurrahman Wahid managed to win a majority of votes to become president. Sukarnoputri was made vice president. The aftermath of the election was chaotic, but the bigger picture was clear: For the first time in their lives, most Indonesians were able to participate in the political system and freely choose their own leaders.

At campaign rallies, in print, and through diverse forms of public and private interaction, Indonesians became citizens able to express their complaints, opinions, and aspirations.

Subsequent parliamentary and presidential elections—as well as various local, mayoral, and gubernatorial elections (instituted as part of *reformasi*)— have included political parties and candidates from across the spectrum. As many as thirty-eight parties contested in the 2009 general elections. New rules for that election demanded a threshold of 2.5 percent of the national vote before parties could claim DPR seats through proportional representation. Nine parties passed the 2.5 percent threshold in 2009, but 29 smaller parties, representing a combined 20 million votes (or one-fifth of all votes cast), were excluded from the assembly. Many parties who lost seats or failed to reach the new threshold were Islamic parties.

Thus far, the institutionalization of particular parties appears a long way off. With the exception of Golkar, most major parties operate around strong figures, their personalities, and even famous families (such as Megawati's PDI-P). Successful leadership succession within parties and greater levels of trust and confidence from the electorate will be important markers of a more stable party system. Unfortunately, money politics, vote-buying scandals, and voter registration fraud are increasing problems in Indonesia and a cause of disillusionment and cynicism among voters. Such problems do not yet delegitimize election outcomes, but if they remain unaddressed, a loss of faith in democracy could grow. Combined with the country's judicial system, which is also prone to corruption, Indonesia's political parties remain a weak element in the country's democratic development.

Political Islam

As the largest Muslim country in the world, Indonesia has a relatively admirable record of integrating Islam into its secular political system. Political Islam, or the participation in political life motivated by Islamic values, has not produced the degree of instability, conflict, or antigovernment rebellion experienced elsewhere in Southeast Asia. Revolutionary Islam has proven more vexing to governments in Thailand and the Philippines. In these countries, Muslim minorities have been oppressed and have engaged in longstanding, Muslim-based separatist movements. In Malaysia, where large, non-Muslim Chinese and Indian minorities live side by side with a Muslim majority, political Islam has proven more divisive than in Indonesia.

Nevertheless, political Islam does animate Indonesian politics, and the more open period of post-Suharto politics has expanded the range and intensity of its recent involvement. Although religious and sectarian clashes erupt on occasion in parts of the archipelago (sometimes with deadly consequences), a broad-based, organized Islamic revolution on the scale experienced in Iran and Afghanistan is not featured in Indonesian experience. Thousands of varied religious institutions and strands of Islamic expression exist in Indonesia. This Islamic milieu weaves itself into the fabric of Indonesian society in a manner that defies traditional or monolithic characterization. Islam in Indonesia is temporally dynamic and socially contested.

Indonesian Muslims have a reputation for practicing a moderate, if syncretic, brand of Islam. About 99 percent of Muslims in Indonesia are Sunni. The heterogeneity that characterizes Islamic belief and practice in the country is rooted in the division between *santri* and *abangan* cultures within Java as well as other forces of *aliran* (i.e., vertical divisions across society produced by ethno-linguistic differences and identity politics). *Santri*, or pious Muslims, generally represent political Islam, whereas *abangan,* or nominal Muslims, lean toward secular politics and absorb cultural influence from *priyayi* traditions (pre-Islamic, Javanese-Hindu customs and supernatural beliefs). In Indonesian politics the dichotomy between *santri* and *abangan* drives much of political Islam, including much of the Islamic antipathy toward a hegemonic *Pancasila* ideology.[12]

Aliran forces influence how Islam is interpreted and practiced from group to group and region to region. Loyalties in Indonesia have traditionally been to the group first, exacerbating ethnic tensions but mitigating the formation of superior Islamic identity or a single Indonesian Muslim narrative. Because of these factors, Islamic revolution is unlikely to emerge or achieve a hegemonic role in Indonesian political life. Moreover, as Indonesia's rulers could attest, it is not easy to mobilize a diverse population of nearly a quarter-billion people for any cause, be it *Marhaenism*, communism, or some singular Islamic vision.

Since independence, Indonesia's leaders have nevertheless remained cautious about the potential for political Islam to coalesce into a larger political movement with revolutionary aims. By embracing the national ideology of *Pancasila*, radical Islamist aspirations have been suppressed by successive regimes that have embraced Islam's presence alongside the security imperatives of ethnic and religious diversity. Further, state patronage and regulation of Islam have often placed serious parameters around Islamic education and influences from outside Indonesia, especially under Suharto. By demobilizing Islam, Suharto, with an *abangan-priyayi* upbringing, began to co-opt Islam for seeming political gain. Suharto become a *hajji* (pilgrim to Mecca) and supported the creation of the Indonesian Association of Muslim Intellectuals (ICMI). He also developed a purposeful program to send the country's Islamic scholars to study at centers in Europe and North America, thus avoiding the more radical mosques in the Middle East.[13]

In Indonesia today, political Islam's largest role is found not in extremist movements but in political parties and mainstream social associations that champion Islamic values without pressing for the creation of an Islamic state. Prominent political parties include the United Development Party (PPP) and the Prosperous Justice Party (PKS). While both claim Islam as their ideology, neither advocates Islamic republicanism or state-based sharia (Islamic law). Together the PPP and PKS garnered over 16 million votes in the 2004 DPR elections but only 13.7 million in 2009. These numbers are strong but pale in comparison to the more politically significant social organizations, such as Nahdlatul Ulama (NU) and Muhammadiyah.

Dating back to the 1920s, Nahdlatul Ulama (Religious Scholars) formed in response to rising European Christian activity, secularism, and communism within Indonesia. During much of the Suharto period, Abdurrahman Wahid served as NU's leader. Wahid formally "removed" NU from politics in 1984 by withdrawing from the Suharto-forced coalition of Islamic parties that composed the PPP. Concentrating instead on the organization's own development, Wahid's NU sought to assist Indonesia's Muslims through the religious and social concerns arising from rapid economic change. Wahid later founded Forum Demokrasi in response to Suharto's creation of ICMI. At the time of Suharto's resignation in 1998, NU was poised to reemerge as a political force with its estimated 35 million members. Though it has thus far resisted the temptation to transform into a political party, NU does throw its support behind Islamic-oriented parties and candidates, such as Wahid himself. Widespread on Java, NU finds support among rural Javanese and in religious schools.

Muhammadiyah and its female organizational arm, Nasyiatul Aisyiyah, claim membership of over 30 million. Muhammadiyah's primary goals are religious and educational. It sets up schools to promote Sunni Islam while also educating about democracy and public health. One of its most recent influential leaders, Amien Rais, helped force Suharto's resignation in 1998 and later led the national assembly. Nasyiatul Aisyiyah, founded in 1917, has sought to define women's roles and, more recently, Arabism within Islam. Expressing disdain for fundamentalist Islam, women in Aisyiyah work against extremist ideologies that give little space for women within Islam.[14] The organization has even partnered with USAID to fund health projects and promote family planning with noted success.[15]

At the other extreme from parties and religious associations that engage Indonesian society through legitimate political channels are Islamist organizations that employ violence and terror to advance their chief cause: destroying the republic and creating an Islamic state. Although on the fringe of Indonesian society (socially and numerically), these groups create significant political problems for Indonesia and overall foreign relations. Some groups, such as Laskar Jihad, instigate communal violence targeting nonbelievers;

others, such as Jemaah Islamiyah (JI), seek international attention by targeting foreign interests.

Movements favoring the creation of an Islamic republic date back to the 1950s; however, the most radical groups in Indonesia formed within the past two decades. Jemaah Islamiyah was formed in 1993. The group was tied to five major bombings in Bali and Jakarta from 2002 to 2005 and later saw its top officials arrested and brought to trial. Yudhoyono in particular launched more aggressive efforts to weaken JI than his predecessors. In 2008, when JI bombers were convicted and executed and the organization was finally declared illegal, few Indonesians came to its defense.

Mainstream society within Indonesia, increasingly convinced of the pernicious effects of radical organizations, currently demonstrates a new willingness to allow elected officials political space to deal with extremist groups. Indonesia's most recent bombings, in July 2009, targeted two Western hotels and killed 9 people, including the two attackers. The architect of these and previous attacks, Malaysian fugitive Nordin Top, was killed in a raid by Indonesian security forces three months later. In 2010, police raided a Jakarta Internet café and killed one of the last suspects in the 2002 Bali bombings. That same year the British-based risk analysis firm Mapelcroft, designer of the Terrorism Risk Index, removed Indonesia from its list of countries at "extreme risk" for terrorist activity. Because of ongoing Islamist unrest in their Muslim-majority provinces, Thailand and the Philippines, nevertheless, remained on the list through 2012.

Military

For much of Indonesia's postindependence period, especially under Suharto, the military pervasively intervened in politics. Aside from Burma, no other Southeast Asian nation had experienced the same degree of military involvement in day-to-day governance. However, the political role of the Indonesian Armed Forces, or the Tentara Nasional Indonesia, has decreased dramatically in the post–New Order era, although its latent power to act remains strong and should not be discounted given the country's history.

Once the political role of the military was enshrined in state doctrine, its leaders set forth the notion of *dwi fungsi*, or dual function, ensuring for itself both a security and a sociopolitical role in Indonesian society. Through legislation, this dual role legitimated the military's involvement as cabinet officers, governors of provinces, members of the legislative body, and leaders of Golkar. Until Suharto's overthrow, it was impossible to imagine an Indonesian administration without the active participation of army generals. The agenda of *reformasi* includes professionalizing the military and dismantling military *dwi fungsi* by removing generals from their designated seats in the assembly and their spots on corporate boards, where many "soldier-tycoons" amassed great wealth in the 1980s and 1990s. Since 2004, no appointed seats for the military or anybody else exist in the MPR. Today, only elected representatives govern Indonesia's lawmaking bodies, as well as the republic's chief executive office.

STATE-SOCIETY RELATIONS AND DEMOCRACY

The diversity of Indonesia's population and its demographic character make the country difficult to control. This diversity, among other forces, has shaped the process of state building, the autonomy and legitimacy of the state, and the development of civil society and democracy.

Like the Philippines, much of Indonesia experienced a long colonial rule (350 years as the Dutch East Indies), during which its economy served Dutch interests through the exploitation of Indonesia's people and natural resources. The impact of the Spaniards and Americans on the Philippines was greater than that of the Dutch on the Indonesians, perhaps because there had been powerful indigenous empires in Sumatra and Java before the Dutch arrived, whereas there had been none in the Philippines before the Spanish arrived. The Japanese occupation of Indonesia, while not as devastating as in the Philippines, was an important event. Moreover, Indonesia waged a four-year war against the Dutch, who returned to retake their former colony after the defeat of the Japanese; thus, a revolutionary war led to rebellions and ethnic-based regional struggles between contenders for power.

Sukarno's fusion of his own political charisma and power to build a young state was effective in bringing unity to diversity, but narrower economic and political failures undid his regime. Never fully autonomous from the powerful forces of a military with praetorian ambitions, a communist insurgency, and Javanese societal prejudice, the political legitimacy of Sukarno's young state was fragile. In spite of his successes in leading Indonesia to independence and fashioning a new state ideology (*Pancasila*), a lingua franca (*Bahasa Indonesia*), and a singular economic philosophy (*Marhaenism*), Sukarno ultimately discovered that grand ideals alone were not enough to sustain state legitimacy and personal authority.

Following the *Gestapu* coup of 1965, Indonesian society experienced a major bloodbath when about half a million Indonesians were killed. The violence spread as racial, religious, ethnic, social, economic, and political differences were judged to be sufficient cause for mass killings. What began as a political cleansing to oust communists became an orgy of killing and a breakdown of law and order. The Communist Party of Indonesia (PKI), tallying 3.5 million members (and 23.5 million in affiliated organizations), was virtually annihilated. The ideals and state institutions created by Suharto collapsed and proved unable to protect vulnerable citizens. His collapsing state was replaced by a repressive military state born from chaos. Gradually, the New Order evolved into a stable state dependent on tight political controls and performance legitimization.

In contrast to the Sukarno era, a strong, autonomous state emerged under Suharto. He brought various groups of people into his ruling circle to create this autonomy. Suharto's oft-celebrated technocrats brought order to the economy and thereby managed to strengthen his claim to power. Even more important, Suharto won the ongoing loyalty of military leaders who consolidated their power around the regime and their access to economic opportunity.

Under New Order rule, the strong state controlled all aspects of political and economic life and was not subservient to particular societal forces. Suharto depoliticized and co-opted all institutional and societal forces to maintain and enhance state power. Forever distrustful of politics, Suharto intimidated some societal groups with military coercion under *dwi fungsi*, emasculated others through administrative corporatism, and bought off others by giving them a stake in rapid economic growth. Consequently, the state's legitimacy found itself fused to Suharto's capacity to meet the economic needs of the citizenry and to his ability to protect the country's security both internally and externally. This troubled legitimacy caused close observers at the time to predict another episode of political tragedy.[16]

Today, all potentially powerful groups are essentially integrated into the polity. The military, once overwhelmingly powerful, is now taking its place as a state-based interest group amidst an array of formal and informal pressure groups. The elected legislature is rising in its importance and proving capable of checking the abuse of presidential power (e.g., Wahid's). Even the most prominent societal groups once left out of the system (political Islam and Muslim parties) are now functioning freely and competing within a democratic constitutional framework. Although the state ideology of *Pancasila* is more openly challenged than in the past, the absence of forced allegiance to it (or prohibition against it) has allowed for its organic development and its own post-Suharto legitimacy.

Vis-à-vis society, Indonesia's state has weakened since the collapse of bureaucratic authoritarianism. Nevertheless, the state is not necessarily vulnerable to hegemonic control by a single group. Here, Indonesia's diversity and growing pluralism are assets to its political development. The current trend embracing constitutionalism strengthens the durability of political order and state capability. The extent to which the diverse set of players in Indonesian politics further legitimate constitutionalism, the rule of law, and sanctioned authority will determine the possibility of a resurgent, strong state. Ethnic groups, political parties, political Islam, Javanese elites, the military, the business community, ruralites, non-Muslims, intellectuals, journalists, and civil society organizations (CSOs) must find consensus in the rules of the game while simultaneously keeping state power at bay and from falling prey to particularistic interests or dominance.

Until 1999, liberal democracy had not flourished in postindependence Indonesia. The one attempt to fashion such a system, which lasted from 1950 to 1957, featured multiple political parties and a parliamentary government. However, that period was a time of great political unrest as the country moved from dependence on its Dutch colonizers to independence. Sukarno, who was president during the transition, paid little attention to necessary day-to-day administrative tasks; nevertheless, the democratic system was blamed for the collapse of the economy and the country's infrastructure. Consequently, Sukarno's notion of a unique, indigenous form of guided democracy was readily embraced as more fitting for Indonesia.

Traditional Indonesian political culture is essentially hierarchical and authoritarian: Authorities at the center do not tolerate opposition that will endanger the potency of the state.[17] Sukarno's notion of democracy appeared to fit traditional Javanese value systems in which power is bestowed on one person, usually a sultan. From an Indonesian perspective, therefore, guided democracy was the most effective way to make policy, even if that process is not compatible with Western notions of representative and accountable government.

From a Western perspective, on the other hand, guided democracy ensured the perpetuation of Sukarno's power at the expense of the liberties and openness available under liberal democracy. From this vantage point, real democracy was destroyed not by a traditional culture but by corrupt, power-hungry politicians who established repressive policies and authoritarian institutions to retain their positions. Similarly, Suharto's New Order can be viewed from this perspective as the archetypal authoritarian administration that mouthed the virtues of democracy but practiced the politics of dictatorship.

Rejecting both of these extreme positions, a younger generation of educated officials emerged to suggest that accountability and civil liberties are not exclusive values of the West, and that as Indonesia's population becomes educated, informed, and economically developed, there is no reason why Western democratic institutions cannot be compatible with Indonesian culture. Adding to the demand for a more open society were the numerous CSOs in Indonesia, representing women's groups, trade unions, student organizations, labor, and various causes. Their growth in the 1990s represented rising dissatisfaction with the lack of liberty and the suffocating restrictions under the New Order.

Emerging from the Suharto era, many Indonesians did not want Indonesia to be viewed as having an anachronistic political system in an era of democratization. The transition from Suharto to Habibie to Wahid was chaotic but set the stage for meaningful constitutional reform. The 1999 elections were a watershed development, setting the precedent for open party competition. Significantly, the willingness of Megawati and Yudhoyono to play by the rules and endure political victory or failure without resorting to power grabs, emergency declarations, or extraconstitutional measures is the greatest contribution they could offer to Indonesia's democratic future. The contrast here with Thai elites and the never-dying impulse to turn to the king or the military during political crisis, and the Philippine practice of presidential-military alliances and martial law declarations, is indeed notable.

Across the Indonesian polity, an expectation of constitutionally correct politics is taking root. A broad-based political settlement between state and society appears to have emerged—one grounded in democratic pluralism. As a state, the Republic of Indonesia has transcended serious challenges by ethnic groups, political movements, and undemocratic leaders. Following Sukarno's highly volatile balancing act, Suharto's authoritarian New Order, and a wretched crisis-driven transition, Indonesia's young constitutionally based regime is showing potential and a will for consolidation. Such a feat, however, must be read against the history of previous regimes and their undoing. Events have overtaken Indonesia's political system before and may do so again in the future. For now, however, state-society relations and the country's democratic institutions appear to be transcending previous threats, including the forces of *aliran* and ethnic separatism.

ECONOMY AND DEVELOPMENT

The Indonesian economy is the largest in Southeast Asia. In the developing world only China, India, Brazil, and Mexico have larger economies when standardized for purchasing power parity. Even as a demographic giant, Indonesia's economic gains in recent decades have rendered the country's per capita GNI ($2,940) higher than many of its less populated regional neighbors (Philippines, Vietnam, Cambodia, Laos, Burma, and Timor-Leste). Having averaged over 6 percent GDP growth each year from 1965 to 1997, during the Asian financial crisis Indonesia sunk to an alarming negative GDP growth of –13.1 percent. Since that nadir, economic growth has climbed back to a high in 2011 of 6.5 percent. Impressively, Indonesia's economy did not contract during the 2008–2009 financial crisis, and from 2000 to 2011 its economy averaged as fairly stable 5.1 percent of annual GDP growth.

Sukarno's "revolutionary" economic system under his guided democracy was isolationist and xenophobic, skewed to meet ideological goals rather than the needs of the citizenry. Suharto's New Order economics sought to provide order to replace disorder and rationality to replace irrationality so that economic development would become the yardstick by which the success of his regime would be measured.

For the most part, the yardstick measured steady although not spectacular growth, but it was enough to buy a substantial share of popular support and political stability. The means to this end were a series of five-year plans to improve the public welfare, realize a financial bonanza from oil revenues, follow the advice of economic technocrats, repair the infrastructure, and begin to rely on the private sector for the necessary capital, structural change, and productivity.[18] The technocrats behind the recovery came to be known as the "Berkeley Mafia," a group of Indonesian economists trained at the University of California–Berkeley in the 1950s. Although the results were generally positive, some difficulties were encountered, including widespread income disparity, corruption, and mismanaged industries. Over time, a countertrend developed within the New Order for greater economic nationalism.

The most badly managed company was the government-owned oil industry, Pertamina, which went bankrupt in the 1970s. Led by President Suharto's colleague General Ibnu Sutowo, Pertamina incurred huge debts from lavish spending on useless projects. When oil prices dropped precipitously from $34 per barrel in 1981 to $8 per barrel in the mid-1980s, economic growth in Indonesia fell correspondingly, ending a decade of greatly increased government outlays for education, infrastructure, and communications. The Indonesian economy's dependence on the oil sector in the 1980s was evident in that oil exports accounted for 78 percent of export earnings, and oil revenues accounted for 70 percent of government income at that time.[19] A decade earlier, by contrast, oil revenues had accounted for less than 20 percent of government income.

During the 1980s, policies to promote exports and foreign investment more aggressively replaced the policies of import substitution favored by economic nationalists and characterized by protectionism and heavy government intervention in distributing capital. The success of the new policy was shown by the fact that foreign investment commitments rose more than threefold over a three-year period, from $1.4 billion in 1987 to $4.7 billion in 1989.

Part of the reason for the great increase in foreign investment under Suharto was that Indonesia, like Thailand, became a major assembly area for manufacturers from Hong Kong, Singapore, Taiwan, South Korea, and even the United States. Most investments were in labor-intensive, low-technology industries such as footwear, food canning, textiles, and wood processing, where Indonesia's low wages attracted entrepreneurs from higher-wage countries.[20] In addition, the indigenous Chinese, who have long been active in the economy, were given greater leeway in return for their support of Golkar. Officials and military officers provided Chinese business executives with protection and useful legislation, while in return the Chinese supplied capital and access to profits from their businesses. These Chinese business-people, called *cukong* (boss), were resented by Indonesian entrepreneurs, who viewed the *cukong* system as corrupt and exclusive.

In addition to growth tainted with corruption, other paradoxical legacies of Indonesia's rapid economy emerged. Although some new wealth trickled down to allow a small middle class to emerge, the rich quickly became richer. Absolute poverty declined markedly, but many Indonesians continued to live a subsistence existence. Foreign investment flooded in, but pleasing investors and ensuring their confidence came at the expense of labor rights and the local environment.

Although foreign investment leveled off in the 1990s as China and Vietnam became cheap-labor competitors, the cumulative effect of investment left the country vulnerable, as demonstrated by massive capital flight caused by the late 1990s "Asian Contagion." While the collapse of the Thai baht triggered a regional crisis, the depths to which Indonesia sunk were a result of the inherent weaknesses of the New Order economy, exacerbated by international exuberance for emerging markets and reckless flows of hot money.

In the years before the crisis, the New Order administration moved in contradictory directions, sometimes supporting market mechanisms and liberalization and other times state intervention and the protection of conglomerates controlled by Suharto's family or cronies. The overall strength of the economy and the high rates of economic growth led to some careless policy choices and regulations, most notably nationalist and protectionist policies Suharto engineered to protect those closest to him.

Hutomo Mandala Putra, known as "Tommy Suharto"—a favored son of the president—benefited greatly from his father's patronage at state expense. He was given rights to produce the "national car," the Timor (which is actually imported from South Korea). Tommy's exclusive tax exemptions and tariff concessions allowed him to sell the Timor at about half the price of competing vehicles. The United States challenged Suharto's support for Indonesia's national car on the grounds that to exempt it from taxes levied against imported cars was unfair. Domestically, many wealthy Indonesians refused to buy the Timor, citing its poor performance as an excuse that often masked their contempt for the family dynasty's use of its economic privileges to attempt to corner one of the most promising markets in Indonesia.

Tommy was also presented with lucrative contracts with the Burmese State Law and Order Restoration Council (SLORC) and was awarded Indonesia's trade monopoly for cloves. Suharto named him head of the Clove Marketing Board, a position that provided him with the ability to generate tremendous revenue. His siblings received similarly lucrative contracts. His eldest sister, Tutut Siti Hadijanti Rukmana, held a controlling interest in a company that collected revenues from Java's principal toll roads, occupied a senior post in

Golkar, and was being groomed as a potential successor to her father. All of Suharto's six children, in fact, were involved in the nation's primary industries: automobiles, petrochemicals, computers, oil, and satellite communications.

Suharto responded to the national community only when the pressure to do so was particularly great. For example, in 1997 he stepped in to block a ministry recommendation that effectively would have forced parents to buy children's shoes from a company owned by the president's eldest grandson. The issue had been on the front pages of national newspapers since it was made public that the ministry had recommended that all elementary schoolchildren wear identical shoes, to be sold for $10.70 a pair. Indonesia's daily minimum wage at the time was about $3. The shoes were dubbed "national shoes" by the public, in reference to the "national car" being manufactured by Tommy Suharto.

In 1997 and 1998, when emergency packages were negotiated with the IMF, new details of Suharto family nepotism and corruption percolated to the surface. Public disdain for the Suharto family grew. The austerity measures imposed as part of loan conditionality proved painful for not only Suharto's family and associates but also, by consequence, Indonesia's general population.

The IMF viewed the economic artifice Suharto had created as the cause of Indonesia's woes and dismantled it virtually overnight. In large part, the Suharto-tied monopolies, as well as importer arrangements, distorted prices of standard goods and items, not just automobiles, cloves, and satellite communications. The IMF-imposed lifting of subsidies, provoking a further slide of the rupiah, caused shortages and huge price increases on rice, cooking oil, instant noodles, paper, and cement. The economic crisis before the IMF measures, itself severely disrupting, demanded economic stimulus, not austerity. At the time when state capital was most needed to buoy an economy suffering capital flight and loss of demand, and when Indonesia's laid-off workers needed subsidized benefits most, IMF measures forced sudden price volatility and sudden budget austerity, and directed $43 billion in rescue funds to pay off international banks and creditors. Unemployment skyrocketed to 15–20 percent. Protesters turned their rage on Suharto's administration, Chinese businesspeople, and the IMF. Social disruption arose. The performance legitimacy of the New Order collapsed.

The Habibie and Wahid administrations suffered the burden of cleaning up the mess. Habibie's tenure, tainted by his Suharto connections, was dominated by political crisis and East Timor's independence, and Wahid, whom many considered incapable of economic thinking, faced economic conditions that would frighten the most skilled policy managers. Sukarnoputri more capably brought stability to the economy, but it was not until Yudhoyono's presidency that "recovery" became more of a reality than a distant hope.

Yudhoyono implemented a set of economic policies designed to reduce unemployment, provide relief to the poorest Indonesians, and restore confidence in the embattled financial sector. To these ends, he invested in infrastructure development and sponsored cash packages and subsidies on rice and housing for the poorest strata. He also developed a deposit insurance scheme while encouraging the growth of sharia banking. Yudhoyono also withdrew Indonesia from membership in OPEC (the Organization of Petroleum Exporting Countries) in 2008 as the country transitioned to being a net oil importer. The move reflected the growth and dynamism of the domestic economy. The outcome of these reforms and others was generally positive; foreign investment confidence improved, as did perceptions related to business corruption.[21] Indonesia's past reputation as a difficult foreign investment environment is now changing. A 2011 BBC survey of 24,000 people across 24 countries discovered that Indonesia was home to the most entrepreneur-friendly culture in the world, ahead of other top countries, the United States, Canada, and Australia.[22]

Despite New Order corruption, severe economic crisis, and years of painful economic recovery, the quality of life of average Indonesians has improved significantly over the past four decades. Life expectancy, under fifty years in 1965, now stands at seventy-one years. Primary school enrollment climbed from 41 percent to 94 percent, and literacy is now at 99 percent. Astonishingly, over a forty-year period when its population grew by 75 million people (the equivalent to two Californias), Indonesia saw its poverty rate lower from 60 percent to 13 percent. In terms of the Human Development Index, Indonesia's value from 1975 to 2011 went from 0.47 to 0.62, a more dramatic swing than that experienced by any other Southeast Asian country or other impressive developers such as China, Mexico, and Brazil.

With these gains, Indonesia is on track to meet many of its UN Millennium Development Goals (MDGs) including poverty reduction, literacy, and female enrollment in school. It will also meet goals to significantly reduce under-five mortality, the prevalence of underweight children, and the incidence of tuberculosis. However, it will not likely meet targeted reductions in the country's maternal mortality rate, HIV/AIDS rates (which continue to increase), and carbon dioxide emissions by the MDG deadline of 2015.

FOREIGN RELATIONS

As in other Southeast Asian nations, the primary goal of Indonesia's postindependence foreign policy has been to sustain the republic's security. Sukarno's means to this end relied on anti-Western nationalism; he was opposed to what he called the "old established forces," or "OLDEFOS," and allied with what he called the "newly emerging forces," or "NEFOS." OLDEFOS included the neoimperialist nations and their allies, led by the

United States. NEFOS, on the other hand, included the "progressive" third world and communist nations, locked in struggle against OLDEFOS. Sukarno's *Konfrontasi* against Malaysia, which began in 1962 and ended in 1965, was described as a classic example of a NEFOS struggle against an OLDEFOS lackey. Supporting Sukarno's foreign policy against the agents of neocolonialism, colonialism, and imperialism was the PKI.

When his New Order was inaugurated, Suharto ended *Konfrontasi*, banned the PKI, and reentered the international arena with a pro-Western, anticommunist foreign policy. New Order Indonesia's quiet support for ASEAN and the Zone of Peace, Freedom, and Neutrality in Southeast Asia reflected its leadership's lower profile in international relations. During the Suharto regime, Indonesia played only a minor role in international affairs, despite the fact that the nation was the fourth-most-populated country in the world and was of immense importance economically, geographically, and strategically.

The major exception to Indonesia's nonintrusive participation in foreign affairs was Suharto's decision to invade East Timor in 1975. This action exacerbated a vigorous guerrilla insurgency movement, which continued throughout East Timor's annexation. Habibie's decision to allow an independence referendum sparked further violence and resulted in the humiliating presence of international peacekeepers and UN authorities.

Relations between Indonesia and the People's Republic of China improved gradually following two decades of tension resulting from the *Gestapu* coup. As part of ASEAN, Indonesia gradually moved foreign policy closer to that of the other ASEAN countries. Sharing interests in checking Vietnamese power, Thailand and China made accommodations with each other in the 1970s. In the 1980s, Sino-Thais began forming connections with their ancestral land, and a vigorous economic relationship began to grow. Indonesia, on the other hand, took until August 1990 to formally establish diplomatic relations with China, ending twenty-five years of hostility. It was not until the presidency of Megawati Sukarnoputri that any significant bilateral efforts were made to expand trade between the two countries. The United States, Japan, Singapore, and other Asian and European countries have continued to be Indonesia's primary markets and sources of investment. Development assistance from the United Nations, the World Bank, the IMF, and bilateral partners continues to shape macro- and micro-level economic policies, but in 2008 Indonesia was invited to join the G-20, the Group of 20 countries that control 85 percent of world GDP.

Unlike Singapore, the Philippines, and Thailand, which emerged as overt and quiet partners in George W. Bush's war on terrorism, Indonesia proved a more reluctant partner and was instinctively leery of U.S. power and its misuse. Sukarnoputri's government publicly opposed the U.S. invasions of

Afghanistan and Iraq following the 9/11 attacks. Susilo Bambang Yudhoyono later welcomed tsunami-related humanitarian assistance from the United States as well as resources to support counterterrorism within Indonesia. General foreign policy skepticism of the United States' relationship with Israel and its war on terrorism persisted through the end of the Bush administration.

Barack Obama's election in late 2008 opened a new door to improving relations between the third and fourth most populous countries in the world. Only days after the historic election, and before Obama had spent a day in office, President Yudhoyono had already called Obama's foreign policy "refreshing" and proposed a strategic partnership with the United States that included stronger people-to-people relations. Obama, he said, "spoke our language, knew our culture, ate our food, played with Indonesian friends . . . [and] experienced the inner soul of Indonesia."[23] In one of his first moves in crafting a new foreign policy direction for the United States, Obama sent Secretary of State Hillary Clinton to Asia in February 2009. Children from the Indonesian school Obama once attended welcomed Clinton with songs and flowers. In a press conference from Jakarta, she celebrated Indonesia's new stability as a Muslim-majority democracy and pledged to work toward a "comprehensive partnership" between the two countries. After two disappointing cancellations, Barack Obama finally visited Indonesia during the 2011 East Asia Summit, which Indonesia hosted.

Indonesia's regional role as a diplomatic mediator and a Muslim-world symbol of democracy continues to rise over time. It constructively helped to resolve the Cambodian crisis and maritime disputes among ASEAN states, and serves as a mediator between Burma and the international community. In the Spratly Islands dispute, Indonesia supports its ASEAN neighbors and even penned a letter to the United Nations stating that Chinese claims lacked a legal basis and "encroach [on] the legitimate interests of the global community."[24] Internationally, Indonesia's status draws considerable attention among the global Islamic community for its successful economic growth and recent political reform toward political openness. Even as it fosters pan-Islamic unity, Indonesia also offers a moderating voice within the Organization of the Islamic Conference.

Conclusion

In terms of stability, democratic political representation, and civil liberties, Indonesia's political direction today is more favorable than at any time in postindependence history. Although the country is forever challenged by geographic and demographic realities, inertia from its current record of economic growth raises the prospects for continued development. The disruption caused by the Asian economic crisis may have been deeper in

Indonesia than elsewhere in Southeast Asia, but a favorable democratic dividend has resulted. Politically, Indonesia today stands in contrast to the troubled eras of instability and authoritarianism in previous decades.

Emerging from the tumultuous years of the Sukarno era, the New Order regime created conditions for economic growth but measured political development in terms of stability. The New Order proved institutionally weak and unable to transcend political crisis when economic growth halted. Of course, millions of Indonesians did see their lives improve during the thirty-year regime of Suharto, but performance legitimacy proves a risky foundation for long-term rule. Suharto, like his predecessor, suffered an ignominious demise. The revelations of Suharto family privilege, cronyism, and corruption paraded before the world—coupled with humiliating, painful, and ill-conceived IMF rescue packages—were more than the Indonesian public could bear. It was thus from the ashes of the New Order's collapse that the country's rising expectations for democracy and demands for accountable government emerged.

How long the current trend in building institutions of representation and accountability will endure remains an open question, but signs of sustainability are undeniable. Unlike the Philippines (troubled by an entrenched oligarchy), Thailand (prone to constitutional crises and extraconstitutional impulses), or Singapore, Malaysia, and Cambodia (controlled by illiberal, hegemonic parties), a growing consensus is emerging across Indonesia that democracy is desirable and possible. Representative government, parliamentary governance, and open party competition are now ideals embraced by ethnic groups, social classes, political Islam, and (importantly) the rising generation. Within this new framework of expectations, political winners are afforded legitimacy and political losers demonstrate a willingness to play a constructive, oppositional role. If the political system can be responsive to those receiving the fewest economic benefits, the consolidation of democracy in the world's largest Muslim country may be within reach. Sukarno's vision of *Bhinneka Tunggal Ika* (Unity in Diversity) remains Indonesia's central challenge, but the nascent institutions of the new era of liberal democratic reform show encouraging potential.

NOTES

1. In Leo Suryadinata, Aris Ananta, and Evi Nurvidya Arifin's *Indonesia's Population: Ethnicity and Religion in a Changing Political Landscape* (Singapore: Institute of Southeast Asian Studies, 2003), the authors use the Indonesian government's 2000 Census to identify eleven major ethnic groups: Javanese (42 percent), Sundanese (15 percent), Malay (3.5 percent), Madurese (3.4 percent), Batak (3 percent), Minangkabau (2.7 percent), Betawi (2.5 percent), Buginese (2.5 percent), Bantenese (2 percent), Banjarese (1.7 percent), and Balinese (1.5 percent). Other ethnic groups compose the remaining 20 per-

cent of the Indonesian population. Many scholars believe the 2000 Census underreported Indonesian-Chinese, who compose up to 3 percent of the total population (compared to the 0.9 percent officially reported). Given Indonesia's history of anti-Chinese activity and riots, the ethnic Chinese can also be considered a major ethnic group of Indonesia.

2. For a sampling of views of the *Gestapu* coup, see Benedict Anderson and Ruth T. McVey, *A Preliminary Analysis of the October 1, 1965, Coup in Indonesia*, Interim Report Series, Modern Indonesia Project (Ithaca, NY: Cornell University Press, 1971); Arnold C. Brackman, *The Communist Collapse in Indonesia* (New York: Norton, 1969); Arthur J. Dommen, "The Attempted Coup in Indonesia," *China Quarterly* 25 (January 1966): 144–168; John Hughes, *Sukarno: A Coup That Misfired, a Purge That Ran Wild* (New York: McKay, 1967); Justus van der Kroef, "Origins of the 1965 Coup in Indonesia: Probabilities and Alternatives," *Journal of Southeast Asian Studies* 3 (September 1972): 277–298; Tarzie Vittachi, *The Fall of Sukarno* (New York: Praeger, 1967); and W. F. Wertheim, "Suharto and the Untung Coup: The Missing Link," *Journal of Contemporary Asia* 1, no. 2 (winter 1970): 50–57.

3. David McKendrick, "Indonesia in 1991: Growth, Privilege, and Rules," *Asian Survey* 32, no. 2 (February 1992): 103–105.

4. See chapter 9 for a more detailed account of Timor-Leste's independence from Indonesia.

5. Rita Smith Kipp, "Indonesia in 2003: Terror's Aftermath," *Asian Survey* 44, no. 1 (January/February 2004): 65.

6. According to the U.S. Geological Survey, the energy released from the earthquake causing the tsunami equaled 474 megatons of TNT or 23,000 Hiroshima-sized nuclear bombs. See http://earthquake.usgs.gov/eqcenter/eqinthenews/2004/usslav/neic_slav_faq .html.

7. Damien Kingsbury, "Indonesia in 2007: Unmet Expectations, Despite Improvement," *Asian Survey* 48, no. 1 (January/February 2008): 46.

8. David G. Timberman, "Yudhoyono's Re-Election: Can SBY and Indonesia Up Their Game?" *East Asia Forum*, July 10, 2009, www.eastasiaforum.org/2009/07/10/yudhoyonos -re-election-can-sby-and-indonesia-up-their-game.

9. Karen Brooks, "Is Indonesia Bound for the BRICs?" *Foreign Affairs* 90, no. 6 (November/December 2011); "Indonesia Surprises with Surge in Economy," *New York Times*, August 6, 2012, http://www.nytimes.com/2012/08/07/business/global/indonesia -surprises-with-surge-in-economy.html.

10. Kingsbury, "Indonesia in 2007," 39.

11. Leo Suryadinata, "Indonesia," in *Politics in the ASEAN States*, ed. Diane K. Mauzy (Kuala Lumpur: Maricans, 1986), 127.

12. Leo Suryadinata, *Interpreting Indonesian Politics* (Singapore: Times Academic Press, 1998), 29.

13. Michael Vatikiotis, *Indonesian Politics under Suharto* (London: Routledge, 1993), 127.

14. Pieternell van Doorn-Harder, *Women Shaping Islam: Reading the Qur'an in Indonesia* (Urbana: University of Illinois Press, 2006), 1.

15. "U.S. Lauds Muhammadiyah Role in Indonesia," *Antara News*, April 3, 2006, www.antara.co.id/en/print/?id=1144054753.

16. Mochtar Pabottigi, "Indonesia: Historicizing the New Order's Legitimacy Dilemma," in *Political Legitimacy in Southeast Asia: The Quest for Moral Authority*, ed. Muthiah Alagappa (Stanford, CA: Stanford University Press, 1995), 255.

17. Ulf Sundhaussen, "Indonesia: Past and Present Encounters with Democracy," in *Democracy in Developing Countries: Asia*, ed. Larry Diamond, Juan J. Linz, and Seymour Martian Lipset (Boulder, CO: Lynn Rienner, 1989), 455.

18. Geoffrey B. Hainsworth, "Indonesia: On the Road to Privatization?" *Current History* 89, no. 545 (March 1990): 121.

19. H. W. Arndt and Hal Hill, "The Indonesian Economy: Structural Adjustment After the Oil Boom," in *Southeast Asian Affairs 1988* (Singapore: Institute of Southeast Asian Studies, 1988), 107.

20. *Far Eastern Economic Review*, April 19, 1990, 42.

21. Kingsbury, "Indonesia in 2007," 41.

22. Andrew Walker, "Entrepreneurs Face Global Challenges: Indonesia 'Top' for Entrepreneurs," BBC.com, May 25, 2011, www.bbc.co.uk/news/business-13547505.

23. Paul Eckert, "Obama 'Experienced Our Soul'—Indonesian President," *Reuters*, November 14, 2008, http://blogs.reuters.com/talesfromthetrail/2008/11/14/obama-experienced-our-soul-indonesian-president/.

24. Ehito Kimura, "Indonesia in 2010: A Leading Democracy Disappoints on Reform," *Asian Survey* 51, no 1 (January/February 2011): 194.

RESOURCE GUIDE

A useful tool for bibliographic and other information on Indonesia is available from Australia National University's WWW Virtual Library: http://coombs.anu.edu.au /WWWVLPages/IndonPages/WWWVL-Indonesia.html. The University of California–Berkeley maintains a useful portal for digital and print resources on Indonesia: www.lib.berkeley.edu/SSEAL/SoutheastAsia/seaelec.html. Northern Illinois University's Southeast Asia Digital Library includes a range of useful links that cover government, academic, and research institutions specific to Indonesia: http://sea.lib.niu.edu. The University of Wisconsin–Madison Libraries maintains a list of digital and print resources on Indonesia: www.library.wisc.edu/guides/SEAsia/resarea.html.

For governmental sites and information, the National Portal of the Republic of Indonesia is available at www.indonesia.go.id/en. For information on Indonesia's Parliament, some English-language content is available on its official page, www.mpr.go .id/index.php?lang=en. Located in Jakarta, the Centre for Strategic and International Studies makes available policy-oriented research on Indonesia and regional issues: www.csis.or.id.

Readers can supplement this chapter with figures and publication information found in the country profile pages of data.UN.org. and ADB.org. Recent and archived news articles are maintained on specific country profile pages by BBC.com and NYTimes.com. Useful country reports are also produced by the Bertelsmann Foundation at www.bti -project.org/home/index.nc.

A full directory of development organizations and civil society organizations operating in Indonesia is available at www.devdir.org/files/Indonesia.PDF. Other sites particularly worth perusing include those of Nahdlatul Ulama, at www.nu.or.id/page.php ?lang=en; the Free West Papua movement, at http://westpapuafree.wordpress.com; and the University of Buffalo's Tsunami Disaster page, which covers all phases of the 2004 disaster, at http://ublib.buffalo.edu/libraries/asl/guides/indian-ocean-disaster.html.

The *Jakarta Post*, Indonesia's most widely read English-language newspaper, maintains a site at www.thejakartapost.com. Tempointeractive.com is a valuable site for finding political punditry and discussion, although content in English is somewhat limited. The Australian-based InsideIndonesia.com publishes interesting feature articles weekly and quarterly that span useful political and social topics.

9

TIMOR-LESTE

OCCUPYING ONLY HALF OF A SMALL ISLAND IN THE EXPANSIVE Indonesian archipelago, the 1.2 million people of Timor-Leste (commonly called East Timor) have drawn considerable worldwide attention in recent decades. Regrettably, East Timor joined the post-Holocaust, "never again" narrative in 1975 when it experienced its first spate of politically motivated mass killings at the hands of Indonesian invaders. The world did nothing to stop the violence then, but it responded with measured effectiveness in the face of a genocide-style reprise in 1999 and internal chaos in 2006. Although episodic bloodshed has continued to torment East Timor in the new international era, foreign occupation and meddling have bedeviled the small island for over five hundred years. Timor-Leste's story, both sad and triumphant, is of a long, painful struggle for political freedom, independence, and unity.

Facing Indonesia to the north and Australia to the south, Timor Island sits prominently in the Timor Sea. It is home to rugged terrain, timber resources, and mountains that reach to 9,000 feet. Three times the size of Cyprus in the Mediterranean, the island is similarly divided into two political entities. East Timor occupies the island's eastern half; Indonesia enjoys sovereign control over its western half (excluding a small East Timor–controlled enclave).

The division of the island runs centuries deep. Portuguese friars first arrived on its eastern flank during the sixteenth century, followed by the Dutch, who gained control of the island's western reaches. By the late eighteenth century, East Timor was under full Portuguese control, although it remained only a minor star in a global empire that celebrated Brazil in the Americas, Mozambique in Africa, and Goa in India. Portuguese rule of East Timor followed a pattern of general imperial neglect, although Catholicism developed deep roots in many areas of the island.

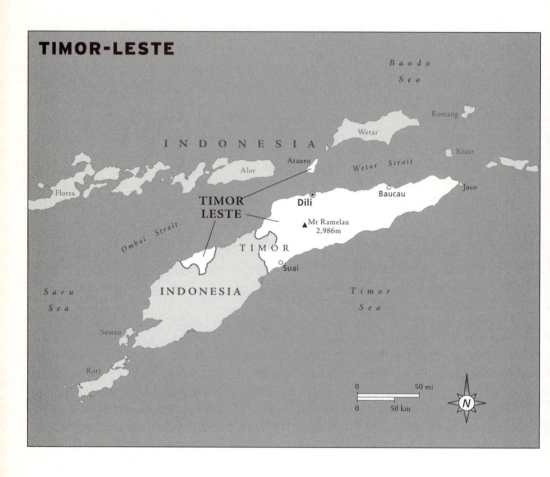

TIMOR-LESTE

Banda Sea

INDONESIA

Romang

Wetar

Kisar

Alor

Atauro

Wetar Strait

Jaco

Flores

TIMOR LESTE

Dili

Baucau

▲ Mt Ramelau
2,986m

Ombai Strait

TIMOR

Savu Sea

INDONESIA

○ Suai

Timor Sea

Semau

Roti

| 0 | | 50 mi |

| 0 | | 50 km |

N

For 460 years, the Portuguese dominated affairs in East Timor. Change did not arrive until World War II, when Dutch and Australian troops, ignoring Portuguese neutrality, overwhelmed the colonists and established East Timor as an Allied military staging ground. Their presence invited Japanese forces, who defeated the Allies in a 1942 battle on the island. As its next occupiers, Japan's warriors brutally demanded submission by East Timor's residents. Tens of thousands were killed, and many islanders were forced into sexual slavery as comfort women. At the end of the war, Timorese leaders attempted independence but without success. The Portuguese subsequently returned to East Timor for an unwanted three-decade encore of colonial rule.

Independence almost came to East Timor in 1975. In that year, half a world away in Lisbon, a coup d'état led by leftist military officers unleashed widespread Portuguese sentiment to decolonize overseas territories. Timorese aspirants encouraged by these events established Fretilin (an acronym for the Revolutionary Front for an Independent East Timor). Its goal was full independence and statehood. Even as Portuguese administrators experimented with local elections and the planned decolonization of the territory, rival groups claiming leadership of the independence movement sparked a civil conflict. Fretilin forces eventually overcame internal challengers and established control of Dili, the administrative capital. With their plans for an orderly transfer thwarted, Portuguese officials retreated in a messy withdrawal. On November 28, 1975, Fretilin declared East Timor independent—a "democratic republic." Nine days later, however, shortly after a visit to Jakarta by U.S. President Gerald Ford, Indonesia invaded East Timor, drawing support from some anti-Fretilin groups within the territory. Jakarta's purpose was full annexation and unification of Timor under the Indonesian flag. Decades later, declassified government documents released in Washington, D.C., confirmed the Ford administration's knowledge and support of the invasion.[1]

Driven by fears of Fretilin's Marxist orientation, and communist victories in Vietnam, Cambodia, and Laos months earlier, General Suharto's armed forces employed vicious tactics in executing Indonesia's annexation of East Timor. The 35,000 Indonesian "volunteer forces" maliciously attacked Timorese civilians, tortured prisoners, and sprayed chemical napalm on villages to ensure the population's complete submission. During the pacification campaign following the takeover, leftists and refugees were placed in camps or otherwise interned for "reeducation." Out of an original population of 650,000, an estimated 100,000 Timorese (about one in six) lost their lives at the hands of the Indonesian military during the invasion, making it among the worst mass atrocities in modern history in terms of loss of life per capita.[2]

Suharto declared East Timor as Indonesia's twenty-seventh province only months after his forces had occupied it. Although most countries refused to recognize the annexation and condemned Indonesia's actions, Suharto's government experienced only minor international repercussions. The United States and many of its Cold War allies in the region were deafeningly silent on the matter. Australia, a key regional player, formally recognized the annexation as legitimate. Alternatively, the United Nations condemned the takeover and granted observer status to Fretilin, inviting its representatives to the General Assembly. However, as with the Palestinian Liberation Organization, observer status in the world's premier organization of nations had little effect on dislodging the occupiers or forcing a political settlement.

The ensuing years of Indonesian control of East Timor were marked by continued suppression. Thousands of Timorese resisting Indonesian control were imprisoned or executed. From 1974 to 1999, almost 20,000 Timorese died as a result of armed clashes with Indonesian troops or from extrajudicial killings by occupation authorities; an additional 80,000 Timorese died from preventable illness or starvation.[3] In total, close to one-quarter of East Timor's pre-1975 population died during the twenty-five years of Suharto's occupation. Armed resistance continued during the period, led principally by Fretilin's military wing Falantil (Forces Amadas de Libertação Nacional de Timor Leste). Over time, Falantil weakened and Fretilin turned increasingly to political means, nonviolence, and efforts to raise international awareness of East Timor's plight.

To dampen foreign sympathy and thwart his critics, Suharto closed the annexed territory to outsiders for many years. The tight control of information worked. During the 1980s, the issue of East Timor largely disappeared from the international consciousness.

Suharto's attempt to integrate East Timor with Indonesia failed miserably. Not only did the Catholic population differ with Indonesia's Muslim majority, but there also was too little by way of shared history, language, or culture to bind the disparate populations together. Neither did East Timor's impoverished, battle-scarred populace share in the rapid economic growth sweeping Indonesia. Economic conditions improved marginally in the 1980s, with meager sums of development aid trickling in from Jakarta, but Java's economic dynamism was worlds away from the Timorese experience. Rather than look to Suharto's New Order government, Timorese turned to their local communities and to Catholic leaders for unity and direction.

In 1988, East Timor was finally reopened by Suharto. It was a significant shift in policy. Pope John Paul II seized the opportunity to visit a year later, a landmark event that sparked proindependence demonstrations, which were forcibly suppressed by Indonesian security forces. Following the papal visit, a pattern of popular protest and harsh military repression emerged. In 1991, an especially appalling massacre of defenseless protesters occurred at the Santa Cruz cemetery in Dili. Congregating themselves to memorialize the death of Timorese students killed days earlier by security forces, scores of young people were suddenly targeted in a vicious melee of bloodshed resulting in seventy dead and countless wounded. Much to the dismay of Indonesian political and military leaders, disturbing video images of the slaughter were smuggled out of East Timor by foreign journalists and broadcasted internationally. Suddenly, East Timor's long saga of occupation drew renewed global attention.

Although never a cause célèbre on the scale of the antiapartheid movement or the ongoing campaign for Tibetan autonomy, East Timor retained a solid core of champions abroad. Throughout the 1990s, numerous international human rights groups stepped up pressure on Suharto's government. The independence movement received a major boost in 1996 when two longtime Timorese leaders, Bishop Carlos Filipe Ximenes Belo and Jose Ramos-Horta, were jointly awarded the Nobel Peace Prize. The movement also featured an important Mandela-esque face for its cause, that of imprisoned poet-warrior Kay Rala "Xanana" Gusmao, known for his leadership of Fretilin guerrillas and his impassioned prison writings during long years of confinement.

In the end, it wasn't renewed international activism, Nobel-level attention, or Xanana's growing status that triggered events that led to independence. In the new international era, the powerful forces of globalizing markets and Asia's financial collapse put into motion events that would end Suharto's occupation.

In May 1998, amidst the financial contagion rocking Southeast Asia, Suharto's government collapsed in spectacular fashion. The economic crisis and IMF rescue programs ignited public anger and revealed the depth of Suharto's mismanagement and his family's corrupt dealings. Social disruption lasting for weeks culminated with intense anti-Suharto street protests in Jakarta and elsewhere. Succumbing to the loss of international legitimacy and facing unyielding domestic pressure, the once-invincible Suharto resigned in political disgrace. Consequently, East Timor's fate followed a new course.

Only weeks after Suharto's resignation, B. J. Habibie, Indonesia's new president, floated the idea of a "special status" for East Timor. A few months later he announced plans for a UN-supervised referendum where Timorese could choose between "autonomy within Indonesia" or "independence." It was a political gamble. Not only might the vote fall in favor of independence, but offering it could fuel separatist aspirations held by other groups within Indonesia. Smoldering irredentist movements in Aceh and Irian Jaya in particular seemed prone to such trajectories. Undeterred, President Habibie pursued the referendum, believing that Indonesian goodwill on the East Timor controversy could foster international respect for his post-Suharto reform agenda. Desperately enmeshed in Indonesia's worsening economic crisis, Habibie saw East Timor as a mechanism to restore confidence among international observers and foreign investors.

In negotiations over the United Nations' role in the planned referendum, Habibie refused to allow foreign peacekeepers as part of the international mission. The civilian authorities of the United Nations Assistance Mission in East Timor (UNAMET), a $50 million endeavor, carried the mandate to train local officials and educate the public in preparation for the referendum. UNAMET officials would thus rely on local security to see the plebiscite through. For anxious Timorese, Habibie's promised referendum was all that stood between them and independence.

On August 30, 1999, after two disorganized postponements, the residents of East Timor finally went to the ballot box to cast votes on their new political status. The run-up to the referendum was marred by various hostilities and dreadful acts of violence perpetrated by proautonomy militias (backed by elements within the Indonesian military). Despite security concerns, the turnout for the referendum was remarkable, surpassing 98 percent of registered voters. The results were equally overwhelming: Nearly four out of five residents (79 percent) voted for full independence.

Reactions to the vote were intense on both sides. Fearful of militias, independence supporters were cautious rather than jubilant. Pro-Indonesia militias, as they had warned, launched a bloody campaign against independence supporters. East Timor suddenly turned chaotic. Enraged thugs attacked civilians with cold brutality. Dili was set ablaze, and disturbing reports of torture and murder surfaced, only to be followed by evidence of mass graves. Fears that political genocide was unfolding grew. Outside Dili, rampaging militias looted and destroyed village after village. Horrific acts of rape and sexual assault accompanied the chaos.[4] The armed militias even attacked UNAMET personnel, killing three staffers and exciting fear among the numerous but defenseless foreign personnel. From Jakarta, Habibie called on the Indonesian military to restore order, but his estranged generals acted slowly while claiming no responsibility for instigating or participating in the turmoil.

International concern developed further as a refugee crisis mushroomed, sending 250,000 Timorese into Indonesian territory and elsewhere over a matter of days. Among those fleeing were leading independence figures such as Nobel laureate Bishop Belo, who fled to Australia for safety. Alindo Marcal, a well-known Protestant leader, was less fortunate—his corpse was found hacked into pieces in a militia-run refugee camp. In two weeks of postreferendum violence, the death toll had risen to well over a thousand. The extent to which Indonesian generals had armed the local militias or Indonesian soldiers had otherwise participated remained unclear. Most observers believed it was significant.

From his New York office, UN Secretary-General Kofi Annan warned the Indonesian government and its military about "crimes against humanity." He then flew to Jakarta to address the situation personally. Lingering feelings of imperial responsibility reverberated in Portugal. Citizens across Lisbon flooded city streets, forming a six-mile human chain and demanding a forceful international response to end the unrest and killings. East Timor's crisis then grabbed the attention of the UN Security Council but, alas, the United States and China, still reeling from recent events in Kosovo, initially balked at authorizing a coordinated intervention.

As events escalated by the day, a solution surfaced in the form of an Australian-led peacekeeping force. The International Force for East Timor (INTERFET) included troops from Australia, Thailand, Singapore, Bangladesh, Brazil, and other willing countries. Conceding his own ineffectiveness on the matter, Habibie granted permission for INTERFET to enter East Timor. With speed unprecedented in the history of assembling and deploying international peacekeepers, INTERFET troops found themselves in East Timor only five days after their initial authorization. Unwilling to relent, the militias pledged death to all outsiders but soon found themselves overwhelmed by the presence and power of the Blue Berets.

With the violence in check and the refugee crisis under international control, the referendum's results were eventually allowed to follow their intended path to Timorese self-rule. In mid-October 1998, the Indonesian Parliament publicly declared the 1976 annexation of East Timor void. INTERFET was also terminated, replaced by a new UN mission designed to manage East Timor's transition to statehood: the United Nations Transitional Administration in East Timor (UNTAET). In the months that followed, UNTAET successfully governed the country, resettled refugees, and managed elections for a new parliament and president. The UN's highly respected Brazilian-born diplomat Sergio Vieira de Mello functioned during this period as East Timor's chief executive.

On May 20, 2002, at midnight, Timor-Leste was reborn as a sovereign, independent nation. The nighttime fireworks and celebrations matched the soaring expectations and aspirations of the Timorese people. Present in Dili to memorialize the event were the world's leaders—Kofi Annan, former U.S. president Bill Clinton, and Australian Prime Minister John Howard. In a show of goodwill, Indonesia's new president, Megawati Sukarnoputri, uncomfortably attended as well. Presiding at the ceremonies was indefatigable freedom fighter and longtime political prisoner Xanana Gusmao, now a free man and the country's first president.

Simultaneous with independence, the United Nations Mission of Support in East Timor (UNMISET) replaced UNTAET to assist the country in early statehood. The new mission included 5,000 security forces and almost 500 foreign advisers. UNMISET, designed to last only one year, stayed three. It expired in 2005 and was replaced by a smaller UN presence of nonsecurity personnel, the United Nations Office in East Timor (UNOTIL).

Timor-Leste's statehood allowed for new opportunities but also created unprecedented challenges. Since its independence, Southeast Asia's newest country has struggled with political infighting, regime instability, and endemic poverty. After a few short years of relative calm, political conditions deteriorated markedly in 2006, less than a year after UNMISET's security forces had left the country. In a sad iteration, political violence returned, and Timor-Leste experienced another round of traumatic street-level chaos, vandalism, mass dislocation, and loss of life. Summoned again to restore peace was an Australian-led peacekeeping contingency, this time under the name Operation Astute. The United Nations followed this event by establishing yet another new mission, the United Nations Integrated Mission in Timor-Leste (UNMIT). Its mandate, originally authorized only through early 2009, included measures to institutionalize democracy with the assistance of civilian advisers and the presence of 1,600 armed UN police officers.

A new round of political hostilities after parliamentary elections in 2007 and a double assassination attempt on the president and prime minister in early 2008 underscored the depth of Timor-Leste's ongoing political fragility. UNMIT troops stayed through 2012 but transferred all policing functions to national police in 2011. In an encouraging sign, presidential elections in May 2012 went off peacefully. Parliamentary elections in July of that year were also conducted without violence. Nevertheless, the necessary presence of international authorities and security forces since *de jure* independence renders the Timorese's hard-won right to self-rule thus far an unfulfilled promise. De facto independence lies somewhere in the future.

INSTITUTIONS AND SOCIAL GROUPS

Catholic Church

The most significant colonial legacy of the Portuguese was religion. Ninety-six percent of Timor-Leste's population is Roman Catholic, in contrast to the Muslim presence that characterizes much of the surrounding region. Catholicism in East Timor actually strengthened under Indonesian rule due to *Pancasila*'s monotheistic imperative (which required citizens to indicate their religious identification). It was also strengthened by active local leaders, whose work was acknowledged by Pope John Paul II and his decision to visit the troubled island in 1989. As the moral voice of Timorese society and the arbiters of Timorese interests, local Catholic leaders fueled the territory's resistance movement during the preindependence period and continue to shape the country after statehood.

Today, the debate over church-state relations is among the central elements of postindependence politics. Timorese political figures are divided on where church-state lines should be drawn. Prime Minister Mari Alkatiri's proposal to restrict religious education in public schools sparked indignation among church authorities and was ultimately defeated upon the threat of social disorder. Tensions between church leaders and Alkatiri, a Fretilin veteran and religious Muslim, persisted until he resigned under great pressure in 2006. Although Fretilin-led governments did not pursue a socialist agenda while in power, church leaders often characterize party leaders, including Alkatiri, as Marxists.

In recent years, the church has developed avenues for a more forceful role in electoral politics. Church policy disallows bishops and priests from formally endorsing parties or candidates during services, but outside church walls they are encouraged to speak openly about their preferences. State funds are also used to support the church, an action justified, in President Ramos-Horta's words, "as an obligation of the State to the oldest and most credible institution in our Nation."[5]

Independence Leaders

Many of East Timor's most prominent independence leaders continue in pivotal leadership roles in the postindependence period. Having emerged from a seminary-trained class of mestizo elites, intellectuals, and civil servants, these leaders took their cues from the political Left in Portugal during their formative years in the 1970s.[6] Less ideological today than before, veteran independence leaders now jockey for positions in government as partners and rivals hoping to navigate the young country through its seemingly insurmountable challenges.

Chief among Timor-Leste's leaders is Gusmao, elected as the country's first president and currently serving as its prime minister. Known best by his pen name, "Xanana," the journalist-turned-revolutionary found himself atop Fretilin in the early 1980s, following a massive Indonesian offensive that eliminated many of the group's leaders. Xanana then worked with Catholic leaders and Fretilin's rivals to create a broad political coalition and an effective clandestine rebel operation. To many Timorese, his legend is part Che Guevara, part Nelson Mandela. When he rejected offers for liberty in exile during his long imprisonment in Jakarta, Xanana became the international face of Timorese courage. Suharto honored Nelson Mandela's request to visit him in prison, and Xanana thanked Suharto by pressuring him with repeated requests to allow an independence referendum.

Jose Ramos-Horta, Fretilin's founder, has also bridged the pre- and postindependence eras as a powerful political actor. In what proved to be entirely consequential, he fled East Timor only days before the Indonesian takeover in 1975. While abroad, he drew attention to East Timor's plight, serving as its observer-representative in the United Nations. Ramos-Horta lobbied governments, legislatures, and human rights organizations in singular fashion to generate international pressure on Suharto's regime. In 1988, he broke with Fretilin to pursue a path of nonviolent resistance. A joint Nobel laureate with Bishop Carlos Ximenes Belo in 1996, Ramos-Horta served as the country's second elected president.

Because of his legendary ambassadorial history, Ramos-Horta wields unparalleled moral authority both inside and outside the new country. Some of this power took a hit when he surprisingly granted clemency to the very assassins who attempted to kill him in 2008. He justified his actions seeking "to close a chapter" and to show that "forgiveness, and preventing a return to instability, trumped punitive justice."[7] Critics, including UN Secretary-General Ban Ki-moon, argued that the act furthered a culture of impunity in East Timor, but the Nobel winner, who had issued over 200 other pardons during his presidency, ignored them. In 2012, he was nominated for reelection but refused to publicly campaign out of respect for his opponents who were former Fretilin guerillas. "I cannot compare myself with them," he said in a *New York Times* op-ed. "They have earned the right to lead as much as I."[8] Defeated in the first round of voting, Ramos-Horta subsequently invited the two run-off candidates for a "heart-to-heart talk," where he pleaded with them to tone down their rhetoric and show greater moderation in their campaigning, for the good of the country. They did. In 2012, presidential power in Timor-Leste was transferred peacefully.

Mari Alkatiri, also a Fretilin founder, remains another prominent figure. He served a tumultuous four-year stint as prime minister, a position with greater constitutional authority and policymaking power than the president has. Interparty divisions and rivalries with Xanana, Ramos-Horta, and Catholic leaders forced him to resign in 2006, but he remains active as a Fretilin party leader in Parliament. Another heroic figure to many Timorese, former Falantil Major-General Jose Maria Vasconcelos, known as "Taur Matan Rauk" (Tetum for "Two Sharp Eyes"), recently rose to the presidency in 2012.

National Parliament and Political Parties

Though weak as institutions, the national Parliament and the country's political parties are important vehicles for political expression and contestation in Timor-Leste's embryonic democracy. The promise of a healthy democracy rests on how well these institutions develop. The extent to which political figures involved in parliamentary politics choose to stay within the bounds of peaceful conflict is among the crucial questions facing the country.

These bounds were pushed after the 2007 election when difficulties surfaced in forming a parliamentary government and choosing a prime minister. Fretilin, now a political party, had won the most seats but was unable to find a partner and attempted to form a minority government. A minority government was unacceptable to other seated parties. The possibility of a unity government of all parties later surfaced, but talks broke down despite President Ramos-Horta's attempts at mediation. Ultimately an alliance government emerged without Fretilin and with Xanana Gusmao, who had recently begun his own party, as prime minister. Fretilin protested the outcome, and Dili's streets exploded with angry house burnings and vandalism. This time, however, no deaths were reported. Alkatiri appealed to Fretilin's supporters to protest using civil methods, but he maintained for months that Xanana's government was illegitimate.

The 65-member unicameral National Parliament currently seats four of the twenty-one parties that contested peacefully in the 2012 general elections. A proportional representation party-list ballot determines seat allocation. By law, at least one in three of all candidates on party lists are required to be women. Fretilin has won nearly 30 percent of the total vote in the past two elections, but it is no longer the most influential faction in Timorese politics. Dampening Fretilin's dominance has been the party work of Xanana Gusmao, who founded the National Congress for Timorese Reconstruction Party (CRNT) prior to the 2007 national elections. CRNT won 24 percent of the popular vote in 2007 and 37 percent of the vote in 2012. Following the 2012 election, CRNT and Fretilin again engaged in discussions to form a unity government.

STATE-SOCIETY RELATIONS AND DEMOCRACY

Timor-Leste's state is dependent and fragile. Technically sovereign, it can be described (somewhat singularly) as an "infant state"—a state engaged in a needy, agnatic relationship with the international community through its UN parentage. Although sometimes classified as a failed state, Timor-Leste is so new as a political entity that it is difficult to equate it with countries that genuinely experienced a measurable loss of sovereign control, central authority, or capacity for self-governance (such as Somalia, Zimbabwe, or Afghanistan). Having yet to achieve a measurable degree of state autonomy or capacity in the first place, Timor-Leste is disproportionately dependent on foreign support for its very being.

In the Timor-Leste experience, it was first the United Nations that accreted and concentrated power to manage sociopolitical disorder. In its first decade, virtually all functions of the Timor-Leste state (security, government, social services, and justice) were at one time or another performed by one of nine UN-led operations: UNAMET (1999), INTERFET (1999), UNTAET

(1999–2002), UNMISET (2002–2005), UNOTIL (2005–2006), Operation Astute (2006), UNMIT (2006–2012), the East Timor Tribunal (2000–2006), and
the Commission for Reception, Truth, and Reconciliation (2002–2005). Essential as these missions have been to the country's emancipation and stability,
Timor-Leste's future as a fully sovereign state depends on how it is weaned
from UN paternalism. President Ramos-Horta, ever conscious of this fact,
has vocally encouraged the United Nations to maintain its presence in
Timor-Leste for at least a decade to lead the country out of its infancy.

Given the country's low level of development, foreign assistance is likely to
continue long after the last UN mission leaves Dili. Countless non-Timorese
members of the international community have expended an immeasurable
amount of human effort, attention, and resources to assist Timor-Leste in its
independence and statehood. Timor-Leste may be decades away from creating a strong state with the autonomy and capability to function independently and effectively.

With respect to the state's legitimacy, questions persist about how Timorese willingly consent to authority. The cultural and moral authority of the
Catholic Church and particular independence figures remain intact, but a
respect for (and submission to) the state and its embryonic political institutions remain questionable. Growing regional divisions between east and
west, known locally as the *firaku-kaladi* (east-west) divide, suggest an added
challenge to the legitimacy of the state and its territorial integrity.

Institutions of democracy in Timor-Leste are weak and underdeveloped.
The greatest threat to the consolidation of democratic institutions may not
be antidemocratic sentiment, authoritarian impulses, or the threat of occupation; it is, rather, the potential of institutional failure by needed functions
of government. An ethos for democracy is taking root in Timor-Leste, but
the country's history is short and its dependence on international support
for regime legitimacy remains considerable. Moreover, the nagging threat of
social disorder and violence that characterizes Timorese political passion
also inhibits confidence in assessing the country's democratization as anything but tenuous. The country fits the definition of what might be called an
"ambiguous" regime.

Indicative of Timor-Leste's weak democratic institutions were the events
of 2006, when, less than four years into its democratic experiment, Dili slid
into another episode of political chaos. A large number of disgruntled government soldiers from the interior west, on strike over low wages and alleged
discrimination, were fired by Prime Minister Alkatiri. In turn, the soldier-
petitioners spurred riots, looting, arson, and clashes with local police and
military loyalists. Multiple deaths occurred, and the homes of military officials were set on fire. The risk of general social disorder grew quickly.
Xanana Gusmao, then president, added fuel to the fire by publicly indicating

sympathy for the soldiers.[9] Echoing earlier incidents, over 150,000 Timorese fled in fear. As the country braced itself for another wave of bloody turmoil, some government ministers and military generals began to distribute weapons to civilians. Only the arrival of another Australian-led peacekeeping force was able to bring calm to Dili's streets.

With respect to democratization, the events of 2006 were especially troubling because this time political violence could not be blamed on Indonesia, outsiders, or some foreign entity. Rather, blame lay within the country, suggesting evidence of a growing regional cleavage and a political culture prone to violent conflict.

The fragile state of Timor-Leste's democracy was further demonstrated in 2007 by electoral violence and again in 2008 when rebels sought President Ramos-Horta's life in a failed assassination attempt that left him hospitalized in Australia with gunshot wounds to his abdomen. An attempt was made on Prime Minister Gusmao's life during the same thwarted coup. Ramos-Horta recovered and rejoined Xanana to lead the struggling country, but the damage the assassination attempts had inflicted on democracy lingered.

Hopeful observers saw the death of Alfredo Reinado, the estranged army major who launched the 2006 mutiny and the 2008 assassination coup, as the beginning of the end of a destabilizing rebel movement that threatened democracy.[10] Nonviolent presidential and parliamentary elections in 2012 have also raised expectations, but it is far too early to label Timor-Leste's transition to democracy complete. Ramos-Horta, favoring forgiveness over punitive justice, and pointing to peaceful elections and recent economic gains, believes that "the country is maturing" and that "a new chapter has begun."[11]

ECONOMY AND DEVELOPMENT

A 1996 report from the UNDP tragically described Timor-Leste as Asia's least developed country—a country "chained to poverty."[12] Independence has improved economic conditions and development in the country but many economic deficiencies remain. Aside from promising revenues derived from oil extraction in the Timor Sea, the young country enjoys limited economic prospects, especially from a household-level perspective. New autonomy and authority to allocate state resources from oil revenues has spawned infighting because there is little institutional capacity to deliver such allocation. A two-tier oil/non-oil economy has emerged, creating both opportunities and risks.

Subsistence agriculture characterizes the country's economy. Seasonal food shortages afflict much of the island's populace. Almost a quarter of the population depends on food assistance during lean months of the year. Little is produced in the overall economy beyond oil, coffee, and some handicrafts.

Manufacturing is negligible. Commercial production of vanilla, palm oil, and other crops awaits more intensive investment before the country's agricultural sector functions profitably in Southeast Asia's trade-based economy. The country is wholly dependent on imports to feed and provide for its population. Without development assistance and oil revenues, the economic situation would be virtually hopeless.

In terms of living standards, no country in Southeast Asia has a higher rate of poverty than Timor-Leste: 41 percent (2011 UNDP). Its record of overall human development is disheartening. Its literacy rate hovers near 50 percent, the lowest in all of Asia. In rural areas, four in ten Timorese lack access to potable water, and only one in three women who give birth do so with a medical professional present. Regionally, only Myanmar ranks lower when measured using the Human Development Index.

Since 2002, the country's oil and non-oil growth rates have risen, especially after 2007, when coffee exports began to generate more revenue. In fact, annual non-oil GDP growth between 2007 and 2011 averaged over 10 percent. As a result, aggregate income figures for Timor-Leste have risen. Evaluating these figures in proper context is important. With a 2010 GNI per capita of $2,730 it may appear the country's population is better off than people in Vietnam and the Philippines, where GNI per capita is much lower.[13] However, non-oil GNI per capita income is actually $599 (2009 UNDP), far lower than even Cambodia and Laos. The reality is that oil revenues are only slowly improving everyday lives, and structural weaknesses in the two-tier economy remain.

Seventy-five percent of Timor-Leste's GDP is derived from oil and natural gas. After hard-fought treaty negotiations with Australia over rival claims, government revenues from oil extraction in the Timor Sea have begun to flow. The oil profits generated by the state are put into a Norway-style sovereign fund, the Timor-Leste Petroleum Fund. This fund, which is managed by government and civil society representatives, has grown dramatically: from $70 million in 2005 to over $10 billion in 2012. The country dollarized its monetary system in part to mitigate the risk a local currency would create for oil revenues. In 2011, Timor-Leste's Parliament passed a bill allowing a greater share of the fund to be invested in equities, prompting some observers to raise questions about market volatility and financial risk.[14]

Outside its nascent tourism sector, weak private investment currently plagues the Timorese economy. Unemployment averages 20 percent across the country and rises even higher in urban areas. Because half of the population is under twenty years old, demographic stress will extend employment pressures well into the future. Prime Minister Gusmao's massive push for new public infrastructure in roads, ports, and electricity is designed to alleviate these problems. The country's annual budget increased from $70 million in 2004 to $1.3 billion in 2011 due in large part to infrastructure initiatives. Indeed, an active state-led economic program will be needed to develop all sectors of the country's economy. Waiting for private investment to arrive will prove a fool's errand. Timor-Leste's Global Competitiveness Index and Bloomberg Economic Momentum Index rankings are both last in Asia.[15] With a small, poorly educated population, and a remote island location, the incentives for foreign investment are minimal.

Of course the greatest risks lie in the oil economy itself. Increasing alongside rising hydrocarbon-driven revenues are the risks of falling into the "oil curse." Common to many small petrostates, the oil curse leads to high-stakes conflict among elites, authoritarian impulses, and corruption. Nevertheless, the opportunity exists for Timor-Leste to learn from mistakes made elsewhere. If political disunity, the temptation for corruption, and inequitable distribution of revenues can be avoided, it is possible that oil wealth will be a blessing to human development, not a curse.

Foreign Relations

As it seeks to wean itself from outside protection, Timor-Leste's relationship with the United Nations remains its most crucial foreign policy priority. Nevertheless, the young country's evolving politics is producing a coherent foreign policy agenda and debate. Dili's principal bilateral relations are with Indonesia, Australia, and (increasingly) China. It also desires a healthy relationship with ASEAN.

Among Timorese, relations with Indonesia remain controversial due to past resentments of Suharto's occupation and the postreferendum mayhem in 1999. A bilateral initiative of the two states, the Timor-Leste Commission of Truth and Friendship, was launched in 2005 to smooth relations. For many Timorese who suffered at the hands of Indonesian perpetrators, the creation of a commission smacked of impunity. Xanana, a supporter of the commission, drew the ire of church officials, UNMIT, and international NGOs that questioned the commission's establishment.[16] At the state-to-state level, however, the Commission of Truth and Friendship has allowed current governments to distance themselves from the sins of the past.

Timor-Leste's relations with other major partners reflect an even more forward-looking posture. Its ties with Australia are complex, multilayered, and asymmetrical. Disputes over territorial waters damaged relations after independence, but Australia willingly returned its peacekeepers to Dili in 2006 to quell civil unrest. Certain parties within Timor-Leste fear that Canberra has neocolonial designs to ensure Dili serves Australian interests. Ramos-Horta and Xanana show less concern about this possibility than do Fretilin and Mari Alkatiri, who looks to China and Portugal as patrons. Portugal was only recently overtaken by Australia as Timor-Leste's largest aid donor.

China, a permanent member of the UN Security Council and long sympathetic to Fretilin's objectives, sent troops to support UNTAET and was the first country to establish diplomatic relations with Timor-Leste. While early support of Fretilin reflects Cold War priorities, more recent moves have sought to preempt Taiwan from courting the new Asian country. China's interests in Timor-Leste may be more economic than political. Oil and resource hungry, China seeks a partnership with Timor-Leste as part of its grand strategy to secure energy sources. Evidence of a deepening relationship between the two countries includes increasing foreign aid from Beijing; the financing of government buildings, including the construction of Timor-Leste's new presidential palace in Dili; and a $1.6 million seismic study for oil and gas in Timor-Leste's interior.[17] In a reversal of roles, as a show of goodwill, the government of Timor-Leste donated $500,000 to China in 2008 in support of recovery efforts following the massive Sichuan earthquake.

With respect to international organizations, Timor-Leste's key relations are with the Asian Development Bank, where membership was established in 2004, and ASEAN, where membership hopes have been inhibited by the criterion that Dili establish foreign embassies in all ten ASEAN capitals. (Timor-Leste has only a handful of diplomatic missions worldwide.) With support from Indonesia, however, ASEAN membership may be realized in 2013. WTO membership is an even more distant hope, although memberships with the IMF and World Bank have resulted in a proliferation of project-based aid initiatives.

CONCLUSION

The full dignity of independence celebrated by Timor-Leste in 2002 came at a heavy price—achieved after 460 years of Portuguese control; three merciless years of Japanese occupation; a thirty-year return of Portuguese rule following World War II; a failed attempt at independence in 1975; twenty-five years of a brutal occupation by Indonesia's Suharto; an independence referendum; a scorched-earth campaign by anti-independence militias; a refugee crisis; a dramatic Australian-led peacekeeping operation; and an ambitious UN mission that governed East Timor's final transition to statehood. Elections, democratic institutions, and membership in international organizations have since followed, but political stability and economic development have remained elusive.

The "never again" narrative, into which Timor-Leste's history is inseparably woven, has recently adopted a new term: *chega!*, Portuguese for "enough!" or "stop!" The title of a UN-commissioned report on the atrocities committed under Indonesia's occupation, *Chega!* might as well be a mantra for independent Timor-Leste as it seeks full self-governance. Realizing an end to episodic disorder, killing, and refugee flows is requisite for the infant state if it is to experience genuine independence and stability. Political order, elusive today, is the keystone in the delicate bridge that may someday lead Timorese to the economic and human development they so sorely deserve.

NOTES

1. See December 6, 2001, press release from George Washington University's National Security Archive, http://www.gwu.edu/~nsarchiv/NSAEBB/NSAEBB62/press.html.

2. Michael Leifer, "Timor, East (Indonesia)," *Dictionary of the Modern Politics of South-East Asia* (London: Routledge, 1995), 236.

3. The figures cited here come from the CAVR Report commissioned by UNTAET and the Timor-Leste National Parliament: See http://www.cavr-timorleste.org/en /chegaReport.htm.

4. Ibid.

5. Extracted from a campaign speech by presidential candidate Jose Ramos-Horta, March 23, 2007, Dili, www.pm.gov.tp/speeches.htm.

6. Michael Leifer, "Fretilin (Indonesia)," in *Dictionary of the Modern Politics of South-East Asia* (London: Routledge, 1995), 97.

7. Aubrey Belford, "East Timor President's Clemency Extends to His Attackers," *New York Times*, November 1, 2010, http://www.nytimes.com/2010/11/02/world/asia /02timor.html.

8. Jose Ramos-Horta, "Elections to Be Proud Of," *New York Times*, April 16, 2012, http://www.nytimes.com/2012/04/17/opinion/elections-to-be-proud-of.html.

9. Joseph Nevins, "Timor-Leste in 2006: The End of Post-Independence Honeymoon," *Asian Survey* 47, no. 1 (January/February 2007): 162–167.

10. Simon Montlake and Nick Squires, "After Foiled Assassination, Timor Rebels' Sway May Lessen," *Christian Science Monitor*, February 12, 2008.

11. Ramos-Horta, "Elections to Be Proud Of."

12. Nevins, "Timor-Leste in 2006," 163.

13. See Table 1.1 in chapter 1

14. "Is Timor-Leste's Plan for Oil Fund Investments a Risk Worth Taking?" *The Guardian*, October 24, 2011, http://www.guardian.co.uk/global-development/2011/oct /24/timor-leste-sovereign-fund-investment.

15. Shamim Adam and Ramsey Al-Rikabi, "East Timor Ends First Decade Fighting Oil Curse," Bloomberg, May 17, 2012, http://www.bloomberg.com/news/2012-05-17 /east-timor-ends-first-decade-fighting-oil-curse.html.

16. Jose Cornelio Guterres, "Timor-Leste: A Year of Democratic Elections," *Southeast Asian Affairs 2008* (Singapore: Institute of Southeast Asian Studies, 2008), 369.

17. Ian Storey, "China and East Timor: Good but Not Best Friends," Association for Asian Research, August 15, 2006, www.asianresearch.org/articles/2920.html.

RESOURCE GUIDE

The University of California–Berkeley maintains a useful portal for digital and print resources on East Timor: www.lib.berkeley.edu/SSEAL/SoutheastAsia/seaelec.html. Northern Illinois University's Southeast Asia Digital Library includes a range of useful links that cover government, academic, and research institutions specific to East Timor: http://sea.lib.niu.edu.

Readers can supplement this chapter with figures and publication information found in the country profile pages of data.UN.org. and ADB.org. Recent and archived news articles are maintained on specific country profile pages by BBC.com and NYTimes.com.

The government's official Web site is www.easttimorgovernment.com. The Useful Links button on the front page of this site provides a comprehensive list of governmental and nongovernmental organizations. UNMIT's address is http://unmit.unmissions.org. The Timor-Leste Commission for Reception, Truth and Reconciliation, and its report, *Chega!*, are available at http://www.cavr-timorleste.org/en/chegaReport.htm. Wikipedia's list of political parties in East Timor provides links to home pages of active political parties. The East Timor and Indonesia Action Network, at www.etan.org, is an excellent source of information about the many dimensions of East Timor's past and present. It also maintains a page with extensive links to Timor-Leste–related topics at etan.org/resource/websites.htm. For current news in English, the monthly magazine *Guide Post* is available online: www.guideposttimor.com.

10

MALAYSIA

MALAYSIA IS IN MANY RESPECTS SOUTHEAST ASIA'S MOST ADMIRABLE achiever. Though generally classified as an illiberal democracy, Malaysia is more pluralist than Singapore, more politically stable than Thailand, and less corrupt than the Philippines. Malaysia has also more successfully managed ethnic and religious conflict than its geocultural cousin Indonesia. With a population of 28.8 million people and a per capita GNI of $8,420, Malaysia recently achieved newly industrialized country status. It currently boasts a poverty rate of only 4 percent. Only the citizens of microstates Singapore and Brunei enjoy a higher standard of living in the region. The Malaysian success story is especially noteworthy because of the country's geographic and racial diversity.

Malaysia consists of the peninsula (formerly Malaya) that is connected to southern Thailand, and Sabah and Sarawak on the island of Borneo, several hundred miles across the South China Sea. Today, eight in ten Malaysians live on the peninsula. Less than 10 percent of Malaysia's land is arable. Half of Malaysia's territory remains forested, and in the Borneo regions of East Malaysia lie some of the world's oldest tropical rainforests. Socially, Malaysia's diversity stems from its geography. Home to the famed Strait of Malacca passage, connecting the Indian subcontinent to Pacific Asia, Malaysia's maritime geography has shaped its history, economy, and society.

There is no more powerful force in Malaysian society than communalism, or the division of the country into racial communities: 55 percent Malay, 25 percent Chinese, 7 percent Indian, and the rest smaller minority and migrant groups.[1] The Malays are Sunni Muslim, predominantly rural and agricultural, or *bumiputra* (sons of the soil). Urban centers are attracting more *bumiputra* from the countryside as the country grows wealthier. Most non-Malays are urban and typically non-Muslim, usually employed in industry, manufacturing, and, more recently, finance. Overall, six in ten Malaysians now live in cities. Smaller indigenous minorities, such as the Dayaks, Iban,

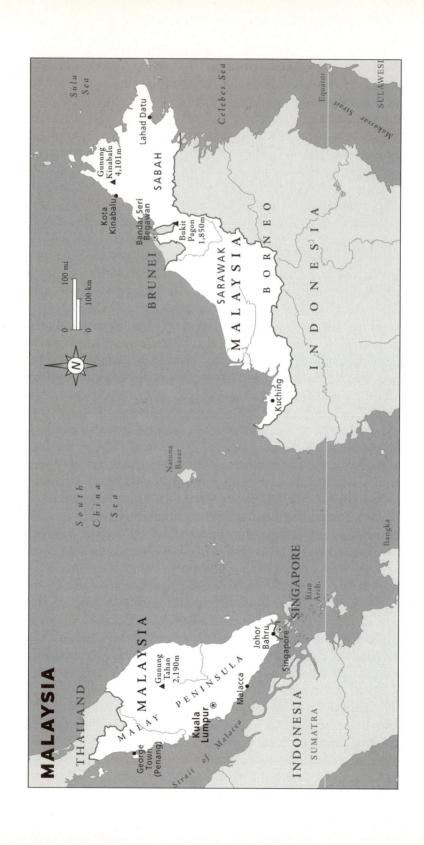

and Orang Asli of Borneo, remain politically weak and culturally vulnerable to the transformative forces of state and market.

Immigrants to Malaysia from 1860 to 1940 were mostly impoverished workers and peasants from southern China or southern India who came during the British colonial administration to work the tin mines and perform labor the Malays scorned. As with overseas diasporic communities elsewhere, their separateness was reinforced even as they expanded their economic roles. The Chinese in particular became Malaysia's money lenders, middlemen, contractors, and manufacturers. Their primary stress on education and ambition provided mobility so that at present the Chinese are the wealthiest businesspeople in most areas of the economy.

Communalism resulted in the stereotyping of Malaysia's ethnic groups. Historically, Malays routinely viewed the Chinese as aggressive, acquisitive, unscrupulous in business dealings, ritually unclean, and politically suspect. Chinese, on the other hand, saw themselves as hardworking, progressive, competitive, and faithful to their families. To the Chinese, the stereotypical Malay was perceived as lazy and superstitious and without motivation for hard work or personal advancement, whereas Malays viewed themselves as scrupulous in their dealings with others and as more concerned with the quality of human relationships than with material acquisition.[2]

Peninsular Malaysia came under formal British rule in 1874, after decades of control over the key ports of Penang, Melaka, and Singapore. North Borneo (now Sabah) and Sarawak also came under British control in the nineteenth century but were administered separately. Following Japanese occupation from 1942 to 1945, the British reestablished governance. Resistance to British rule emerged from communist guerrillas led by Chin Peng and from anticommunist Malay nationalists led by Tunkul Abdul Rahman. The latter group cooperated with British governors, and full independence, *merdaka*, was arranged for peninsular territories on August 31, 1957, under the UN-recognized name the Federation of Malaya. Tunkul Abdul Rahman was named prime minister. Within two years of independence, the communist insurgency was neutralized and the defeated Chin Peng fled to Beijing.

By 1963, the newly titled Federation of Malaysia, inclusive of all peninsular states—Sabah, Sarawak, and Singapore (but not Brunei)—was fully formed. To offset the integration of 3 million Chinese from Singapore into the federation, Sabah and Sarawak were brought in to maintain a favorable proportion of non-Chinese in the population. All of these areas shared a common colonial heritage under Great Britain, and all feared that without collaboration, they could not function as viable and autonomous nation-states.

To mitigate ethnic differences, the British arranged "the Bargain" when they relinquished colonial authority. The Bargain included such arrangements as constitutional advantages to the Malays; support for a Malay as head of state, chosen from among the sultans of nine peninsular Malay states; Malay as the country's official language; and Islam as the official religion. Also, the constitution provided special privileges to Malays in land acquisition, educational assistance, and civil service employment.

To meet the terms of the Bargain, the leading Malay, Chinese, and Indian political parties formed a coalition known as the Perikatan (Alliance) with the understanding that non-Malays would prevail in the economic sector while Malays would control the political sector. As long as that formula was accepted by all groups, the Malaysian political system was stable. When the formula was challenged, however, instability threatened, as in 1969 when, following a national election, deadly riots ensued and a state of emergency was declared lasting almost two years.

The original federation itself lasted only two years. It fell apart in August 1965 when Tunku Abdul Rahman expelled Singapore for many complex reasons inextricably bound up with communal problems. Singapore's leader, Lee Kuan Yew, called for a "Malaysian Malaysia"—that is, for a Malaysia with equal participation from all areas and groups. His call opposed and contrasted with Tunku Abdul Rahman's design for a "Malayan Malaysia," with special privileges reserved for the dominant ethnic group. When Lee Kuan Yew attempted to influence the larger area of Malaysia, Tunku Abdul Rahman regarded the attempt as a direct threat to continued political dominance by the Malays.

The May 1969 communal riots were a watershed event in Malaysia's postindependence era, and their immediate cause was the erosion of support for Abdul Rahman's Alliance coalition of parties in the 1969 elections. In the preceding two elections, in 1959 and 1964, the Alliance had won an overwhelming majority of the parliamentary seats. In 1969, for the first time the opposition parties won a majority (51.5 percent) of the votes against the Alliance's 48.5 percent. Although Alliance candidates still controlled a majority in the Parliament despite losing 23 seats, the 1969 election showed that the Alliance coalition's capacity to govern was seriously impaired. To celebrate their "victory," anti-Alliance forces marched in the streets of the capital, Kuala Lumpur. Later, on May 13, Alliance supporters paraded, which led to communal tensions reaching the point of provoking mob action that raged for four days and tragically ended in 196 deaths (official count).

The Malaysian government viewed the race riots as a threat to the ethnic Bargain that had been the formula for civic stability. To ensure that Malays retained political power, a state of emergency was proclaimed, Parliament was temporarily disbanded, civil liberties were curtailed, and total authority was granted to a new body, the National Operations Council. The council worked to restore order and sought to return Malaysia to parliamentary democracy. The twenty-one-month period was a time of suspended democracy.

Believing that economic tensions were mainly responsible for the communal riots, Tun Abdul Razak, the new prime minister, proposed the New Economic Policy (NEP) to promote national unity and a just society, and to attack poverty by "reducing and eventually eliminating the identity of race with economic function." Under the NEP, the rights of Malays were extended by reserving for them a proportion of positions in higher education and certain businesses, and sedition acts were passed that prohibited discussion of such "sensitive issues" as the prerogatives of Malay rulers, special rights for Malays, and official status for the Malay language. In essence, this meant that Malay participation in the economic sphere was to be increased by granting special privileges in terms of business ownership, tax breaks, investment incentives, and employment quotas—a pro-Malay affirmative action program for the majority.

By 1972, parliamentary democracy returned, albeit within the constraints of the sedition acts and the reworking of the Alliance into the Barisan Nasional (National Front), or BN. Tun Abdul Razak established the BN to ensure dominance of the political system by Malays and to preclude upheavals such as the 1969 riots. His party, the United Malays National Organization (UMNO), the lead member of the BN coalition, co-opted most of the opposition parties and won 90 percent of the parliamentary seats in the 1974 election.

When Abdul Razak died in 1976, he was succeeded by Tun Hussein Onn, who, like his predecessors, came from prestigious ancestry and great wealth and had a Western education. He continued BN policies until 1981 when, following a serious illness, he resigned and was succeeded by Deputy Prime Minister Dr. Mahathir bin Mohamad. Mahathir, the first commoner prime minister, with no aristocratic ancestry or family wealth and with a local education in medicine, symbolized the new Malaysian technocrat. His brash and confrontational style was the opposite of that of his refined predecessors.

Mahathir became an articulate spokesman in modern Malaysia's bid to develop economically. His "Look East Policy" argued that Western nations were not appropriate models for Malaysia. He believed that Malaysia should emulate the methods of Japan, South Korea, and Taiwan, all Asian countries whose values were more in tune with those of Malaysia. He also introduced the concept of "Malaysia Incorporated," whereby business and government leaders would work together as in a modern corporation.

In the 1982 parliamentary election, Mahathir and the UMNO-led BN coalition of parties triumphed, winning 132 of 154 seats. Again in 1986, the BN coalition won a landslide victory, winning 148 of the 177 parliamentary seats, but this election marked the beginning of a period of political and economic difficulties. The leaders of the major parties in the BN fell into strife as the country underwent a major recession, which resulted in negative economic growth for the first time since independence.

The major problem was within UMNO, the dominant party of BN and the "political home" of Mahathir (as well as all former prime ministers). Strife in UMNO led to the resignation of high-ranking officials, some of whom joined a faction known as Team B, who then challenged the leadership of Mahathir and his followers, known as Team A. In the elections for the leadership of UMNO in April 1987, Mahathir barely beat his challenger, Team B leader Trade and Industry Minister Tunku Razaleigh Hamzah, when he won by only 43 votes, 761 to 718. In a shocking display of internecine factionalism, Team B officials accused Mahathir of blatant abuse of power, authoritarian leadership, economic mismanagement, and corruption.[3]

Razaleigh had run against Mahathir following five years of a recessionary economy, including a 1 percent decline in the GNP, which disillusioned the Chinese and the new Malay middle class. Mahathir's confrontational administrative style had also become controversial. The challenge to Mahathir was especially noteworthy because it is the custom of Malays not to challenge their leaders; generally, Malaysians believe in *taat setia* (absolute loyalty) to their rulers. It is considered a case of *kurang ajar* (impropriety) to question the leadership. The electoral challenge undermined this important custom in Malay politics.[4]

In response, Mahathir purged Team B members from his cabinet and from UMNO leadership, and he invoked the Internal Securities Act, ordering the arrest of persons critical of government actions. Also, three opposition newspapers were closed, and Operation Lallang was ordered: a sweep by the Malaysian police on October 27, 1987, that took into custody 119 people who had been accused of threatening internal security by provoking communal conflict. All those arrested were members of religious, political, and social organizations that, merely by criticizing regime policies, had qualified themselves as "thorns in [Mahathir's] side."[5]

In still another stunning incident related to UMNO factionalism, the Malaysian high court decreed that since unregistered regional branches had participated in the UMNO elections, UMNO was an illegal organization. Immediately there was a scramble to register a new party with UMNO in its name and to lay claim to the party's considerable assets. After rejecting Team B's applications, Mahathir was able to get UMNO Baru (New UMNO) registered. A dissident faction, again led by Razaleigh, formed a new party, Semangat '46 (Spirit of '46, the year of UMNO's birth), and allied itself with other opposition groups to form an alternative coalition known as Angkatan Perpaduan Umnah (APU), or the United Movement of the Faithful. Subsequently, the Barisan Nasional, led by UMNO Baru, won six of eight by-elections against the APU as well as the national election in October 1990.

Because of high-court decisions against the interests of the BN, Mahathir reduced the power of the courts by taking away their right to judicial review of executive decisions on internal security and matters concerned with the administration and operation of political parties. Ostensibly, this reduction of the courts' power was to ensure that, in case of threat to the nation's security, an executive could move with dispatch rather than having to wait for the cumbersome courts to deliberate. Eventually, at Mahathir's instigation, a specially created tribunal removed a majority of court justices from office.

In early 1989, Mahathir suffered a heart attack and underwent a successful multiple coronary bypass operation. His rapid recovery restored him as the central figure in contemporary Malaysian politics. A strong recovery from economic recession was the principal factor in the overwhelming election victory Mahathir and the multiethnic BN coalition achieved in October 1990. After only a ten-day political campaign, one of the shortest in contemporary Southeast Asian history, he won a two-thirds majority, thus ensuring control over constitutional amendments.

The primary political issue of the early 1990s concerned the role of Islam in Malaysian society. Islamization had made inroads into the state of Kelantan, with the state assembly controlled by an Islamic-dominated coalition between the Parti Islam Se-Malaysia (PAS) and Semangat '46. Mahathir reacted against the notion of an Islamic state, which he deemed inappropriate for a multiracial society. The issue did not become a crisis at the time because high economic growth rates provided a cushion that softened societal tensions.

In 1992–1993, a social reformation of great significance occurred when Mahathir decided to confront the nation's sultans, the traditional hereditary rulers of most of peninsular Malaysia's states, whose positions were largely ceremonial. The prime minister moved to reduce their power and prerogatives, notwithstanding laws and acts precluding discussion of the sultans' roles. By 1993, Mahathir had thus tamed the bureaucracy, political parties, judiciary, press, and sultans. Through confrontation and co-optation, he had successfully undermined the major forces once competing with him for political power.

The period from 1990 to 1996 was positive for the ruling Barisan Nasional coalition and for its leader, Mahathir. Winning its ninth general election in April 1995, with 64 percent of the popular vote, the BN enjoyed a two-thirds parliamentary majority. In addition, the it won control of every state assembly except one (that of Kelantan), and the opposition was left in disarray. Both the Democratic Action Party (DAP) and Semangat '46 were shut out throughout the nation. The Barisan Nasional coalition of UMNO, the Malayan Chinese Association, the Malayan Indian Congress, and the largely Chinese Parti Gerakan were united after the election. Malaysians supported the BN because of the strong economy, the disarray of the opposition, and the BN's monopoly of the mass media. At seventy years of age, Mahathir had never been more secure in his position.

As Mahathir's health stayed strong and his international stature increased, few politicians were brave enough to question his preeminence. His main competition came from a former Muslim youth activist and deputy prime minister, Anwar Ibrahim, but Mahathir kept him off balance with intraparty rules that banned confrontations with the leader. Mahathir became Malaysia's longest-serving premier and the only BN chairman to lead his coalition through five successive elections.

Mahathir's international reputation widened after a series of speeches in which he praised the virtues of "Asian values" and condemned "Western values." He often spoke passionately about his nation's sovereignty and, appearing to revel in the role of "West-basher," about the Americans, whom he deemed to be neoimperialist in their desire to control Malaysia and Malaysia's neighbors. In 1996, Mahathir was responsible for backing the construction of the world's tallest building, the Petronas Towers in Kuala Lumpur (eclipsing America's Sears Tower in Chicago). He built a gleaming high-tech research park, dubbed "Technopolis," and the Multimedia Super-Corridor, linking Kuala Lumpur with an immense new international airport.

In 1997, when the Asian economic crisis hit Malaysia, Mahathir was in his sixteenth year of tenure and in sole command of his country. A new problem arose when the Malaysian ringgit lost much of its value as a result of the Thai currency's devaluation. For the first time, Mahathir was in the midst of a crisis he could not control directly because the crisis was partly caused by international and not domestic factors. His first reaction was to blame outsiders, and he ridiculously pointed his finger at the "Jewish conspiracy" he believed had long wanted to undermine Malaysia because of its predominantly Muslim population. Mahathir later explained that he was referring to only one Jew, Hungarian-born American financier George Soros, whom Mahathir accused of maliciously speculating on the Malaysian currency. Most of the world's press criticized Mahathir for refusing to accept that a large reason for the currency crisis was domestic, and not external.

Since 1991, Mahathir had focused on "Vision 2020," a plan to lift Malaysia into the ranks of developed nations by 2020. The economic crisis blunted his goal, which may explain the depth of his anger and his shocking anti-Semitic accusation. Mahathir emphatically rejected emergency aid from the IMF and, defying economic orthodoxy, imposed capital controls. Foreign investors, stunned by the announcement that their investment funds must remain in Malaysia for at least one year, reacted sourly. Although pundits predicted a policy disaster, Mahathir, who accused the IMF of trying to recolonize Asia, eventually won admiration for guiding the country through the turbulent Asian economic crisis without an IMF bailout.

In 1999, Mahathir dismissed his deputy prime minister, Anwar Ibrahim, for alleged corruption and sodomy. Serious scholars of Malaysia believed that Ibrahim was actually sacked because he was increasingly popular among Malaysians and a potential threat to Mahathir's continued leadership. The entire issue of trumping up charges against a rival minister proved to be an immense international embarrassment to Mahathir and provided his critics with evidence that Malaysia was no longer a nation of laws, but instead a nation of personalities, many of whom were above the law.

Despite the debacle, Mahathir felt confident to set national elections for the Parliament in November 1999, six months before his term was even up. Campaigning was minimal, and many topics were banned. The election was an excellent example of electoral politics designed to perpetuate the leading party's power. The short eight-day campaign led to the BN winning an overwhelming majority, 57 percent of the popular vote (down from 65 percent in 1995). Several provinces voted against the UMNO-led coalition, choosing Islamic parties. UMNO lost nearly half the Malay vote, particularly in Sabah and Sarawak, but the BN maintained Malay support in key peninsular districts and won a majority of the total votes.

By 2001, Mahathir had run Malaysia for over twenty years and, like many overstaying leaders, he began to lose his edge and became surrounded by yes-men who failed him by pointing out only his successes and not his weaknesses. Mahathir stepped down as prime minister in 2003, believing it was time for new leadership. He left a paradoxical legacy from his twenty-two years in office. Because of his vision and leadership, the nation had enjoyed two decades of ever-improving living standards for all classes of people. With an intolerance of pettiness, disdain of opposition, and fervent commitment to Malaysian sovereignty, Mahathir sidelined rivals while lifting the country out of its third-world status. He embraced strategic alliances with Chinese and Indian elites but also left his UMNO colleagues (and his fellow Malays) as the beneficiaries of a political system stacked in their favor. During his tenure, Mahathir brashly disciplined the bureaucracy, political parties, judiciary, press, and sultans, all of whom once dared to challenge his political power.

Going out in true Mahathir style, the prime minister gave the world some parting thoughts. During a high-profile speech in 2003 at the Organization of the Islamic Conference (OIC), which Malaysia hosted, he claimed that the U.S. invasion of Iraq proved the West's intention to recolonize the developing world. He also claimed that Jews were controlling the world by proxy, adding defiantly that "1.3 billion Muslims cannot be defeated by a few million Jews." Then, as conference host, he turned on his OIC guests and rebuked the Muslim community for its backwardness, deriding its tolerance for religious fanaticism. "Islam is not just for the seventh century," he proclaimed. "Islam is for all times. And times have changed."[6]

Abdullah Ahmad Badawi, a low-key but longtime UMNO minister, replaced Mahathir as prime minister only to struggle to find his own political style and support base. During his initial years as prime minister, a number of official scandals erupted and communalism reared its ugly head with resurgent Malay nationalism. Mahathir's party edifice was both crumbling and rallying at the same time. Caught in corruption imbroglios, UMNO elites came to one another's defense. Badawi's support suffered a blow in 2008, however, when Mahathir left UMNO, pledging not to return to the party until Badawi was relieved of his position.

Mahathir's dissatisfaction with his successor stemmed in large part from UMNO's poorest performance in general elections in twenty years. In the March 2008 elections, UMNO won less than 30 percent of the vote and lost 30 seats in the 222-seat lower assembly. The Barisan Nasional retained power, but with its weakest coalition victory ever and a slim 51 percent of the popular vote. The Pakatan Rakyat (PR), or People's Front, a three-party coalition led by Anwar Ibrahim's People's Justice Party, secured 47 percent of the vote. In terms of assembly seats, the PR won 82 to the BN's 140. The first post-Mahathir election had resulted in the BN's loss of its previous two-thirds majority, needed to pass constitutional amendments.

The changes in UMNO leadership caused by Mahathir's departure and election woes opened new political space for democracy activists and opposition groups. Ibrahim, released from prison in 2004 when the previous verdict on the sodomy was overturned, reemerged on the political scene. Wan Azizah Wan Ismail, Anwar's wife, was elected by opposition parties as opposition leader. NGOs began to form their own coalitions, and an increasingly vocal Internet community pushed for an end to UMNO's dominance. Facing massive street protests in 2007, UMNO appeared vulnerable for the first time in decades.

Parliament opened in May 2008 with a palpable sense that UMNO's majority was in jeopardy. Pledging to end government corruption, and the privileged position Malay business oligarchs derived from the New Economic Policy, the opposition parties began wooing members to their side, hoping to shake UMNO's grip on Parliament. Facing serious threats, UMNO leaders initially returned to harassing and intimidating their opponents. Activists and antigovernment Internet bloggers found police at their doorsteps and, amazingly, Ibrahim was rearrested, again on specious charges of sodomy.

Subsequent criticism for Badawi to resign led the embattled prime minister to offer up a meager package of political reforms. Ultimately, the economic downturn caused by the 2008–2009 global financial crisis brought Badawi down. In April 2009, in an event confirming Malaysia's first intergenerational political dynasty, Badawi was replaced by Najib Abdul Razak, son and nephew of previous Malaysian prime ministers (Abdual Razak and Hussein Onn, respectively).

With UMNO facing unprecedented political pressure, Najib announced a program of reform under the slogan "1Malaysia. People First, Performance Now." It sought to appease the non-Malay voters, as well as many younger Malays, who had abandoned BN. New policy initiatives included reducing NEP quotas requiring compulsory *bumiputra* ownership in private companies and a new government scholarship program based on merit rather than race. Claiming that "Malaysians have reached a high level of maturity," Najib also lifted long-standing emergency decrees, reassessed restrictions on public demonstrations, and repealed the 1960 Internal Security Act, which had permitted indefinite detention without charge or trial.[7]

Though welcomed by some reform advocates, Najib's reforms were not enough; many others interpreted the new Peaceful Assembly law as a vehicle to expand state powers. Angered by ongoing UMNO corruption scandals and Badawi's failed leadership, Malaysia's traditionally apolitical youth were also amidst a political awakening by the time Najib came to power. New vehicles of civic expression were emerging in Malaysia: online activity, political blogs, and planned rallies.

Organized in 2007 under the name Bersih ("clean," in Malay), antigovernment youth and opposition PR figures launched massive rallies and protests in 2007, 2011, and 2012—commonly referred to as Bersih 1.0, 2.0, and 3.0, respectively. Donning distinctive canary yellow T-shirts, tens of thousands of protestors from Bersih (a coalition of sixty-two civil society groups) have assembled to demand electoral reform, access to government-controlled media, and an end to bureaucratic corruption.[8] Intended to be peaceful and festive, Bersih rallies have turned violent, with protestors testing public security forces. To disperse crowds, police have resorted to chemical-laced water cannons, tear gas, and excessive force. Over 2,000 detentions resulted from Bersih 2.0 and 3.0. The episodic clashes have emboldened Bersih's resolve to end Malaysia's illiberal electoral authoritarianism; and thus far, UMNO's usual strategies of co-opting, depoliticizing, or intimidating opponents have proven futile. Chatter in the blogosphere about another major demonstration began shortly after the 2012 rally; "Global Bersih 4.0" was set up as a Facebook page.

In 2012, Najib thus found himself governing a Malaysia that Mahathir never knew. Not only did Najib face a more troubled global economy, a more active civil society, and a generation of angry urban youth, but political Islam was also strengthening in certain areas of the federation. In addition to ongoing communalism, a newer and more complex array of domestic political forces now coexisted alongside Malaysia's march of economic success.

Under the constitution, a general election must be held before March 2013, but it may be called sooner. When elections do occur, fifty-five years of continuous BN rule will be up for referendum. Najib, whose own approval ratings have increased since taking office, could lead UMNO to another victory. Bersih's rising street power notwithstanding, the opposition in Malaysia remains divided ideologically and organizationally. Where the Pakatan Rakyat coalition has won control of state governments, bickering, defections, and factionalism have inevitably followed. Nevertheless, further BN losses or defections could fundamentally change Malaysia's long-standing government-party configuration. Malaysia's governing elites, and the illiberal democracy they created, face unprecedented political challenges going forward.

INSTITUTIONS AND SOCIAL GROUPS

Political Parties

The Alliance (in the pre-1969 period) and the Barisan Nasional (National Front) are coalitions of parties, joined together by the common goals of winning elections and securing societal stability. These goals have for the most part been achieved. Three parties composed the Alliance: the United Malays National Organization (UMNO), the Malayan Chinese Association, and the Malayan Indian Congress. Representing the three major ethnic groups, these parties accepted the Alliance formula to legitimize the interests of these ethnic groups. The formula required that each group accept the basic societal division: Malays dominate the political sphere, and Chinese and Indians dominate the economy.

When the formula broke down in 1969, the Alliance was transformed into the Barisan Nasional, which consisted of the three Alliance parties as well as a coalition of former opposition parties led by the Parti Islam Se-Malaysia (PAS), or the Islamic Party of Malaysia, the country's strongest Islamic party. In all, Barisan Nasional was composed of eleven component parties, but UMNO remained the senior partner, with final say over coalition decisions.[9]

In 1988, a Malaysian court stunned the country when it found UMNO unlawful on the grounds that the delegates sent to the assembly had not been properly chosen. The rapid transformation of UMNO into UMNO Baru (with "Baru" subsequently deleted) was important for retaining the government's legitimacy. For the first time since independence, UMNO was challenged by a party organization, Semangat '46, led by a Malay and strong enough to defeat the BN. Having allied with Razaleigh's United Movement of the Faithful (APU) coalition (which included the PAS), Semangat '46 provided a viable alternative to the UMNO-dominated BN.

However, the APU's strength was found wanting in the 1990 elections, in which some 8 million registered Malaysians voted. Candidates representing the BN capitalized on the issues of economic growth and political stability to achieve another electoral victory. The opposition's focus on issues of human rights, press freedom, lower taxes, and Mahathir's combative personality was not as credible to Malaysia's voters.

Other efforts to develop a party coalition to oust the UMNO-led BN have followed the APU's path but with increasing success. The Barisan Alternatif coalition formed in the wake of Ibrahim's arrest in 1999. The Barisan Alternatif included the Islamic-oriented PAS, the Chinese-oriented Democratic Action Party (DAP), and other Malay parties. Barisan Alternatif parties, especially PAS, competed well in the 1999 general elections, but the DAP left the coalition shortly after September 11, 2001. The oppositional infighting was again put aside in the 2008 election, when the People's Front coalition was formed to challenge UMNO. It included PAS, the DAP, and the People's Justice Party, led by Wan Azizah, Anwar's wife.

The BN also has long enjoyed the advantage of UMNO's access to funds. UMNO has transformed itself into a huge business conglomerate with assets in numerous corporations. Although conglomerates throughout Southeast Asia rely on government patronage, no assemblage of companies owned directly by a political party appears to have benefited from government largesse to the same extent as UMNO's holdings.[10] Neither opposition nor allied parties within the BN have access to such funds. One of UMNO's greatest vulnerabilities, as demonstrated by intermittent scandals, rests in its own missteps in allocating the state budget.

The three-party Pakatan Rakyat (People's Front) coalition that challenges UMNO and the thirteen-party BN today is not an ideologically cohesive opposition but a tactical alliance. The People's Justice Party's main goal, for example, is to end preferential policies favoring Malays under the NEP. Offended by the corruption that preference has bred, the party of Anwar Ibrahim (who is the de facto head) and Wan Azizah, his wife (the official leader), is viewed by some as a viable alternative to UMNO for the federation's leadership. Anwar, a former Muslim activist, holds acceptable Muslim credentials for most Malays but his economic leanings have alienated economic nationalists in the PR coalition.

Parti Islam Se-Malaysia (PAS), or the Islamic Party of Malaysia, is a rising force in Malaysia. With an implicitly communalist platform, PAS is dedicated to advancing conservative Malay Muslim interests. PAS's platform has included the unrealistic goal of creating an Islamic state. Some within the party favor sharia-based administration at the state level. PAS enjoyed a brief stint in a government coalition in the 1970s but soon parted ways with the business-oriented UMNO. Although it has largely jettisoned the objective to transform Malaysia into an Islamic state, many moderate Muslims, Chinese, and Indians remain leery of further PAS gains. PAS may never dominate Malaysia, but its supporters remain committed partisans, and the party's Malay identity threatens UMNO's core communal support.

The third party in the Pakatan Rakyat, the Democratic Action Party (DAP), is a secular, multiethnic party oriented toward furthering Malaysia's modernity. Advocating a "Malaysian Malaysia," the DAP is resurrecting jargon made prominent decades earlier by Lee Kuan Yew, before Singapore left the federation. While the DAP platform is somewhat compatible with that of the People's Justice Party, the three parties of the PR share little more than anti-UMNO ambitions. If the parties were to someday replace the current UMNO-led government, they are unlikely to match UMNO's decades-long stability. A change in government may herald a new pattern of government instability.

Compared to political parties in Thailand, the Philippines, and Indonesia, UMNO is a highly institutionalized party coalition. Unseating it will be difficult. Every Malaysian prime minister has reached that position because he has led UMNO, whereas leaders elsewhere in the region have reached the top governmental positions in other ways, reflecting the lesser importance of their parties and the weaker institutionalization of their party systems. Highly institutionalized parties, nevertheless, can be dangerous engines of patronage; ongoing revelations of corruption and scandal render UMNO far from invincible in a system with an increasingly savvy and demanding public.

State Royalty

Malaysia's means of choosing its monarch is unique among Southeast Asia's constitutional monarchies. Nine states have hereditary rulers (sultans) and Malaysia's king, or *Yang di-Pertuan Agong* (Supreme Ruler), is elected from this body (usually on the basis of seniority) for a five-year term. The king, who has ceremonial and religious duties and powers of appointment, can officially delay certain legislative bills (although this power has been circumscribed). The Malaysian king is not held in the same awe as the king of Thailand; nevertheless, he plays an important symbolic role as the head of state.

The sultans' role changed dramatically in 1993 when Mahathir moved to place them under the law. The prime minister's actions were precipitated by an incident in which the sultan of Johore allegedly assaulted a field hockey coach with whom he was displeased. Mahathir lifted the hereditary rulers' immunity from legal action and revoked their right to grant pardons to themselves and their families.

Mahathir's moves were accompanied by daily press reports on the sultans' rampant corruption, philandering, and high living. These reports were shocking to the citizens both because of the extent of the alleged debauchery and because the reports appeared to break sedition-act regulations forbidding criticism of the sultans. Rural Malays were stunned to read such reports about their sultans, who had long commanded their loyalty and were viewed as their symbolic protectors.

Serving as head of state in Malaysia's federative constitutional monarchy, the people's many rotating monarchs nevertheless bear the global distinction of rarely outlasting the government's prime ministers. Consequently, prominent prime ministers such as Tunku Abdul Rahman and Mahathir bin Mohamad became de facto symbols of the Malaysian state, both inside and outside of Malaysia. Political insignificance is thus the price of a system championing royal fairness.

Federal Parliament

Malaysia's political system is based on the British model, with a bicameral Parliament that elects one of its own members to the prime ministership. The prime minister must sit among the 222 seats in the lower chamber, the House of Representatives (Dewan Ra'ayat) and must command majority support. The upper chamber, the Senate (Dewan Negara), has 70 members: 26 appointed by state legislatures and 44 appointed by the king after the prime minister's recommendation. Senators hold office for six years; representatives serve five years unless Parliament is dissolved sooner than that. Although representation is based on single-member constituencies, a weighting of constituencies in favor of rural areas traditionally enhances Malay representation—in effect almost guaranteeing Malay political power.[11]

The potential of Malaysia's Parliament to alter the course of the federation's politics is significant. Given the fragmentation of political interests in the party system, and the multitude of viable parties (seventeen with House seats following the 2008 elections), UMNO is more likely to lose its coalition partners in the Parliament before it loses general elections outright to another party. Even with a more active civil society than in the past, the locus of political change in Malaysia's future is likely to be found in the parliamentary institution; that is, the electoral politics that determines who sits in it and the coalition governments it creates.

Political Islam

The religious element is central to Malaysians' political party orientations. Parties among the Malay majority are defined largely in terms of their degree of Islamic orthodoxy. Although moderate Islamic parties have been dominant in the ruling alliance, the rise of the conservative Islamic Party of Malaysia (PAS) in many states, and as a major partner in the current Pakatan Rakyat opposition coalition, is a noteworthy development.

In Malaysia, all Malays are Muslim by legal definition. Islam provides both legal and political privileges to Malays that, if lost, are tantamount to renouncing the Malay way of life. The state's new high-tech national identity cards, or MyKads (which include fingerprint biometrics), prominently list one's race and religion. Traditionally, Malay Muslims did not emphasize

distinctions between secular and religious activities. Islam was tightly organized from the village up to the state level; hence, Muslims could be easily
mobilized. Following the communal violence of 1969, proliferating *dakwah*
(Muslim revivalist groups) made calls for Islamic fundamentalism, promoting rigid codes of conduct and the implementation of Islamic law. Many of
these revivalist groups were filled with educated youth, often affiliated with
the University of Malaya. Indeed, many of the movement's leaders came to
hold radical Islamic ideas from the Arab world while studying in Britain.[12]

In the 1980s, Mahathir sought to defuse the Islamic resurgence by a program of "absorption of Islamic values," but this fanned the contentious
flames of communalism. Sentiment for an Islamic state grew as organizations found inspiration from movements in Egypt and Pakistan.[13] Even before the September 11, 2001, terrorist attacks, Mahathir aggressively applied
pressure on Islamist fundamentalists groups with international ties. As
Washington, D.C., launched its war on terrorism following the attacks,
Malaysia cooperated with U.S. intelligence to uncover cells of al-Qaeda and
Jemaah Islamiya in the country. Arrests, rumors, and discoveries of terrorist
activity fueled anxiety in the region. The Petronas Towers were thought to be
especially vulnerable to attack (authorities emptied the towers on September
12, 2001, for example). Terrorist bombings in neighboring Indonesia put
Malaysian authorities on full alert about the nebulous threat the federation
faced. Mahathir may have railed against Jews and the West in passionate
speeches, but he also made no room for terrorists in Malaysia.

Similarly, Abdullah Badawi worked both sides of the Islamist extremism
issue. Experienced in state security and antiterrorism as a former home
minister, Badawi carried strong Muslim credentials as the son and grandson of Islamic scholars. Advocating a policy addressing fundamentalism's
"root causes," Badawi stepped up his government's antipoverty agenda for
rural areas following bombings in Indonesia. Standing before the UN General Assembly, he also promoted the concept of *Islam Hadhari* (Civiliza-
tional Islam)—that Islam is compatible with both modernity and equitable
development.

Domestically, the opposition Islamic Party of Malaysia (PAS), which
competes with BN's UMNO for the Malay-Muslim vote, has increased its
presence in national and state assemblies. Some areas where conservative
Islam is predominant have begun to permit underage marriage; others have
banned yoga, dark lipstick, and high-heeled shoes. Sharia courts are also on
the rise. Sentences of corporal punishment for women involved in extramari-
tal sex and beer drinking spawned international outcry and condemnation
from international human rights groups. Under Najib, Malaysia's international reputation as a moderate Islamic society remains intact, but political
Islam and fundamentalism are on the rise.

Notwithstanding recent trends, Islam and modernity have generally evolved to complement each other in Malaysia. Because political Islam is largely moderate and finds expression through the party mechanism and other legitimate political channels, Islamist terrorism in multiethnic Malaysia has thus far remained limited. Malaysia's leaders also gain recognition for dampening the threat of communalism and the dangerous marriage between identity politics and Islamic fundamentalism. Nevertheless, the globalization of Islamist terrorism in the new international era leaves Malaysia exposed to pernicious influences beyond its borders.

STATE-SOCIETY RELATIONS AND DEMOCRACY

Malaysia was granted independence under peaceful circumstances, and it adopted and adapted British governmental institutions; thus, the country emerged from colonialism with a strong and stable political system. Because of the communal character of their society, Malaysian leaders adapted Western democratic structures in an attempt to provide Malays with dominance of the political realm. This required that the principal institutions of the society be merged with the state. This fusion has been both a blessing and a curse to Malaysia's political development.

The clearest example of this close association is the integration of the Alliance (after 1969, the Barisan Nasional) with the state. As in Indonesia, where Golkar was in essence a state institution, the BN (led by UMNO) merged with the state—dominating the bureaucracy, the Parliament, the media, and the courts. This has set Malaysia apart from Thailand and the Philippines, where political parties are relatively autonomous from the state. If UMNO's control of Parliament is overturned, however, the state could achieve new separation from its long-dominant partner.

One characteristic of strong states is their ability to project their power into the countryside. Through the co-optation of local Malay elites and the provision of roads, financial credit, medical facilities, recreational programs, and other benefits, the Malaysian state has succeeded in tying local power brokers to the central authorities through either UMNO or local-level governmental agencies.

In economic affairs as well, the Malaysian state has asserted its control. No facet of the economy is excluded from governmental intervention, intended to ensure that the goals of the NEP are met and to provide resources to UMNO. The state has co-opted most of those who could challenge it. Indeed, oppositionists are established supporters of the state, differing only in terms of their desire to replace its political leaders. Thus, the Malaysian state is not subservient to societal forces, such as an autonomous military or insurgency, or to such external powers as a former colonial ruler or present-day international financial institutions.

Malaysia's postindependence prime ministers have also strengthened state institutions as a means to promote political stability, economic development, and ethnic harmony. Malaysia experienced strong leadership from Tunku Abdul Rahman, the father of Malaysian independence, and Mahathir bin Mohamad, the manager of Malaysia's economic success. These leaders did not undermine the state's institutions in a manner similar to that of Ferdinand Marcos in the Philippines, Ne Win in Burma, or Hun Sen in Cambodia.

Thus, as opposed to its neighbors, Malaysia has managed to sustain basic institutions of democratic rule. The major exception, following the 1969 riots, was a temporary state of emergency, but it was carried out less as a coup d'état than as an interlude during which parliamentary democracy could be rebuilt. Unlike in Thailand, Indonesia, and Burma, the Malaysian military has not played a major role in politics. In the early years of independence, priority was given to socioeconomic development rather than to building substantial armed forces.[14] Despite significant upgrades in the military's profile in recent years, and new purchases of fighter jets, submarines, and weapons systems, Malaysia's military remains far from being a praetorian force.

The granting of independence by Great Britain was carried out peacefully and was received with some reluctance by Malaysians, who feared their country's viability would be jeopardized without British support. Nevertheless, the Malaysians adopted the Westminster model of governance, including regularized competitive elections, a representative parliament, the separation of powers, civilian supremacy, and civil liberties. These adoptions are especially noteworthy because Malaysian elites tend to hold a formalized view of democracy that crumbles when it faces more deeply held values; stability and security, for example, take precedence over democratic values.[15]

Since independence, Malaysia has witnessed an impressive twelve national elections. Remarkably, UMNO has won all twelve, and the right to form a government, although sometimes with coalition partners. Although their numbers in the Parliament have been few, opposition candidates generally win about 40 percent of the votes. Over the course of these twelve elections, there have been five orderly successions of power.

Despite this admirable election record, Malaysia is generally regarded as a quasi- or illiberal democracy because of serious limitations on civil liberties.[16] Until it was repealed by Najib in 2012, the country's Internal Securities Act imposed a culture of silence on citizens and prohibited discussion of "sensitive issues." Even after its repeal, newspapers, television, radio, and the Internet are government (read: UMNO) regulated and generally compliant vis-à-vis all communalism issues. Web sites, magazines, and newspapers that overstep boundaries can be, and have been, shut down. "Religious freedom" for Muslims in Malaysia includes the criminality of apostasy and, in many states, the criminality of conversion to another religion. In Malaysia's democracy, non-Muslims may not marry Muslims without converting first. Local sharia courts often hold authority over Muslims in such matters of marriage and conversion, and where federal law or state law is silent or ambiguous.

According to the system's defenders, the explanation for the necessity of quasi-democracy rather than full, Western-style democracy is that Malaysia's polycommunal situation is unique. Such a society cannot carry out its affairs in a fully democratic way if one segment of the society must be given special privileges of governance. In the context of communal issues, an election loss or BN-coalition collapse would mean the perceived end of the Malays' primary rights. Emergency rule became necessary in 1969, the argument goes, because Malays and Chinese reacted to that possibility.

The rules for Malaysian democracy, which had to be modified after 1969 to ensure that Malay political supremacy would continue, were changed to include opposition parties in the Alliance.[17] Dividing the nation along ethnic lines between those in power and those not in power would only worsen communal issues. To mitigate divisiveness, the Barisan Nasional was created to accommodate a wider range of parties. Even the Islamic PAS was initially included in the BN, but it later withdrew to join the Chinese-oriented DAP in leading the opposition. The BN formula was uniquely Malaysian, reflecting the difficult ethnic sensitivities that have long been at the core of Malaysian politics.

Malaysia's illiberal democracy, or what might be called a competitive authoritarian regime, has been sustained by the continuing strength of the economy, which mitigates extremist demands by the growing urbanized middle class (which favors moderate policies) and by the country's modern history of British-style democratic institutions. Mahathir's emphasis on "Asian values" opposed democratic tendencies, especially regarding the rights to protest and question governmental leaders. Until recently, most Malaysians seemed content with the notion of quasi- or illiberal democracy, which they viewed as appropriate to their values. Nevertheless, the government's treatment of opposition politicians and UMNO corruption scandals are causing many to push for greater civil liberties and fuller democracy.

ECONOMY AND DEVELOPMENT

Malaysia is one of the few success stories of economic development in the third world. With a nominal per capita GNI approaching $9,000 ($15,600 using purchasing power parity) there has been a clear improvement in the standard of living since independence in 1957. In 1966, only 18 percent of households in a typical Malaysian village had piped water. By 1978, this figure was 71 percent and by 1993 close to 100 percent. Electricity was available to 45 percent of households in 1966; this increased to 79 percent in 1978 and

100 percent by 1987. In 1966, only 4 percent of Malay families owned a television; by 1997, the figure was just under 100 percent. During this period, dirt roads were paved, telephone lines were installed, and mosques were built.[18] By 2011, Malaysia's Human Development Index global ranking was 61 (out of 179), higher than resource-rich Venezuela and Brazil, and former superpower Russia.

In 1971, by means of the unprecedented New Economic Policy (NEP), the Malaysian government initiated an extraordinary twenty-year plan designed to eradicate poverty and eliminate ethnicity as a function of economic prosperity. The plan was meant to change Malaysia's fundamental structures and ethnic divisions by directing the increments of rapid economic growth disproportionately to the Malay sector without expropriating Chinese assets or weakening the vigor of Chinese enterprise.[19]

The NEP was the government's response to the 1969 riots and the perceived need for a dramatic attack on the ethnic divisions in the economy. According to government data, in 1971 the ownership of share capital was 63 percent foreign, 34 percent non-Malay, and less than 3 percent Malay. The goal was to raise the Malay share of capital ownership to 30 percent and reduce the foreign share to 30 percent, while allowing the Chinese share to rise to 40 percent.[20] The means to this end were tax breaks, investment incentives, employment quotas, and the granting of special privileges in business ownership. The government required all banks to earmark a significant proportion of their business loans for Malays.

The NEP was to end in 1990; however, because the target of 30 percent capital ownership by Malays had not been met (it stands at about 20 percent), the government appointed a commission to design a new twenty-year policy. The foreign share had fallen from 63 percent to 33 percent, and the difference was taken up by non-Malays, whose share increased from 34 percent to 47 percent. Other goals were substantially achieved, including the reduction of the poverty level, which had fallen from 30 percent in 1977 to 17 percent by 1987. Many more *bumiputra* Malays were engaged in businesses in which they had formerly been underrepresented. Investments in rural development and agricultural programs increased many times over during the twenty-year NEP.

Like other successful Asian economies, Malaysia's economic achievements are not the result of Washington Consensus policies. Under Mahathir, Malaysia did emphasize market-oriented mechanisms, featuring the privatization of public utilities, communications, and transportation; at the same time it also featured state-owned heavy industrialization and large state-managed holding companies. Mahathir's "Look East Policy" stressed the adoption of the work ethic and other principles followed by companies in Japan and South Korea as well as increased trade with Asian neighbors.

The success of these programs led economists to claim that Malaysia had joined Singapore, Taiwan, South Korea, and Hong Kong as Asia's fifth tiger.

Over time, Malaysia became the world's largest exporter of semiconductors and one of the largest exporters of single-unit air conditioners, textiles, and footwear. Manufacturing accounted for 50 percent of total exports by 1990, compared to just 20 percent ten years earlier. These increases in manufacturing output, stimulated largely by export-oriented industrialization, have resulted in a much more broadly based economy.

During the 1990s, Malaysia's economic growth rate was one of the highest in the world, averaging 8.3 percent. The country enjoyed low unemployment and inflation rates, along with increases in manufacturing production and foreign investment. However, Malaysia's economic success was mitigated by continuing reports that the percentage of Malays sharing in the new wealth had not increased appreciably, despite the stated goals of the NEP. Hence, in 1991, Prime Minister Mahathir introduced a ten-year new development policy, which sought to achieve 30 percent equity for Malays in the economic system. Mahathir also set forth his ambitious "Vision 2020" goal for Malaysia: developed country status. Such a noteworthy goal would require an annual growth rate of 7 percent during the intervening thirty years.

Despite the country's economic growth trajectory, several challenges emerged, including the need to import migrant labor for plantation work, improving infrastructure, and keeping wages competitive for foreign investment. Most consequentially, the 1997 currency crisis undermined Malaysians' pride in their "miracle" economy and threatened to bring Mahathir's 2020 project crashing down. The crisis meant the new millennium was greeted with non-performing loans, large debts, rising unemployment, and lower-than-expected economic growth rates.

Malaysia's economy strengthened after the Asian economic crisis, notwithstanding Mahathir's refusal to accept IMF loans. His decision to place controls on capital account transactions went against the decisions of other Southeast Asian leaders. But criticism of the capital controls ended when Malaysia's economy began to flourish again. From 2003 to 2008, Malaysia's GDP growth rate averaged 5.7 percent. After contracting to –1.7 percent in 2009 due to the global financial crisis, Malaysia's GDP growth rebounded to an average rate of over 6 percent. Throughout the global downturn, Malaysia maintained an unemployment rate below 4 percent. By 2012, the World Economic Forum rated Malaysia fourth in the world for protecting investors and twenty-first for doing business overall—ahead of South Korea, China, and all of Latin America. In Southeast Asia only Singapore ranked higher.

Malaysia's economy today reflects increasing diversity founded on the base of its nationalized oil company, Petronas; manufacturing exports in electronics and information technology; and a natural-resources sector built on logging, rubber, palm oil, and liquefied natural gas. (Malaysia is the world's leading exporter of tropical wood, natural rubber, and palm oil, and the world's second-largest producer of liquefied natural gas.) Small and medium enterprises focusing on textiles, wood products, and services prosper in Kuala Lumpur, Penang, Johor Bahru, and other urban areas. A market capitalization of close to $400 billion shores up the Kuala Lumpur Stock Exchange, one of Southeast Asia's oldest. Malaysia's financial sector is internationally recognized for its efficiency and consistent performance.

In negotiating free trade agreements with the United States (bilaterally) and with China (via ASEAN), Malaysia has forged ahead with a long-term internationalization strategy for its economy. Talks with Washington stalled even as negotiations began for the newly proposed Trans Pacific Partnership, involving free trade between Malaysia and eleven Asian and North and South American countries. Also, with Malaysia seeking to become a financial center for Islamic banking, the country's economic ties to the Muslim world are growing fast. After the United States, Malaysia is Saudi Arabia's largest trading partner, sending it and its oil-rich neighbors in the Persian Gulf furniture, electronics, and construction materials.

FOREIGN RELATIONS

Malaysia has not been an interventionist country, nor has it participated prominently in international affairs since its independence in 1957. During the Cold War, it joined the Non-Aligned Movement but it actively worked to eliminate communist insurgency along its Thai border. Regional cooperation through ASEAN has long been a first priority for Malaysia as a means to enhance both the nation's security and its economic objectives.

Following independence, Malaysia's main adversary was China because of the support the People's Republic gave to communists during the Emergency in the 1950s and because of distrust of Malaysia's indigenous Chinese. Nevertheless, in 1974 Malaysia normalized relations with China, although the domestic communal situation remained a concern in the relationship for decades. Favoring the development of ASEAN, Malaysia adopted a "strategically exclusive" approach to regional security that favors the view that outside powers abstain from interference.[21]

Mahathir was principal spokesman for the ASEAN Free Trade Area (AFTA) and for Asian trade groups, which, he argued, could counter the North American Free Trade Agreement (NAFTA) as well as the European Union. Mahathir also became a spokesman against "Western values," which he viewed as inappropriate for Malaysia and other developing countries. He joined Singaporean leaders and others promoting "Asian values" as a superior alternative to the West's social disorder and moral indifference.

Malaysia supported the admission of Burma, Laos, and Vietnam into ASEAN. In 1996, tensions with Singapore increased when Singaporean Senior Minister Lee Kuan Yew made the comment that if Singapore ever was forced back into Malaysia, it would be a catastrophe for Singapore's ethnic Chinese because the Malaysian system was "racist." Eventually, the issue was handled diplomatically, but the disagreement reflected the long-running unease between the two neighbors.

In the new international era, Malaysia's foreign policy focus has been economic. Its strategy for the twenty-first century is built on global trade and investment by enhancing direct links to three of the world's largest markets: the United States, Japan, and China. Under Abdullah Badawi's watch, Malaysia became the United States' tenth-largest trading partner. Japan, for its part, remains one of Malaysia's most important foreign investors and export markets; and Malaysia's trade with China is now experiencing double-digit growth, although the balance is in the latter's favor. The opening of the ASEAN-China Free Trade Zone in 2010 deepened Sino-Malaysian economic ties, and China's appetite for Malaysia's palm oil, as well as its crude oil, continues to grow unabated. One of Prime Minister Najib's first overseas visits after assuming office was to China, the country's former adversary. China reciprocated six months later by sending Hu Jintao to Kuala Lumpur.

Malaysia's global significance is now following its economic success. Its delicate position in the relations between the Muslim world and the West reflects its new role. Muslim commentators note that "the entire Muslim world views it [Malaysia] as a successful model of a modern Islamic state."[22] Indeed, of the most successful developers of the Organization of the Islamic Conference's fifty-seven countries (representing 1 billion Muslims), only Malaysia can boast that it is neither a petro-kingdom nor a microstate. Malaysia's increasing economic ties to the Muslim world are also complicating its relations abroad. After China, Malaysia is the largest foreign investor in Sudan's oil industry, drawing criticism that refined Malaysia supports a pariah, genocidal regime. Malaysia's foreign policy, moving beyond Asia-Pacific concerns, is now framed with a greater international dimension.

CONCLUSION

Since 1969, the desire for stability has kept Malaysians from relapsing into destructive identity politics and communalism. The political will of its Malay, Chinese, and Indian citizens to impose order on society found positive expression through political party alliances and by acquiescing to visionary leadership. Symbiotically, rapid economic growth and political order led Malaysia up the development ladder in tandem, hand over hand, foot over foot. By combining market forces, international openness, strong state guidance, and policies designed to benefit those most unlikely to benefit, Malaysia's leading party, UMNO, and its Barisan Nasional alliance partners engineered enviable degrees of order, development, and equality.

Sacrificing certain civil and political liberties was, of course, a substantial price for stability and success. Mahathir, champion of "Asian values," often offended Westerners by gloating about Malaysia's brand of development, but it is difficult to imagine Malaysia's success in the absence of any trade-offs. As witnessed too often elsewhere, communalism does not generally escape asymmetrical structures of power and inequitable patterns of allocation.

Even as the Barisan Nasional coalition faces unprecedented challenges today from opposition parties, urban protesters, and conservative Islamists, the formula for political success in Malaysia is perhaps more clearly understood than in any other Southeast Asian system: cross communal alliances with willing Malay, Chinese, and Indian partners underpinned by a Malay-led "fidelity to the icons of indigenousness, protection, Malay unity, dominance, and Islam."[23] Existing institutions serve this formula well, but institutions are human creations that demand guidance and leadership if they are to endure. Malaysia's history suggests considerable risk for leaders who choose to alter this formula or the institutional legacies of Tunku Abdul Rahman and Mahathir bin Mohamad.

NOTES

1. In the study of Malaysia, the terms "ethnicity" and "race" are widely used to distinguish the same communities of Malays, Chinese, and Indians. In this chapter, both terms are used loosely and are not intended to imply narrower definitions of either term.

2. Milton J. Esman, *Administration and Development in Malaysia* (Ithaca, NY: Cornell University Press, 1972), 20–22.

3. Diane K. Mauzy, "Malaysia in 1987," *Asian Survey* 28, no. 2 (February 1988): 214.

4. Hari Singh and Suresh Narayanan, "Changing Dimensions in Malaysian Politics," *Asian Survey* 29, no. 5 (May 1989): 517.

5. Stephen A. Douglas, "How Strong Is the Malaysian State?" paper presented to the Association for Asian Studies, Chicago, April 1990, p. 2.

6. The full transcript of Mahathir's OIC speech is on ASEAN's Web site: www .aseansec.org/15360.htm.

7. James Chin, "Malaysia: The Rise of Najib and 1Malaysia," *Southeast Asian Affairs 2010* (Singapore: Institute of Southeast Asian Studies, 2010); Teo Cheng Wee, "Najib Scores on Repeal of ISA," *Asia News Network*, April 12, 2012, http://www.asianewsnet.net/home /news.php?id=29566&sec=3.

8. Liz Gooch, "Police Clash with Malaysia Protesters Seeking Electoral Reforms," *New York Times*, April 28, 2012, http://www.nytimes.com/2012/04/29/world/asia/malaysian -capital-braces-for-rally-by-democracy-activists.html.

9. Zakaria Haji Ahmad, "Stability, Security and National Development in Malaysia: An Appraisal," in *Durable Stability in Southeast Asia*, ed. Kusuma Snitwongse and Sukhumbhand Paribatra (Singapore: Institute of Southeast Asian Studies, 1987), 125.

10. Doug Tsuruoka, "UMNO's Money Machine," *Far Eastern Economic Review*, July 5, 1990, 48.

11. Zakaria Haji Ahmad, "Malaysia: Quasi Democracy in a Divided Society," in *Democracy in Developing Countries: Asia*, ed. Larry Diamond, Juan J. Linz, and Seymour Martin Lipset (Boulder, CO: Lynne Rienner Publishers, 1989), 373.

12. Michael Leifer, "Dakwah," *Dictionary of the Modern Politics of South-East Asia* (London: Routledge, 1995), 83.

13. Ibid.

14. Zakaria Haji Ahmad, "The Military and Development in Malaysia and Brunei, with a Short Survey on Singapore," in *Soldiers and Stability in Southeast Asia*, ed. J. Soedjati Djiwandono and Yong Mun Cheong (Singapore: Institute of Southeast Asian Studies, 1988), 235.

15. For an in-depth analysis of this point, see James C. Scott, *Political Ideology in Malaysia* (New Haven, CT: Yale University Press, 1968).

16. Ahmad, "Malaysia: Quasi Democracy in a Divided Society," 349.

17. Ibid., 358.

18. These figures come from Marvin Rogers, "Patterns of Change in Rural Malaysia: Development and Dependence," *Asian Survey* 29, no. 8 (August 1989): 767–770.

19. Milton J. Esman, "Ethnic Politics and Economic Power," *Comparative Politics* 19, no. 4 (July 1987): 403.

20. Ibid.

21. Donald Emmerson, *Hard Choices: Security, Democracy, and Regionalism in Southeast Asia* (Stanford, CA: The Walter H. Shorenstein Asia-Pacific Research Center), 21.

22. Abdulaziz Sager, "Saudi-Malaysia Alliance Could Help Reshape the Islamic World," *Arab News*, January 29, 2006, http://www.arabnews.com/node/279598.

23. William Case, "Malaysia: Aspects and Audiences of Legitimacy," in *Political Legitimacy in Southeast Asia: The Quest for Moral Authority*, ed. Muthiah Alagappa (Stanford, CA: Stanford University Press, 1995), 107.

Resource Guide

A useful tool for bibliographic and other information on Malaysia is available from Australia National University's WWW Virtual Library, which has a specific page for Malaysia, at https://sites.google.com/site/wwwvlmalaysia. Northern Illinois University's Southeast Asia Digital Library includes a range of useful links that cover government, academic, and research institutions specific to Malaysia: sea.lib.niu.edu. The University of Wisconsin–Madison Libraries, at www.library.wisc.edu/guides/SEAsia/resarea.html, similarly maintains a list of digital and print resources on Malaysia. Ohio University's Berita Database is a useful tool for resources on Malaysia: http://cicdatabank.library .ohiou.edu/opac/berita.php.

Readers can supplement this chapter with figures and publication information found in the country profile pages of data.UN.org. and ADB.org. Recent and archived news articles are maintained on specific country profile pages by BBC.com and NYTimes.com. Useful country reports are also produced by the Bertelsmann Foundation at www.bti -project.org/home/index.nc.

Official government statistics for Malaysia are easily obtained at www.statistics.gov .my/portal/index.php?lang=en. The Central Bank of Malaysia maintains useful economic information: www.bnm.gov.my. To follow happenings of Malaysia's Parliament, visit www.parlimen.gov.my/index.php?lang=en.

An excellent place to get a sense of Malaysian political activism is Aliran Online: http://aliran.com. Associated with a magazine under the same name, the site provides links to its magazine issues, the NGO community, human rights reports, and reform agenda politics. The Bersih coalition can be followed at www.bersih.org and www.globalbersih .org. A Malaysian blogger who became a parliamentarian continues a blog on Malaysia politics: http://tonypua.blogspot.com.

The *New Straits Times*, published from Kuala Lumpur, is the oldest English-language daily in the region, established in 1845: www.nst.com.my. The Malaysian National New Agency can be found at www.bernama.com. An excellent privately owned interactive Web site with real-time news, videos, and cultural features is www.malaysiakini.com; a similar Web site is also timely on current issues: www.themalaysianinsider.com. An English-language newspaper specific to East Malaysia is the *Daily Express*: www.dailyexpress .com.my.

11

SINGAPORE

THE QUEST FOR SURVIVAL, ORDER, AND PROSPERITY IS A DOMINANT theme of contemporary Singaporean politics. Surrounded by countries hundreds of times larger in area, with populations twenty to fifty times greater, this island city-state is in many respects a speck in a region of giant nations—even tiny Hong Kong is twice its size. As an urban entrepôt with virtually no agricultural base, Singapore stands alone, bereft of the resources and land of its Southeast Asian neighbors.

Singapore's principal resource is its people. Multiethnic and multicultural, Singapore's 3.3 million citizens are about 76 percent Chinese, 15 percent Malay, 7 percent Indian, and 2 percent other minorities. Singaporean citizens are the wealthiest (with per capita GNI of $42,930), best-educated, best-housed, and healthiest population in Southeast Asia. Interestingly, only 64 percent of the 5.2 million people actually living on the densely populated island are officially citizens; the remaining 36 percent, nearly 1.9 million, are nonresident foreign workers or permanent residents.

In 1999, B. J. Habibie, then president of Indonesia, unflatteringly referred to Singapore as a "little red dot," just a speck on the map compared to its massive neighbors. Insulted as they were at the time, Singaporeans began to consider the contemptuous label as a source of pride, symbolic of the republic's remarkable economic success. The country's leaders, prone to strategies of co-optation, embraced the "red dot" label and Singaporeans inside and outside of government now celebrate their new soubriquet with affection.

Ironically, despite its achievements, Singapore has one of the highest rates of emigration in the world. In 1990, about 36,000 Singaporeans lived in other countries. By 2006, over 143,000 émigrés had formally registered with the republic's embassies abroad. A large number of unregistered exiles render the Singaporean diaspora even larger—as high as 192,000 according to one estimate.[1] It is often Singapore's young and most talented who leave. The primary reasons emigrants give for leaving are advanced education and job

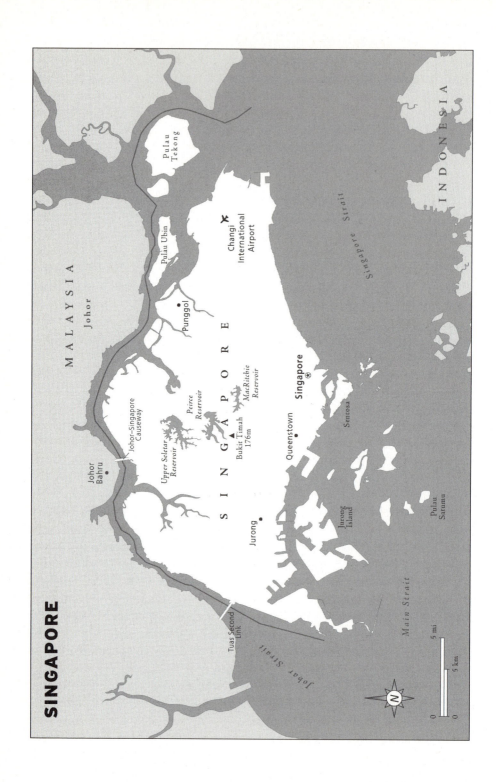

SINGAPORE

INDONESIA

MALAYSIA

Johor

Johor Bahru

Johor-Singapore
Causeway

Tuas Second
Link

Upper Seletar
Reservoir

Peirce
Reservoir

MacRitchie
Reservoir

Bukit Timah
176m

SINGAPORE

Pulau Tekong

Pulau Ubin

Changi
International
Airport

Punggol

Singapore

Queenstown

Jurong

Sentosa

Jurong
Island

Pulau
Satumu

Singapore Strait

Main Strait

Johor Strait

5 mi

5 km

N

opportunities, but for many, the city has become devoid of spirit, heart, and vitality, characteristics that have been displaced by a materialistic coldness symbolized by the nation's ubiquitous rules and prohibitions.

No noncommunist society in Southeast Asia regulates its citizens' behavior as much as Singapore. For example, rules on traffic, street cleanliness, shops and markets, gum chewing, landscaping, and food preparation are strictly enforced by the authorities and rigorously followed by the citizenry. Regulation extends to residential choice. Land poor, Singapore's Housing and Development Board manages a large-scale program housing over 80 percent of citizens in multistory buildings. Since the 1960s, Singaporean authorities have engineered public housing allocations to diffuse ethnic-based residential clustering. Chinese, Malays, and Indians must live amongst each other in government-controlled, but affordable, "housing estates." The government's Central Provident Fund, derived from mandatory payroll contributions, functions as a compulsory savings program that supports the housing program as well as medical care and retirement pensions.

One might expect such bureaucratization would engender corruption. However, less corruption exists in Singapore than in any other Southeast Asian nation. Although a part of the political system, patronage is less salient in political recruitment and policymaking than it is in the systems of Singapore's neighbors. The republic's clean reputation is reflected in Transparency International's annual rankings, where Singapore is listed among the five least corrupt countries in the world.

To achieve order, Singapore has fashioned one of the world's most effective and efficient governments. Characterized by democratic institutions but within the context of authoritarian order, Singapore's government has been controlled by a single party, the People's Action Party (PAP), since full independence was obtained in 1965. Until November 1990, Singapore had known only one leader, Lee Kuan Yew, who had led the island since 1957. Only two others, including Lee's own son, have ruled Singapore since 1990.

The themes of survival, prosperity, and order have become fused in Singapore to produce a unique style of politics and economic life.[2] The fusion stems from colonial times, when the British controlled Singapore, making it dependent on British economic policies. After achieving limited independence in 1957, Singapore granted Britain control over its external affairs and security matters out of fear of a seizure of power by the communists or by external intervention. To achieve full independence, the Singaporean economic system established interdependence in the global economic system, and the country allied with its northern neighbor, Malaya, which complemented Singapore economically.

The concern for survival was the major impetus for the decision by Malaya and Singapore to forge the Federation of Malaysia in September

1963, which included Sabah and Sarawak as well. Tunku Abdul Rahman, Malaysia's founding prime minister, feared that Singapore might become communist, an "Asian Cuba." The solution was to accept the city-state as a member of the federation. From the Singaporean perspective, Malaya's agricultural resources were necessary for their own development. Lee Kuan Yew did not originally believe that Singapore was viable by itself.

The federation lasted only two years, until August 1965, because the Alliance government in Kuala Lumpur perceived that the Chinese in Singapore were threatening the Malays' privileged political position. Lee Kuan Yew had called for a "Malaysian Malaysia," with the implication that all Malaysians, regardless of race, could participate equally in all phases of life. This view was contrary to Tunku Abdul Rahman's belief that a "Malay Malaysia" was in the society's best interest. Unable to reconcile, the parties agreed to remove Singapore from Malaysia.

After separating from the federation, Singapore again faced the challenge of survival in an era of grave tensions, which stemmed mostly from the global Cold War and the *Konfrontasi* threat from Indonesia. Rather than seek a complementary alliance to attain security, Singapore fashioned policies designed to achieve rapid and far-reaching economic development to ensure its sovereignty. By 1969, the government had consolidated the republic's independence, stability, and viability, a consolidation that has lasted to the present. This success has depended on continued economic development and the inculcation of values supportive of a unified, highly educated, quality-oriented Singapore in people from diverse backgrounds.

When Lee Kuan Yew stepped down in November 1990, he sponsored his protégé Goh Chok Tong to become Singapore's second prime minister. Just nine months after becoming the nation's leader, Goh called a snap election to legitimize his administration. Goh needed to step out of the shadow of Lee, who continued in an official capacity as "senior minister." In contrast to Lee's more authoritarian style, Goh used a more consensual approach to governing. He did not yet have a popular mandate and wanted to take advantage of the country's excellent economy to ensure widespread support for the PAP.[3]

The August 1991 election resulted in a decisive victory for the PAP; only 4 of the 81 seats were won by the opposition Singapore Democratic Party. To shore up his administration even more, in December 1992 Goh stood in a by-election and received a significant victory, capturing 73 percent of the vote in his own constituency. There was special poignancy in this victory because in the previous month he had informed the populace that his two deputy prime ministers were both suffering from cancer. The better known of these two was Lee Hsien Loong, minister of trade and industry, the son of Lee Kuan Yew and presumed heir apparent to the position of prime minister. Indeed, many commentators suggested that Goh was only an interim leader until Lee Hsien Loong was ready to assume the top position. The other deputy prime minister diagnosed with cancer was Ong Teng Cheong. Both deputies were immediately treated with chemotherapy and soon recovered.

Indeed, in 1993 both men made remarkable comebacks. Ong Teng Cheong was elected for a six-year term as the country's first executive president in August, and Lee Hsien Loong returned as next in line for the prime ministership. Ong faced weak opponents, but he received only 58 percent of the votes cast (voting was compulsory). The PAP interpreted this as a rebuke from the public because candidates endorsed by the PAP are usually expected to win about 70 percent of the vote. The position of executive president was intended to be subordinate to the prime ministership, and it has not subsequently become more influential. In 1999, S. R. Nathan, a Hindu diplomat and the only candidate of the PAP, won a 70 percent majority for the presidency.

In 1995 and 1996, both Lee Kuan Yew and Goh Chok Tong engaged in a series of libel suits against their adversaries, winning every case and thus again demonstrating that the Singaporean judiciary has little autonomy from the executive branch. The PAP routinely wins multimillion-dollar defamation awards against political opponents and has even imprisoned some opposition candidates without charge.

In 1995, *New York Times* columnist William Safire described Singapore as a family dictatorship, characteristic of "old-fashioned European totalitarianism."[4] Goh responded with rhetorical shots of his own and a trans-Pacific debate about "Asian values" played out for months on editorial pages and in academic circles. Goh, Lee, and others (including Malaysia's Mahathir bin Mohamad) claimed Asian superiority over Western societies where crime, disorder, and corruption tainted economic success. They argued that a cultural emphasis on order, family, individual sacrifice, and hard work explained Asia's rising status. Critics responded by claiming that rule of law in Singapore was a sham and that "Asian values" justified strong-armed "authoritarian capitalism."[5] During this same time, the formerly impeccable Lee Kuan Yew and his son Lee Hsien Loong were revealed to have received discounts on two exclusive private condominiums. Lee explained that "it is an unfair world," which did little to mollify those who had supported the government's claim to meritocracy.

On January 2, 1997, parliamentary elections were held, but there was never any question about the outcome. The opposition contested only 36 of the 83 available seats, and the PAP won 63.5 percent of the total votes cast and 81 of the parliamentary seats. This strong showing reversed a downward trend that had reduced the PAP vote in 1991 to 59.3 percent. The Singapore

Democratic Party lost every seat it had held. The victory was viewed as a vindication for Goh Chok Tong and his party's economic achievements. Goh interpreted the result as a sign that voters had rejected Western-style liberal democracy; he also saw the outcome as his liberation from the long shadow of Lee Kuan Yew.

Similar election results in 2001 and 2006 perpetuated PAP legislative dominance, with winning margins of 75 percent and 67 percent, respectively. In 2004, Lee Hsien Loong took over as prime minister. Goh, credited for sound economic management and for bolstering education and medical assistance during his tenure, stayed on as senior minister. Lee Kuan Yew, ever present, took on yet another new cabinet title as minister mentor. The 2006 election affirmed Lee Hsien Loong's new position, as the 1997 election had for Goh.

The political effects of the 2008 global financial crisis later produced what Lee Hsien Loong described himself as a "watershed election" in 2011. Problems in the real estate market, rising inflation, and Singapore's worst recession since independence turned a record number of voters away from the PAP. Returning one of its worst election results since 1965, the PAP garnered only 60 percent of the vote. The opposition Worker's Party won 6 seats in parliament (the PAP retained 81). Somewhat symbolically, after the election, eighty-seven-year-old Lew Kuan Yew resigned from his cabinet post as minister mentor, claiming the time had arrived for a new generation of leaders to guide the country.

In spite of recent gains, Singapore's opposition still remains effectually powerless in crafting legislation. Decades of single-party rule have "reduced the parliamentary function down to passing the annual government budget and making new laws"[6]; elections remain loyalty tests and referendums on PAP performance, not contests between rival party platforms.[7] Under Lee Hsien Loong's leadership, Singapore continues the political patterns made familiar by his father: one-party dominance and technocracy, unapologetically focused on order, security, and material prosperity.

INSTITUTIONS AND SOCIAL GROUPS

Lee Kuan Yew

Few leaders in Southeast Asia have had the impact on their societies that Lee Kuan Yew has had in Singapore. Ho Chi Minh, Sukarno, Suharto, Ne Win, and Norodom Sihanouk had comparable influence, but none ruled a society with as much effectiveness. Lee, who won a Queen's Scholarship to study law at Cambridge, was a brilliant and pragmatic politician with more popular support than almost any other world leader.

By placing highly educated and technically proficient officials in charge of his development programs, Lee relied on his subordinates to establish effective policies free from corruption. By combining the advantages of Western-style democratic institutions with an Asian-style hegemonic political party system, Lee was able to dominate the country's politics and still achieve universal support and legitimacy.

In the late 1980s, Lee's consummate political skill lost some of its edge as he moved toward authoritarianism and away from open and pragmatic policies. In a series of decisions concerning the jailing of dissident politicians and the restriction of newspapers printing articles critical of his administration, Lee veered from the careful balance he had achieved between civil liberties and order during the previous decades. Lee rationalized the new direction toward tighter order as necessary for the continued stability of the country and as appropriate for Asian culture.

Following his resignation as prime minister in 1990, Lee officially became senior minister and continued as the country's most visible statesman. He traveled extensively, advising developing nations on how to achieve the economic miracle he had overseen in Singapore. He stressed the importance of discipline and denigrated Western-style democracy as inappropriate for developing countries. He also gave up his position as secretary-general of the PAP to allow Goh to assume the legitimacy he needed to govern effectively.

In November 1991, the Parliament passed the Elected President Act, which provided for a stronger presidency but retained the cabinet, headed by the prime minister. Initially, it was believed that Lee would be nominated for the presidency, but he denied interest in a position he judged too subordinate. When his son Lee Hsien Loong assumed the prime ministership in 2004, Lee Kwan Yew became minister mentor. Through this position, which he kept until age eighty-seven, Lee maintained a spot in the cabinet, where his policy influence could continue. Even during his advanced age, Lee has commanded respect, visiting with U.S. presidents, Chinese officials, and the world's powerful. Forever in the shadow of the minister mentor, Lee Hsien Loong, a skilled leader in his own right, has failed to exhibit his father's magnetism or visionary leadership.

Political Parties

The People's Action Party is virtually synonymous with Lee Kuan Yew and with governance in Singapore. The PAP has been in power since 1959; more striking than its uninterrupted rule, however, is that since 1968 the PAP has won all but a handful of hundreds of parliamentary seats, garnering as high as 84 percent of the vote.

The only party ever to provide credible opposition was the left-wing Barisan Sosialis (Socialist Front), which split from the PAP in the 1960s. Since that time, opposition parties have been allowed to function, but none have provided meaningful competition to the PAP. The reasons for the

PAP's dominance include the effectiveness and incorruptibility of most PAP politicians, the factionalization of the opposition, and the rigid rules that circumscribe the activities of political parties and opposition groups; these rules were especially important in the late 1980s, when newspapers were censored and suspected communists arrested. The other major reason for the PAP's success is the reluctance of the electorate to risk undoing a system that has been working so well by voting in alternative leadership. To many Singaporeans, the PAP is indispensable for continuing the extraordinary economic development and societal stability the city-state has enjoyed since independence.

Unlike most hegemonic parties, the PAP does not have a large staff to perform research and stage functions.[8] Instead, civil bureaucrats outside the party perform these functions, leaving the PAP visible only before general elections. To ensure its continued dominance, the PAP has prepared for succession through its self-renewal program, choosing young candidates who are more in tune with the electorate. Between 1980 and 2012, the PAP's winning percentage in legislative elections fell below 60 percent only once. Over fifty years following its first victory in 1959, the People's Action Party controls 81 of 87 elected seats.

So overwhelming is PAP's dominance that opposition parties, such as the Singapore Democratic Party and the Worker's Party, consider winning 2 or 3 seats an electoral success. Winning six in 2011, as did the latter, was considered to be a historic success.

Singapore's most visible opposition politician is Chee Soon Juan, a labor rights advocate and secretary-general of the Singapore Democratic Party, a Singapore Democratic Alliance partner. Chee's activities include verbal attacks and publicity events that often allege PAP corruption and undemocratic practices. Legal tangles with all three of Singapore's prime ministers have landed Chee and his activist sister, Chee Soik Chin, in and out of jail and in bankruptcy. Barred from international travel and running for office, Chee Soon Juan draws support from Amnesty International and other rights groups that contend Singapore's leaders restrict political speech and abuse the judiciary to crush PAP opponents.

Legislature

Singapore's parliamentary system is a legacy of British colonialism, even though its practice is much different from that of today's Great Britain. In contrast to the British bicameral system, the Singaporean parliamentary system is unicameral and has presented no meaningful opposition to the administration. Legislators are elected to five-year terms, unless the prime minister dissolves Parliament before the term ends.

To ensure a semblance of bipartisanship, in 1984 the Parliament provided for 3 opposition seats to be awarded if opposition candidates did not win at least 3 in constituency races. These 3 nonconstituency members (later changed to a possible 9) would be appointed from among the highest-polling opposition candidates as long as they had won at least 15 percent of the votes cast in the constituency.[9] Nonconstituency oppositionists were not accorded full voting rights; they were prohibited from voting on motions relating to constitutional amendments, money bills, or votes of no confidence in the government. The opposition views this provision as tokenism rather than a meaningful commitment to open politics.

Another feature in parliamentary procedures is the "Team MP" scheme. Since the 1988 election, in certain constituencies, the electorate votes for a team of candidates instead of only one candidate. These constituencies are declared Group Representation Constituencies (GRCs), and each is represented by three members of Parliament. No more than half of the total number of constituencies can be GRCs. At least one of the three candidates in a GRC is required to be an ethnic minority (non-Chinese). The team that wins a plurality of the total vote is elected.[10]

The primary purpose of group representation is to institutionalize multiethnic politics by ensuring that minorities will be represented in Parliament by getting them elected on the coattails of others.[11] The PAP was confident that the change would not threaten its ability to win. Indeed, since 1988, minority population representation within the PAP has expanded while seats won by opposition parties remain rare.

In another attempt to bring alternative ideas to Parliament, nine distinguished individuals from the community, academia, the military, the professions, and trade unions are now appointed to serve as independent members, or Nominated Members of Parliament (NMPs). Nominated members are technically unaffiliated with any party, but a PAP-dominated committee makes their appointment. Voting rights of NMPs are restricted similarly to those of nonconstituency members. Some NMPs have been active parliamentarians. The only non-PAP-initiated legislation ever to pass the Singapore Parliament came from a nominated member.

Nevertheless, Singapore's institutional tinkering of adding opposition quotas, ethnic diversity, and independent experts has done little to develop a consequential parliamentary opposition in Singapore. In the 2011 elections, for example, 3 nonconstituency opposition seats and 9 nominated members were added to 87 elected delegates who came from fourteen GRC districts and nine single member districts, yet the PAP still controlled all but 9 elected seats. Almost half of the PAP's elected members ran unopposed, winning their seats upon nomination. Only 6 of the legislature's 99 total members were actually elected by Singaporeans to represent a parliamentary opposition.

Foreign Workers and Permanent Residents

In 1990, only 16 percent of Singapore's active labor force was composed of foreign workers. That number increased to 35 percent by 2010 (or 25 percent of the total population). Over that same period, the number of permanent residents in Singapore increased from 3.6 percent to 11 percent. These changes mean that alongside every six Singapore citizens in the city there exist roughly three foreign workers and one nonnative permanent resident.

One in five foreign workers comes to Singapore to work at the high end of the economy in business, finance, or other white collar jobs. The other four in five arrive via work permits as construction laborers, factory workers or, increasingly, as service workers in homes, restaurants, night clubs, and discotheques. Many nonresident workers are Chinese; others are Indian, Sri Lankan, Indonesian, and Filipino. As Singapore has grown wealthier, meeting demand for low-skill work has led to rapid, though largely legal, immigration. Today, the increased presence of foreign workers animates much of Singapore's Internet chatter and blogosphere. Public debates over job competition, workers' rights, wages, and even the smell of cooking curry have created a new type of social turbulence in the multiethnic city-state.

Although foreign workers are politically powerless in representative politics, NGOs are emerging to address issues related to disadvantaged nonresidents. Advocacy by such groups is beginning to make a difference. For example, in 2013 a new law goes into effect mandating that all nonresident domestic workers be allowed at least one day off each week.[12]

STATE-SOCIETY RELATIONS AND DEMOCRACY

Debate exists about how to best characterize the Singaporean state. Through a Chinese cultural lens, Singapore can be viewed as a "patriarchal state," where traditional elders wield influence over a compliant society. The country is also frequently characterized as a developmental state, due to the state's active management over investment and trade-oriented sectors. Its critics label it an authoritarian state, pointing to its high degree of centralization and power over dissenting voices. The island's own leaders may implicitly see their state in Hegelian terms, as an altruistic state prioritizing solidarity and order over interest-group competition.[13] Debate notwithstanding, analysts agree that Singapore is, if nothing else, a strong state.

Upon first glance, Singapore does not have the requisites for a strong state. Geographically, the country is minuscule and has no important natural resources. Although it boasts the highest per capita income in Southeast Asia, its total GNP is far smaller than that of fellow dragons South Korea, Taiwan, its total GNP is far smaller than that of fellow dragons South Korea, Taiwan, or Hong Kong. Singapore's military is capable of only minor defensive operations. Viewed in these terms, Singapore would not have the wherewithal to be a strong state.

Nevertheless, using standard criteria, Singapore's state can be considered strong. Its leaders use the agencies of the state to get Singaporeans to do what they want them to do. In no other Southeast Asian society do the citizens follow the state's dictates with the same regularity as in Singapore. Taxes are paid, young men accept compulsory military conscription, and traffic rules are followed. Few autonomous groups compete for influence in the society. Indeed, the state has co-opted the bureaucracy, the military, and interest groups, while the hegemonic PAP—itself a creature of Lee Kuan Yew—has co-opted the state.

In explaining or understanding the high capacity of the state in Singapore, it becomes apparent that the country's small size is a major advantage in strengthening the state. Although Singapore is heterogeneous in the ethnic sense, more important is that its society is quite homogeneous culturally. Singaporeans are urban and largely united in their goals for their society. Living in fewer than 225 square miles, citizens have little room for nonconformity.

Singapore developed a strong sense of the politics of survival due to its wrenching expulsion from Malaysia and its subsequent Cold War experience. The impact of aid and overseas investment during the Vietnam War strengthened the role of the Singaporean state. In the 1960s, when the PAP was factionalized into left-wing and moderate groups, Lee Kuan Yew's victory over the Left was interpreted as a victory over communism and, therefore, as a victory for the survival of the country's capitalist system. Lee justified his "administrative state" as necessary to concentrate power and repress the state's internal and external enemies.

Singapore is the quintessential example of a strong state built from skillful leadership. For many Singaporeans, Lee Kuan Yew *was* the state. His strength came less from charisma or repression than from his extraordinary capabilities to fashion an effective state. The technocrats that Lee cultivated were among the most educated and skilled in Southeast Asia. Incorruptible and effective, they appear to be unbeholden to any particular societal groups. Instead, they are integrated into the state through the PAP or the ministries. Their lack of any mass political base reinforces their loyalty to the state.

The case of Singapore also raises the question of whether a one-party state can be democratic. From a Western perspective, the governmental system of Singapore does not meet the criteria of full civil liberties and competitive choices of leaders. From a culturalist Chinese perspective, the government's paternalistic nature is appropriate, providing, as it does, law and order as well as economic achievement without relying on oppression. Lee Kuan Yew agrees with Sukarno's rationale for guided democracy in Indonesia and has said that Western-style majority rule leads to chaos, instability, dissension, and inefficiency. For Yew and his successors, legitimization is sought not through democracy but through performance, which is viewed as a technical matter. In Singapore, the critical factor in politics is the technocratic power of the elite, not the government's ability to ideologically mobilize its citizenry.[14] Thus, technocrats, not democrats, characterize Singapore's hegemonic electoral authoritarian regime.

Singapore is the most disciplined society in Southeast Asia, in part because its citizens fear being fined or punished and in part because these citizens genuinely believe lawful obedience to be in the public interest.[15] Certainly, the government has set forth strict and often ridiculed measures to ensure orderly behavior (such as installing urine detection devices in housing block elevators that, if the rider urinates, lock the elevator door until authorities arrive). Although the Chinese heritage is one of discipline for the common good, at the time of independence, Singaporeans behaved no differently from their neighbors. The difference is that, since then, the Singaporean state has had the capacity to exploit that heritage to help it achieve its aims of survival, economic development, meritocracy, and order. The price it has paid is a lack of meaningful popular participation in the affairs of state and a sanitized society that has lost much of its soul.

While building Singapore, Prime Minister Lee argued that in the Chinese tradition there was no concept of a loyal opposition. For example, it was not possible to support an opposition candidate without withdrawing total support from the government. This tradition stemmed from Confucian philosophy, which stressed the principles of centralized authority. Obligation to those in authority was the cement of the Confucian order. As long as the authorities were meeting the people's needs and leading according to moral principles, the ruler was considered to have the mandate of heaven and was therefore deemed legitimate by the public. From this cultural perspective, a strong one-party system is most conducive to effective rule.[16]

One-party systems can provide policy alternatives if there are differences in opinion among the party leaders. Moreover, if two-way communication between the government and the people is established, the citizenry can assert influence over public policy. In Singapore, a high degree of intraparty factionalism occurs, with varying points of view aired publicly; differences, nevertheless, tend to be issue specific, not ideological. In addition, the PAP has established grassroots organizations, including Citizens' Consultative Committees, designed to elicit ideas from the public. These corporatist groups do provide input but do not indicate the development of an autonomous civil society, which the government views as potentially destabilizing. The government's claim to moral authority rests on public recognition of its performance record. Public compliance within this one-party system is rooted in a "broad-based recognition that politics is the business of the government, not the people."[17]

For five decades Singapore's technocracy has provided the republic with effective, but not always accountable, government, consistent with its traditions and history and supportive of the goals of development, order, and merit. Singapore's capacity to deliver on these goals over time is the fundamental question going forward. Founding father–cum–mentor minister Lee is the first to admit this fact, as he did in 2008 to a large crowd of Singaporeans and international delegates at the World Cities Summit. Speaking extemporaneously, Lee fretted that the island's voters might soon become bored and vote for a "vociferous opposition" out of "light-heartedness, fickleness, or sheer madness." A non-PAP government, he claimed, would ruin the city-state in as little as five years. "When you're Singapore," he clarified, "your existence depends on performance—extraordinary performance, better than your competitors—when that performance disappears because the system on which it's been based becomes eroded, then you've lost everything."[18]

ECONOMY AND DEVELOPMENT

It is impossible to make generalizations about Singapore's economic development because the nation's status as a city-state sets it fundamentally apart from its neighbors. With no agricultural base, Singapore is destined to become increasingly interdependent with the global economic system to ensure its survival.

Singapore is a mixture of capitalist and socialist economics, with emphasis on the former. The PAP leadership inherited a capitalist economic system from the British and has created state institutions to manage key aspects of the economy including housing, transportation, and shipping. Home to the world's busiest trans-shipment port, Singapore enjoys a geographic location that is its greatest economic asset. Although Singapore typically ranks among the world's most free economies, its government also controls large, state-owned holding companies that invest in manufacturing, communications, and foreign securities markets.

Singapore consistently posts the region's highest growth rates. These growth rates are largely the result of an outward-looking, export-oriented strategy begun after 1965 to accelerate the manufacture of consumer products, reduce unemployment, and obtain needed outside capital. Since 1965, Singapore's annual GDP growth has averaged above 8 percent. Only once, between 2000 and 2003, did Singapore experience more than two consecutive years with growth below 7 percent. Moreover, relatively low rates of inflation and unemployment have accompanied this growth. Inflows of foreign capital have been staggering. Foreign investment ballooned from

$300 million in 1967 to a stock of over $39 billion in 2010 (ninth in the world).[19] In anticipation of changes in the world economy, Singapore launched its "Second Industrial Revolution" in 1979, designed to restructure the economy toward high-tech industries. The plan was to manufacture exports of superb quality, win higher salaries for workers, upgrade job skills, and reduce dependence on foreign workers. The economy emphasized automotive components, machine tools, computers, electronic instrumentation, medical instruments, and precision engineering.

The revolution was a success until 1985, when the protectionist tendencies of developed countries hurt Singaporean exports. Low petroleum prices dealt a sharp blow to the ship-repair and shipbuilding industries (which made up one-quarter of the manufacturing sector), and high wages were not matched by growth in productivity.[20] Finally, the continued high rate of national savings (42 percent of GDP) could not become a part of productive domestic investments.

After state intervention had corrected each of these difficulties, the economy responded rapidly, leading Singapore to a period of remarkable growth. As the economy diversified, financial and business services displaced manufacturing as the economy's leading sectors. Not content with the level of economic development, Lee Kuan Yew set forth a controversial program to improve the country's gene pool. He determined that the quality of the people was the most important factor in a country's rapid development, and he arranged a program to encourage the marriage and procreation of the well-educated populace, giving incentives for educated mothers to have more children.

The early 1990s continued with solid 6–7 percent growth rates, although these percentages were down from previous years. Despite this record, the economy faced several problems. Seventy percent of domestic exports were produced by multinational corporations, perpetuating the nation's dependence on foreign-owned companies. Exports were not broadly based, with almost two-thirds of exports (in terms of value) in electronics and with the United States buying fully one-third of all exports.

Initially, the 1997 Asian economic crisis did not seriously jeopardize the Singaporean economy, because it was tied into the global rather than just the Southeast Asian economy. However, the worldwide economic slowdown in the United States and Japan that followed proved a challenge for the globalized economy. Singapore slipped into recession, with a –2.4 percent economic growth rate in 2001, a dramatic and significant drop from a remarkable 9.9 percent growth rate in 2000. Singapore recovered in 2002 only to find itself gripped by the SARS crisis that crippled the local economy, closed shopping malls, and devastated its Asian-based tourism sector.

The 2001 recession and economic effects of SARS raised questions about Singapore's export-oriented development model and recent efforts at regional integration. The PAP's answer: develop a knowledge-based economy highlighting financial services and cross-regional free trade agreements. By the mid-2000s, foreign investment in financial and insurance services surpassed manufacturing as the largest sector of foreign direct investment. Nevertheless, manufacturing still matters greatly to the country. Singapore's GDP growth rate in 2010 shot up to 14.1 percent based on a surge of electronic and biomedical manufacturing output.

Internationally, the country has negotiated twenty-four bilateral and regional trade agreements with major economic players in the global economy, such as ASEAN, the United States, India, Mexico, Switzerland, Korea, Panama, Australia, and oil-rich states in the Persian Gulf. It has also pursued closer economic ties with China. China needs assurance that oil will flow freely through Singapore's ports. Two-thirds of the world's oil flows through waters near Singapore each year, and only the port cities of Houston and Rotterdam refine more petroleum. As a new decade approaches, increasing demand for oil, particularly in Asia, leaves the city-state well positioned to benefit. Singapore's leaders are anxious about a regional settlement over the Spratlys dispute.

As a founding member of ASEAN, Singapore has supported efforts to further integrate the region's economies. Its economic relations with neighboring Malaysia are of vital significance. Singapore imports nearly half of its water supply from Malaysia, a fact Malaysian leaders frequently cite when relations turn sour. Singapore's investments in Southeast Asian countries are extensive and can invite trouble, such as when Temasek, a public holding company, bought Shincorp, Thaksin Shinawatra's telecommunications empire—a transaction that helped to trigger the 2006 military coup in Bangkok and left the ousted Thai prime minister awash in legal troubles and Thailand in political turmoil.

The 2008 global financial crisis pushed Singapore into a serious recession and leaders opted for an expansionary budgetary response rather than formulaic neoliberal austerity. Initiatives included a $3 billon jobs credit scheme that subsidized employers' wage bills; a cash subsidy to low-income workers; and an 18,000 jobs expansion plan for the public sector, among other measures. These programs are credited for assisting a quick recovery to growth and showed the flexibility of Singaporean leaders to pragmatically respond to economic stress.[21]

The Singaporean economy is interdependent with the global economic system. With a diversified economy, one of the best infrastructures for transportation in the world, superb medical care, the highest standard of living in all Southeast Asia, a highly educated population, and peaceful relations with its neighbors, Singapore's prospects for long-term economic growth are excellent. Even with periodic domestic inflationary pressures, the prospects for Southeast Asia's wealthiest population look strong.

FOREIGN RELATIONS

Singapore did not take charge of its foreign relations until 1965, when the republic was expelled from the Federation of Malaysia. Since then, the basic theme of foreign policy has been survival. As a small city-state with only minimal military capacity, Singapore has looked to Western powers and Japan to balance the influence of the Soviet Union (in the 1970s and 1980s) and China in Southeast Asia. Unabashedly anticommunist, Singapore supported the U.S. war in Vietnam and was a principal advocate for a hard-line policy toward the Vietnamese government. More recently, Singapore has become a major investor in the Vietnamese economy and seeks close relations with China.

Despite its pro-U.S. stance, Singapore often enunciated a policy of neutrality, avoiding embroilment in major power conflicts. Nevertheless, certain issues have strained Singapore-U.S. relations. In 1988, Singapore accused Washington of interfering in its domestic affairs and expelled a U.S. diplomat who allegedly encouraged a high-profile dissident to organize a group of opposition candidates. Bad feelings also arose when President Ronald Reagan removed Singapore from the Generalized System of Preferences. The Generalized System of Preferences had allowed selected goods to enter the United States duty free, but Singapore had attained the status of an NIC and was no longer eligible for this benefit.

Relations between Singapore and the United States reached a low in 1994 over the case of Michael Fay, an American teenager who was caned for an act of vandalism. U.S. public opinion polls indicated that most Americans supported Singapore's corporal punishment for the delinquent youth. The Clinton administration campaigned for a pardon for Fay, but Singapore's contemptuous response was to reduce his sentence from six lashes of the cane to four.

By the beginning of the millennium, Singapore had achieved its goal of survival. It was no longer threatened by internal insurgency or external intervention, and it was surrounded by large nations that had no capacity or desire to seriously intervene in the republic's affairs. But the events of September 11, 2001, reopened old concerns and caused Singapore's leaders to imagine new ones.

As a porous hub of trade, oil shipments, and transportation, Singapore developed a renewed sense of vulnerability in 2001, which resulted in a warming of relations with the United States. In December 2001, an al-Qaeda sleeper cell with plans to terrorize Western embassies was discovered in Singapore. A year later, President George W. Bush traveled to the republic to sign a bilateral free trade agreement. The post-9/11 United States-Singapore Free Trade Agreement (USSFTA) proved to alter more than just economic relations between the two countries.

During the war on terrorism, Singapore became a vital staging ground for U.S. operations in Afghanistan and Iraq (although it has prohibited the permanent establishment of a U.S. base). Goh Chok Tong even sent a token military unit to the Persian Gulf as part of U.S. Secretary of Defense Donald Rumsfeld's "Coalition of the Willing." Then, adding to its existing array of F-16s, Apache helicopters, and Harpoon missiles, purchased in the 1990s, Singapore later inked an arms deal with Washington in 2005 worth upward of $1.8 billion. The USSFTA led to the purchase of twelve Boeing F-15SGs and millions of dollars' worth of missiles, ordnance, and other supplies.[22]

In addition to economic benefits and coordination on regional terrorist threats, Singapore's pursuit of stronger cross-regional relations with the United States hedged against an increasingly assertive China. Like its neighbors, Singapore both celebrates and fears China's rise. It is Southeast Asia's largest investor in China, fourth overall behind Japan. The massive Singapore-Suzhou industrial park in Jiangsu Province, negotiated at the highest levels by the two governments, typifies the countries' growing economic relations.

In the new international era, Singapore seeks to interpret China to the United States and the United States to China. Just before signing the USSFTA, it signed a strategic partnership agreement with China. At the same time, it fears being perceived by its Muslim neighbors as an "unrepentant China beachhead."[23] Although fears of communism have disappeared, uncertainty about a rising China and new threats of Islamist terrorism keep Singapore desirous of a U.S. presence in Asia. By balancing economic and security interests between both powers, Singapore seeks strategic relations with each in a way that China and the United States could never imagine between each other.

CONCLUSION

Singapore's singularity does not always allow for meaningful comparisons with other countries. Indeed, the "little red dot" is an exception in Southeast Asia in terms of culture, ethnicity, geography, state capacity, and level of economic development. Only the less globalized citizens of oil-rich microstate Brunei, with one-tenth the population of Singapore, enjoy such a high income in the region. Singapore's small size notwithstanding, its geographic location remains significant. The city-state is destined to play a role in international trade, commerce, and finance as long as ships need the Malacca Straits to transport food, manufactures, and oil between Asia and the world. New bilateral trade agreements with major trading partners are likely to reap economic results in the future for Singapore. The smooth succession of power from Lee Kuan Yew to Goh Chok Tong to Lee Hsien Loong bodes well for continued PAP dominance and political stability.

NOTES

1. Brenda S. A. Yeoh and Weiqiang Lin, "Rapid Growth in Singapore Immigrant Population Brings Challenges," Migration Information Source, April 2012, http://www .migrationinformation.org/feature/print.cfm?ID=887.

2. Lee Boon Hiok, "Political Institutionalization in Singapore," in Asian Political Institutionalization, ed. Robert A. Scalapino, Seizaburo Sato, and Jusuf Wanandi (Berkeley: Institute of East Asian Studies, University of California, 1986), 202.

3. This section relies on Shee Poon Kim, "Singapore in 1991," Asian Survey 32, no. 2 (February 1992): 119–125, and Hussin Mutalib, "Singapore in 1992," Asian Survey 33, no. 2 (February 1993): 194–199.

4. William Safire, "Honoring Repression," New York Times, July 10, 1995, A13.

5. Christopher Lingle, Singapore's Authoritarian Capitalism: Asian Values, Free Market Illusions and Political Dependency (Fairfax, VA: The Locke Institute), 1996.

6. Chua Beng Huat, "Singapore in 2006: An Irritating and Irritated ASEAN Neighbor," Asian Survey 47, no. 1 (January/February 2007): 208.

7. Cho-oon Khong, "Singapore: Political Legitimacy through Managing Conformity," in Political Legitimacy in Southeast Asia: The Quest for Moral Authority, ed. Muthiah Alagappa (Stanford, CA: Stanford University Press, 1995), 132.

8. Lee, "Political Institutionalization in Singapore," 207.

9. Chan Heng Chee, "The PAP in the Nineties: The Politics of Anticipation," in ASEAN in Regional and Global Context, ed. Karl D. Jackson, Sukhumbhand Paribatra, and J. Soedjati Djiwandono (Berkeley: Institute of East Asian Studies, University of California, 1986), 173.

10. Thomas Bellows, "Singapore in 1989," Asian Survey 30, no. 2 (February 1990): 146.

11. Lee Lai To, "Singapore in 1987," Asian Survey 28, no. 2 (February 1988): 203.

12. This section draws from Yeoh and Lin, "Rapid Growth in Singapore Immigrant Population Brings Challenges."

13. Terrence Chong, "Why Labels for the Singaporean State Fall Short," Straits Times, February 8, 2007.

14. Khong, "Singapore: Political Legitimacy through Managing Conformity," 132.

15. Donald K. Emmerson, "Beyond Zanzibar: Area Studies, Comparative Politics, and the 'Strength' of the State in Indonesia," paper presented to the Association for Asian Studies, Chicago, April 1990, p. 28–29.

16. Asia Yearbook, 1991 (Hong Kong: Far Eastern Economic Review, 1990), 214–215.

17. Khong, "Singapore: Political Legitimacy through Managing Conformity," 132.

18. Lydia Lim, "5 Years All It Takes to Ruin Singapore," Straits Times, June 26, 2008.

19. Figures from the Singapore Department of Statistics and the United Nations Conference on Trade and Development.

20. Jon S. T. Quah, "Singapore in 1987," in *Southeast Asian Affairs 1988* (Singapore: Institute of Southeast Asian Studies, 1988), 249.

21. Narayanan Ganesan, "Singapore in 2009," *Asian Survey* 50, no. 1 (January/February 2010): 267–257.

22. Eul-Soo Pang, "Embedding Security into Free Trade: The Case of the United States-Singapore Free Trade Agreement," *Contemporary Southeast Asia* 29, no. 1 (April 2007): 10.

23. Ibid., 22

Resource Guide

The National University of Singapore maintains a useful bibliography of major scholarly and governmental works on Singapore at www.lib.nus.edu.sg/bib/sh/. The Southeast Asia Digital Library maintained by Northern Illinois University includes a range of useful links that cover government, academic, and research institutions specific to Singapore: http://sea.lib.niu.edu.

To get a full sense of the People's Action Party, browse its Web page: www.pap.org.sg. Useful economic information and news is available from Singapore's Ministry of Trade and Industry: http://app.mti.gov.sg. Official government statistics for Singapore are easily obtained at www.singstat.gov.sg. To keep pace with Singapore's ever-expanding free trade agreements, visit www.fta.gov.sg.

Singapore's most well-known English-language daily, the *Straits Times*, was first published in 1845: www.straitstimes.com. Channelnewsasia.com provides an interactive Web site with real-time news, videos, and cultural features. Infopedia.nl.sg, maintained by the National Library of Singapore, covers a full range of political, economic, and social issues of interest to Singaporeans.

Readers can supplement this chapter with figures and publication information found in the country profile pages of data.UN.org. and ADB.org. Recent and archived news articles are maintained on specific country profile pages by BBC.com and NYTimes.com.

12

BRUNEI

Brunei, known formally as Negara Brunei Darussalam (Brunei, Abode of Peace), is on the island of Borneo facing north to the South China Sea. It is divided into two sectors surrounded by the Malaysian state of Sarawak. With a population of only 408,000, and with the second highest GNI per capita in Southeast Asia ($31,800), Brunei, together with Singapore, is unlike other nations in the region. About 70 percent of the people of Brunei are ethnically Malay, and most of this group works in the public sector. The Chinese community, which makes up nearly one-fifth of the population (but for the most part does not have Bruneian citizenship), supplies most of the nonpublic workforce. Indigenous, non-Muslim ethnic groups who live in the interior regions compose about 10 percent of Brunei's population. Imported laborers from neighboring countries supply additional labor to the microstate. Islam is the state religion.

Brunei achieved internal self-government in 1959 when the sultan promulgated the country's first constitution, thereby ending British administration and ensuring that power would be transferred to the ruling dynasty rather than to the people. The British still handled foreign and military affairs, however, until full independence was achieved in 1984. Ironically, the sultan was reluctant to accept independence because he feared his new nation would be vulnerable to attack from its larger neighbors, Indonesia and Malaysia.

Brunei's reluctance to assume full independence also stemmed from the monarch's fear that internal revolts could undermine the royalty's prerogatives. The most threatening incident occurred in 1962 when about a thousand followers of A. M. Azahari revolted. Shortly after attacking royal-owned oil installations, Azahari, who dreamed of an independent federation of Brunei, Sabah, and Sarawak, declared himself premier of Kalimantan Utara (North Borneo). Within two days, the rebellion was crushed by the Bruneian government, supported by Gurkha fighters flown

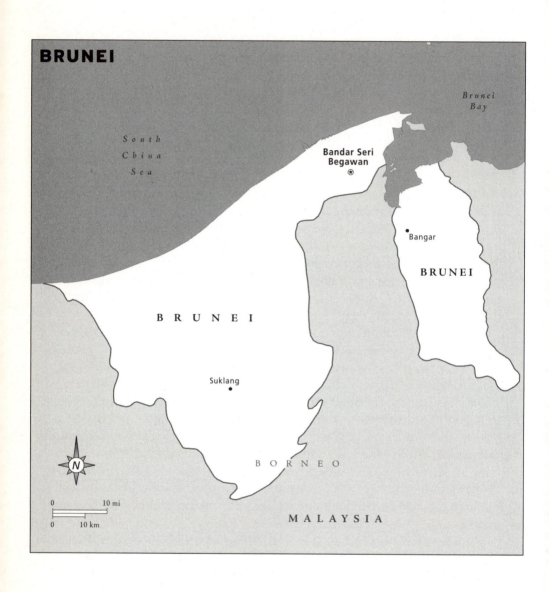

BRUNEI

Brunei Bay

South China Sea

Bandar Seri Begawan
⊛

• Bangar

BRUNEI

B R U N E I

• Suklang

B O R N E O

MALAYSIA

N

| 0 | 10 mi |
| 0 | 10 km |

in from British bases in Singapore.[1] The sultan dismissed Parliament and declared a state of emergency yet to be lifted. (Azahari fled to Indonesia, where he died in exile in 2002.)

Following independence, Brunei achieved political stability and economic development primarily because of enormous revenues from oil and natural gas. These funds allowed the government to establish a cradle-to-grave welfare system (facetiously known as the "Shellfare" state) that provided, among other things, free education and health care programs as well as subsidies for rice, housing, cars, funerals, and pilgrimages to Mecca. Moreover, Bruneians enjoy no income tax.

The national ideology of Brunei is *Malay Islamic Beraja* (MIB), which means "Malay Muslim Monarchy." The ideology emphasizes Malay-style Islam, with the monarchy as the defender of the faith and the people. It also discourages westernization and secularism. All public ceremonies and the school curriculum include MIB teachings.

When the sultan celebrated twenty-five years on the throne in 1992, he strengthened the concept of MIB, drawing from traditional Malay kingship and binding it with traditional Islam. *Malay Islamic Beraja* provides special status for Brunei's indigenous Malays and requires unquestioning deference to the throne. Its purpose is ostensibly to keep unwanted foreign influences out of Brunei.

In honor of his jubilee year (1992), the sultan built a new state mosque on the outskirts of Brunei's capital, Bandar Seri Begawan, at a cost of $30 million. Many Bruneians believed the sultan would establish democratic institutions during the celebrations. Instead, he announced that political parties and elections would remain proscribed and that the monarchy was the proper institution to bring benefits to the people. He tightened internal security, increased defense spending, purchased jet fighters from Great Britain, and announced plans to diversify the economy to lessen the nation's dependence on oil and gas revenue.

In 2004, the sultan revived the moribund Legislative Council, which had not met since before independence. It then passed constitutional amendments to reform the Parliament, including the direct election of one-third of its 45 delegates. Direct elections never followed. Rather, the sultan has since appointed and then disbanded three separate legislatures. He constructed a new parliament building in 2008 and later permitted the indirect election of 9 district representatives through peer-based secret balloting.[2] Beyond limited budgetary oversight, legislators function merely as advisors to the powerful sultan. In 2010, the first female cabinet member in the country's history was appointed. In spite of changes, the system is still fully authoritarian, and the country is one of the word's five remaining absolute monarchies.

INSTITUTIONS AND SOCIAL GROUPS

Sultanate

The sultanate is the embodiment of the state, and Sultan Sir Muda Hassanal Bolkiah—the twenty-ninth ruler in a dynasty that originated in the thirteenth century—is an absolute monarch whose legitimacy derives from his heredity, not from popular elections or accountability to Bruneians. He is the son of Sultan Haji Omar Ali Saifuddien Sa'adul Khairi Waddien, ibn Al-marhum Sultan Mohammad Jamulul Alam, who was known as the Sultan Seri Begawan. Brunei's capital, Bandar Seri Begawan, is named in his honor. Although Sultan Seri Begawan abdicated in favor of his son Hassanal Bolkiah in 1967, he attempted to keep ultimate power for himself, so the present sultan was not able to rule unconditionally until his father's death in 1986.

The sultan has ceremonial responsibilities and exercises total control over day-to-day affairs as the nation's prime minister, defense minister, and finance minister. The cabinet is made up principally of members of the sultan's own royal family. There is no dissent from the populace because the sultan has absolute power. He even amended the constitution to include his own immunity from any form of legal prosecution. His power is enhanced by the fact that he oversees the government bureaucracy, which employs an estimated two-thirds of Brunei's total workforce. The hierarchical nature of Bruneian society has made open communication with the sultan impossible for the common people. He is the head of state, head of government, and leader of the faith.

Despite announcements that Brunei would remain free from bourgeois decadence, the microstate has loosened up in an effort to attract tourism and Western business elites. Bookstores and movie theaters have opened, and satellite TV is ubiquitous. New Western-style restaurants (including McDonald's and KFC) have been established. Even hard liquor is available (although the nation is legally dry). In 1996, the American pop singer Michael Jackson presented a free concert for the sultan's fiftieth birthday, although he apparently was asked to swivel less than usual. Wealth is bringing new social problems to Brunei. A new generation of "bored youth" has emerged, as have graffiti, theft, and inhalant and methamphetamine use.[3]

There is no distinction between the state's wealth and the sultan's personal riches. Only four years after independence, the sultan was the richest man in the world, and he remains counted among its richest billionaires (worth about $30 billion). All the state's revenues and reserves are his, and he alone decides what portion goes for state expenditures.[4] The sultan of Brunei resides in a palace forty times the size of the White House, with 1,700 rooms. He rules in the style of classic potentates, albeit with modern tastes. Millions of dollars are spent on exotic collections of art, jewelry, and automobiles, including hundreds of Bentleys, Mercedes-Benzes, and Ferraris. A polygamist—married at one point to three wives (two of whom he later divorced)—the sultan has multiple children born over a forty-year span. Known more as a philanderer than a philanthropist, numerous stories of his activities have undermined his attempt to create an image of a responsible, benevolent ruler.

In 1993, Filipino senators investigated reports that some of their country's best-known actresses, models, and singers had engaged in prostitution while visiting Brunei. The senators reported a "high-class white slavery ring." A former Miss USA later made headlines with allegations of sexual abuse by Bruneian royalty. The sultan has attempted to shed his playboy image and shore up his credentials as a devout Muslim with three pilgrimages to Mecca.

In 2000, the sultan issued a lawsuit against his brother, Prince Jefri, and about seventy other officials for allegedly having wasted billions of dollars of state funds. The prince was fired from his position as finance minister and cited for particularly gross corruption that included extravagant purchases of planes, yachts, and jewelry, and high-priced sex orgies. The prince entertains a retinue of wives and mistresses and is the father of at least thirty-five children.[5]

Prince Jefri fled Brunei and initially made an out-of-court settlement with his brother to repay losses and change his lifestyle. When he failed to live up to the agreement, a legal case was sent to Britain's Privy Council for further settlement. In full tabloid drama, the Bruneian royal scandal was followed with shock as court documents revealed how both royals had spent billions of dollars on selfish luxuries and services ($900 million on jewelry, $475 million on Rolls Royces, hundreds of millions on a family fleet of jets, and even $3.6 million on badminton lessons and acupuncture). When the court found the prince liable for $8 billion of the missing $15 billion, he fled to France and began to sell off many luxury assets. A 2008 warrant for his arrest from a London judge remains outstanding. In Prince Jefri's wake is the royal family's latest conspicuous spender, Prince Azim, the third in line to the throne. A paparazzi favorite in London, the younger Prince Azim is known for his legendary birthday parties; for his thirtieth birthday, in 2012, he spent over $100,000 on flowers alone and drew tabloid attention with his guest list of "mature divas" including Raquel Welch, Faye Dunaway, and Pamela Anderson.

The heir apparent to the throne is Crown Prince Al-Muhtadee Billah, born in 1974, three years before his father's third wife. After studying in England, Prince Billah married Pengiran Anak Sarah, a half-Swiss teenager thirteen years his junior. Their first son, Prince Abdul Muntaqim, born in 2007, is the youngest living person with rights to the world's oldest monarchical line.

Military

The Royal Brunei Armed Forces (RBAF), with about 4,500 members (the strength of a brigade group with support elements), is the smallest military force in ASEAN. This voluntarily recruited, highly paid national defense force represents a state that spends a higher proportion of its budget on defense than any other ASEAN nation.

Since 1962, the RBAF has been augmented by a battalion of British Army Gurkhas paid for by the sultan (the only permanent deployment of British troops in the region). This force helps to ensure that there will be no revolt against the sultan's rule. The RBAF regularly engages in joint exercises with the U.S. Marine Corps, as well as armed forces from Malaysia and Australia. The RBAF also contributed peacekeepers to international operations in Cambodia, the Philippines, and Lebanon. The sultan recently purchased twelve Polish-made Black Hawk helicopters with a capacity to monitor Brunei's 200-nautical-mile Exclusive Economic Zone of the South China Sea.

Political Parties

Brunei has no viable political parties, nor has the government mobilized its own party as did Indonesia and Burma. Brunei's sultan draws support through patrimonialist programs and by depoliticizing society. Government employees are banned from joining political parties. The country's short history is punctuated by failed attempts by actors outside the sultan's circle of patronage to effect change by forming political parties. The left-leaning, proindependence Brunei People's Party, for example, briefly held seats in the Legislative Council in the early 1960s but was forced into exile along with its leader, A. M. Azahari, following the 1962 rebellion. The Brunei National Democratic Party, established in 1985, sought to promote a moderate platform based on Islam and liberal nationalism. Its primary goal was to restore parliamentary democracy. When party leaders called for elections and asked the sultan to give up his position as prime minister, they were arrested and the party was forcibly deregistered.

The Brunei Solidarity National Party, formed in 1995, remains Brunei's only registered political party as of 2012. Outwardly supportive of the sultan's right to rule, its platform is vague beyond its support for small-business owners, from whom it draws support. The party remains unconnected to the royal family or Chinese entrepreneurs and is essentially powerless. Its only hope is to compete for elected seats in the Legislative Council, assuming the sultan delivers on his 2003 pledge to permit direct elections.[6] Other parties, such as the Brunei National Solidarity Party and the Brunei People's Awareness Party, have been deregistered in recent years for technical reasons. They join the Brunei People's Party and the National Democratic Party on the growing list of defunct political parties in Brunei's meaningless party system.

STATE-SOCIETY RELATIONS AND DEMOCRACY

Brunei's small size makes governance far easier than in the larger and more diverse countries elsewhere in Southeast Asia. The state has brought virtually all institutions into its fold, leaving no autonomous societal groups to compete with the state apparatus.

There is an essential identity between the state and the person of the sultan. Almost every official, technocrat, and military officer in Brunei is related—directly or indirectly—to the sultan, his family, and his advisers. These people do not have another base of social control independent of the state. The lack of any mass political base in Bruneian society has reinforced these officials' loyalty to the state. Even the Chinese community is loyal to the state, despite the fact that most Chinese in Brunei are not even citizens. However, their businesses depend on the sultan's continued largesse and support.

The welfare state provides all basic needs of most Bruneians; thus, there is little dissension with the sultan's absolute powers. His lineage and royal aura and his leadership of Islam in Brunei further strengthen his position. Moves by groups calling for the formation of democratic institutions, and the relegation of the sultan to ceremonial rather than administrative functions, have failed.

There is no major external threat to Brunei's security today, nor has there been since 1962, when Indonesia supported the Azahari revolt. Since that time no dissident groups have been allowed to grow to the point that they pose a meaningful threat to the regime. Brunei has received considerable aid and support from its former colonial ruler, Great Britain, and the presence of the Gurkhas has strengthened the state by intimidating potential dissidents.

There is no democracy in Brunei. The country's political system is an absolute monarchy with no representative form of government—a politically closed regime. The 1984 constitution consolidated the monarchy's power by suspending parliamentary institutions. The reconvening of the Legislative Council in 2004 allowed for nonelected appointees to participate in some constitutional amendments and policy-level decisions at the sultan's behest. Even if the Legislative Council is reformed with directly elected seats, as the sultan has announced, the capacity of elected representatives to exercise power would be limited at best.

Civil liberties in Brunei include freedom of movement but little else. Journalists must practice self-censorship or risk charges of sedition. Labor rights are circumscribed and abuse of foreign workers by employers is rarely prosecuted. Brunei is considered "not free" by Freedom House, a rating shared in Southeast Asia by Cambodia, Laos, Vietnam, and Myanmar. The presence of forced labor and prostitution in the sultanate caused the United States to add Brunei to its human trafficking watch list in 2010.

ECONOMY AND DEVELOPMENT

Vast oil reserves make the dynamics of Brunei's economy different from the agriculturally based economies of other Southeast Asian nations. Oil and natural gas are the main sources of government revenue, foreign investment, and employment. Together they account for about 90 percent of total export earnings, 80 percent of government revenue, and 40 percent of GDP. After rising oil prices in 2007, Brunei's revenues from the oil sector dropped significantly as a result of the global financial crisis. Negative GDP growth followed in 2008 and 2009, and low growth rates have since continued. Its top economic priority, therefore, is to diversify its economy to reduce vulnerability. The problem of oil-export dependency is exacerbated by estimates that, at current extraction rates, reserves could disappear in twenty to thirty years. New drilling concessions begun in 2008 could extend the life of the oil-based economy past 2050.

Over the past twenty years, officials have worried about which industries to pursue as oil and gas reserves are depleted. Formal plans were developed in the 1990s to promote the private sector, especially in pharmaceuticals, cement, steel, chemicals, ceramics, and high technology.[7] Garment manufacturing and cash crops were also pursued but largely failed after global quotas on textiles were abolished. Restructuring the economy has proven difficult, and investors have been slow to come to Brunei. A large industrial park aimed at downstream petrochemical industries opened in 2009, drawing only mild interest from some European and Japanese investors.

Brunei's government views ecotourism as a promising alternative to the energy sector. Relatively untouched tropical forests make tourism attractive, but Brunei's remote location renders it unlikely that tourism will ever bring the economic returns that hydrocarbons now produce. Another initiative proposed by the sultan, following Malaysia's lead, is for Brunei to become a center for Islamic banking and finance. Outside investors have shown interest in Brunei, but the microstate's principal neighbor currently dominates Islamic-based banking in the region.

A final economic concern is employment. About 40 percent of Brunei's workforce is made up of foreign workers. Brunei's private sector, weak as it is, does not attract the country's own graduates. A rising rate of unemployment among younger Bruneians, who are often holding out for better government jobs, troubles officials. Increasingly, foreign workers are filling skilled positions in the private sector, adding to the already large base of immigrant laborers. Brunei's dependence on human resources from outside the country shows little sign of abating.

Foreign Relations

Just one week after gaining full independence in 1984, Brunei joined ASEAN, strengthening its relationships with former adversaries such as Indonesia and Malaysia. Today, Brunei's foreign policy focuses on security attained through international legitimacy and expanding economic relations. ASEAN membership has been the primary means to that end. Brunei also cultivates relations beyond Southeast Asia with key partners.

Since independence, Brunei's relations with the United States have been close. Indeed, according to media sources, Brunei channeled some $10 million to help the U.S.-backed Contras in Nicaragua after depositing the money in a Swiss bank account in 1986, and the Bruneian government confirmed that "His Majesty the Sultan of Brunei Darussalam had made a personal donation to the United States to be used for humanitarian purposes in Central America."[8] This incident became part of U.S. president Ronald Reagan's "Irangate" imbroglio, and it was the first time that most Americans had ever heard about Brunei.

In keeping with the country's generally pro-Western foreign policy, Brunei supported the U.S.-led liberation of Kuwait (an allied sultanate) from Iraq in 1990, as well as post–September 11 efforts at intelligence sharing to target Islamist terrorists. In December 2002, Sultan Hassanal visited President George W. Bush in Washington to personally pledge support for U.S. counterterrorism efforts in Southeast Asia.

Because Brunei is not threatened by any external power, the country has adopted a low-key foreign policy that is more reactive than proactive. Its main concerns are participating in ASEAN programs and building its diplomatic missions abroad to ensure trade and investment for the Bruneian economy. Brunei supported efforts to create AFTA, the ASEAN Free Trade Area, and successfully negotiated a free trade agreement with Japan, which imports 90 percent of Brunei's liquefied natural gas. It also became a member of the Trans-Pacific Strategic Economic Partnership, a free trade body inclusive of Brunei, Singapore, Chile, and New Zealand that aims to eliminate all tariffs between members by 2015. In 2013, Brunei assumes the chair of ASEAN amidst growing tensions surrounding the Spratly Islands dispute.

Conclusion

As is true of most other states in the region, there are discrepancies in the explanation of conditions for a strong state in Brunei, whose absolute monarchy is increasingly an anachronism in the changing world of Southeast Asia. As the world moves toward open societies and governmental accountability to the people, Brunei continues to more closely resemble a Middle

Eastern kingdom. The country's capacity to sustain absolutism results from the great wealth brought in by the sale of oil and gas. In a country surrounded by agricultural societies in which most of the people are poor, the sultan has bought his legitimacy by providing his subjects with all of life's necessities and, indeed, with luxuries.

NOTES

1. Justus M. van der Kroef, "Indonesia, Malaya, and the North Borneo Crisis," *Asian Survey* 3, no. 4 (April 1963): 177.

2. William Case, "Brunei Darussalam: An Electoral Feint," *East Asia Forum*, May 26, 2012, http://www.eastasiaforum.org/2012/05/26/brunei-darussalam-an-electoral-feint.

3. William Case, "Brunei in 2006: Not a Bad Year," *Asian Survey* 47, no. 1 (January/February 2007): 192.

4. D. S. Ranjit Singh, "Brunei Darussalam in 1987: Coming to Grips with Economic and Political Realities," in *Southeast Asian Affairs 1988* (Singapore: Institute of Southeast Asian Studies, 1988), 63.

5. Seth Mydans, "Brunei: From Oil Rich to Garage Sales," *New York Times*, August 17, 2001, http://www.nytimes.com/2001/08/17/world/brunei-from-oil-rich-to-garage -sales.html?pagewanted=all&src=pm.

6. Case, "Brunei in 2006," 190.

7. *Asia Yearbook, 1990* (Hong Kong: Far Eastern Economic Review, 1990), 91.

8. K. U. Menon, "Brunei Darussalam in 1986," in *Southeast Asian Affairs 1987* (Singapore: Institute of Southeast Asian Studies, 1987), 99.

RESOURCE GUIDE

Links to government Web pages and the official policy line, updated daily, can be found at www.brunei.gov.bn. A list of active international development organizations in Brunei can be found at www.devdir.org/files/Brunei.PDF. Daily headlines and news are available from the *Borneo Bulletin Online* at www.brunei-online.com.

Readers can supplement this chapter with figures and publication information found in the country profile pages of data.UN.org. and ADB.org. Recent and archived news articles are maintained on specific country profile pages by BBC.com and NYTimes.com.

Because freedom of speech is strictly controlled by the Bruneian government, do not expect to find critical journalism or scholarship sourced from within the country.

Index

Abinales, Patricio, 220n12
Abdul Rahman, Tunku, 6, 279–280, 291, 294, 300, 306
Abdual Razak, Tun, 281, 286
Abu Sayyaf, 209–210, 217
Aceh, 232, 234–235, 263
Afghanistan, 12, 18, 89, 241, 253, 319
AFTA (ASEAN Free Trade Area), 21, 68, 298, 331
Aguinaldo, Emilio, 202
Ahmad, Sakaria Haji, 301n9, 301n11, 301n14
Alagappa, Muthiah, 134n12, 219n2, 256n16, 301n23, 320n7
Alave, Kristine L., 220n27
Albritton, Robert B., 71n13, 71n19
Alkatiri, Mari, 267–270, 273
Allen, Douglas, 183n3
All Burma Monks Alliance, 83, 93
Al-Queda, 66, 209, 217, 233, 292, 318
Amnesty International, 176, 310
Anand Panyarachun, 33, 35, 50, 52
Anderson, Benedict, 255n2
Angka ("the organization"), 141–142
Angkor Wat, 44, 67, 137, 160, 163
Annan, Secretary-General Kofi, 265
Anwar, Ibrahim, 284, 286, 289
Antara News, 256n15
Aquino, Benigno, Jr. 190, 192, 199, 202–204, 206, 208, 209, 211, 215
Aquino, Corozon "Cory," 192, 201, 204–209
 communism and, 208
 dynastic family, 210
 "Freedom Constitution" of 1986, 202

 last-minute U.S. support for, 216
 political parties in support of, 203–204
 as woman in politics, 206
Arifin, Evi Nuridya, 254n1
Aris, Michael, 82
Arndt, H. W. 256n19
ASEAN (Association of Southeast Asian Nations), 7, 18, 21
 Brunei, 328, 331
 Cambodia, 145, 162–163
 Indonesia, 252–253
 Laos, 178, 182
 Malaysia, 298–299
 Myanmar (Burma), 85, 87, 97, 99–101
 Philippines, 195, 208, 214, 218
 Singapore, 317
 summits, 46, 100, 132
 Thailand, 65
 Timor-Leste, 273–274
 Vietnam, 113, 129–132
ASEAN Free Trade Area (AFTA), 21, 68, 298, 331
ASEAN Plus Three process, 68
ASEAN-China Free Trade Agreement, 68, 163
Asian Development Bank (ADB), 180, 183, 215, 274
Asian Economic Crisis (1997), 15–17
 Brunei, 330
 Indonesia, 228–231, 247, 249–251, 233–234
 Laos, 179
 Malaysia, 284, 297
 Philippines, 196–197, 214

333